TSUBASA

16

CLAMP

TRANSLATED AND ADAPTED BY
William Flanagan

LETTERED BY
Dana Hayward

BALLANTINE BOOKS · NEW YORK

Tsubasa, volume 16 is a work of fiction. Names, characters, places, and incidents are the products of the author's imagination or are used fictitiously. Any resemblance to actual events, locales, or persons, living or dead, is entirely coincidental.

A Del Rey Manga/Kodansha Trade Paperback Original

Published in the United States by Del Rey Books, an imprint of The Random House Publishing Group, a division of Random House, Inc., New York.

Publication rights arranged through Kodansha, Ltd.

First published in Japan in 2006 by Kodansha, Ltd., Tokyo.

ISBN 978-0-345-50148-6

Printed in the United States of America

www.delreymanga.com

9 8 7 6 5 4 3 2 1

Translation and adaptation—William Flanagan
Lettering—Dana Hayward

Contents

Tsubasa crosses over with *xxxHOLiC*. Although it isn't necessary to read *xxxHOLiC* to understand the events in *Tsubasa*, you'll get to see the same events from different perspectives if you read both series!

Honorifics Explained

Throughout the Del Rey Manga books, you will find Japanese honorifics left intact in the translations. For those not familiar with how the Japanese use honorifics and, more important, how they differ from American honorifics, we present this brief overview.

Politeness has always been a critical facet of Japanese culture. Ever since the feudal era, when Japan was a highly stratified society, use of honorifics—which can be defined as polite speech that indicates relationship or status—has played an essential role in the Japanese language. When addressing someone in Japanese, an honorific usually takes the form of a suffix attached to one's name (example: "Asuna-san"), is used as a title at the end of one's name, or appears in place of the name itself (example: "Negi-sensei," or simply "Sensei!").

Honorifics can be expressions of respect or endearment. In the context of manga and anime, honorifics give insight into the nature of the relationship between characters. Many English translations leave out these important honorifics and therefore distort the feel of the original Japanese. Because Japanese honorifics contain nuances that English honorifics lack, it is our policy at Del Rey not to translate them. Here, instead, is a guide to some of the honorifics you may encounter in Del Rey Manga.

-san: This is the most common honorific and is equivalent to Mr., Miss, Ms., or Mrs. It is the all-purpose honorific and can be used in any situation where politeness is required.

-sama: This is one level higher than "-san" and is used to confer great respect.

-dono: This comes from the word "tono," which means "lord." It is an even higher level than "-sama" and confers utmost respect.

-kun: This suffix is used at the end of boys' names to express familiarity or endearment. It is also sometimes used by men among friends, or when addressing someone younger or of a lower station.

-chan: This is used to express endearment, mostly toward girls. It is also used for little boys, pets, and even among lovers. It gives a sense of childish cuteness.

Bozu: This is an informal way to refer to a boy, similar to the English terms "kid" and "squirt."

Sempai/Senpai: This title suggests that the addressee is one's senior in a group or organization. It is most often used in a school setting, where underclassmen refer to their upperclassmen as "sempai." It can also be used in the workplace, such as when a newer employee addresses an employee who has seniority in the company.

Kohai: This is the opposite of "sempai" and is used toward underclassmen in school or newcomers in the workplace. It connotes that the addressee is of a lower station.

Sensei: Literally meaning "one who has come before," this title is used for teachers, doctors, or masters of any profession or art.

-[blank]: This is usually forgotten in these lists, but it is perhaps the most significant difference between Japanese and English. The lack of honorific means that the speaker has permission to address the person in a very intimate way. Usually, only family, spouses, or very close friends have this kind of permission. Known as *yobisute*, it can be gratifying when someone who has earned the intimacy starts to call one by one's name without an honorific. But when that intimacy hasn't been earned, it can be very insulting.

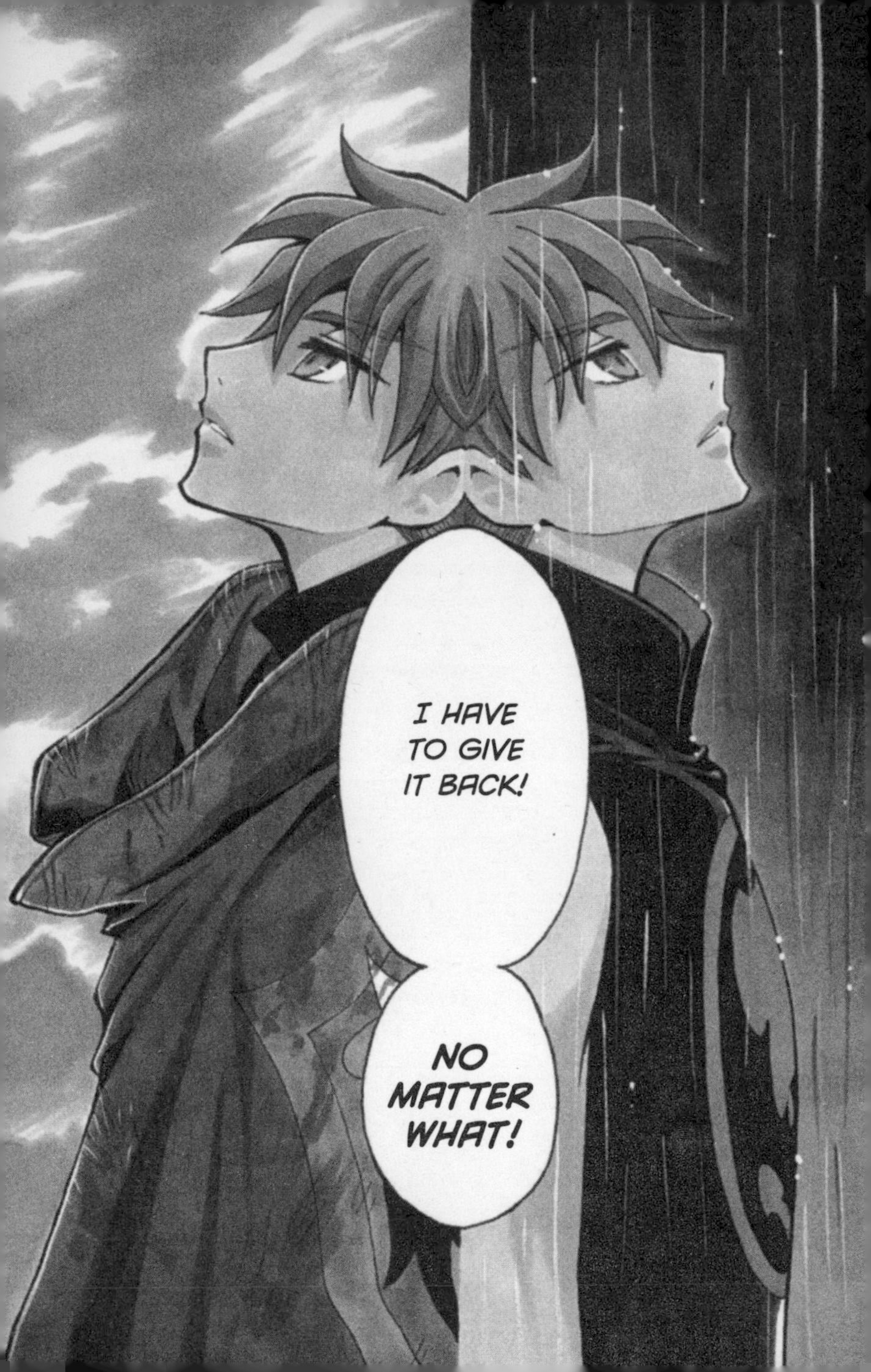
I HAVE TO GIVE IT BACK!
NO MATTER WHAT!

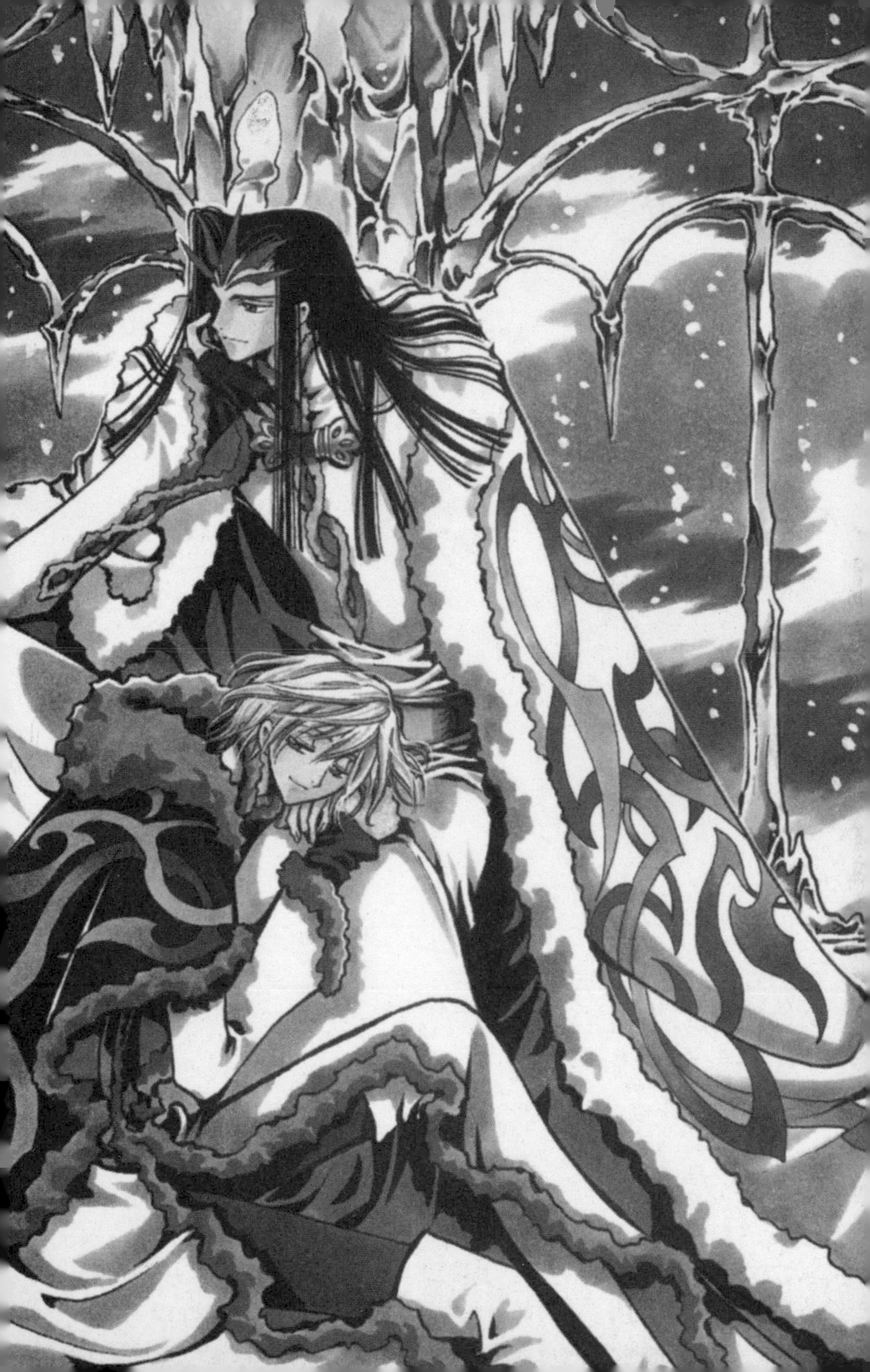

Chapitre. 117
The Wandering Soul

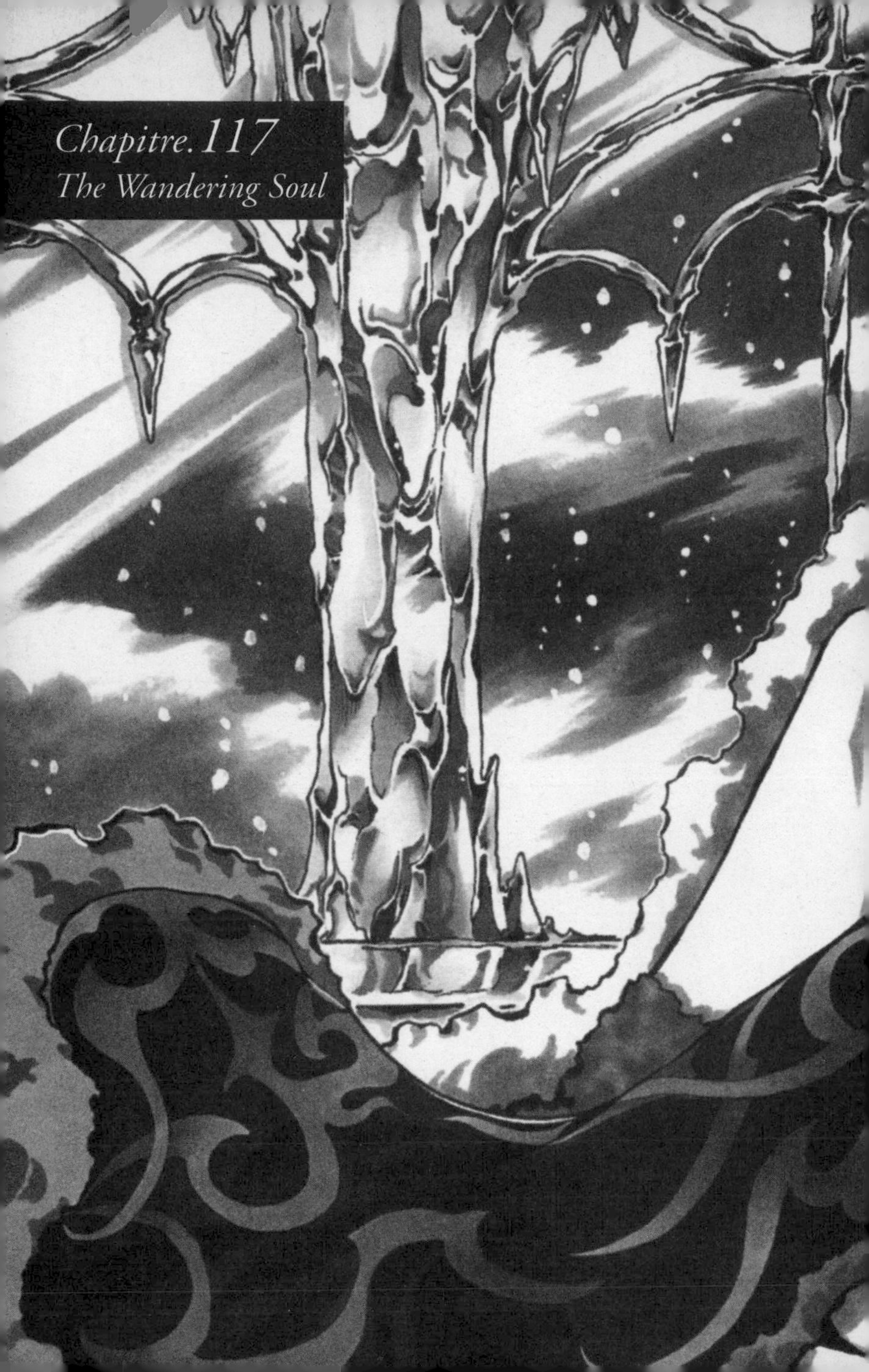

ツバサ

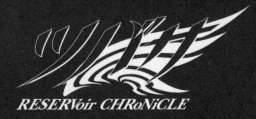

RESERVoir CHRoNiCLE

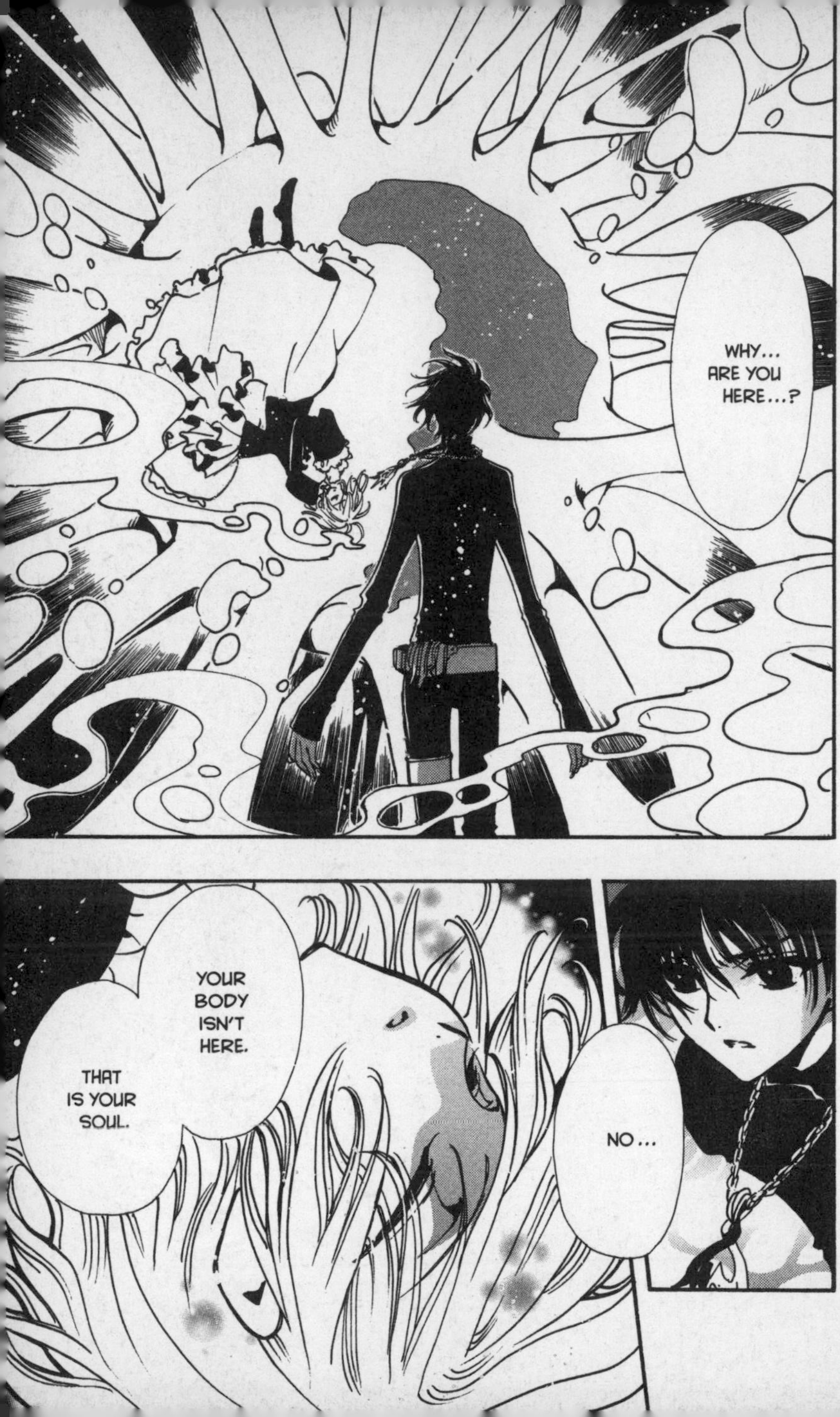
WHY... ARE YOU HERE...?
NO...
YOUR BODY ISN'T HERE.
THAT IS YOUR SOUL.

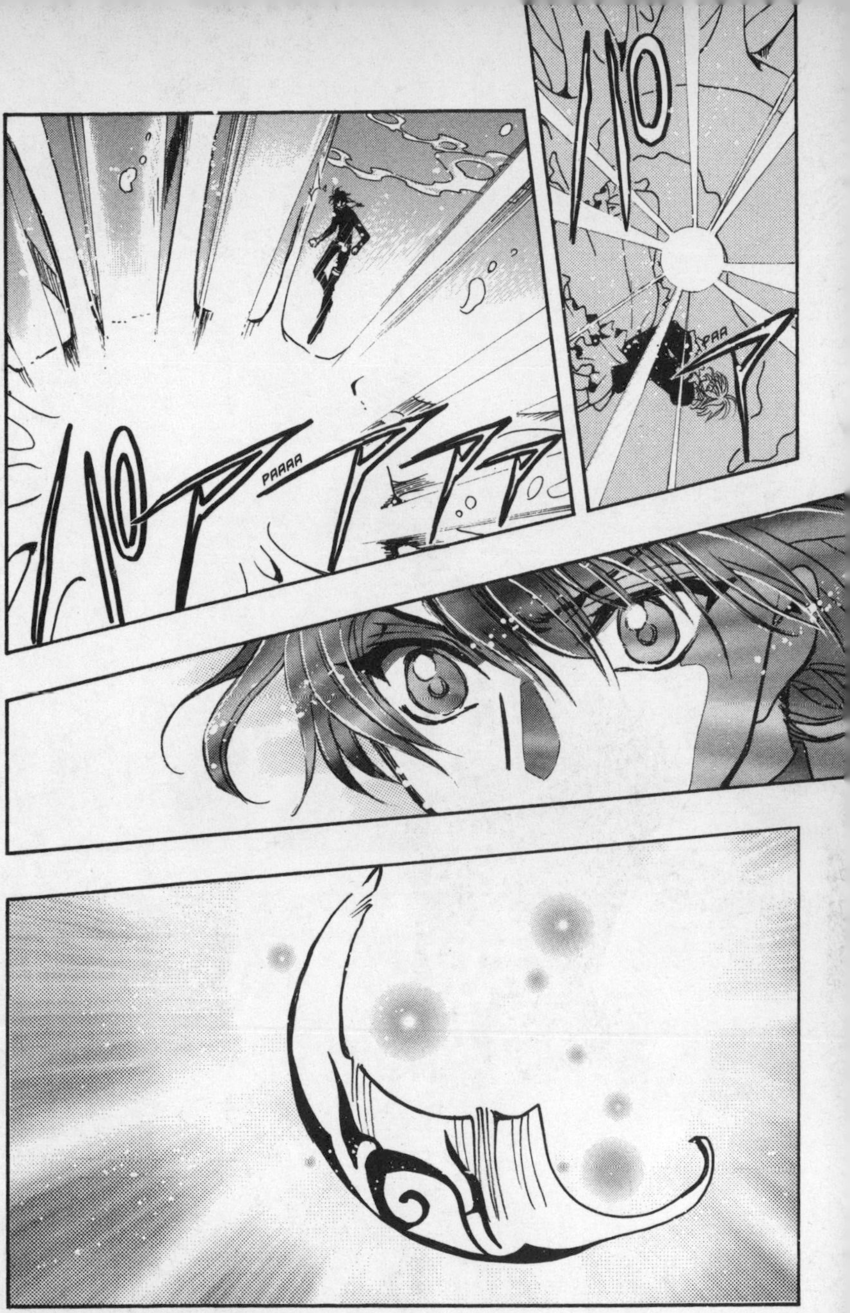
PAA
PAAAA

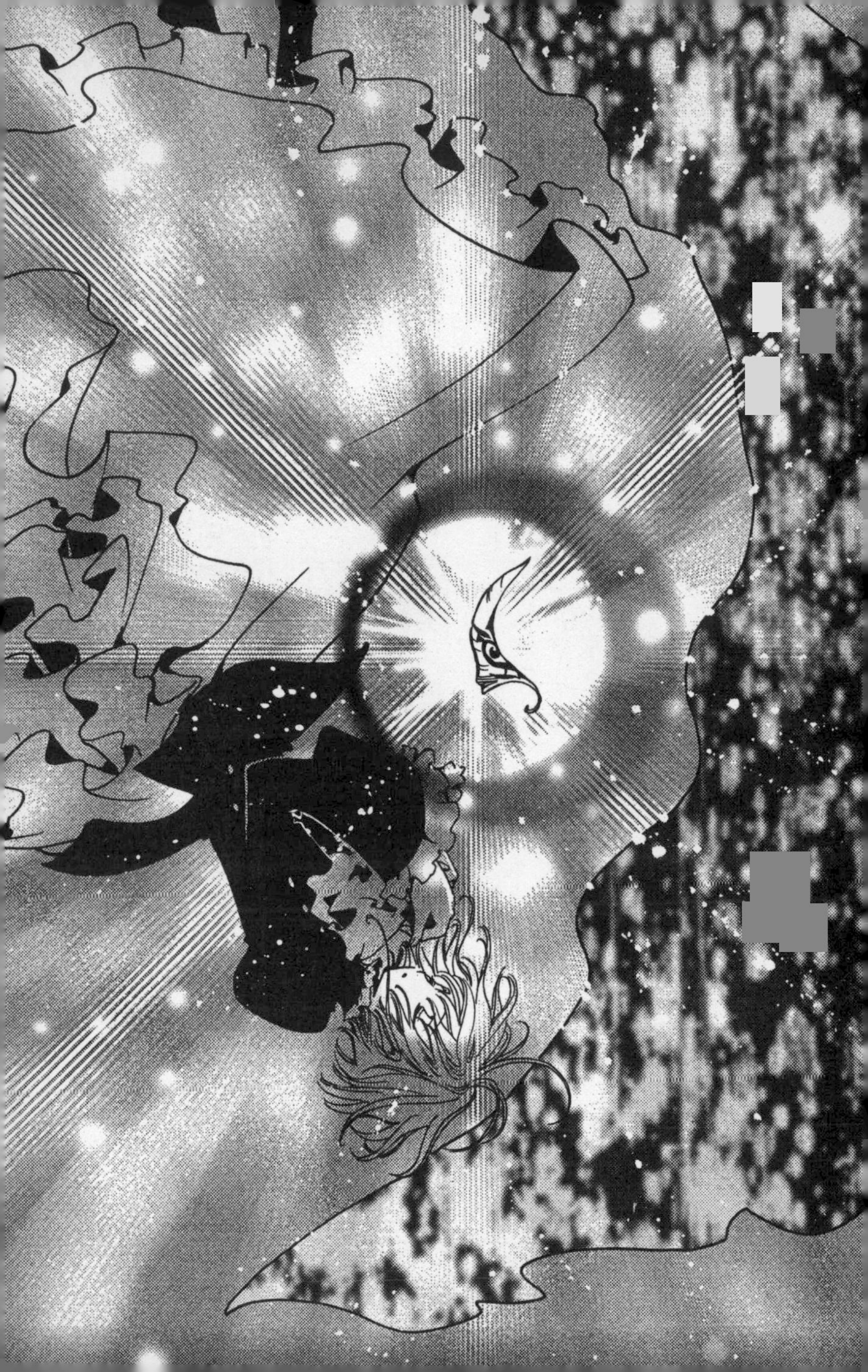

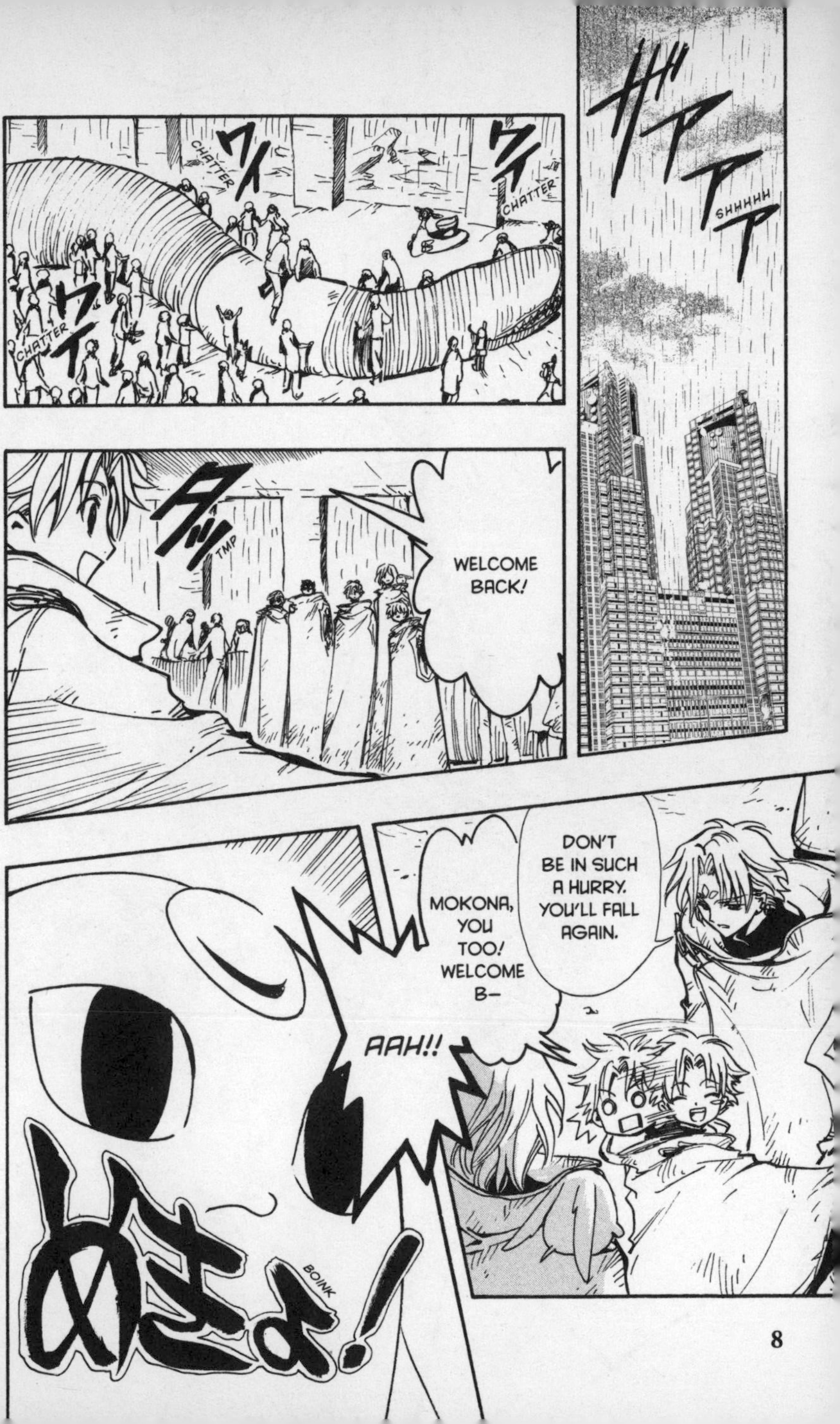
SHHHHH
CHATTER
CHATTER
CHATTER
TMP
WELCOME BACK!
DON'T BE IN SUCH A HURRY. YOU'LL FALL AGAIN.
MOKONA, YOU TOO! WELCOME B–
AAH!!
BOINK

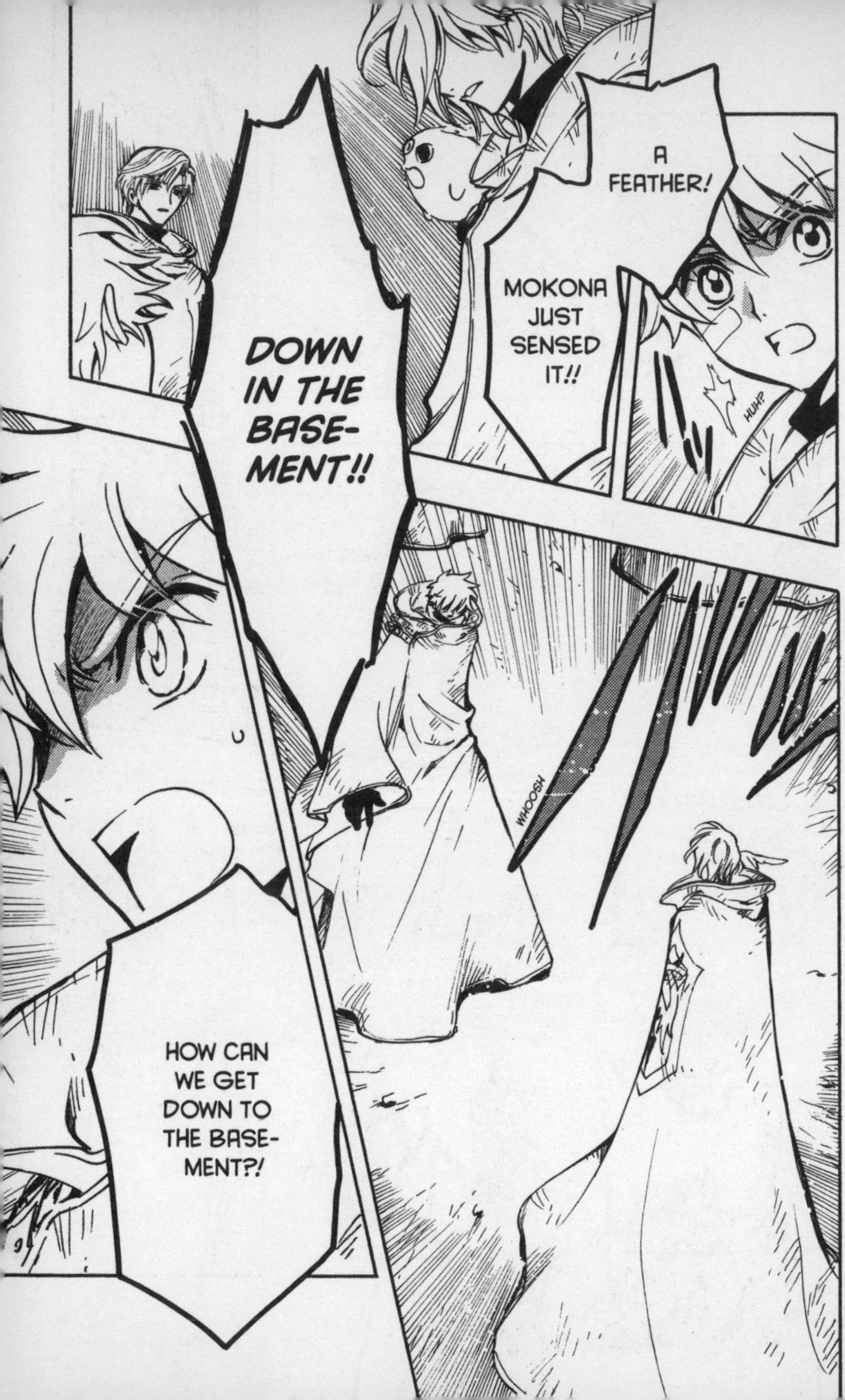
A FEATHER!
MOKONA JUST SENSED IT!!
HUH?
DOWN IN THE BASEMENT!!
WHOOSH
HOW CAN WE GET DOWN TO THE BASEMENT?!

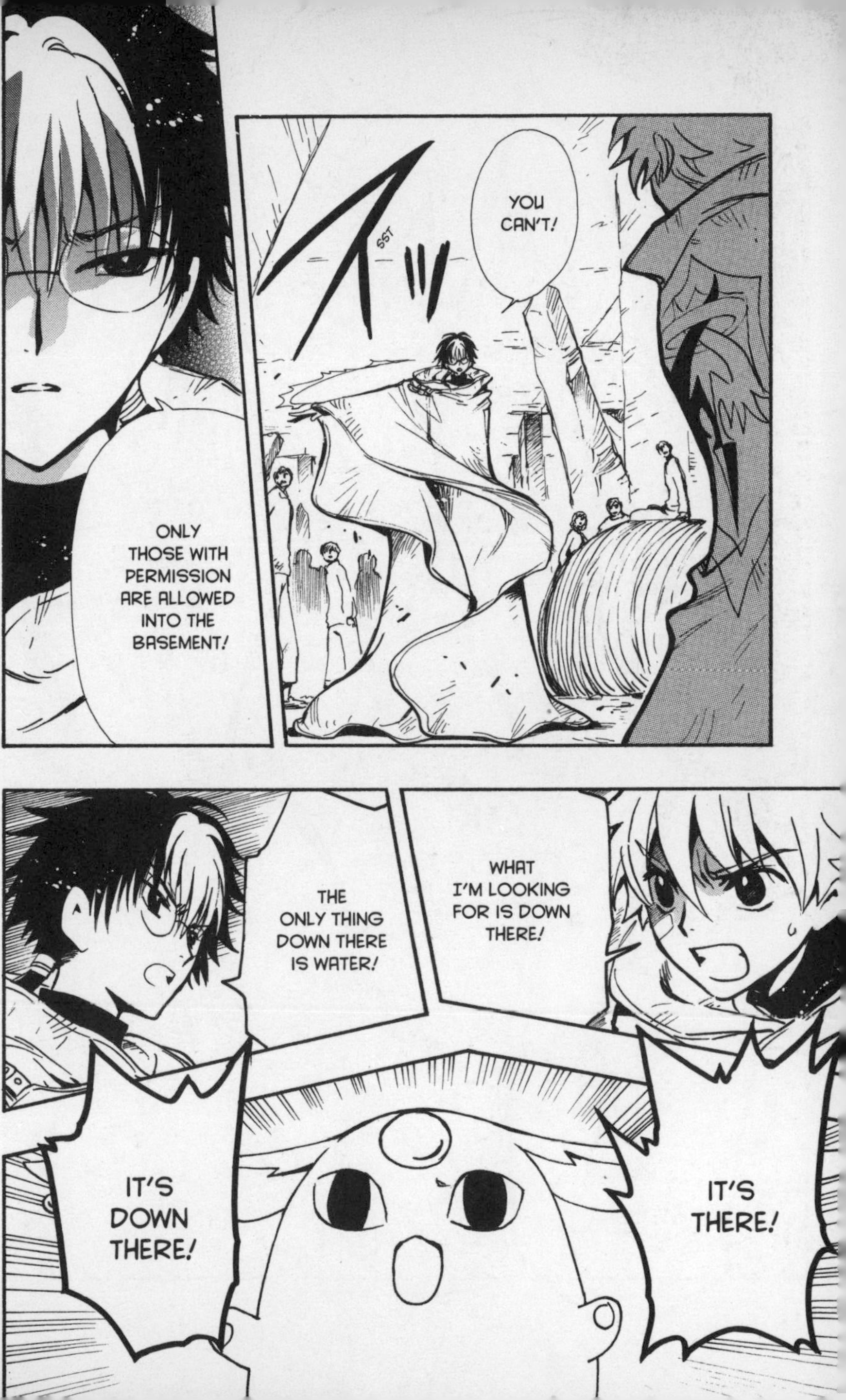
YOU CAN'T!
SST
ONLY THOSE WITH PERMISSION ARE ALLOWED INTO THE BASEMENT!
WHAT I'M LOOKING FOR IS DOWN THERE!
THE ONLY THING DOWN THERE IS WATER!
IT'S THERE!
IT'S DOWN THERE!

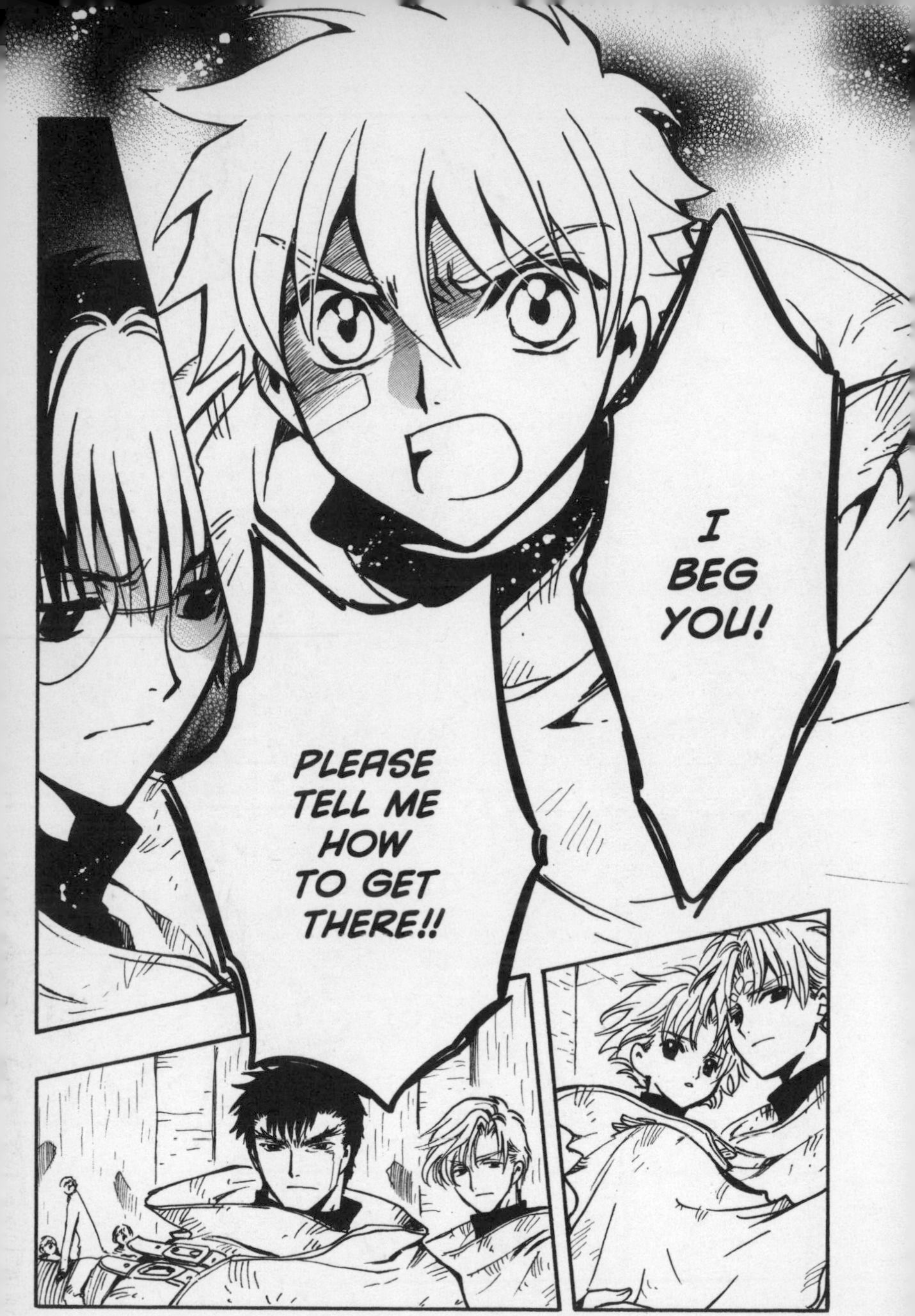
I BEG YOU!
PLEASE TELL ME HOW TO GET THERE!!

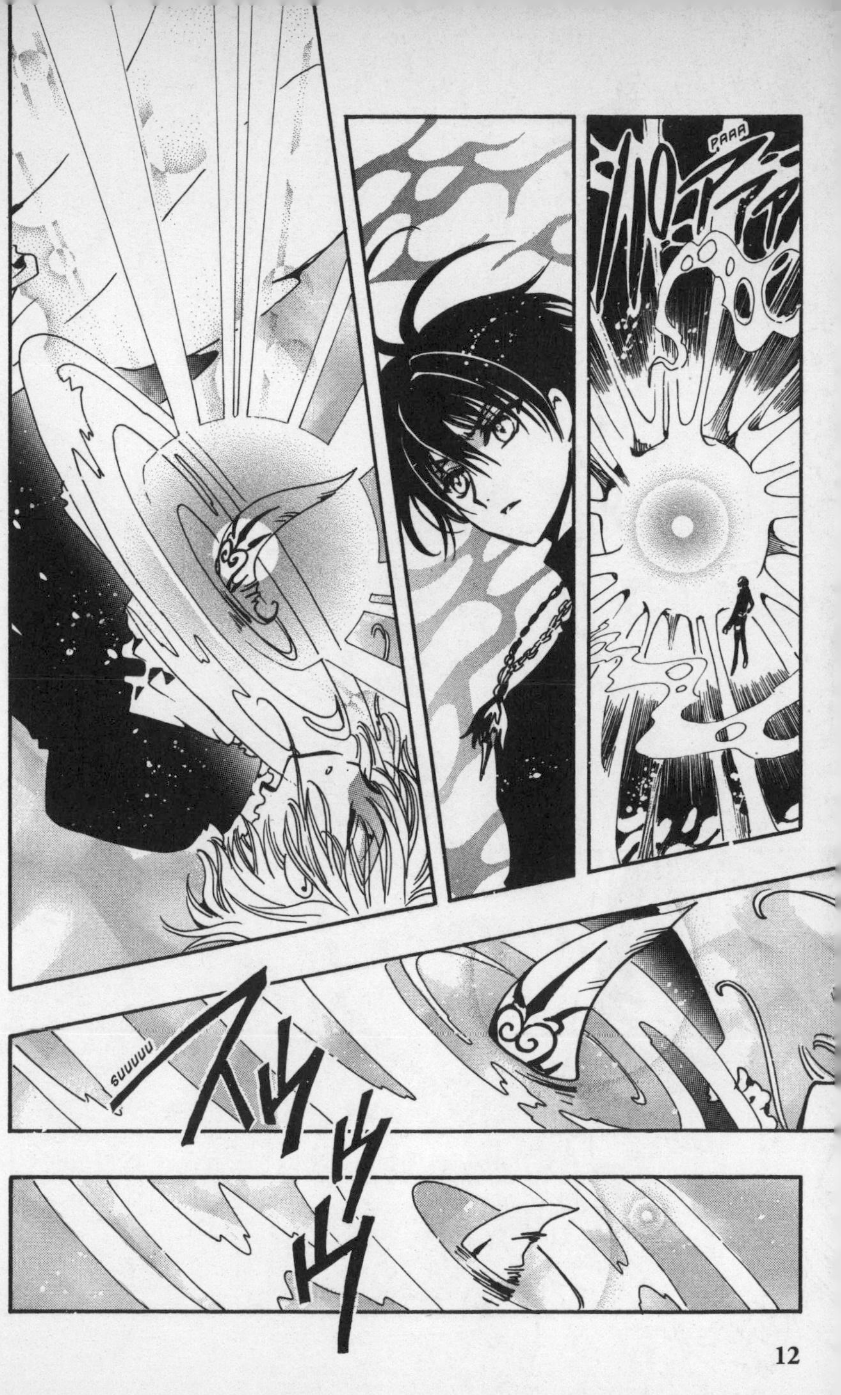
PAAA
SUUUUN

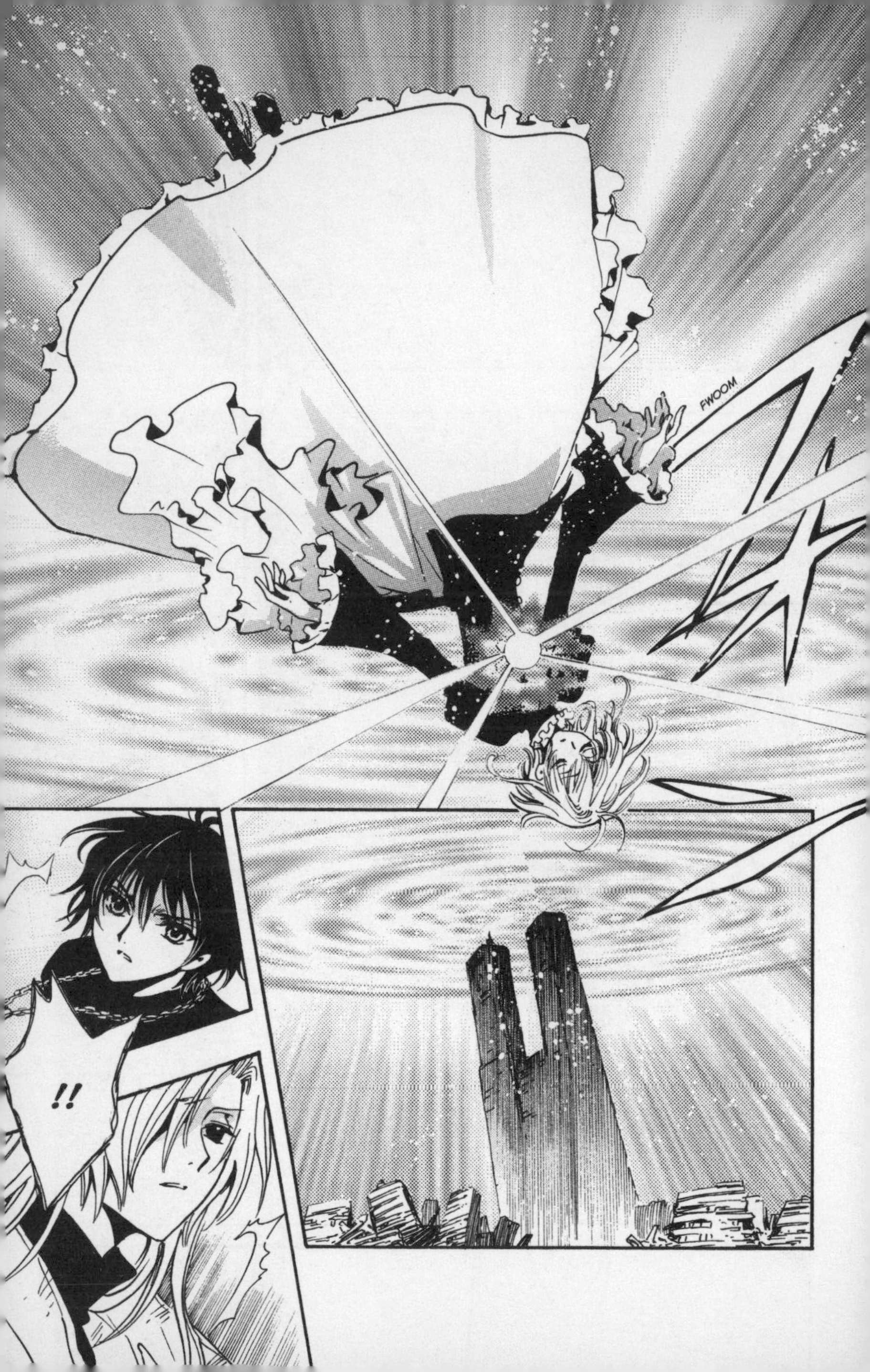
FWOOM
!!

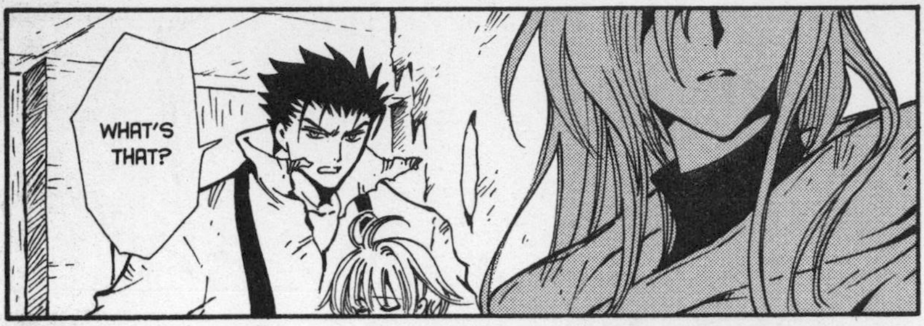
WHAT'S THAT?
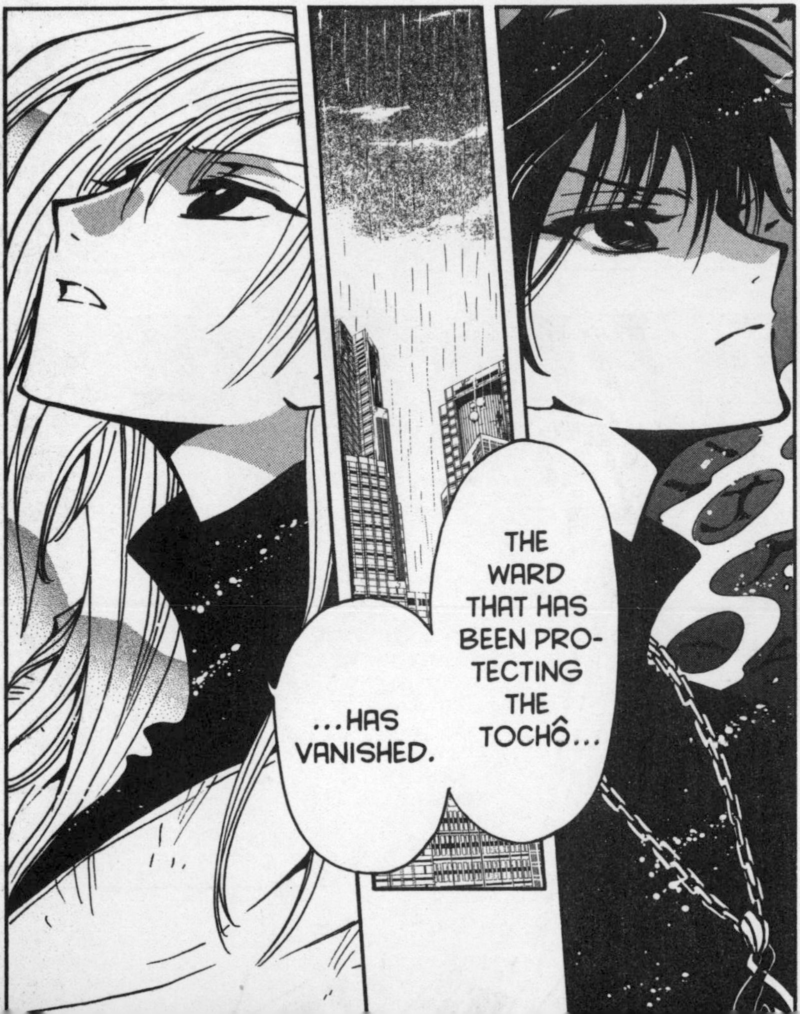
THE WARD THAT HAS BEEN PROTECTING THE TOCHÔ...
...HAS VANISHED.

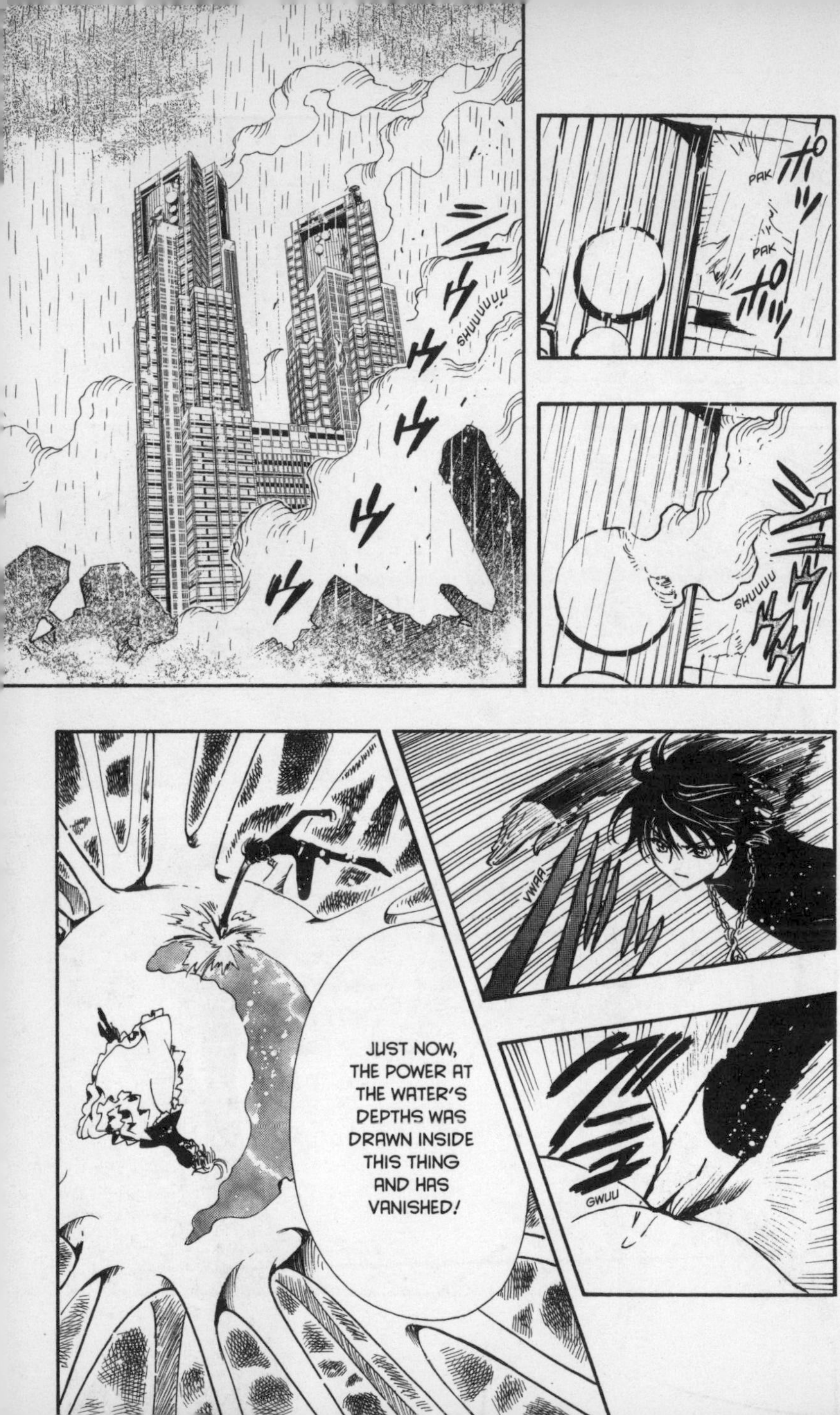
PAK
PAK
SHUUUU
SHUUUUUU
VWAA
GWUU
JUST NOW, THE POWER AT THE WATER'S DEPTHS WAS DRAWN INSIDE THIS THING AND HAS VANISHED!

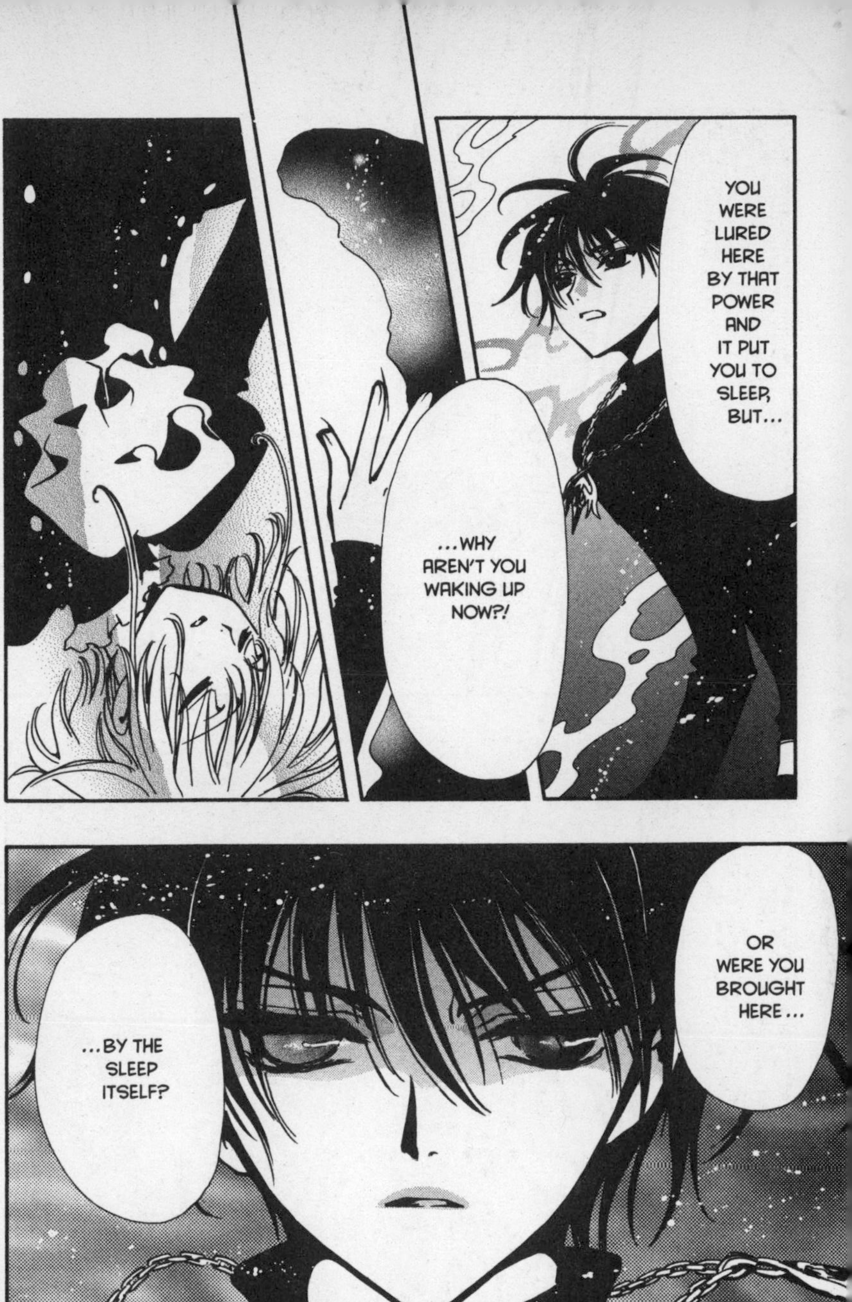
YOU WERE LURED HERE BY THAT POWER AND IT PUT YOU TO SLEEP, BUT...
...WHY AREN'T YOU WAKING UP NOW?!
OR WERE YOU BROUGHT HERE...
...BY THE SLEEP ITSELF?

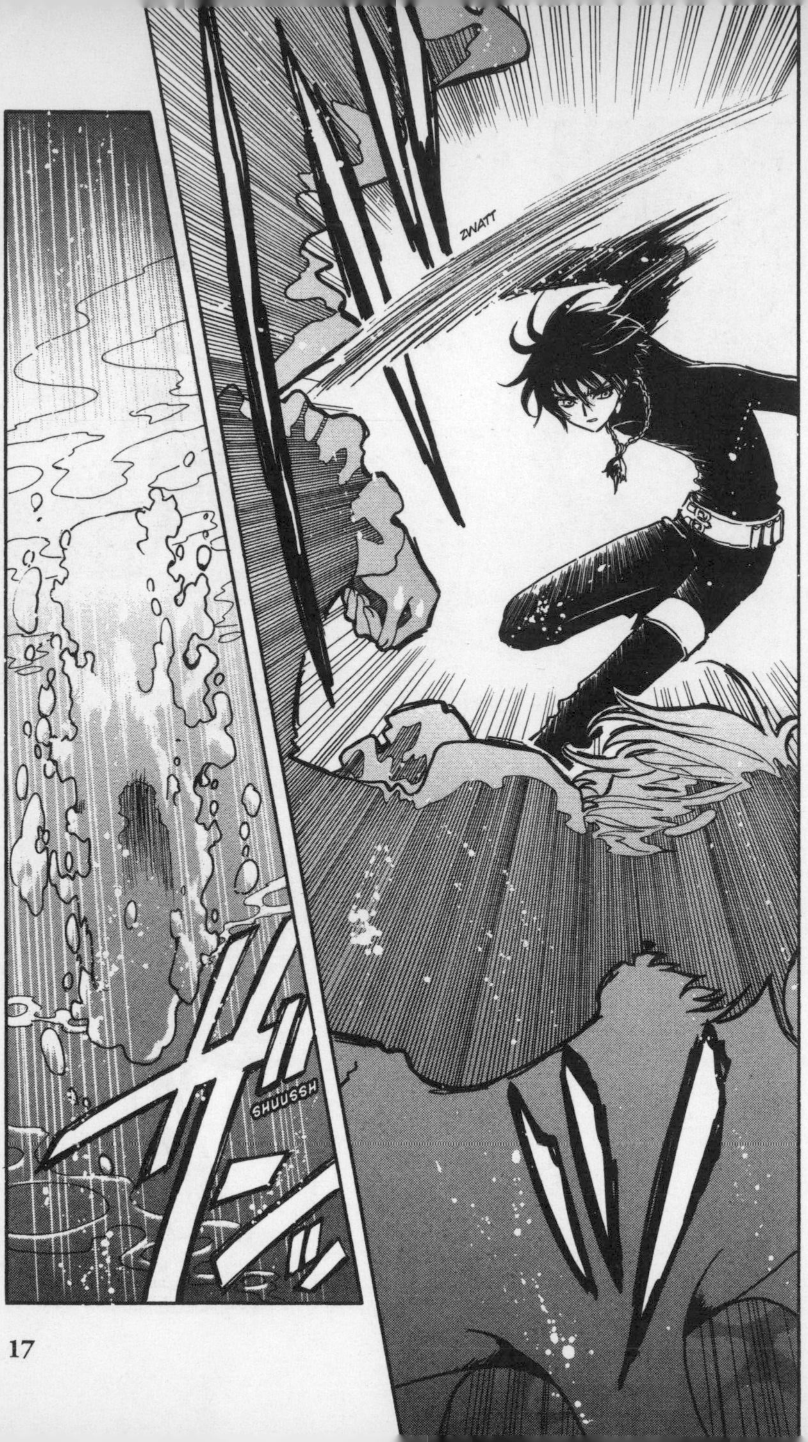
ZWATT
SHUUSSH

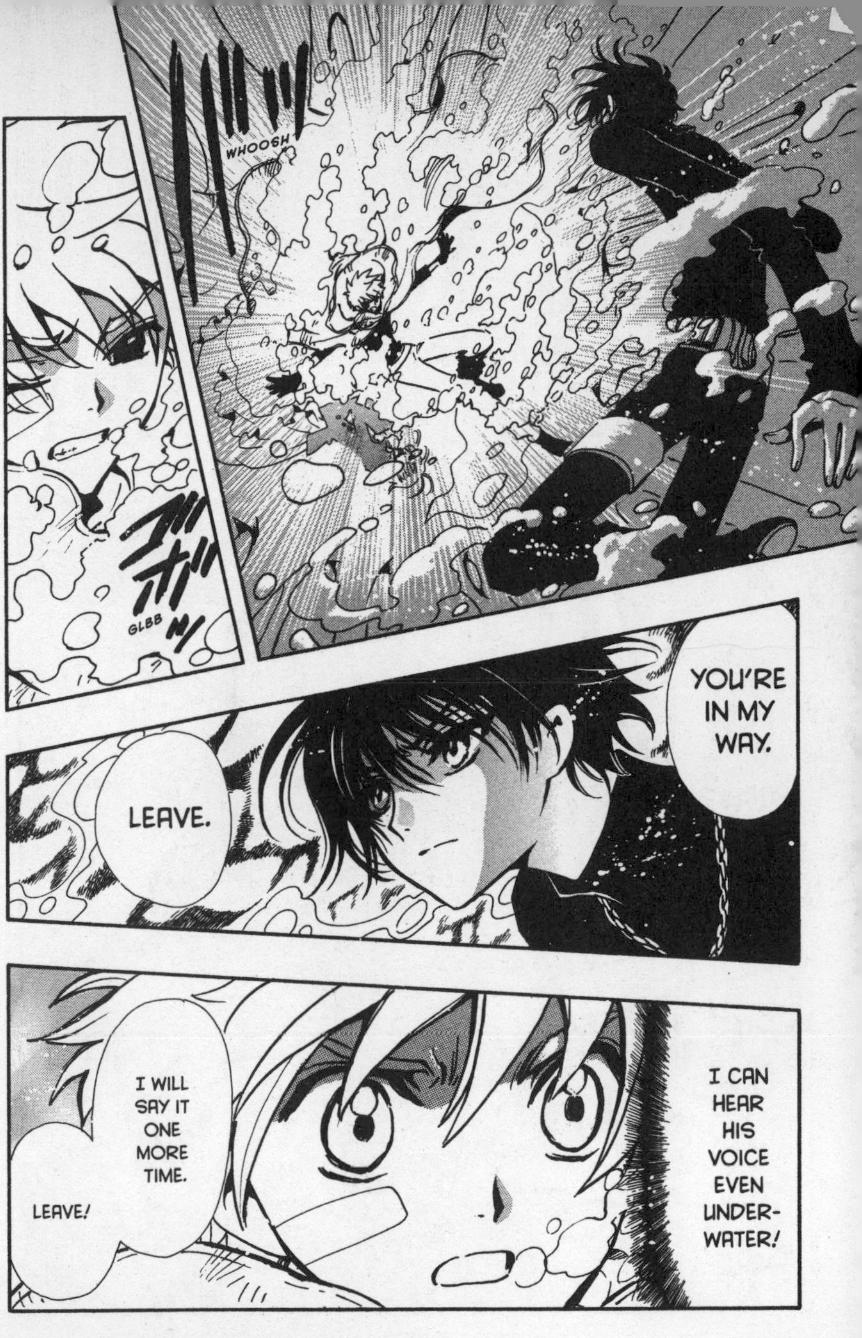
WHOOSH
GLBB
YOU'RE IN MY WAY.
LEAVE.
I CAN HEAR HIS VOICE EVEN UNDER-WATER!
I WILL SAY IT ONE MORE TIME.
LEAVE!

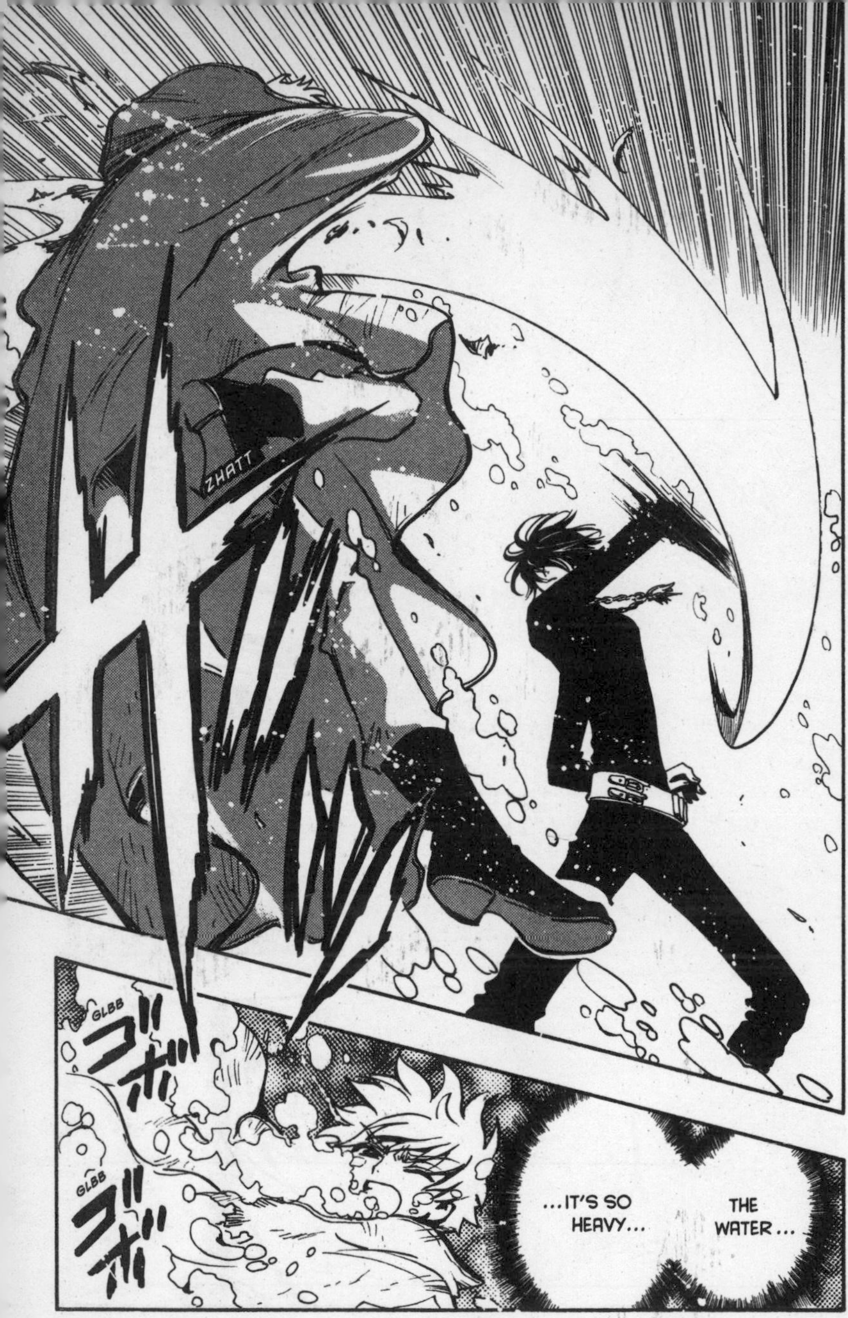
ZHATT
THE WATER...
...IT'S SO HEAVY...
GLBB
ゴボ
GLBB
ゴボ

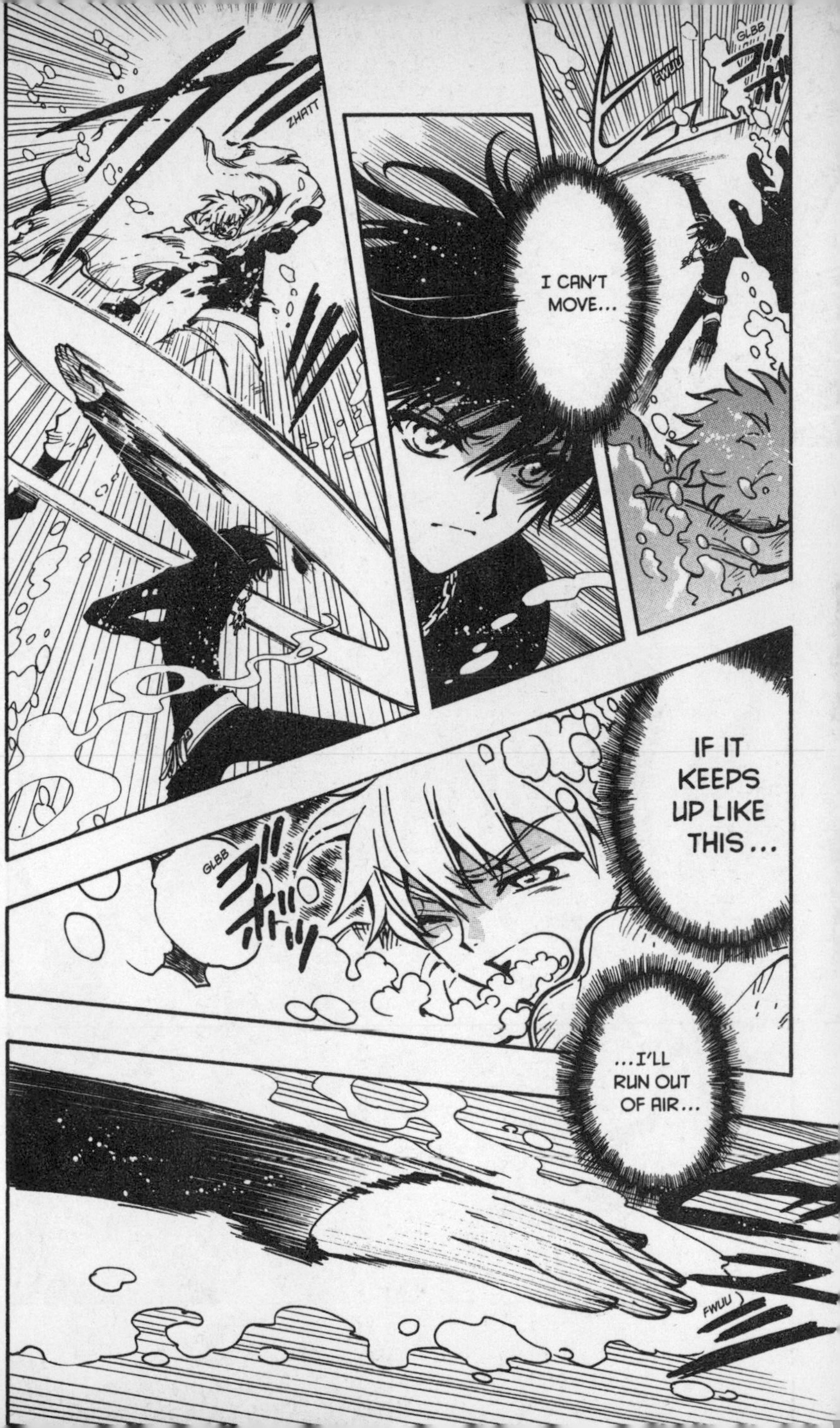
FWUU
GLBB
I CAN'T MOVE...
ZHATT
IF IT KEEPS UP LIKE THIS...
GLBB
...I'LL RUN OUT OF AIR...
FWUU

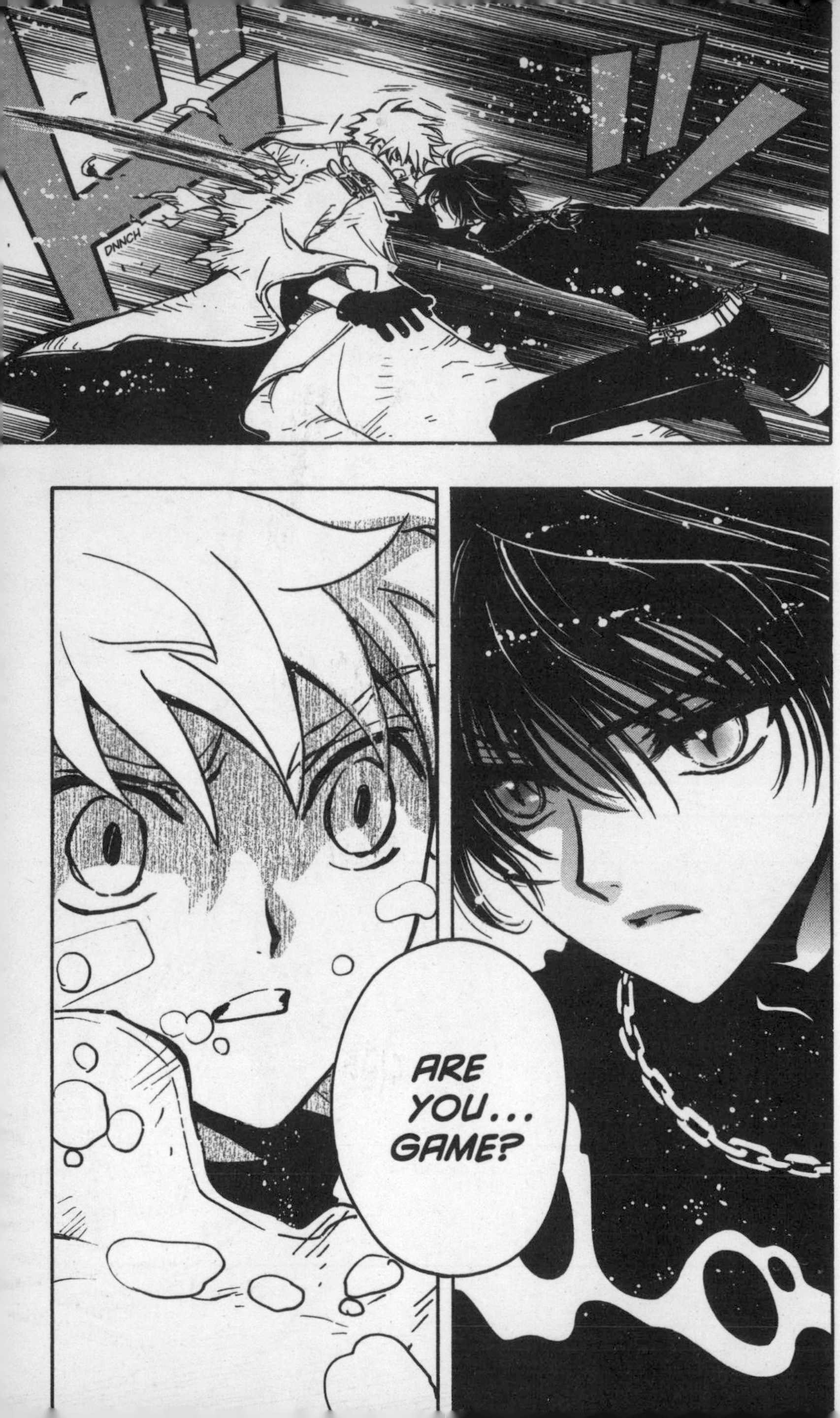
DNNCH
ARE YOU... GAME?

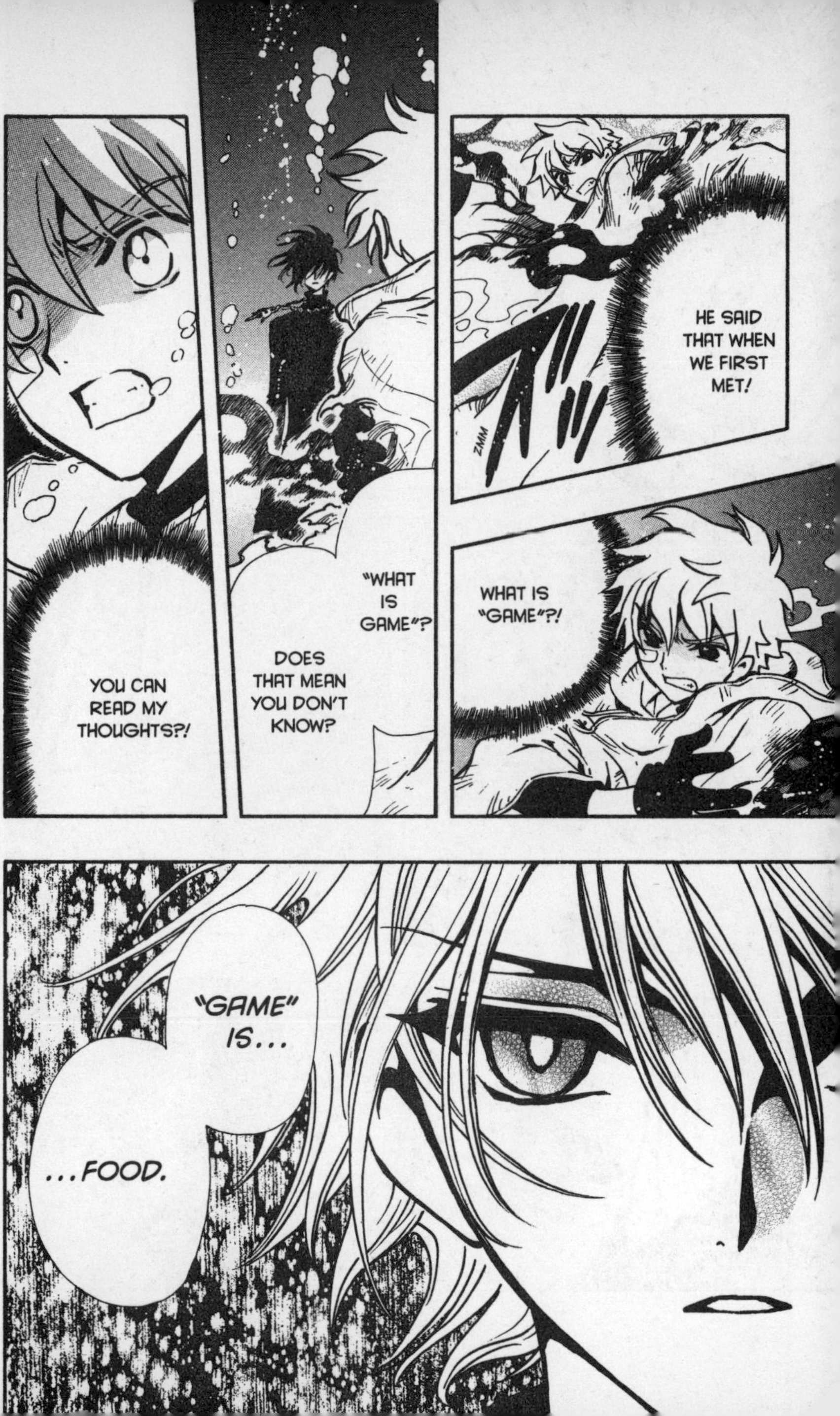
HE SAID THAT WHEN WE FIRST MET!
ZMM
WHAT IS "GAME"?!
"WHAT IS GAME"?
DOES THAT MEAN YOU DON'T KNOW?
YOU CAN READ MY THOUGHTS?!
"GAME" IS...
...FOOD.

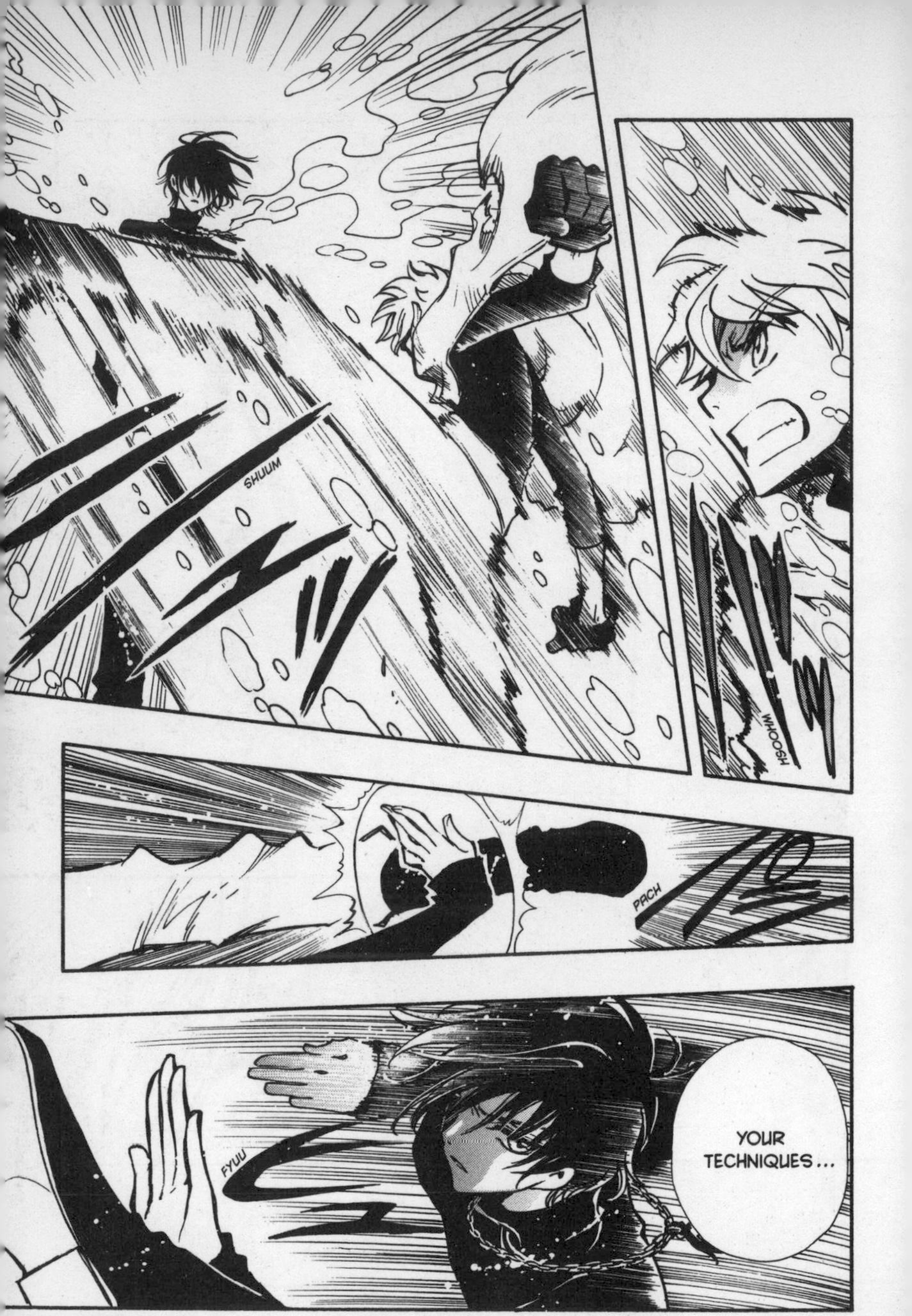
WHOOSH
SHUUM
PACH
YOUR TECHNIQUES...
FYUU

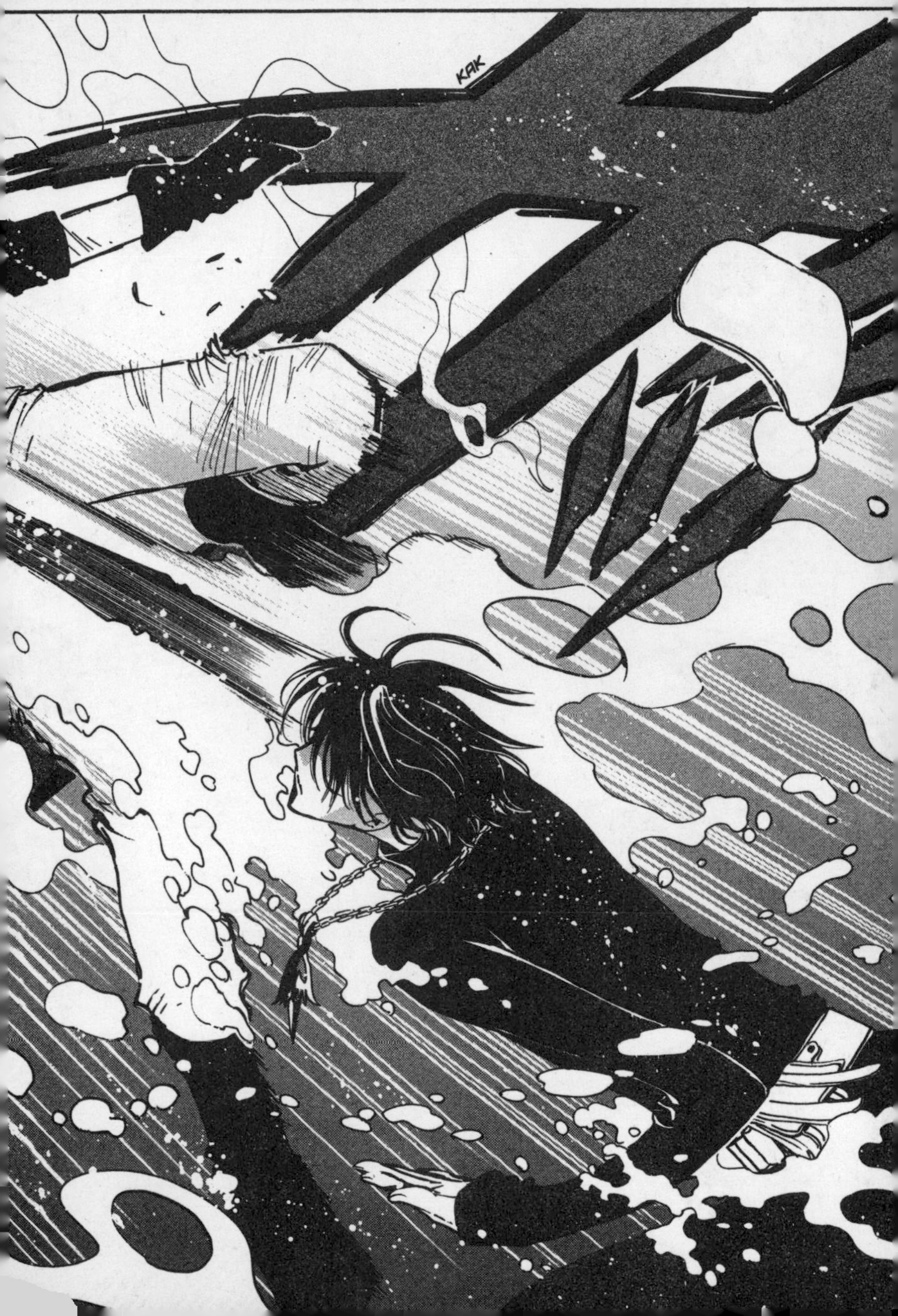
KAK

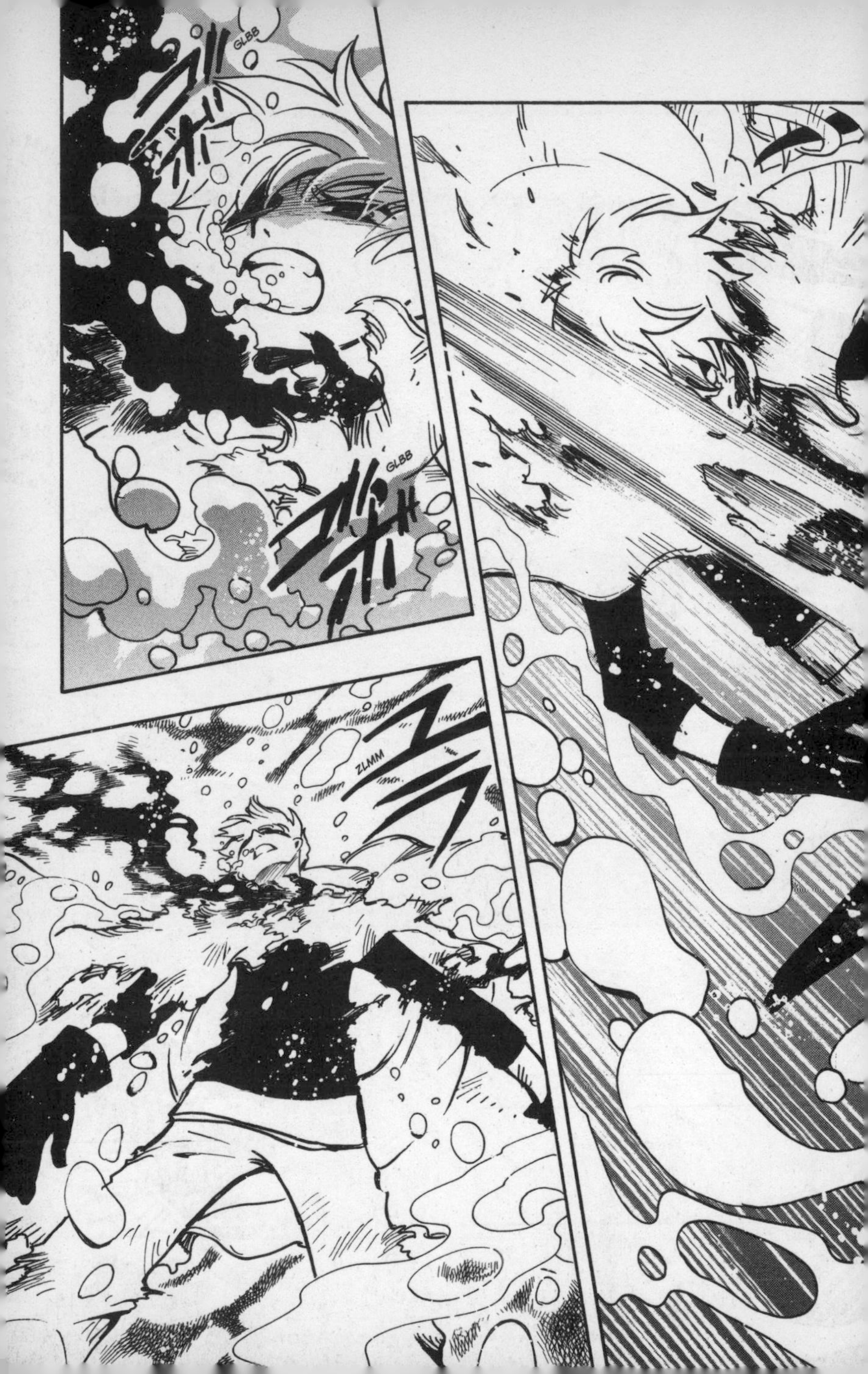
GLBB
GLBB
ZLMM

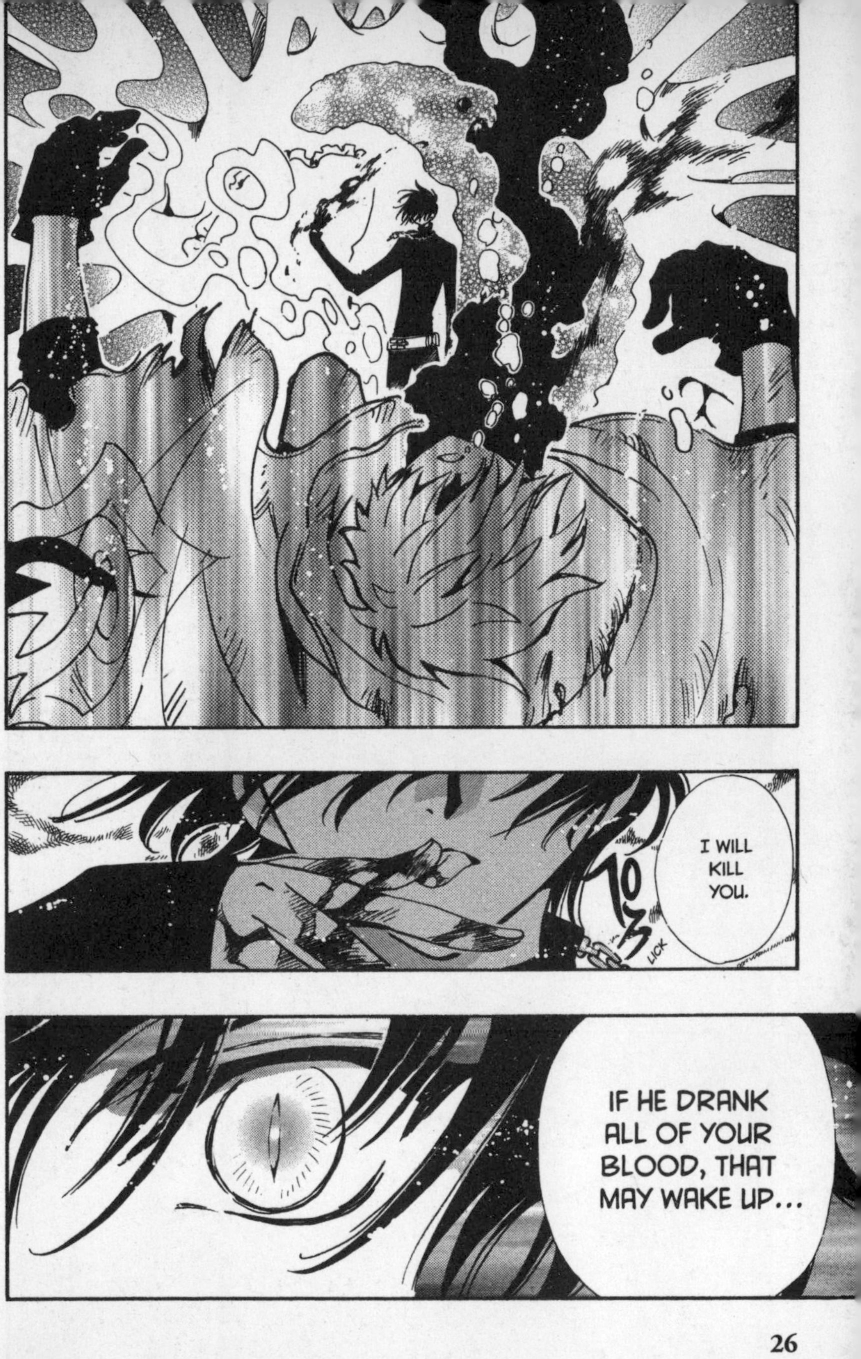
I WILL KILL YOU.
LICK
IF HE DRANK ALL OF YOUR BLOOD, THAT MAY WAKE UP...

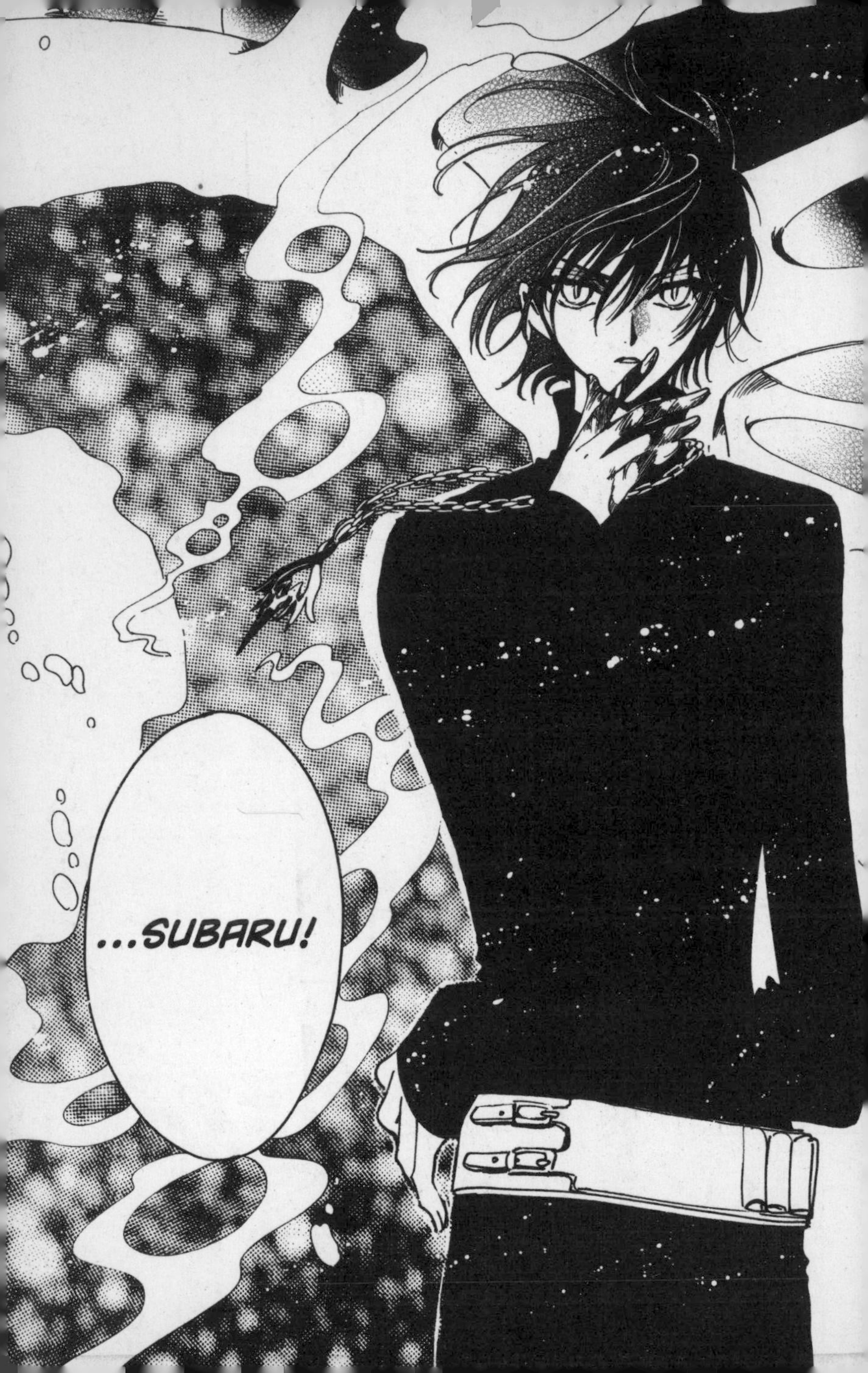
...SUBARU!

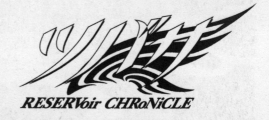

RESERVoir CHRoNiCLE

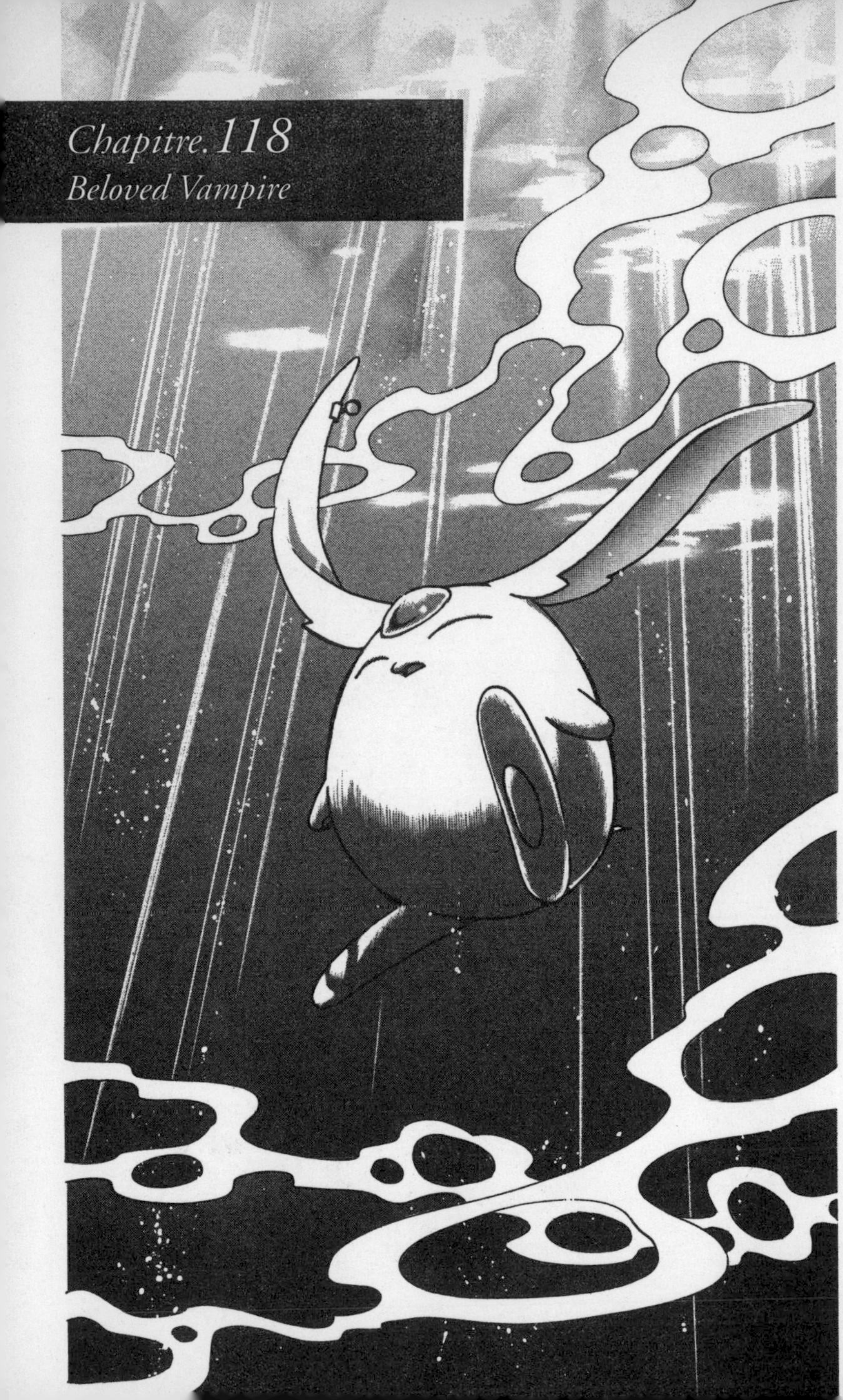
Chapitre. 118
Beloved Vampire

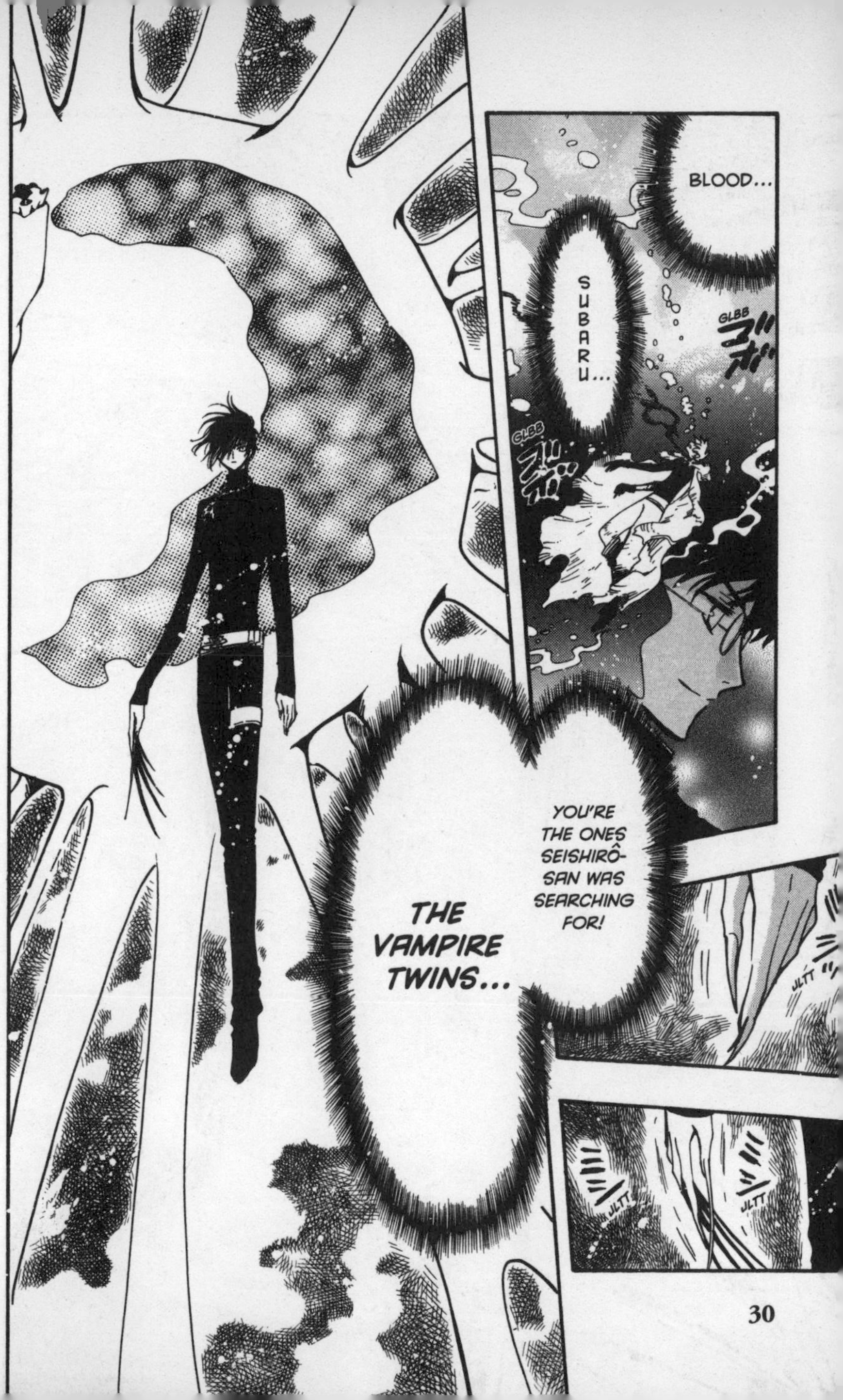
BLOOD...
SUBARU...
GLBB
GLBB
YOU'RE THE ONES SEISHIRÔ-SAN WAS SEARCHING FOR!
THE VAMPIRE TWINS...
JLTT
JLTT
JLTT

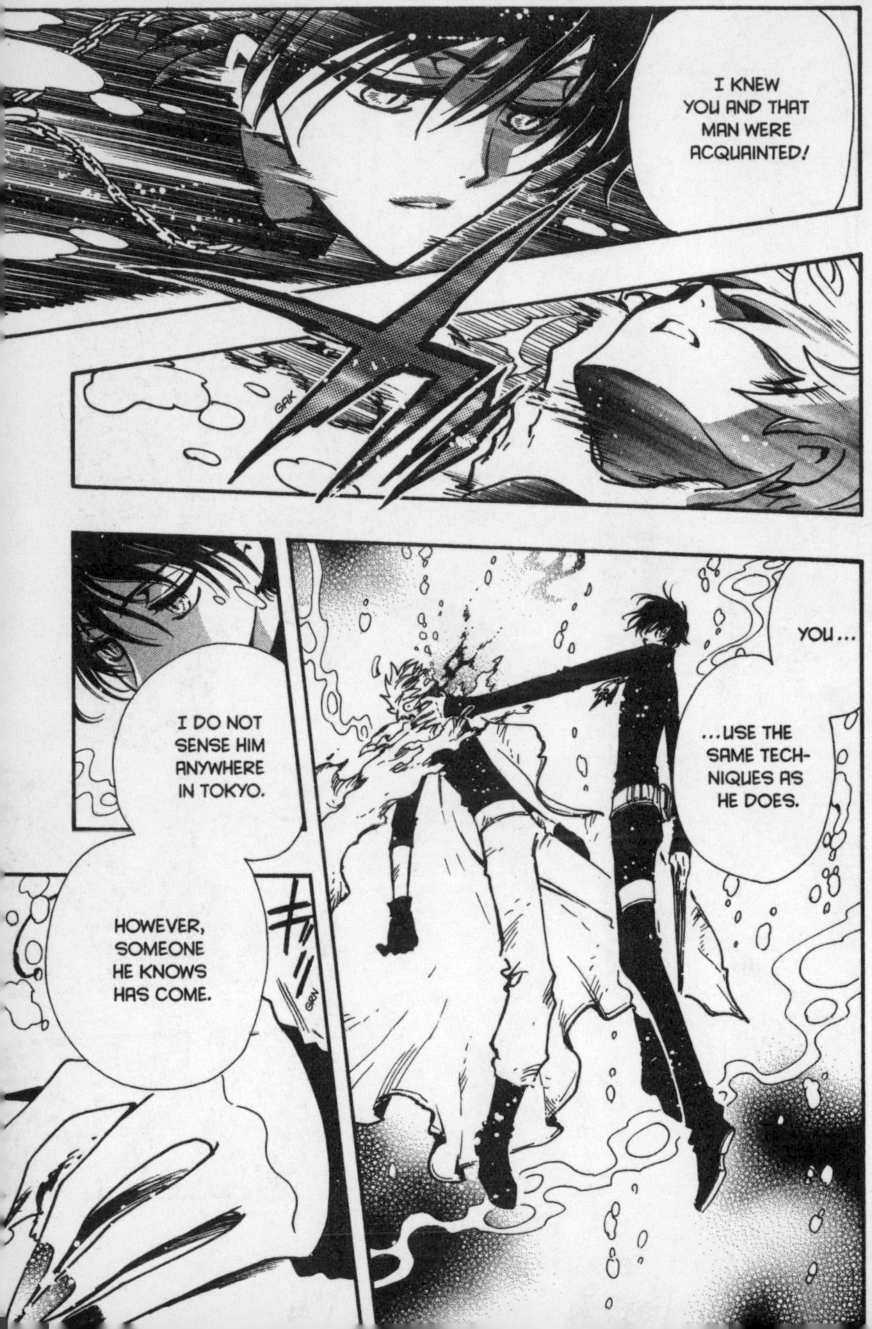
I KNEW YOU AND THAT MAN WERE ACQUAINTED!
GAK
YOU...
...USE THE SAME TECHNIQUES AS HE DOES.
I DO NOT SENSE HIM ANYWHERE IN TOKYO.
HOWEVER, SOMEONE HE KNOWS HAS COME.
GRN

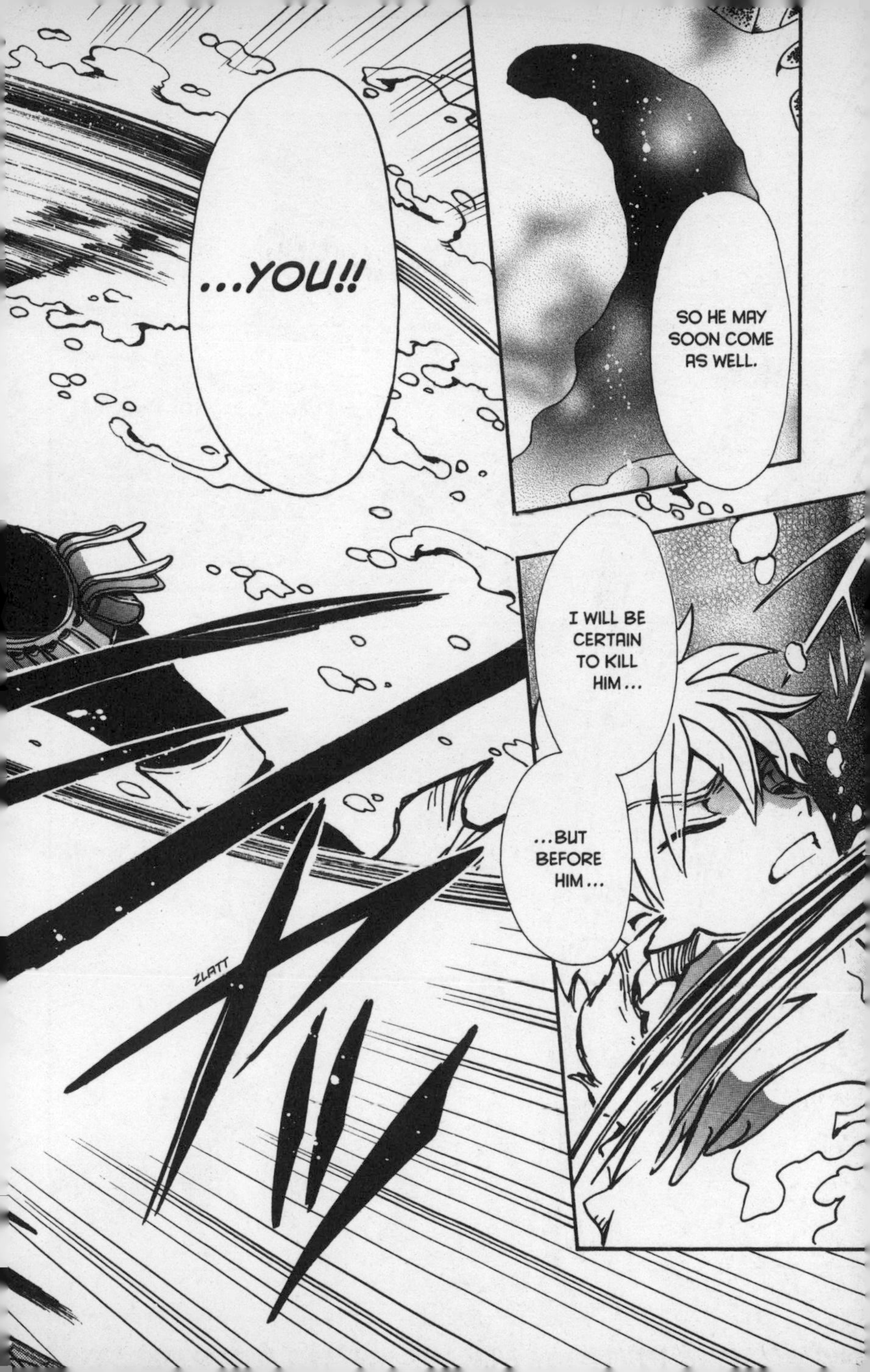
SO HE MAY SOON COME AS WELL.
I WILL BE CERTAIN TO KILL HIM...
...BUT BEFORE HIM...
...YOU!!
ZLATT

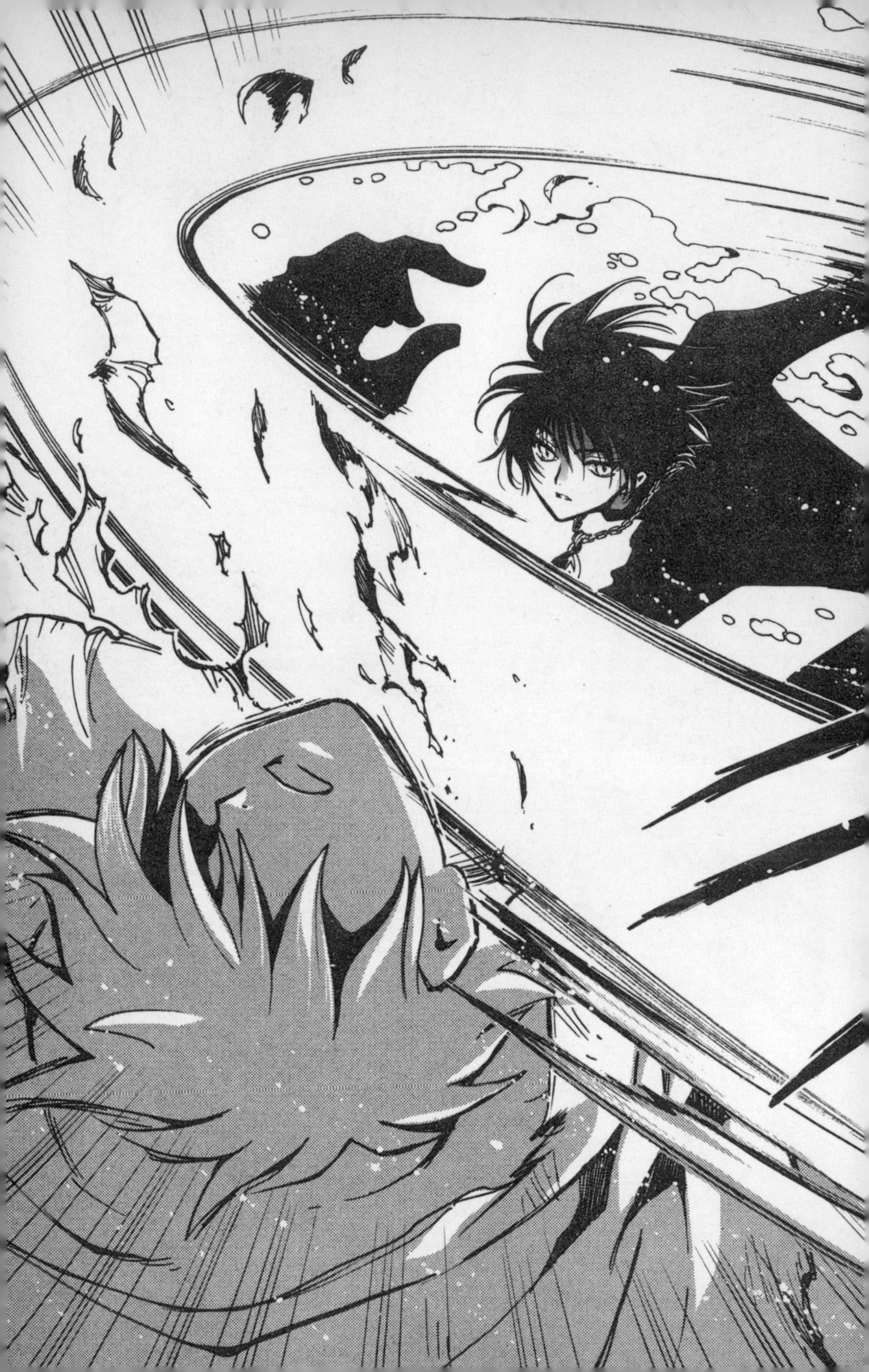

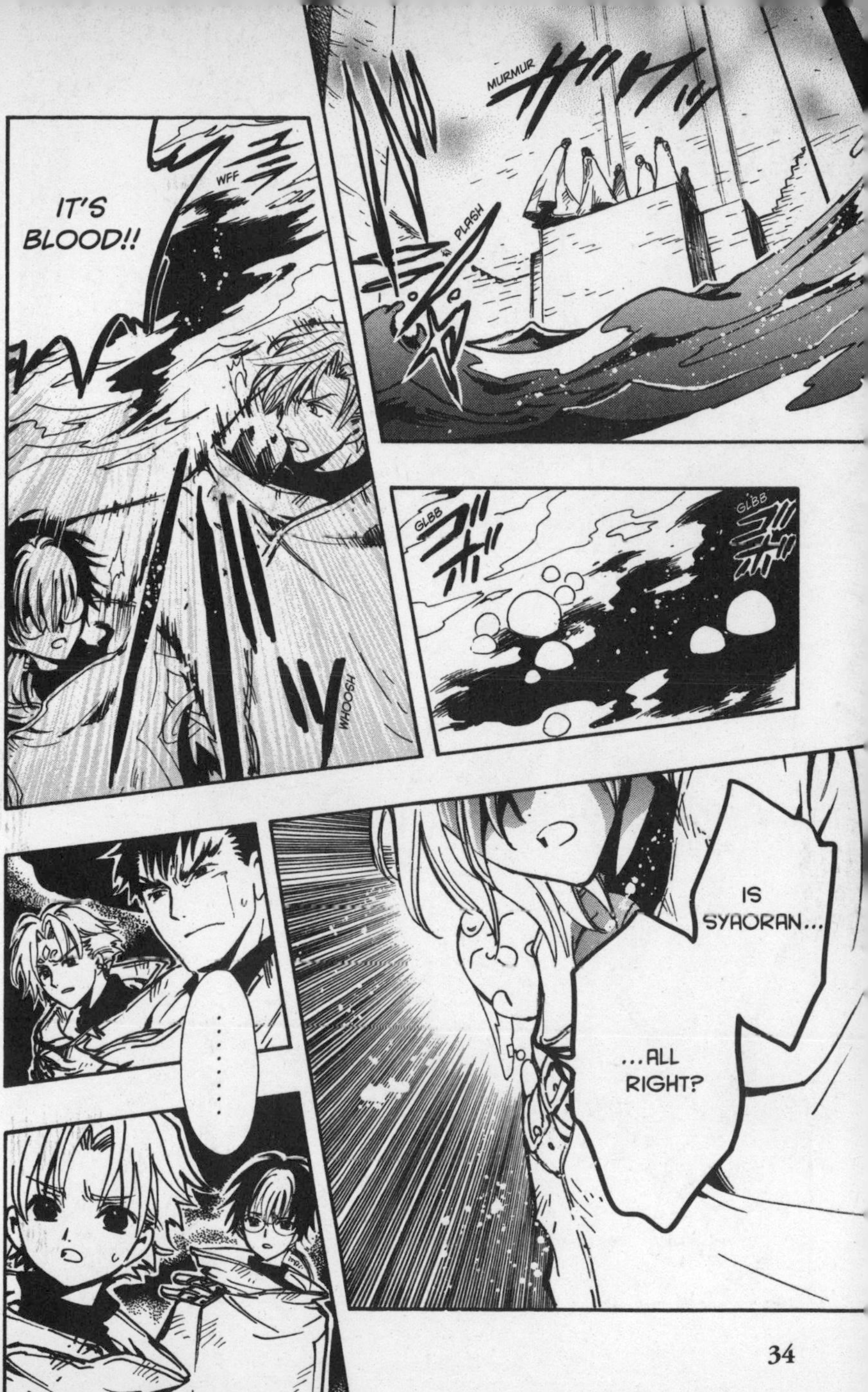
MURMUR
PLASH
GLBB
GLBB
IT'S BLOOD!!
WFF
WHOOSH
IS SYAORAN...
...ALL RIGHT?
......

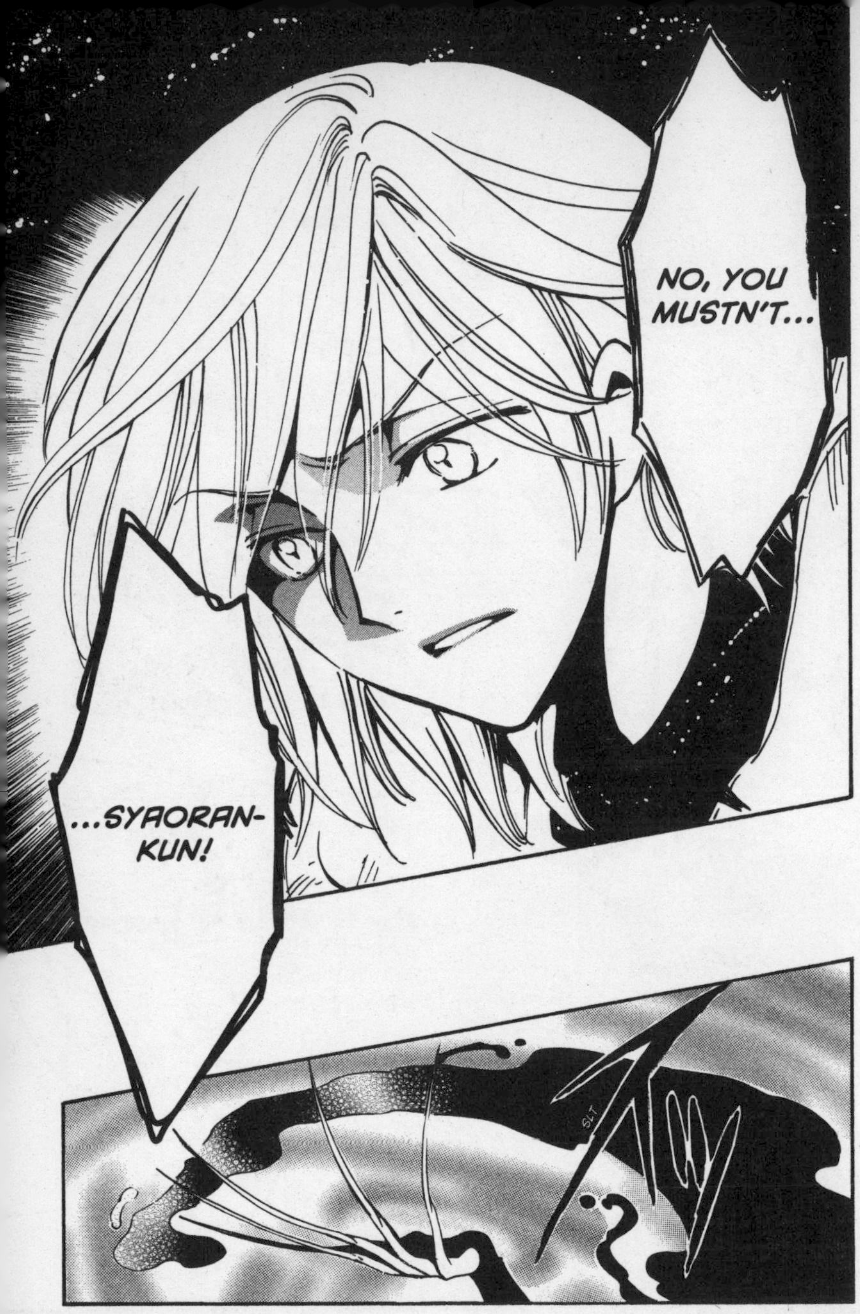
NO, YOU MUSTN'T...
...SYAORAN-KUN!
SLT

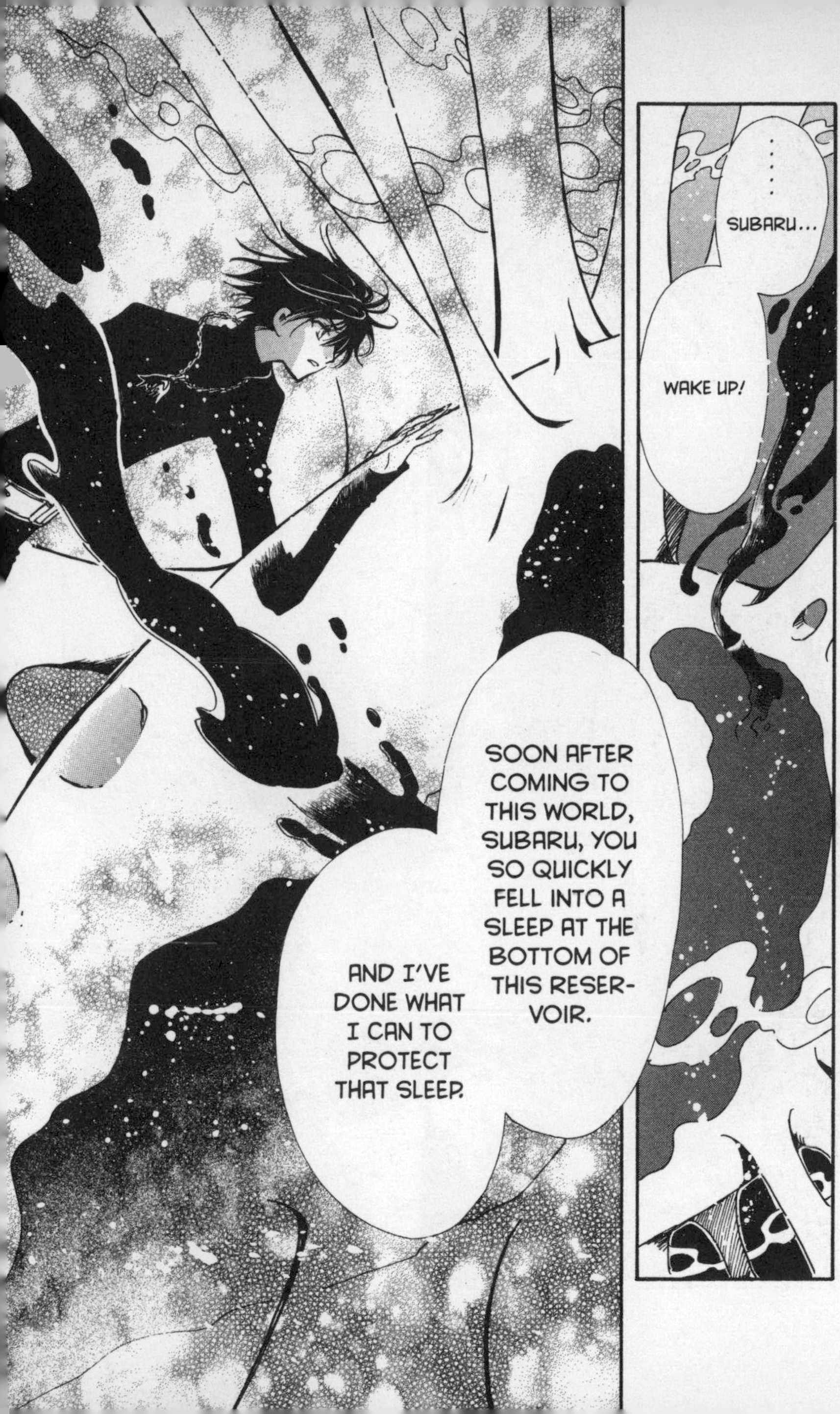
......
SUBARU...
WAKE UP!
SOON AFTER COMING TO THIS WORLD, SUBARU, YOU SO QUICKLY FELL INTO A SLEEP AT THE BOTTOM OF THIS RESER-VOIR.
AND I'VE DONE WHAT I CAN TO PROTECT THAT SLEEP.

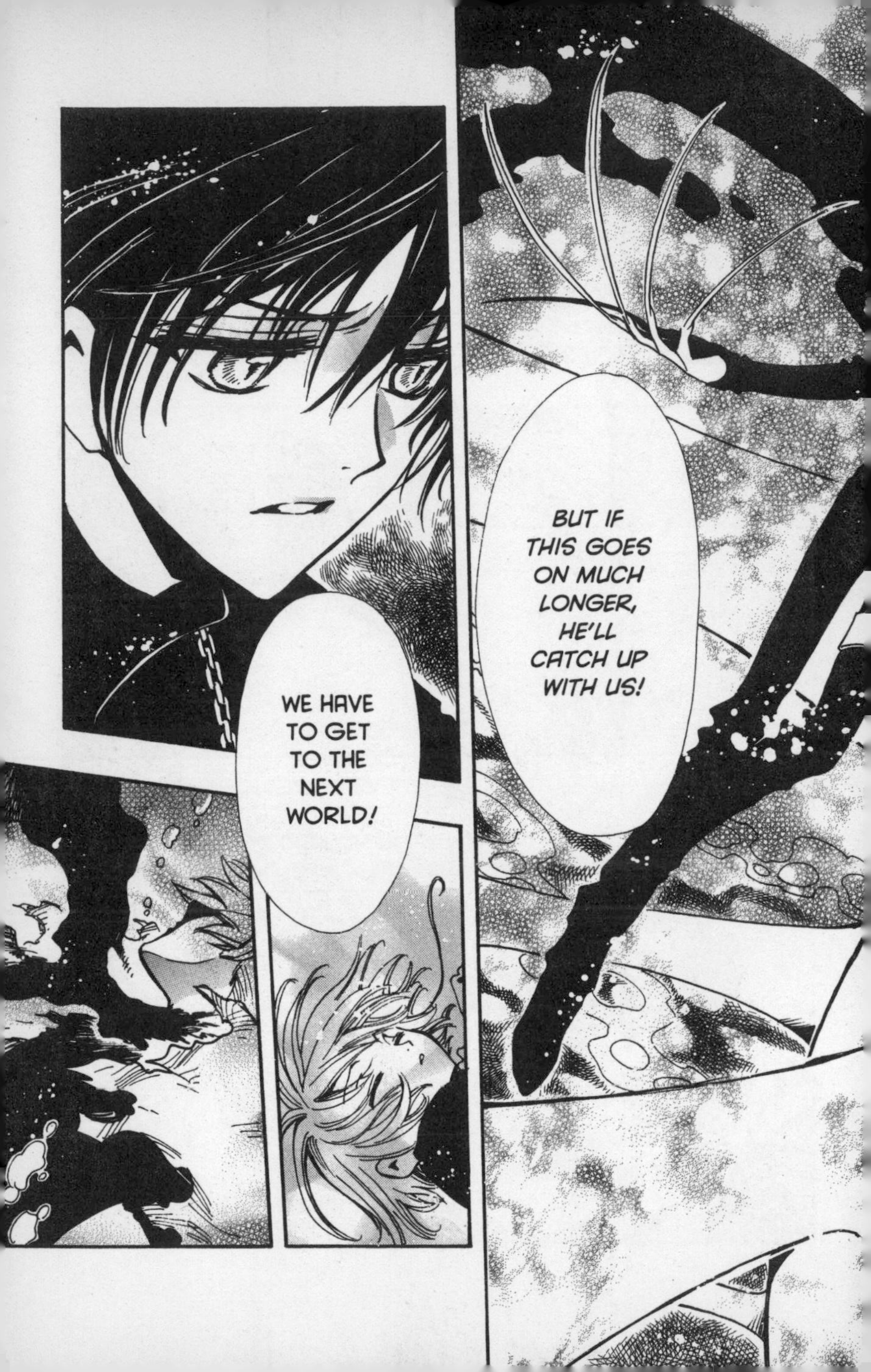
BUT IF THIS GOES ON MUCH LONGER, HE'LL CATCH UP WITH US!
WE HAVE TO GET TO THE NEXT WORLD!

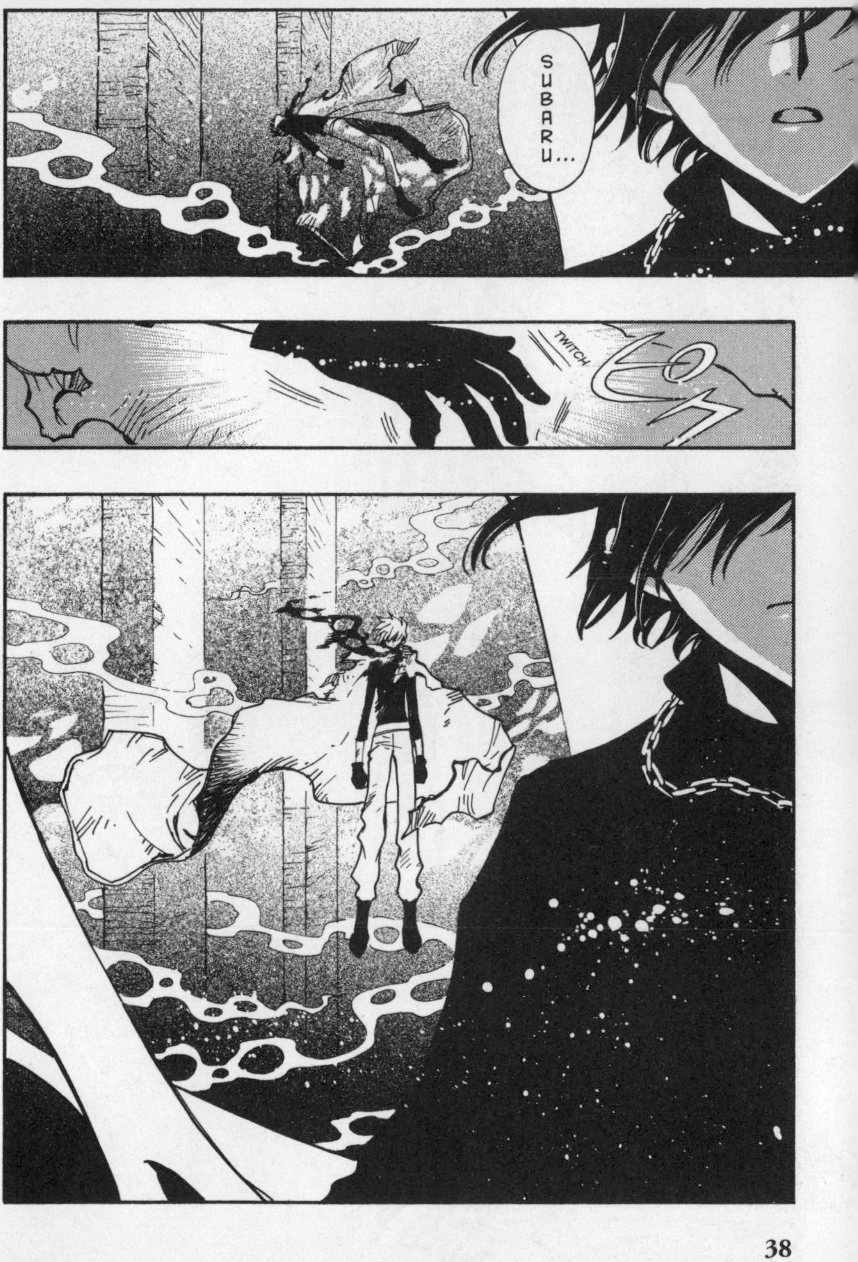
SUBARU...
TWITCH

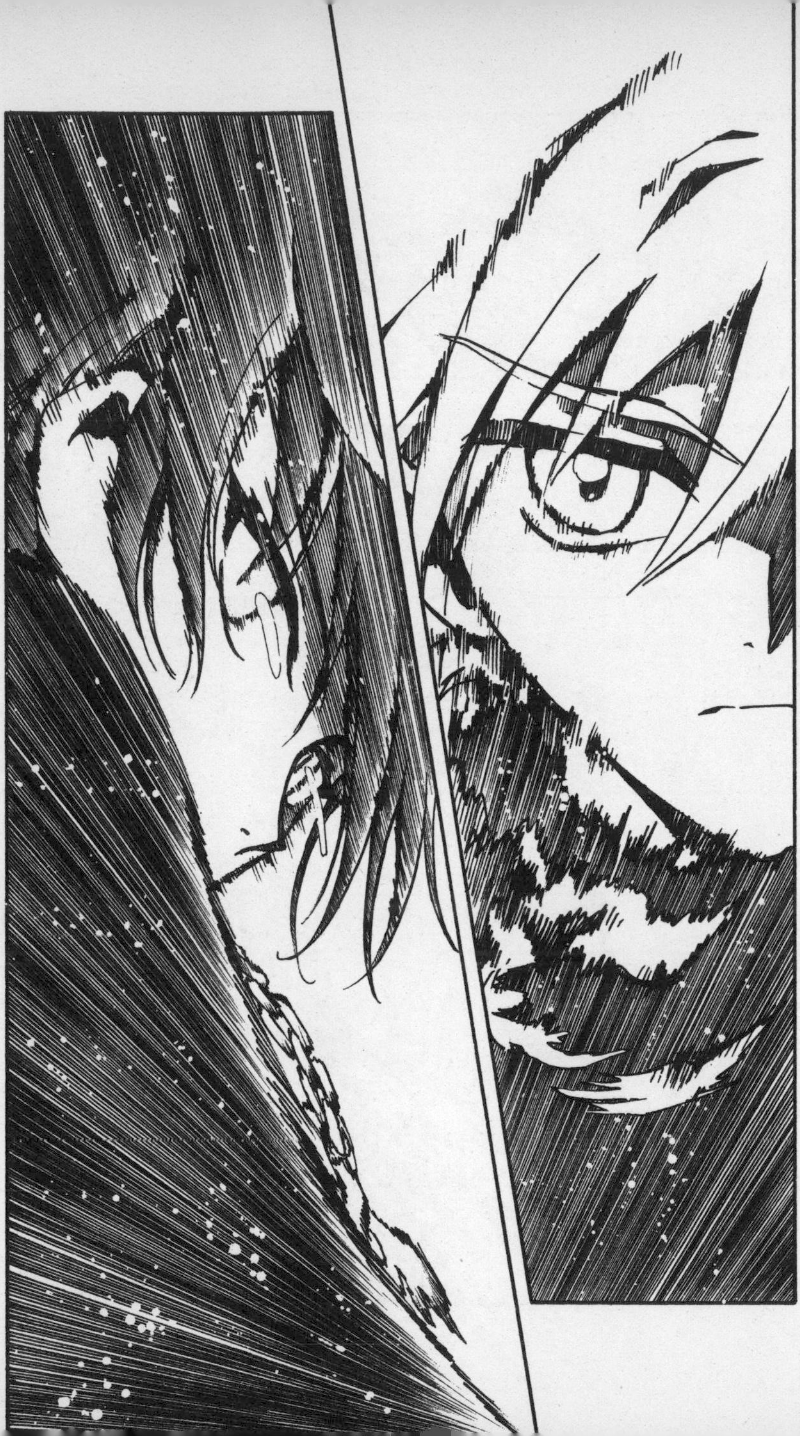

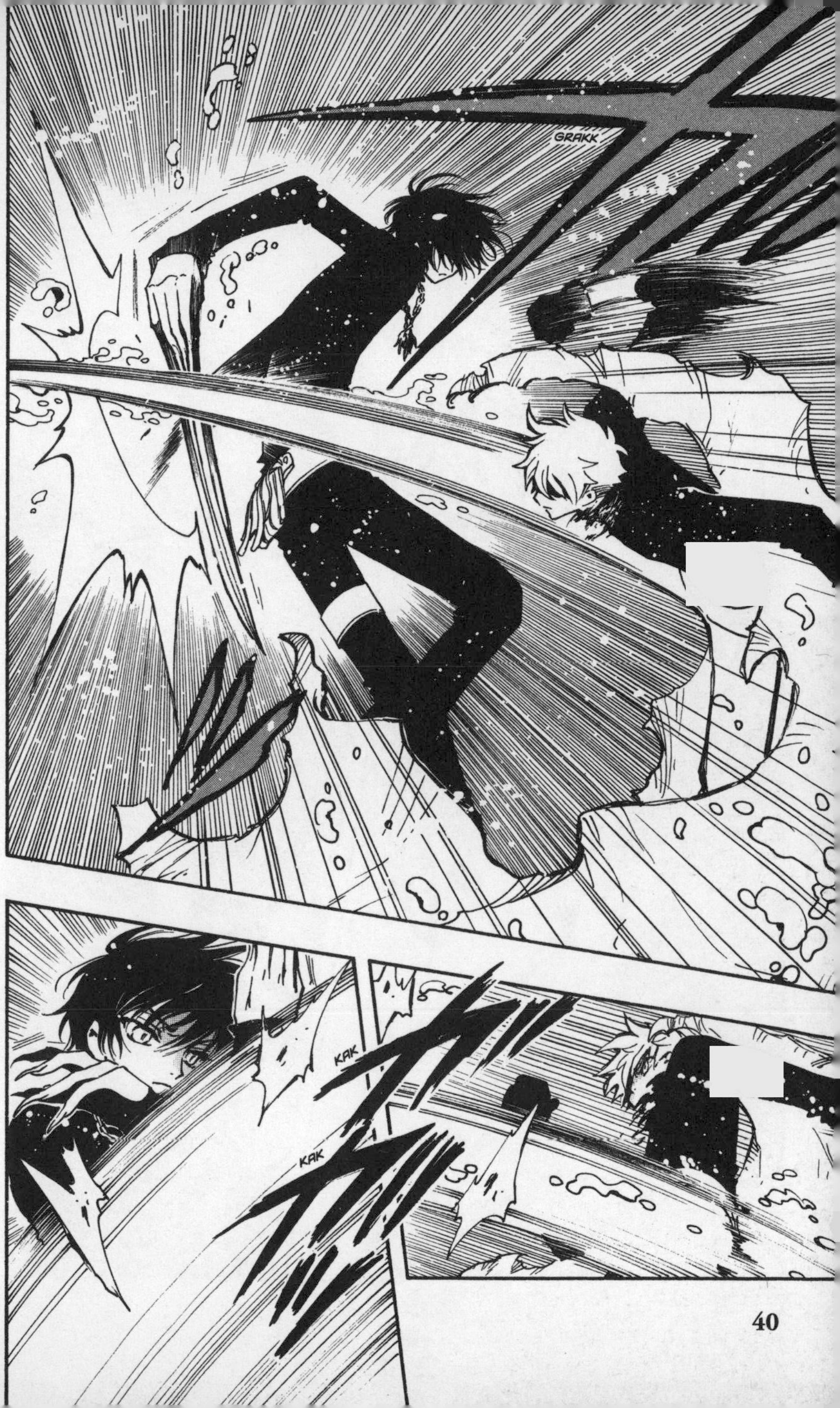
GRAKK
KAK
KAK

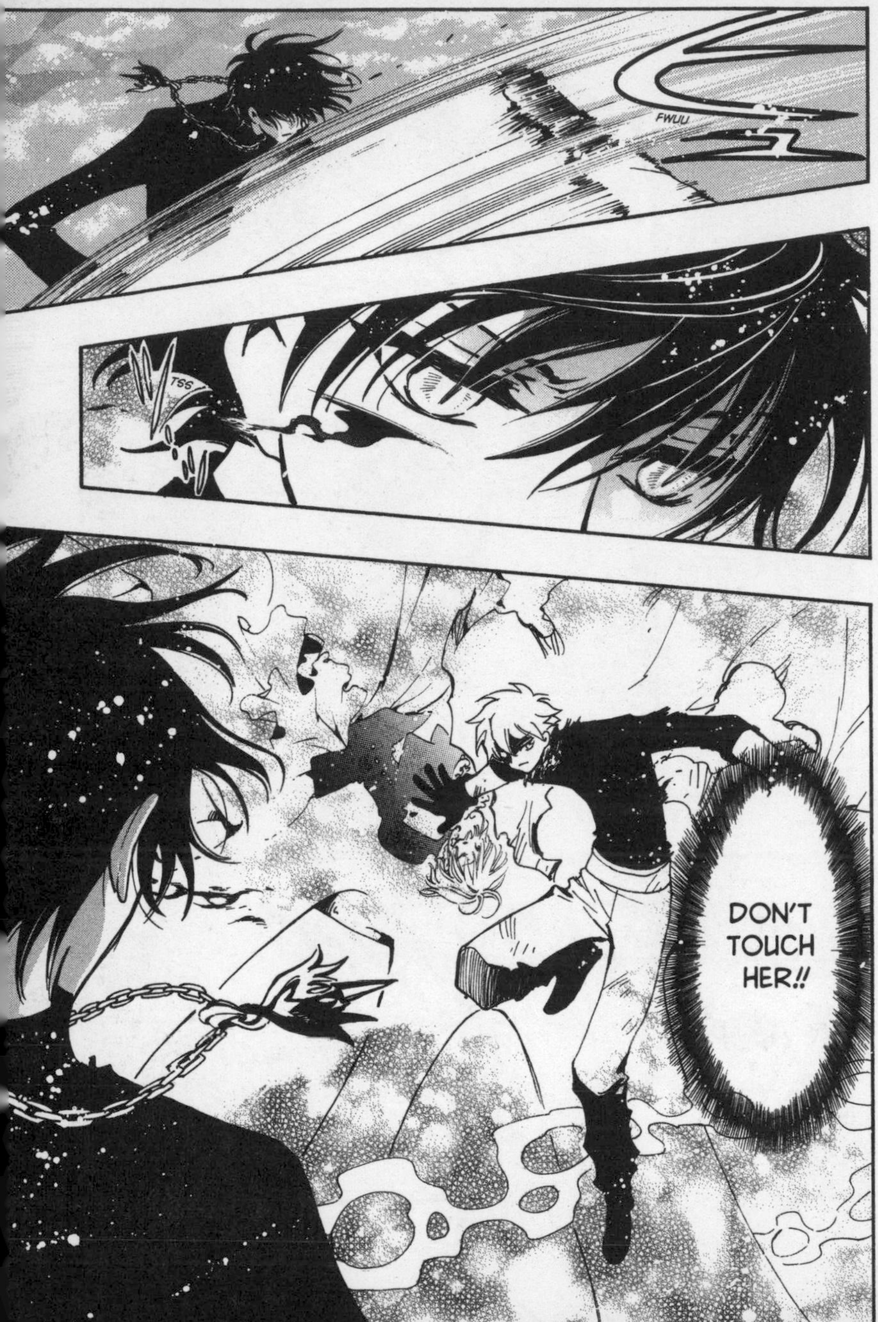
FWUU
TSS
DON'T TOUCH HER!!

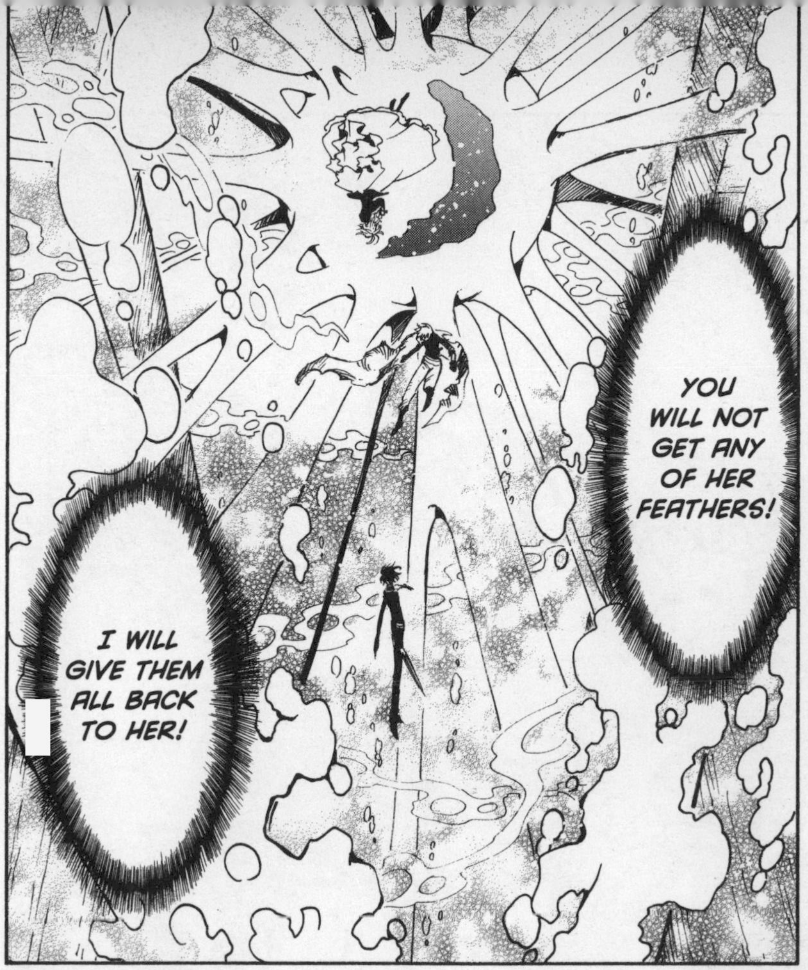
YOU WILL NOT GET ANY OF HER FEATHERS!
I WILL GIVE THEM ALL BACK TO HER!

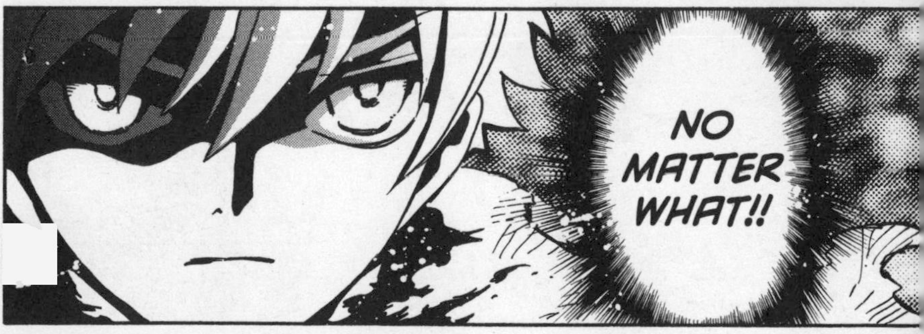
NO MATTER WHAT!!

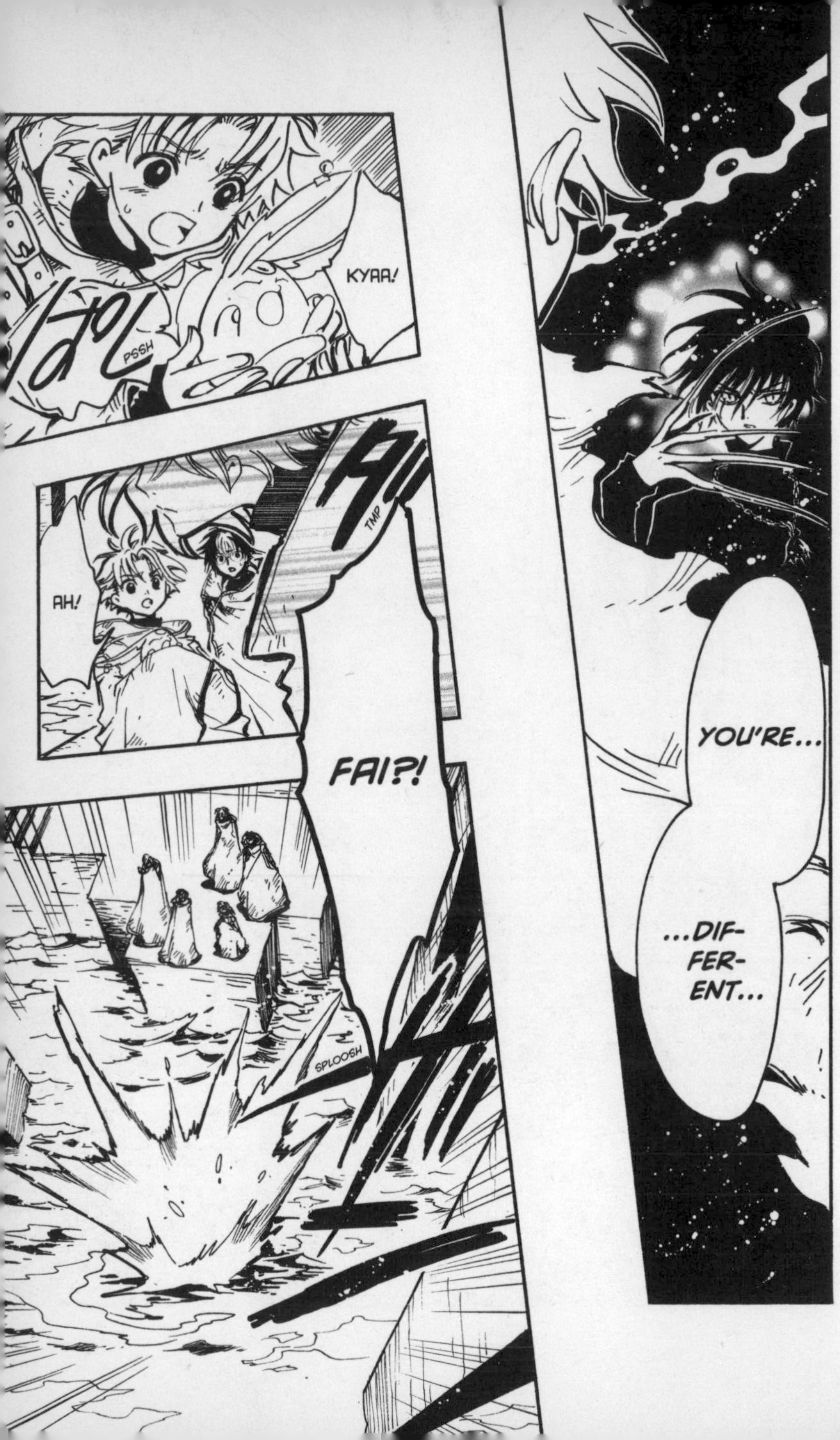
YOU'RE...
...DIF-
FER-
ENT...
KYAA!
PSSH
AH!
TMP
FAI?!
SPLOOSH

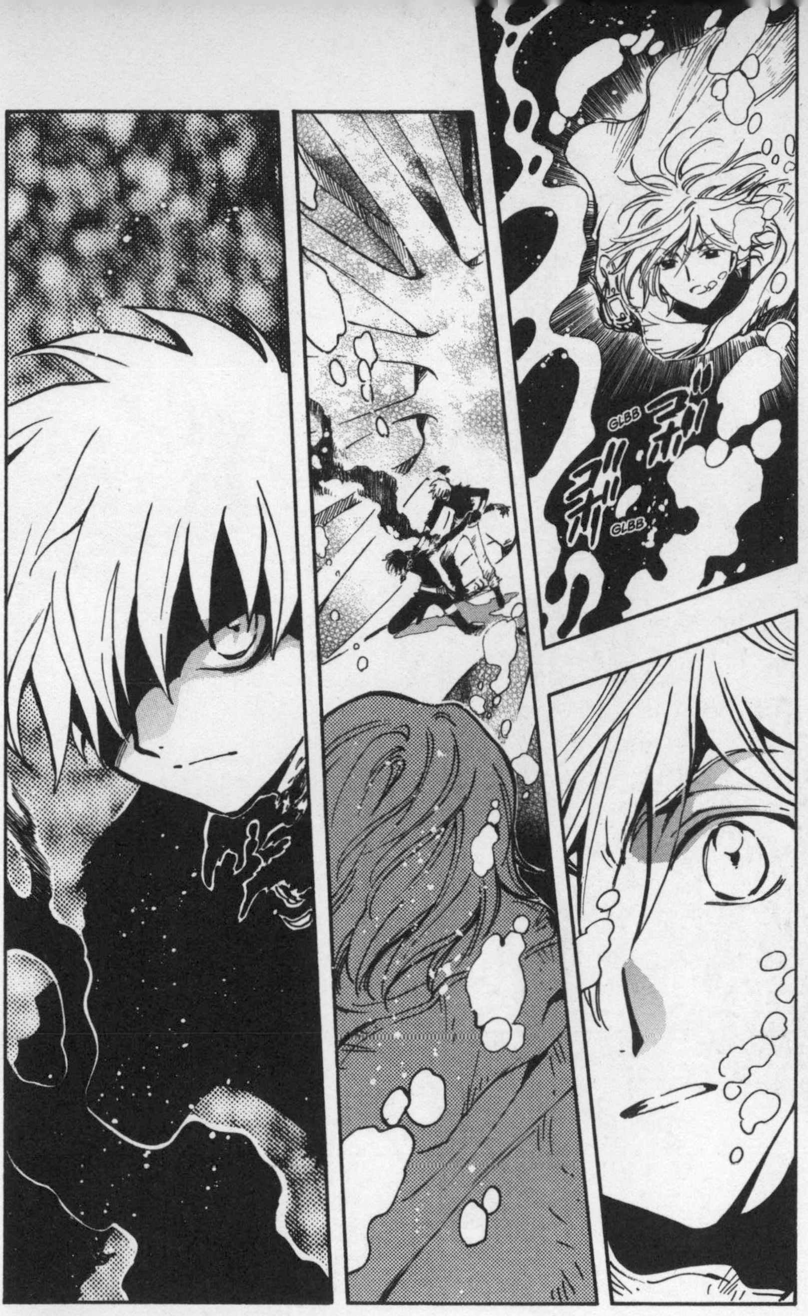
GLBB
GLBB

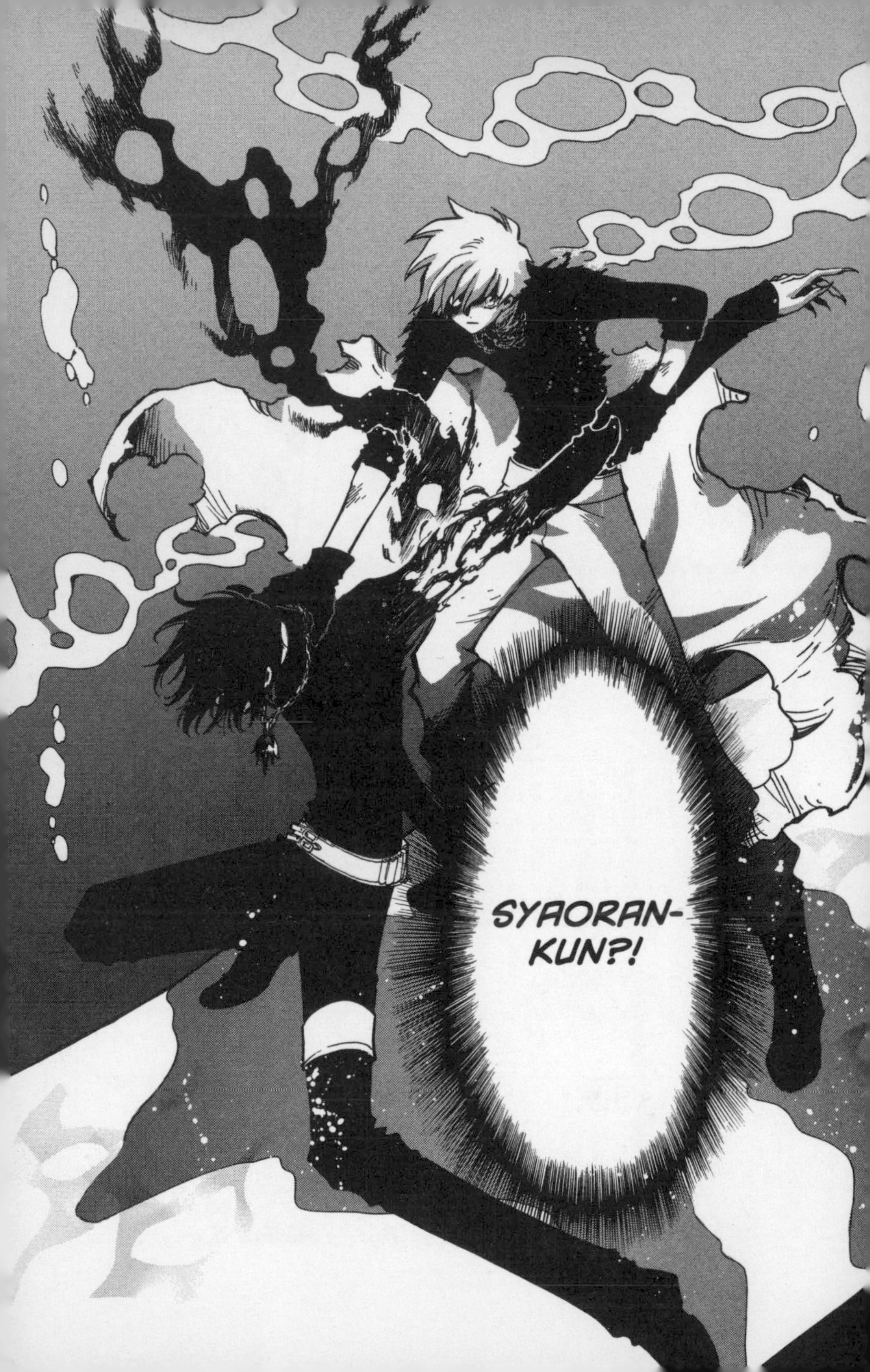
SYAORAN-KUN?!

ツバサ

RESERVoir CHRoNiCLE

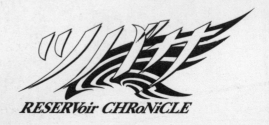

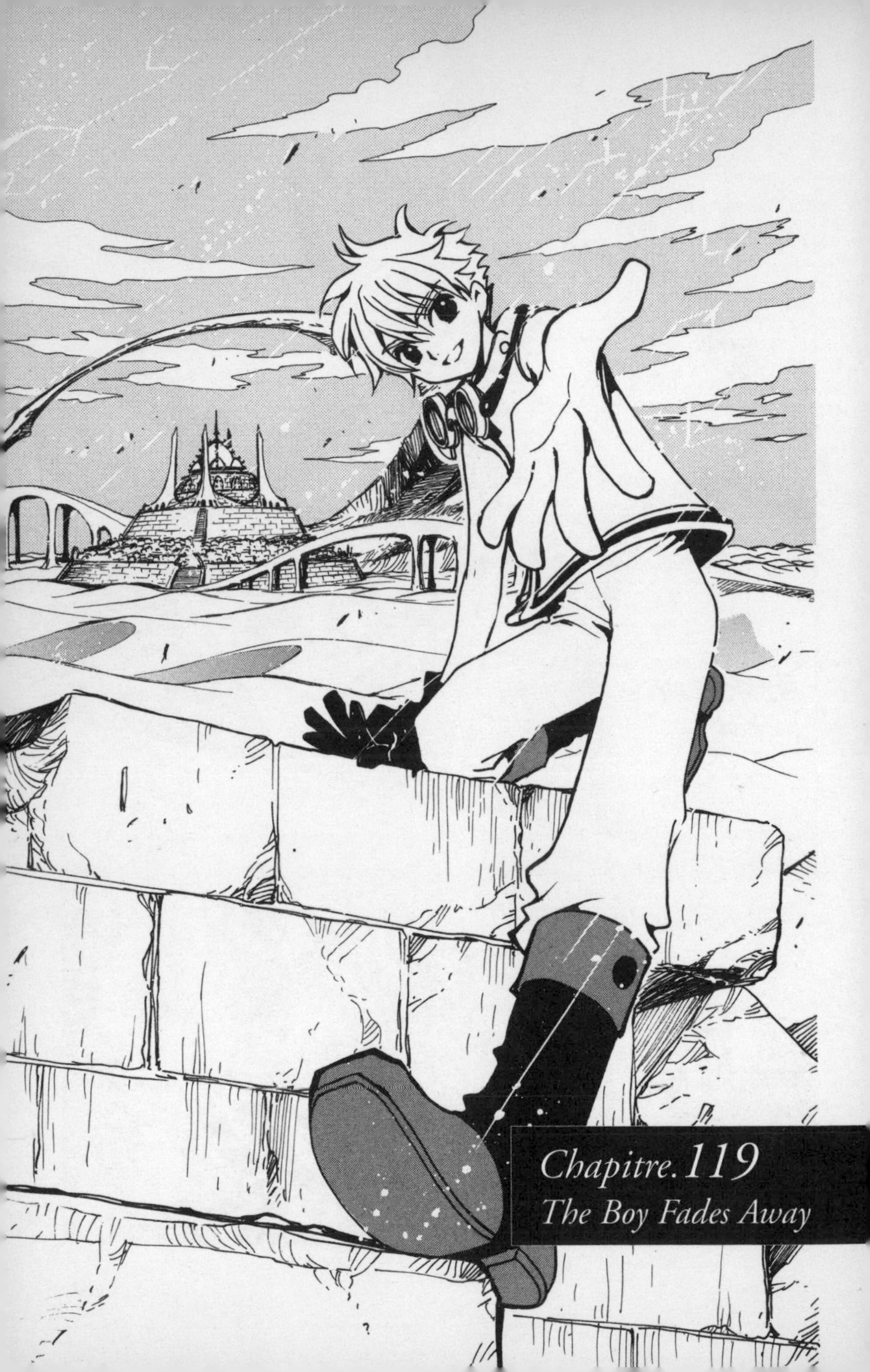
Chapitre.119
The Boy Fades Away

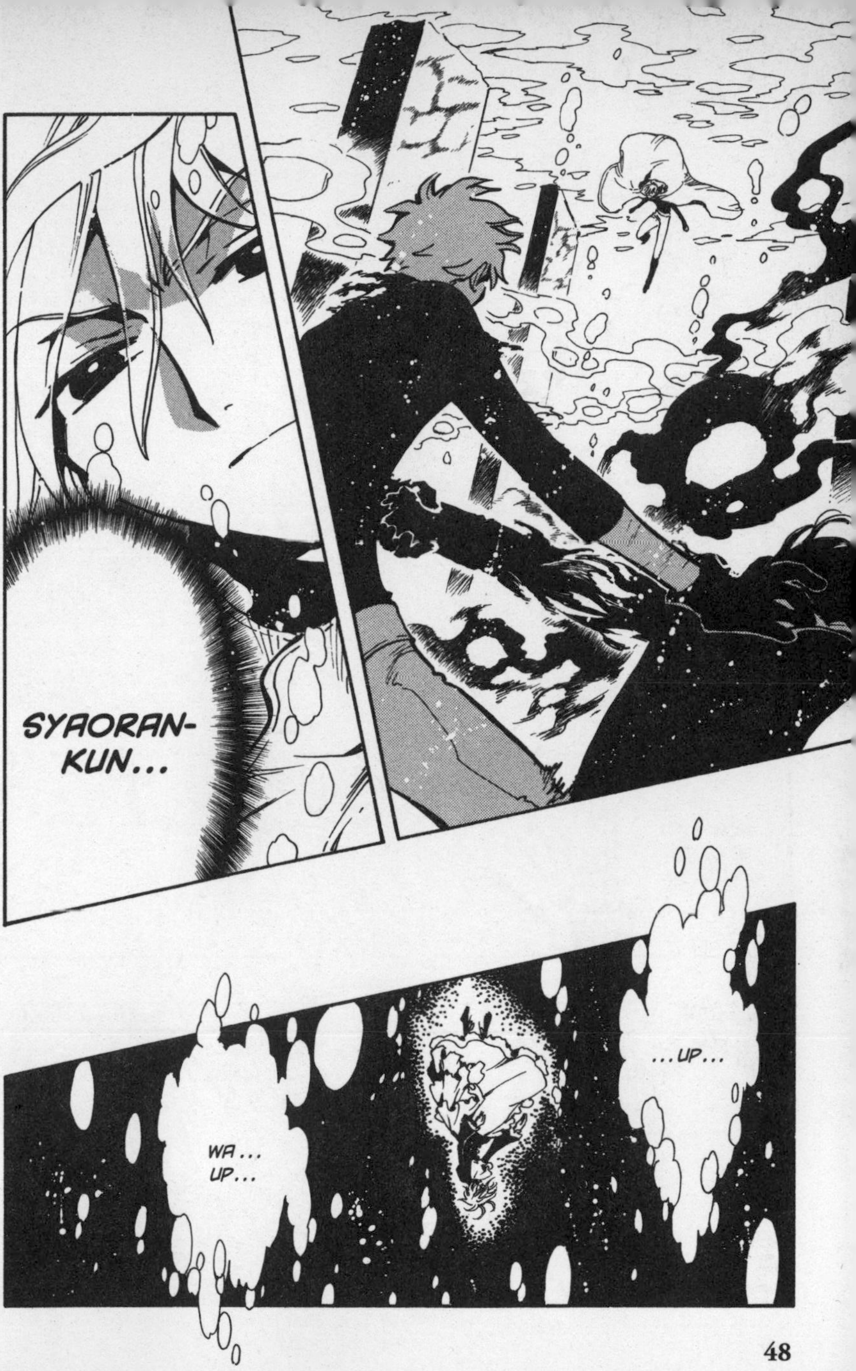
SYAORAN-KUN...
...UP...
WA...
UP...

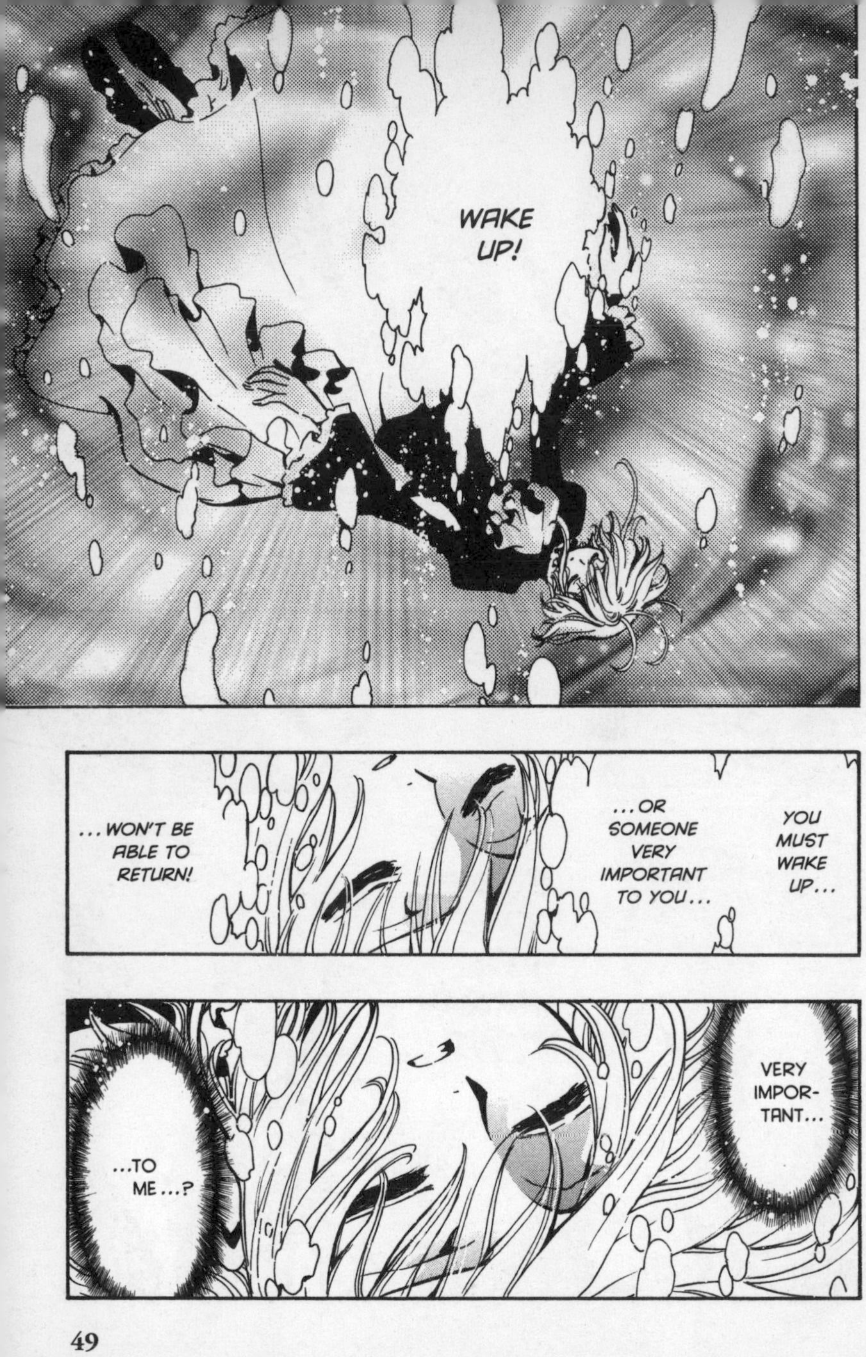
WAKE UP!
YOU MUST WAKE UP...
...OR SOMEONE VERY IMPORTANT TO YOU...
...WON'T BE ABLE TO RETURN!
VERY IMPOR-TANT...
...TO ME...?

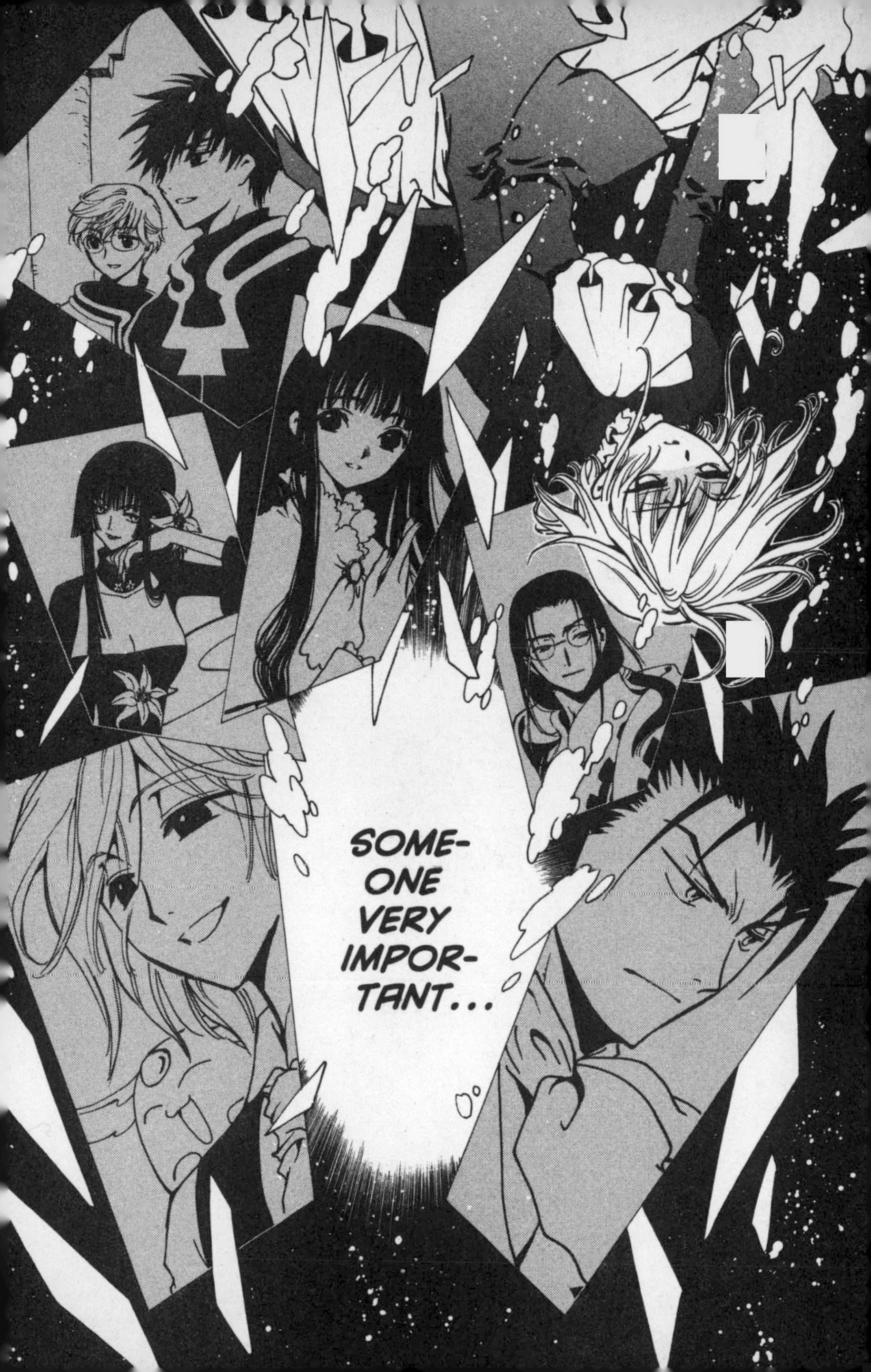
SOME-ONE VERY IMPOR-TANT...

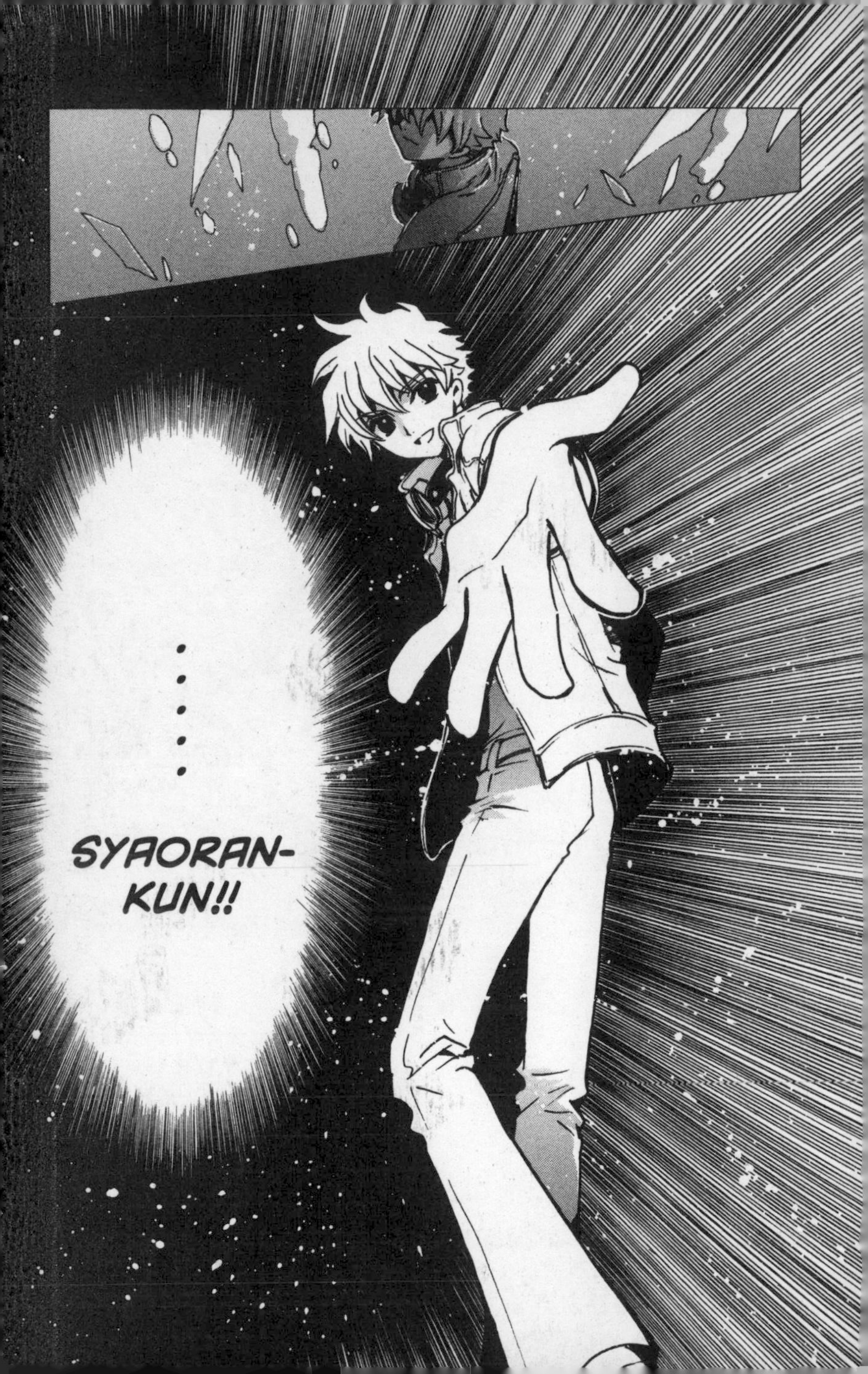
.....
SYAORAN-
KUN!!

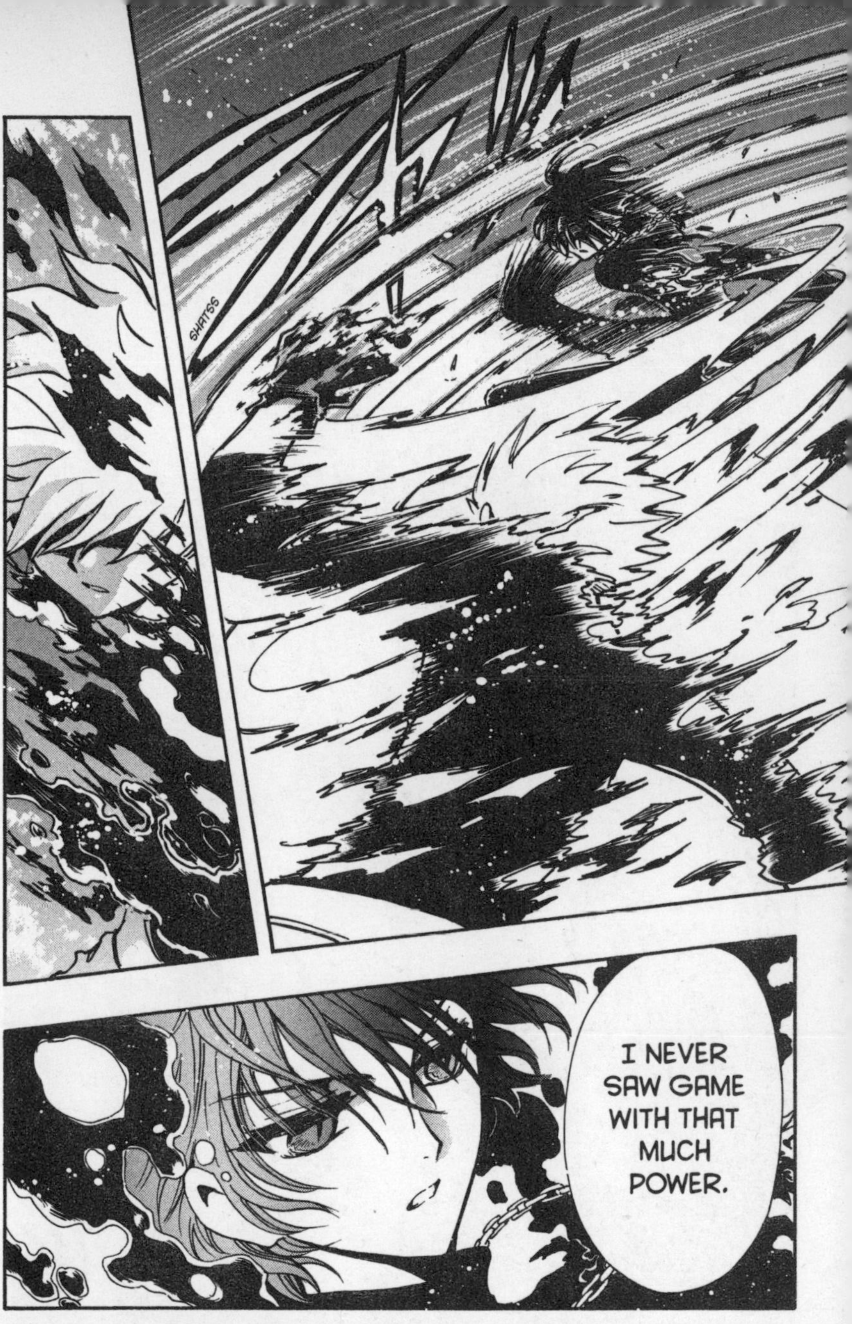
SHATSS
I NEVER SAW GAME WITH THAT MUCH POWER.

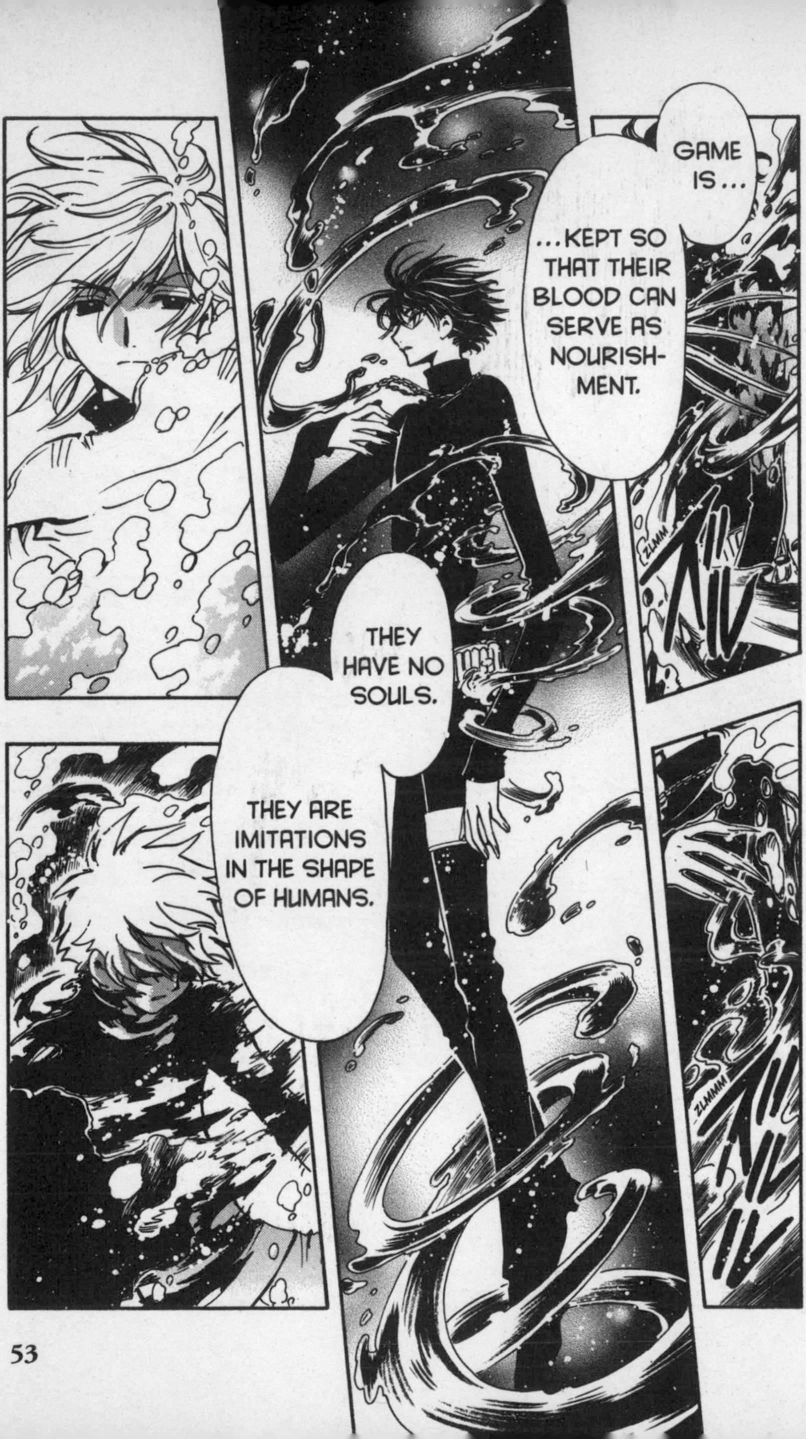
ZLMMM
ZLMMM
GAME IS...
...KEPT SO THAT THEIR BLOOD CAN SERVE AS NOURISH-MENT.
THEY HAVE NO SOULS.
THEY ARE IMITATIONS IN THE SHAPE OF HUMANS.

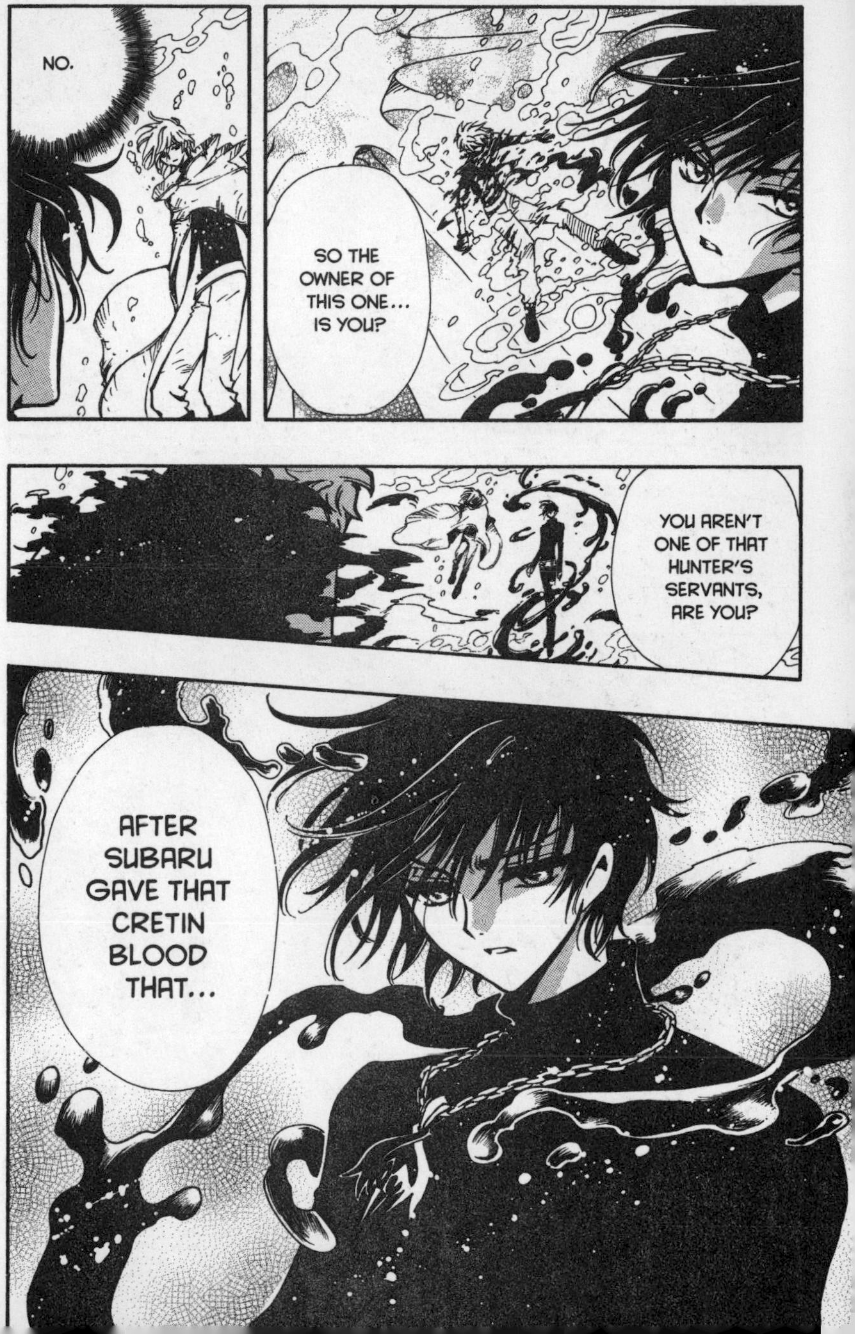
SO THE OWNER OF THIS ONE... IS YOU?
NO.
YOU AREN'T ONE OF THAT HUNTER'S SERVANTS, ARE YOU?
AFTER SUBARU GAVE THAT CRETIN BLOOD THAT...

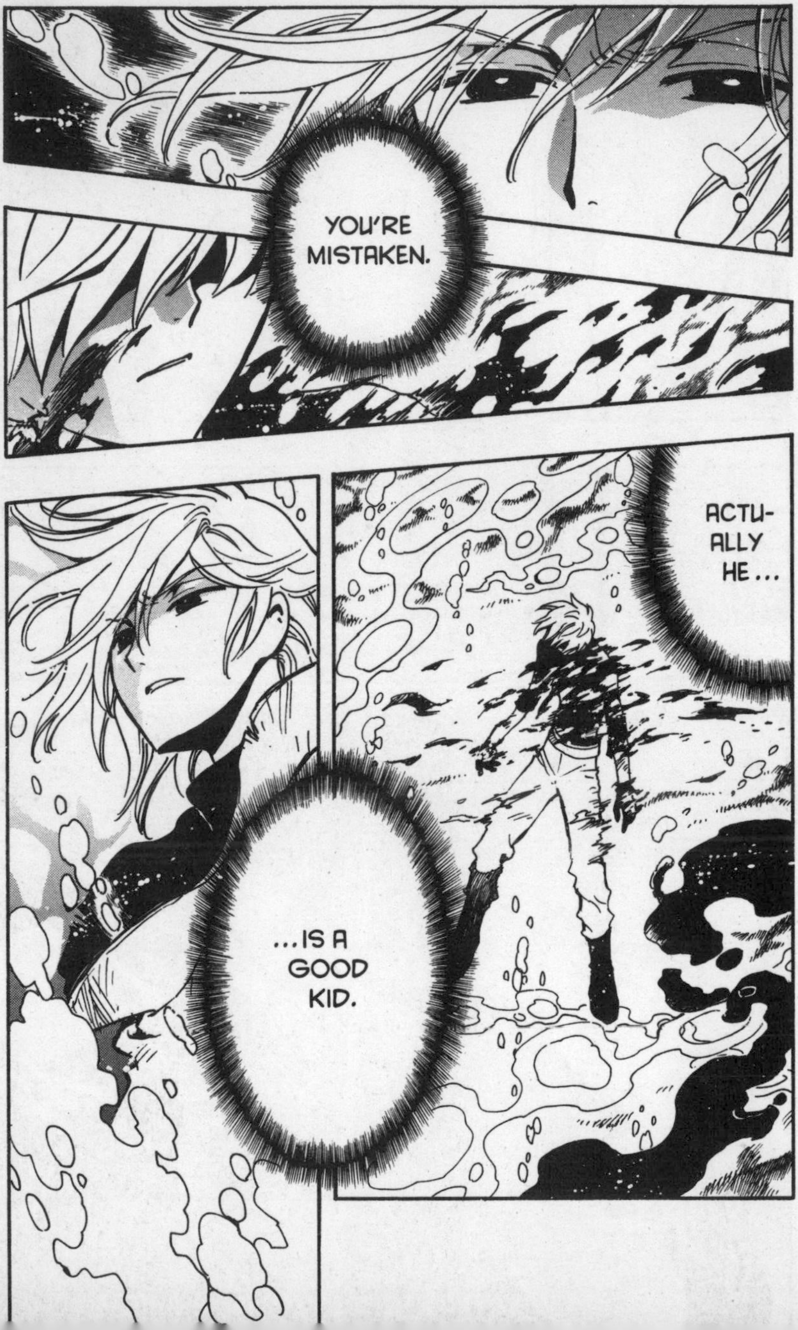
YOU'RE MISTAKEN.
ACTU-ALLY HE...
...IS A GOOD KID.

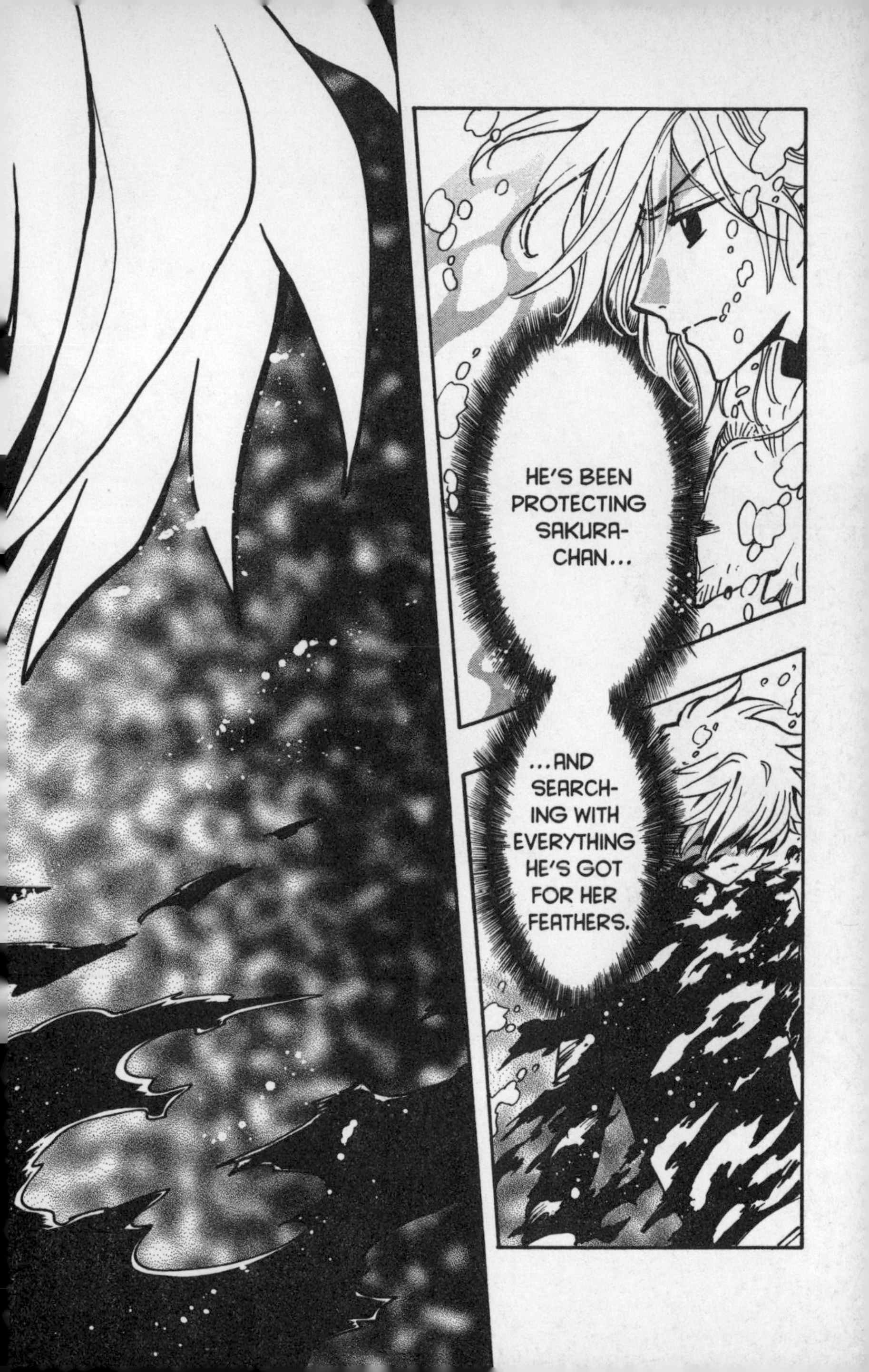
HE'S BEEN PROTECTING SAKURA-CHAN...
...AND SEARCH-ING WITH EVERYTHING HE'S GOT FOR HER FEATHERS.

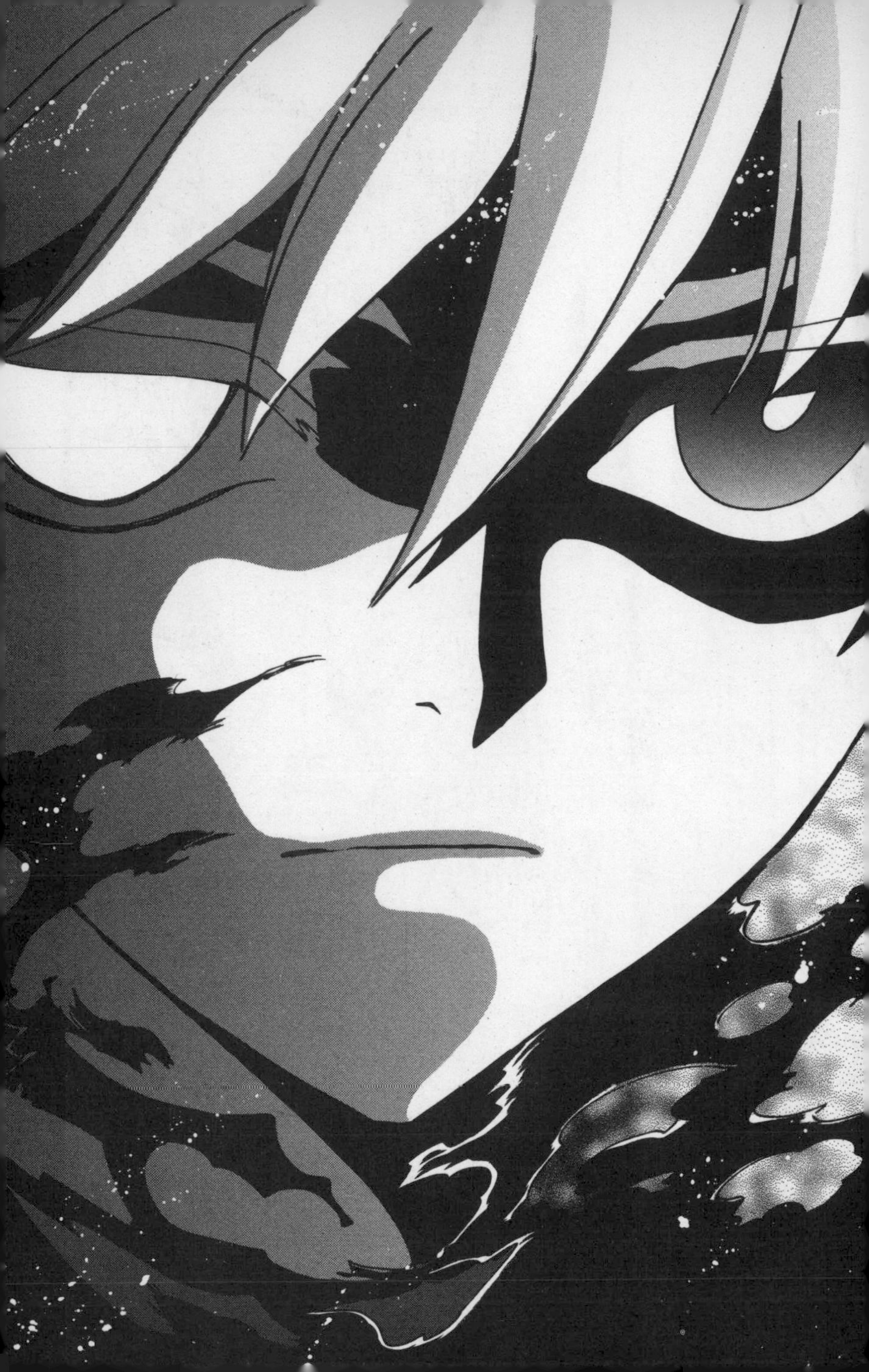

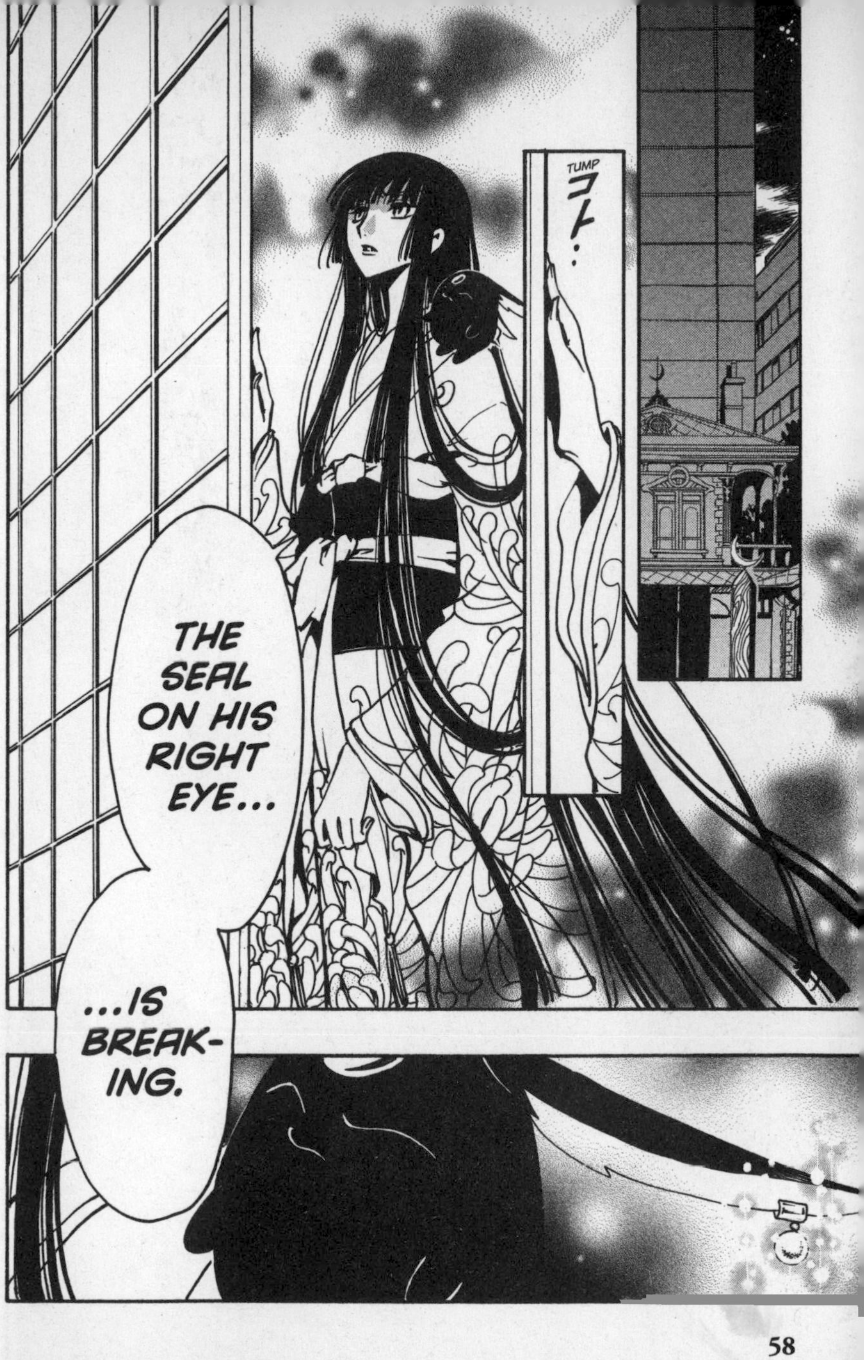
TUMP
コト…
THE SEAL ON HIS RIGHT EYE...
...IS BREAK-ING.

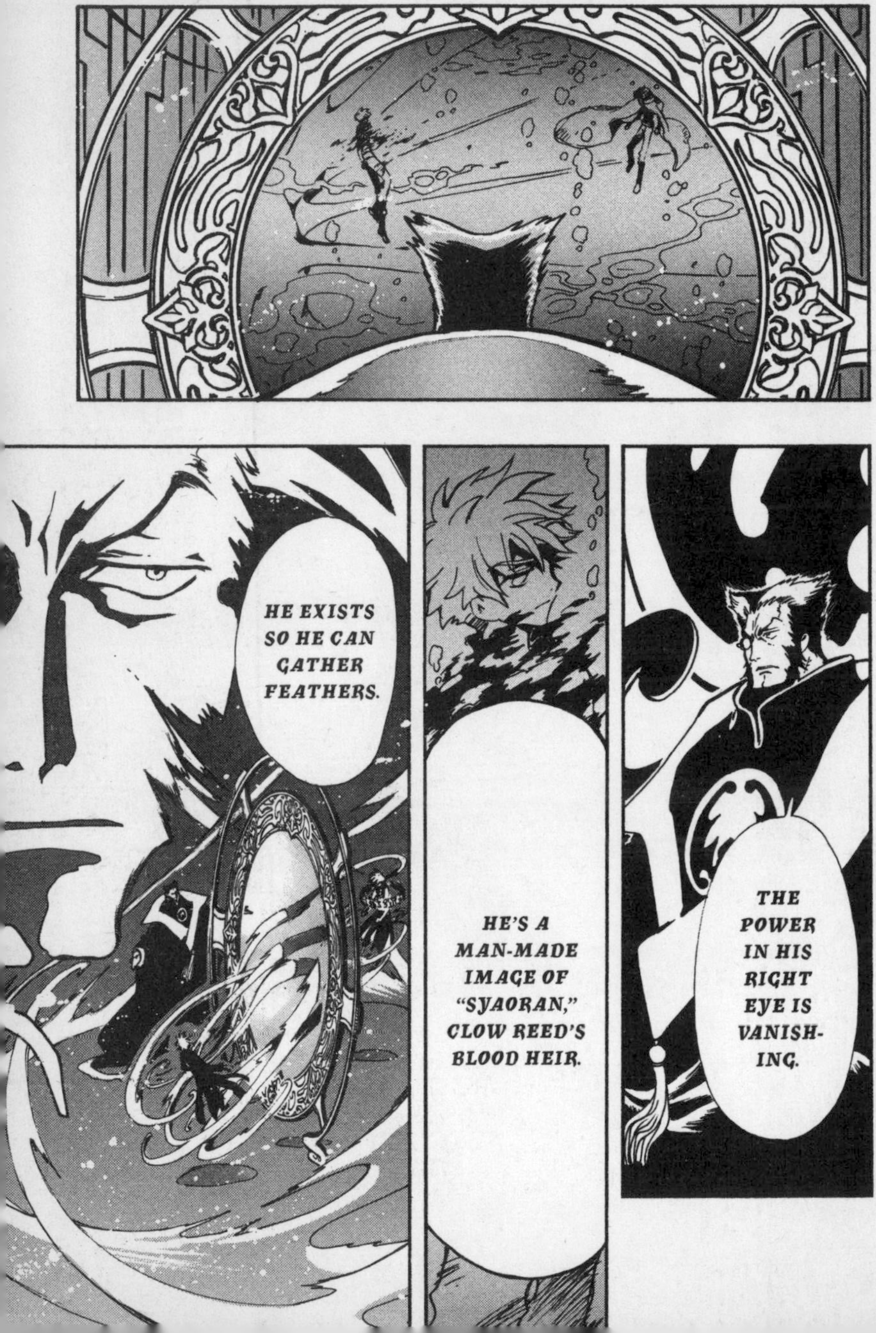
THE POWER IN HIS RIGHT EYE IS VANISH-ING.
HE'S A MAN-MADE IMAGE OF "SYAORAN," CLOW REED'S BLOOD HEIR.
HE EXISTS SO HE CAN GATHER FEATHERS.

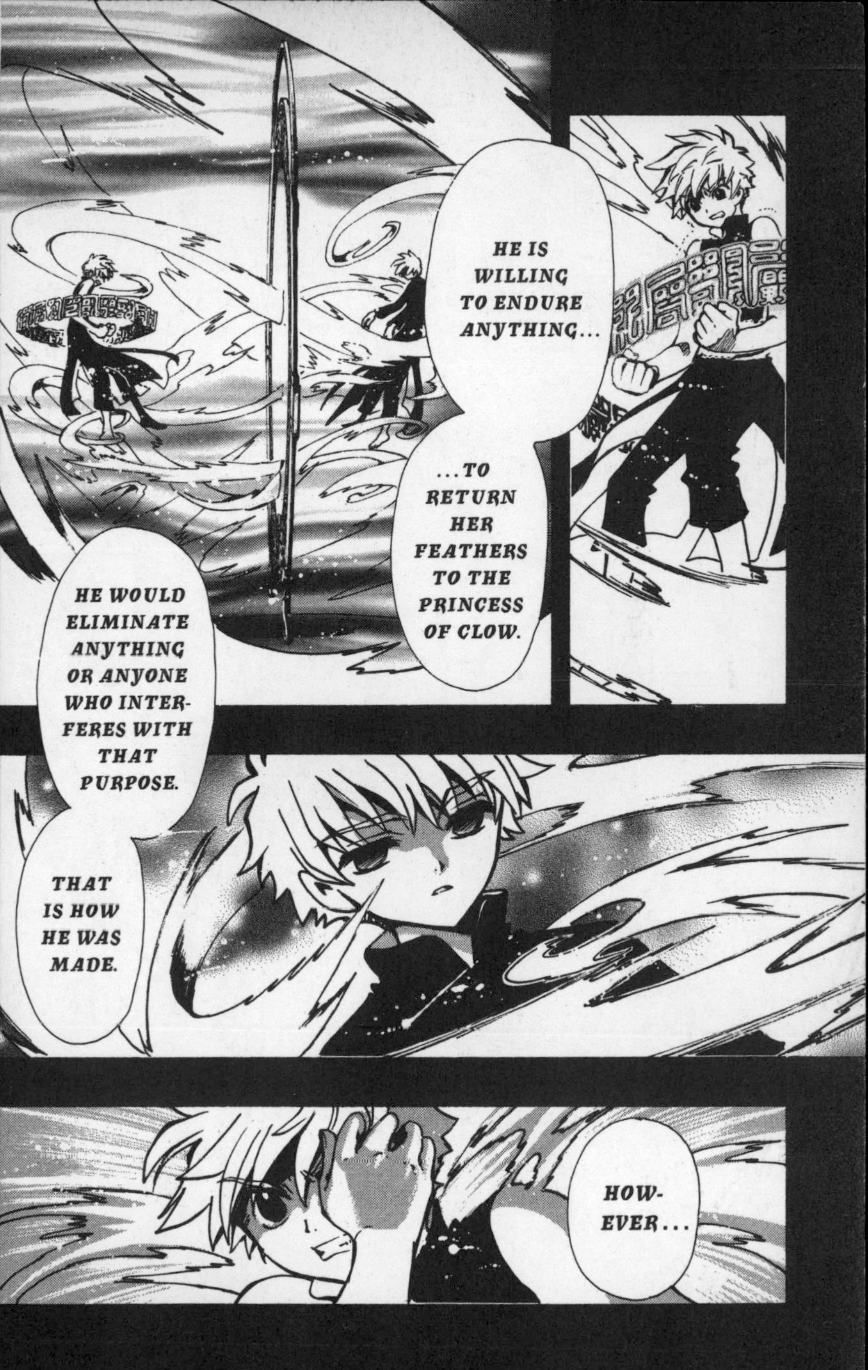
HE IS WILLING TO ENDURE ANYTHING...
...TO RETURN HER FEATHERS TO THE PRINCESS OF CLOW.
HE WOULD ELIMINATE ANYTHING OR ANYONE WHO INTER-FERES WITH THAT PURPOSE.
THAT IS HOW HE WAS MADE.
HOW-EVER...

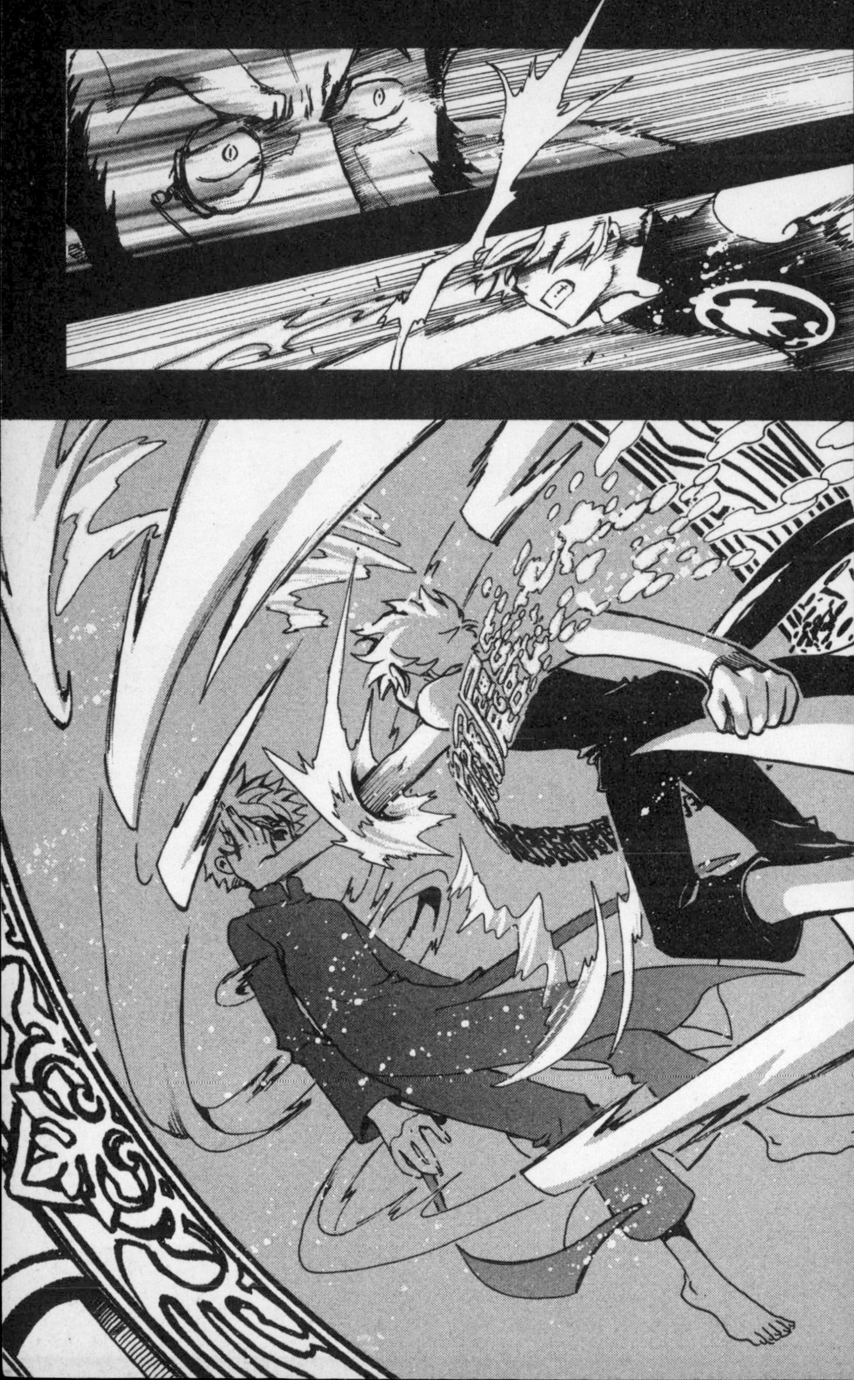

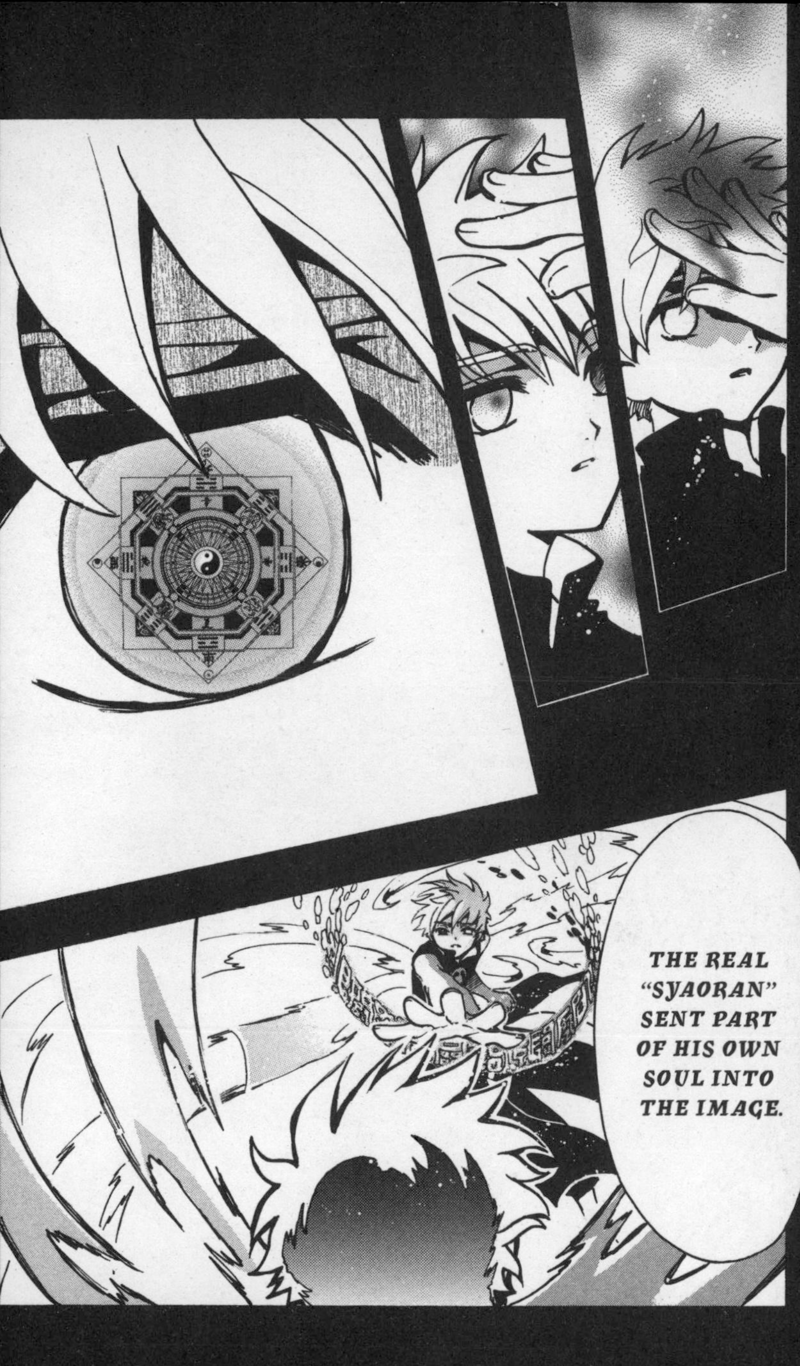
THE REAL "SYAORAN" SENT PART OF HIS OWN SOUL INTO THE IMAGE.

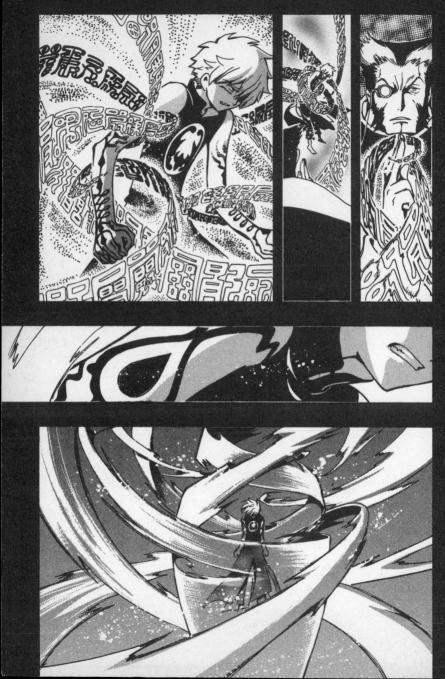

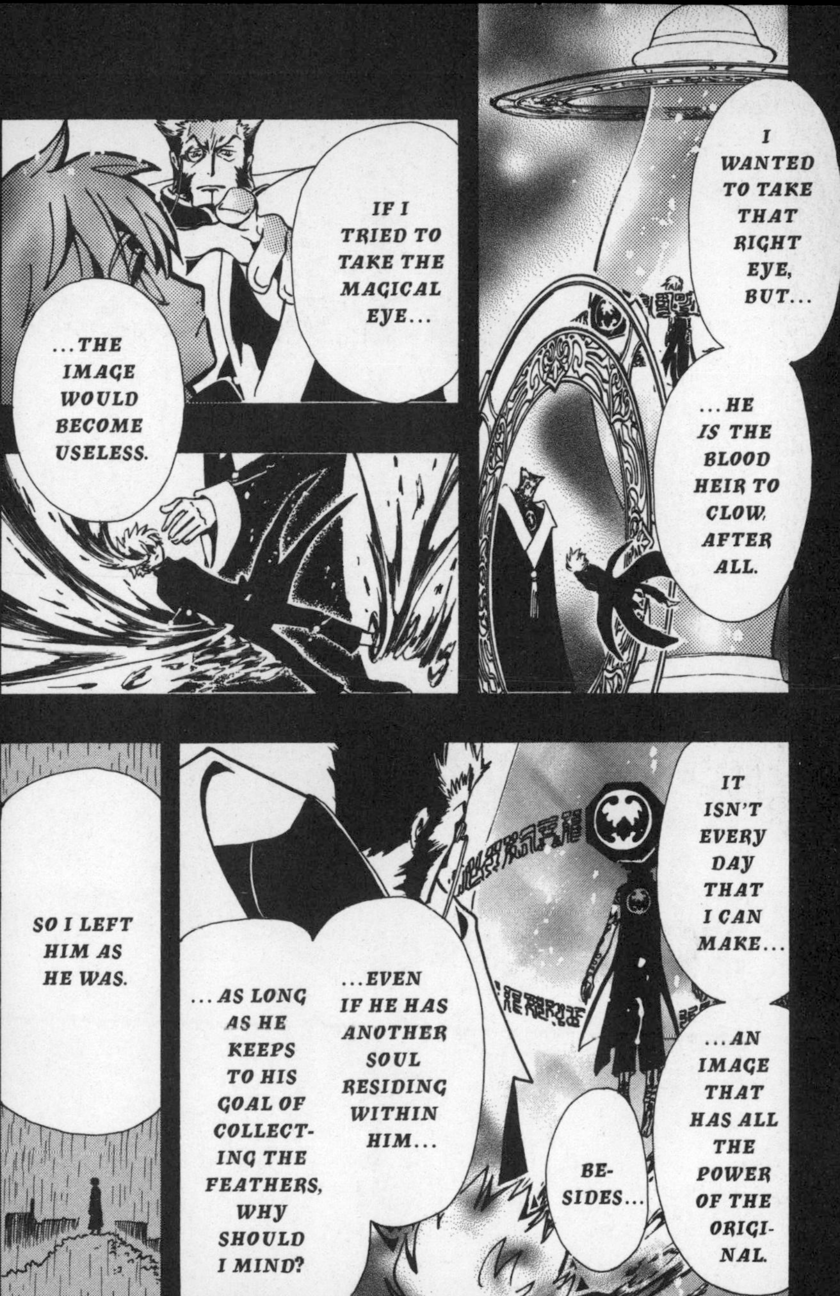
I WANTED TO TAKE THAT RIGHT EYE, BUT...
...HE *IS* THE BLOOD HEIR TO CLOW, AFTER ALL.
IF I TRIED TO TAKE THE MAGICAL EYE...
...THE IMAGE WOULD BECOME USELESS.
IT ISN'T EVERY DAY THAT I CAN MAKE...
...AN IMAGE THAT HAS ALL THE POWER OF THE ORIGINAL.
BESIDES...
...EVEN IF HE HAS ANOTHER SOUL RESIDING WITHIN HIM...
...AS LONG AS HE KEEPS TO HIS GOAL OF COLLECTING THE FEATHERS, WHY SHOULD I MIND?
SO I LEFT HIM AS HE WAS.

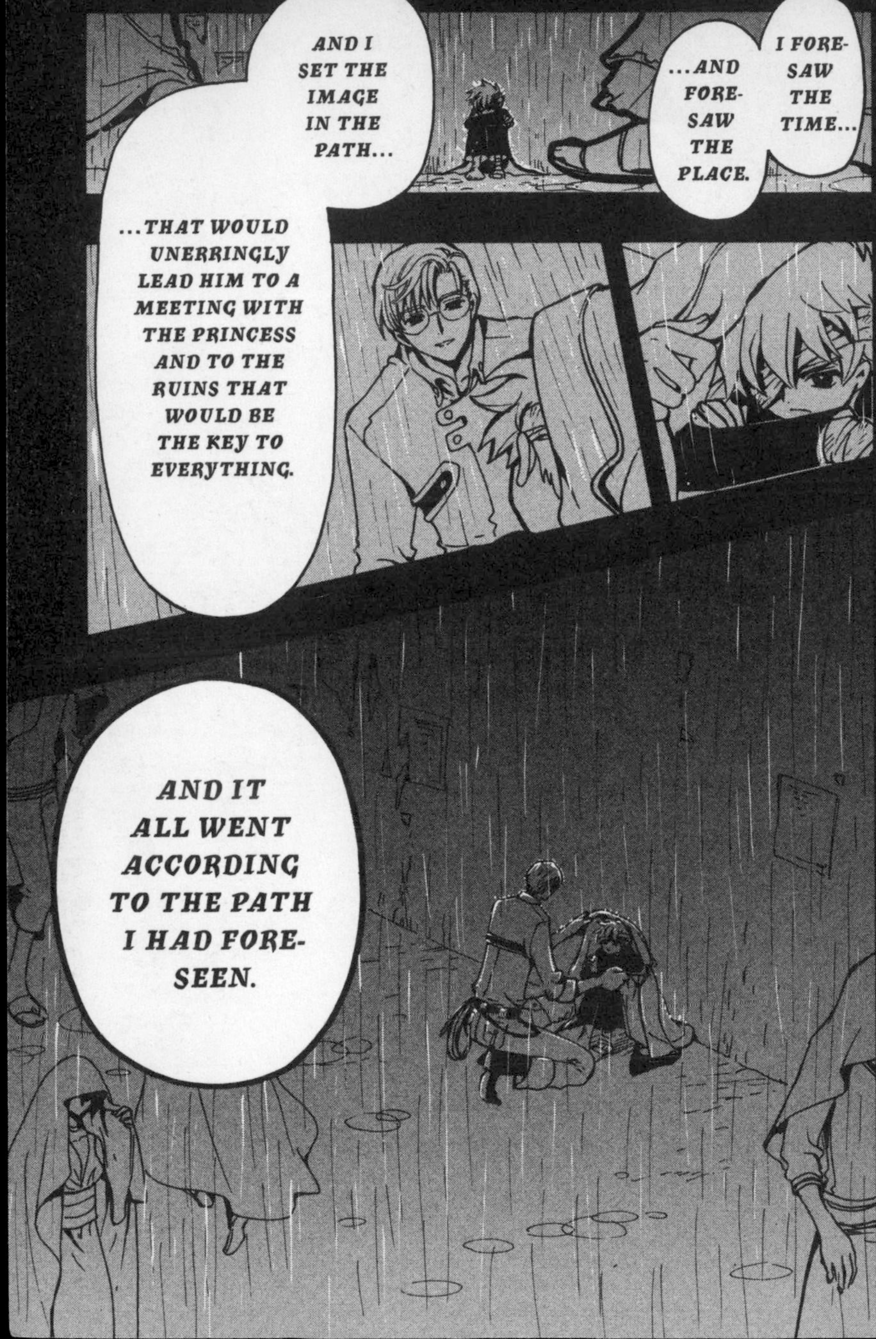
I FORESAW THE TIME...
...AND FORESAW THE PLACE.
AND I SET THE IMAGE IN THE PATH...
...THAT WOULD UNERRINGLY LEAD HIM TO A MEETING WITH THE PRINCESS AND TO THE RUINS THAT WOULD BE THE KEY TO EVERYTHING.
AND IT ALL WENT ACCORDING TO THE PATH I HAD FORESEEN.

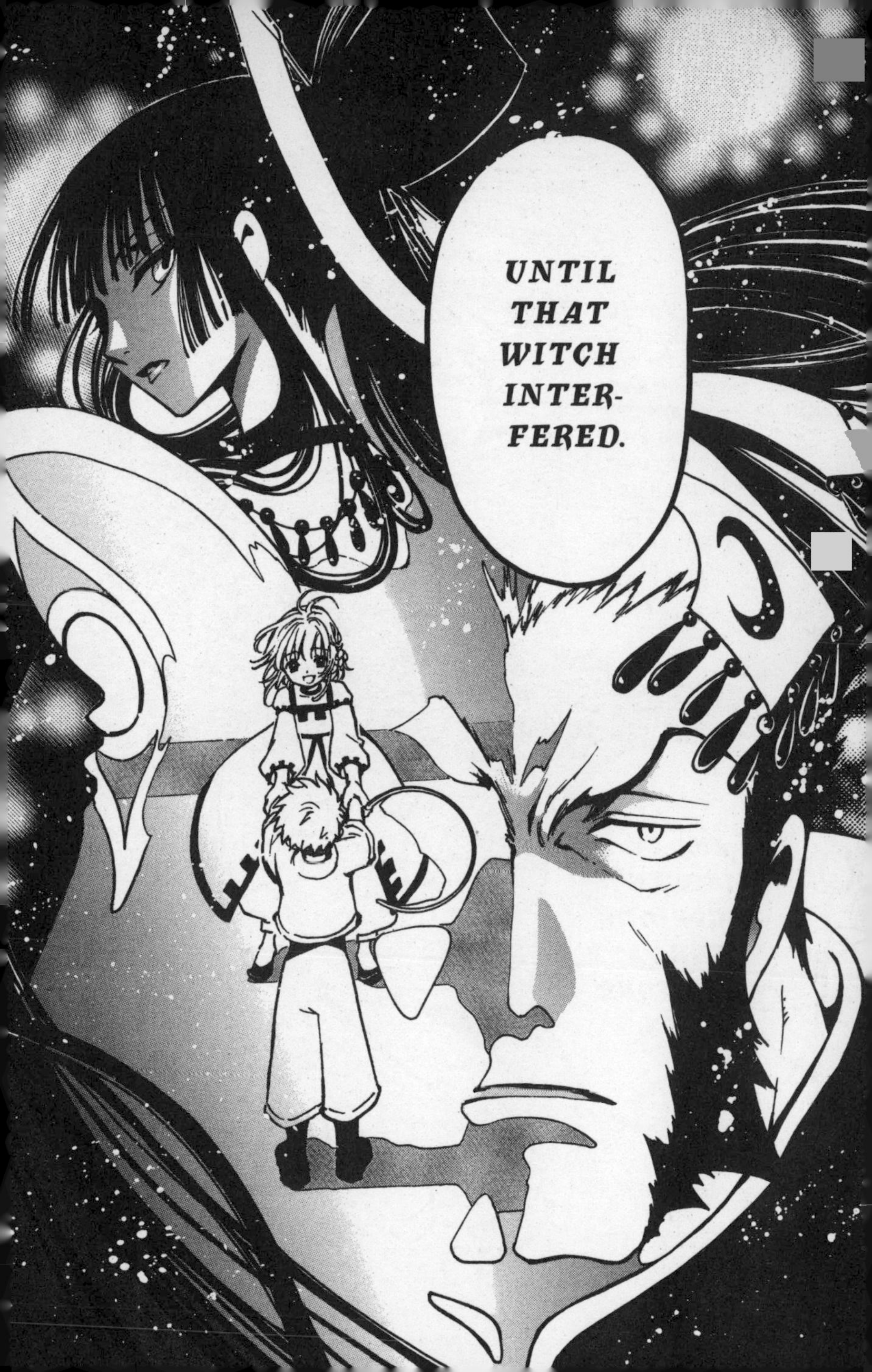
UNTIL THAT WITCH INTER-FERED.

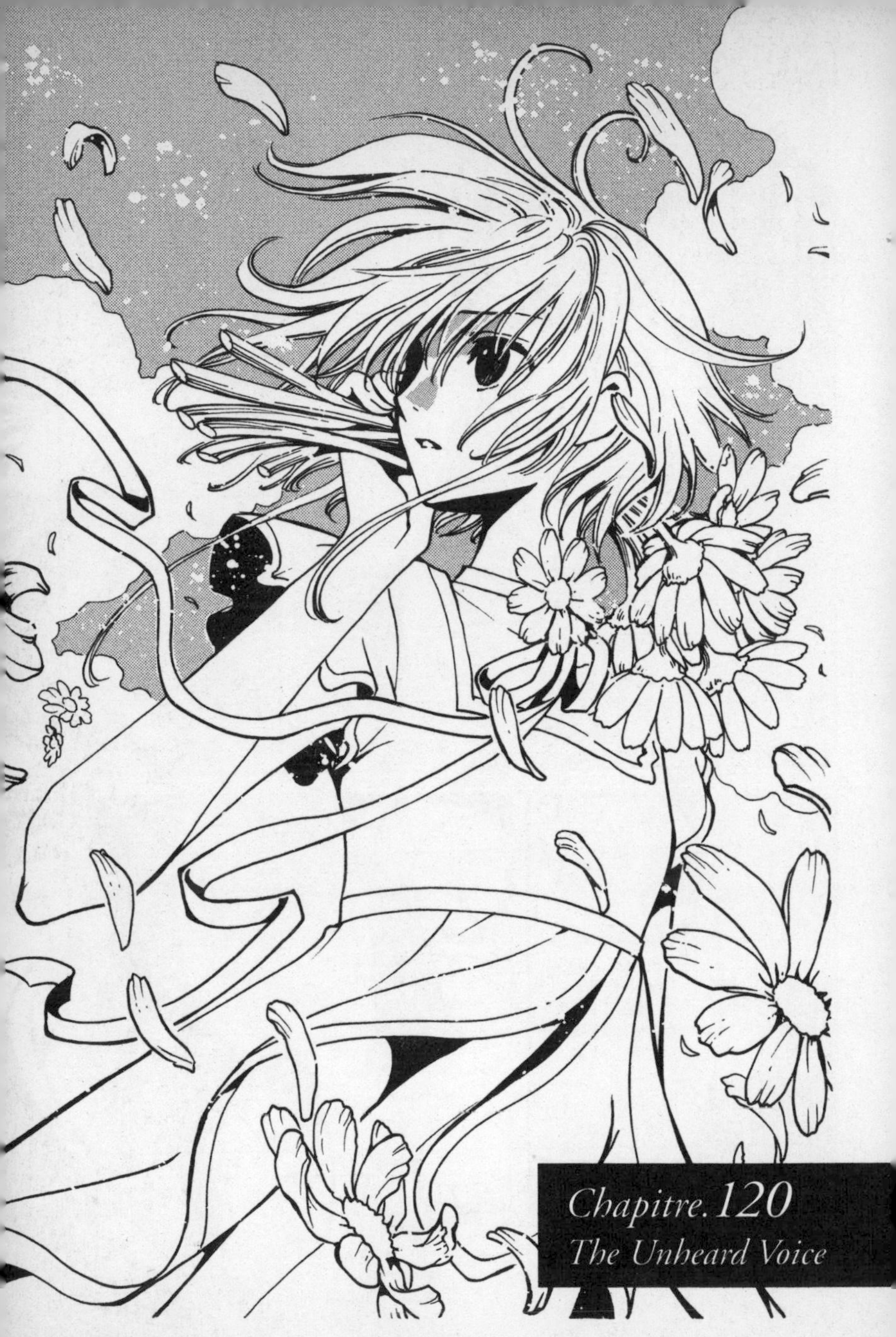Chapitre. 120
The Unheard Voice

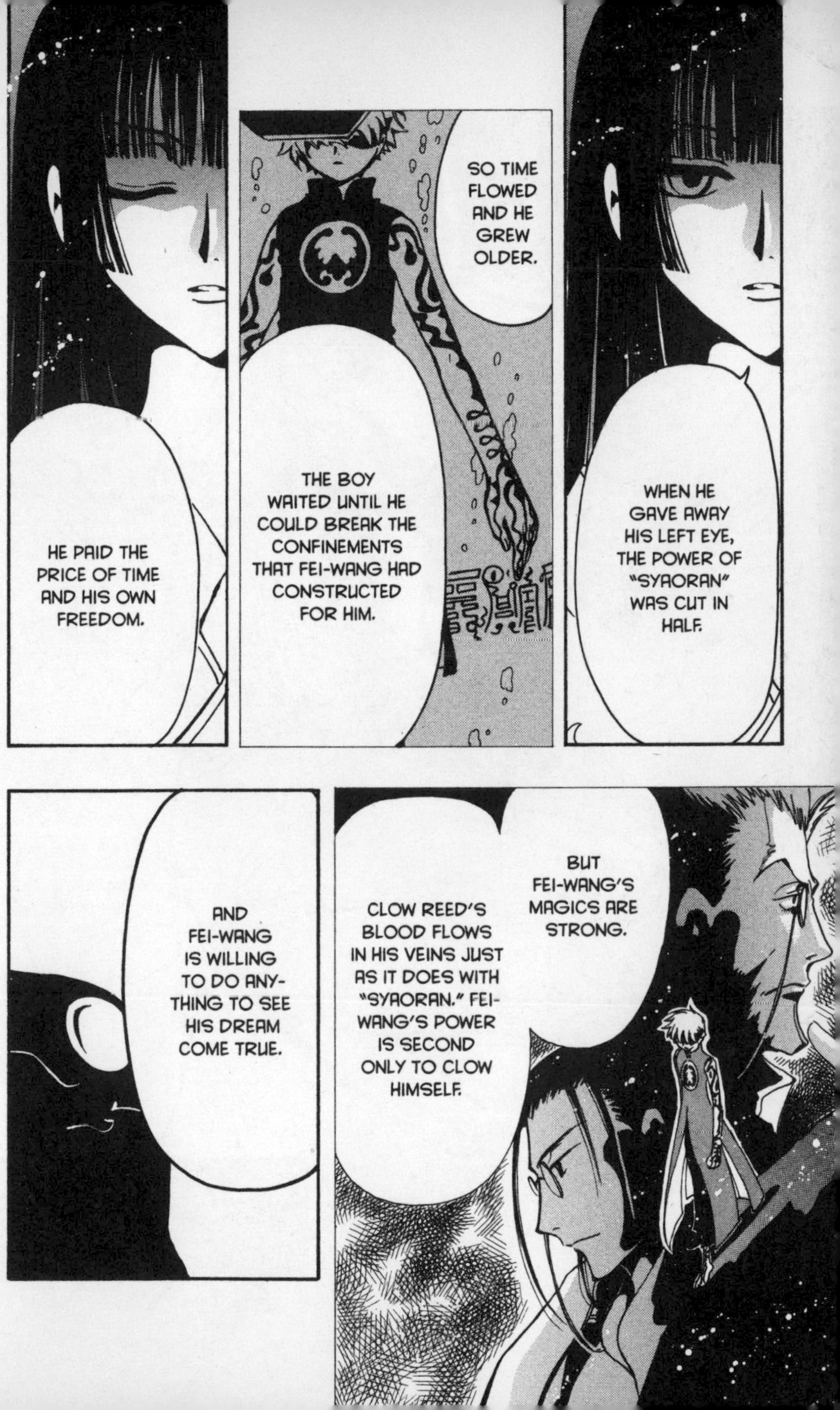
WHEN HE GAVE AWAY HIS LEFT EYE, THE POWER OF "SYAORAN" WAS CUT IN HALF.
SO TIME FLOWED AND HE GREW OLDER.
THE BOY WAITED UNTIL HE COULD BREAK THE CONFINEMENTS THAT FEI-WANG HAD CONSTRUCTED FOR HIM.
HE PAID THE PRICE OF TIME AND HIS OWN FREEDOM.
BUT FEI-WANG'S MAGICS ARE STRONG.
CLOW REED'S BLOOD FLOWS IN HIS VEINS JUST AS IT DOES WITH "SYAORAN." FEI-WANG'S POWER IS SECOND ONLY TO CLOW HIMSELF.
AND FEI-WANG IS WILLING TO DO ANYTHING TO SEE HIS DREAM COME TRUE.

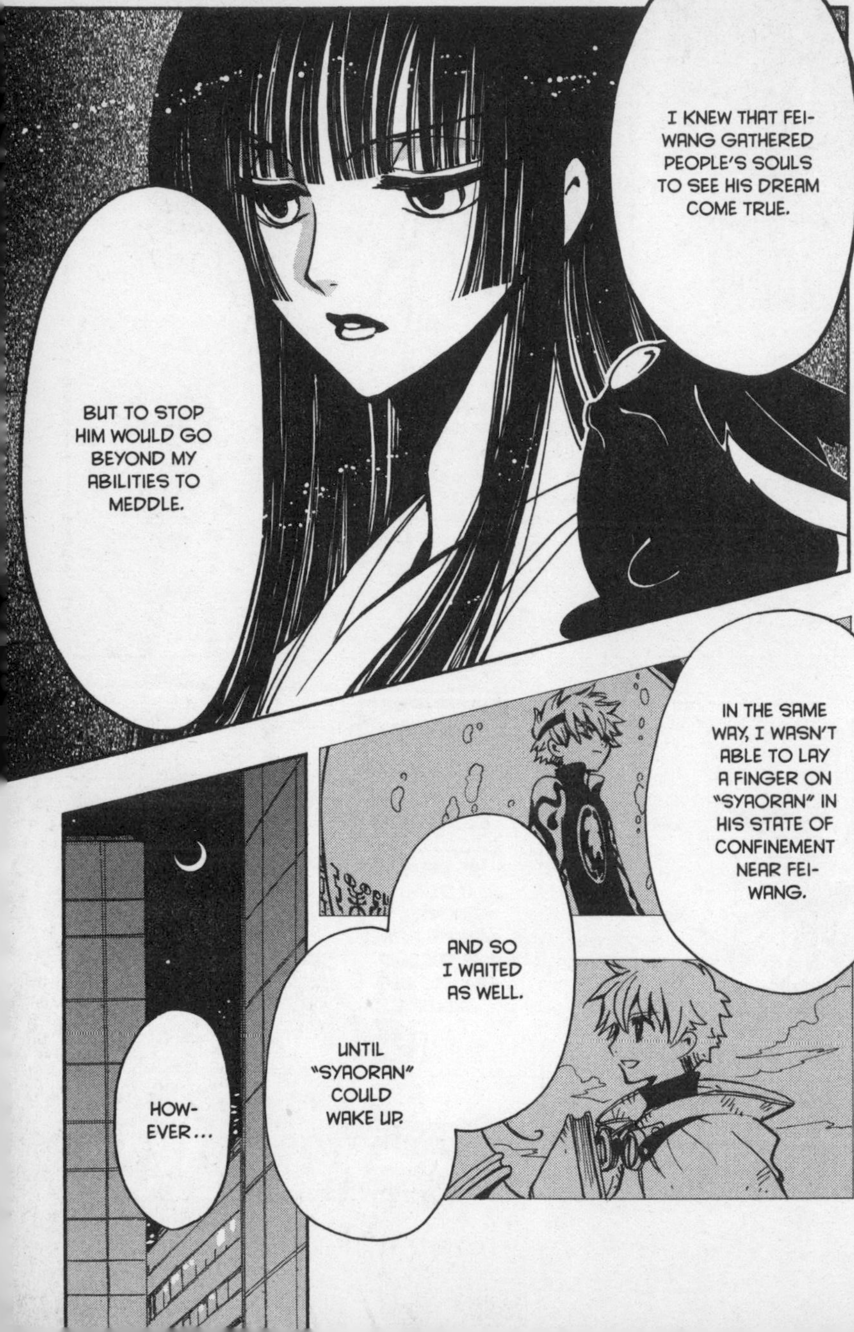
I KNEW THAT FEI-WANG GATHERED PEOPLE'S SOULS TO SEE HIS DREAM COME TRUE.
BUT TO STOP HIM WOULD GO BEYOND MY ABILITIES TO MEDDLE.
IN THE SAME WAY, I WASN'T ABLE TO LAY A FINGER ON "SYAORAN" IN HIS STATE OF CONFINEMENT NEAR FEI-WANG.
AND SO I WAITED AS WELL.
UNTIL "SYAORAN" COULD WAKE UP.
HOW-EVER...

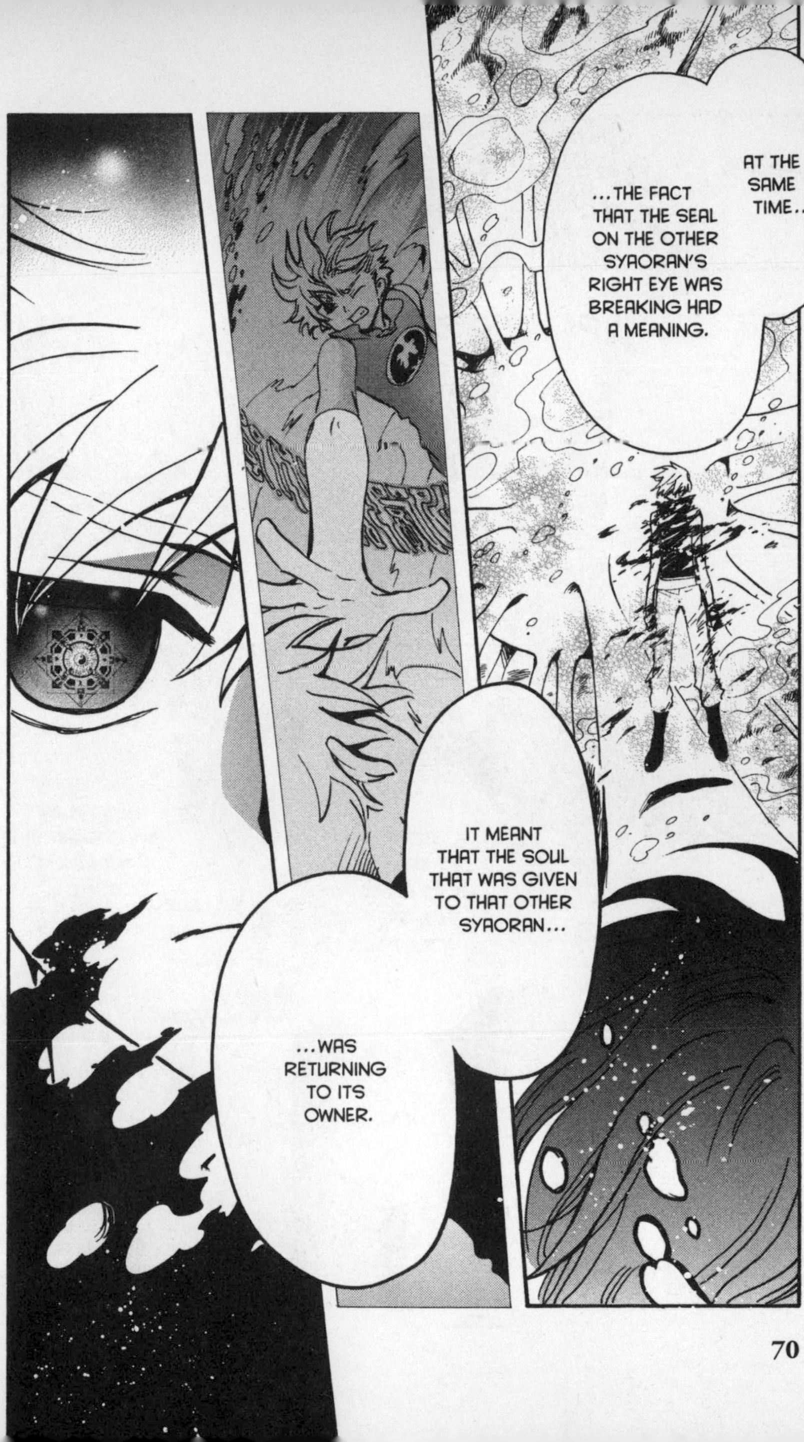
AT THE SAME TIME...
...THE FACT THAT THE SEAL ON THE OTHER SYAORAN'S RIGHT EYE WAS BREAKING HAD A MEANING.
IT MEANT THAT THE SOUL THAT WAS GIVEN TO THAT OTHER SYAORAN...
...WAS RETURNING TO ITS OWNER.

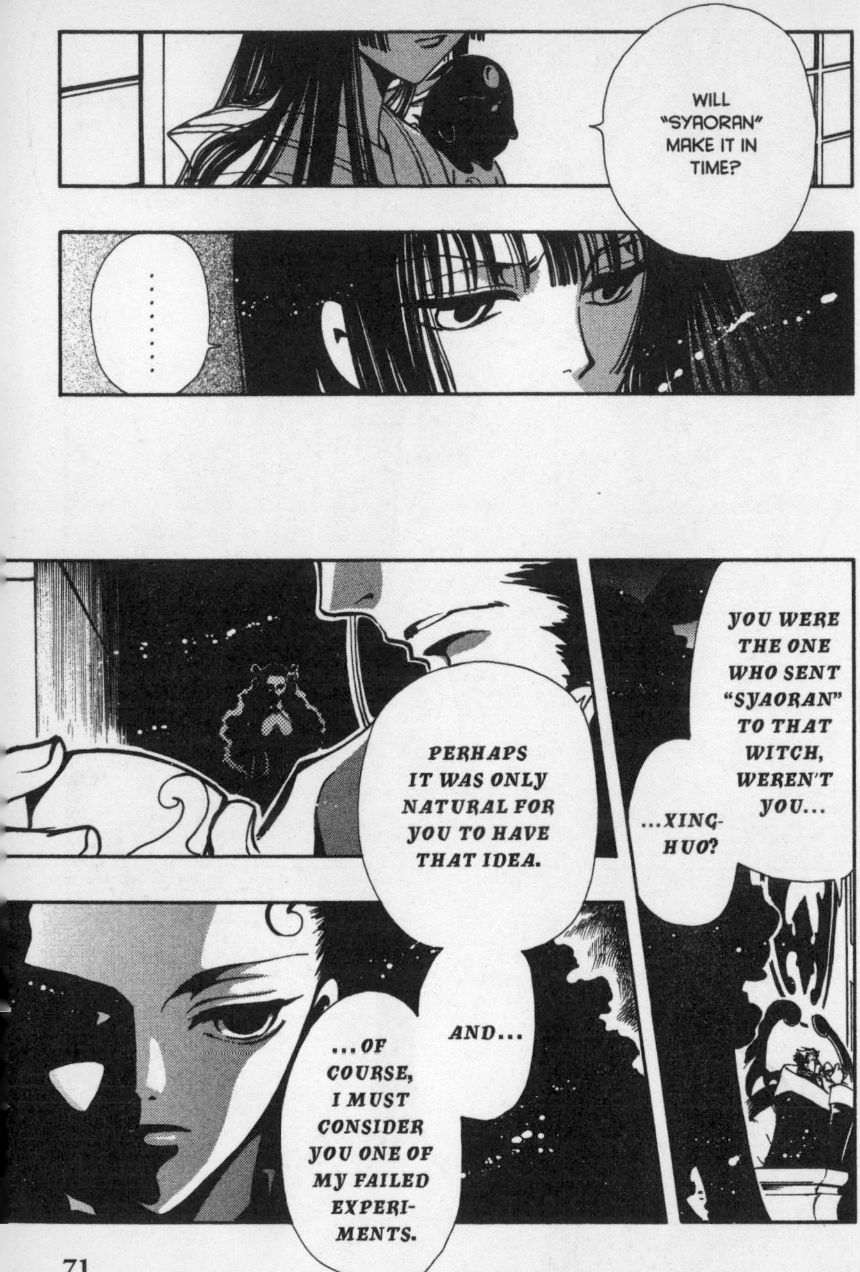
WILL "SYAORAN" MAKE IT IN TIME?
......
YOU WERE THE ONE WHO SENT "SYAORAN" TO THAT WITCH, WEREN'T YOU...
...XING-HUO?
PERHAPS IT WAS ONLY NATURAL FOR YOU TO HAVE THAT IDEA.
AND...
...OF COURSE, I MUST CONSIDER YOU ONE OF MY FAILED EXPERI-MENTS.

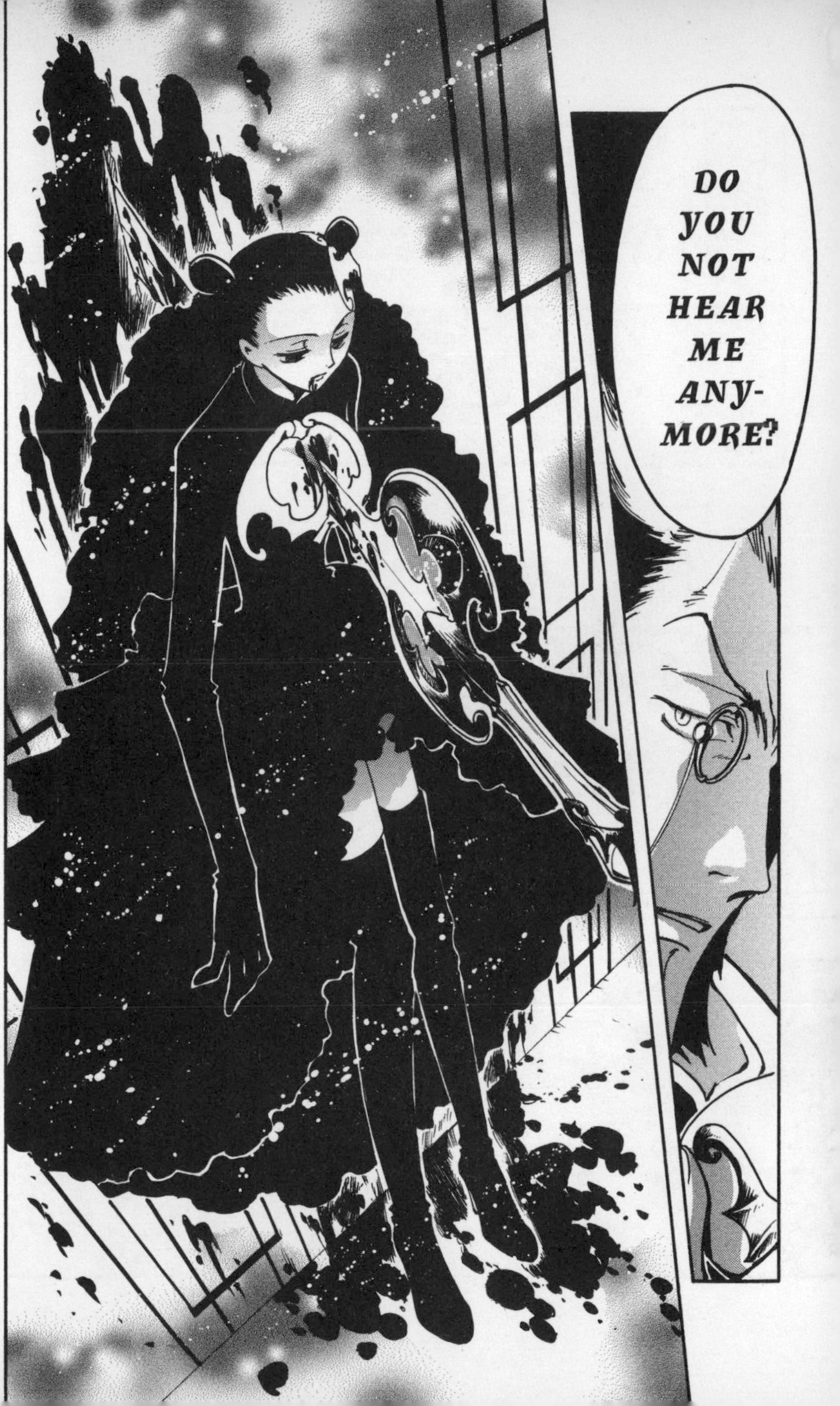
DO YOU NOT HEAR ME ANY-MORE?

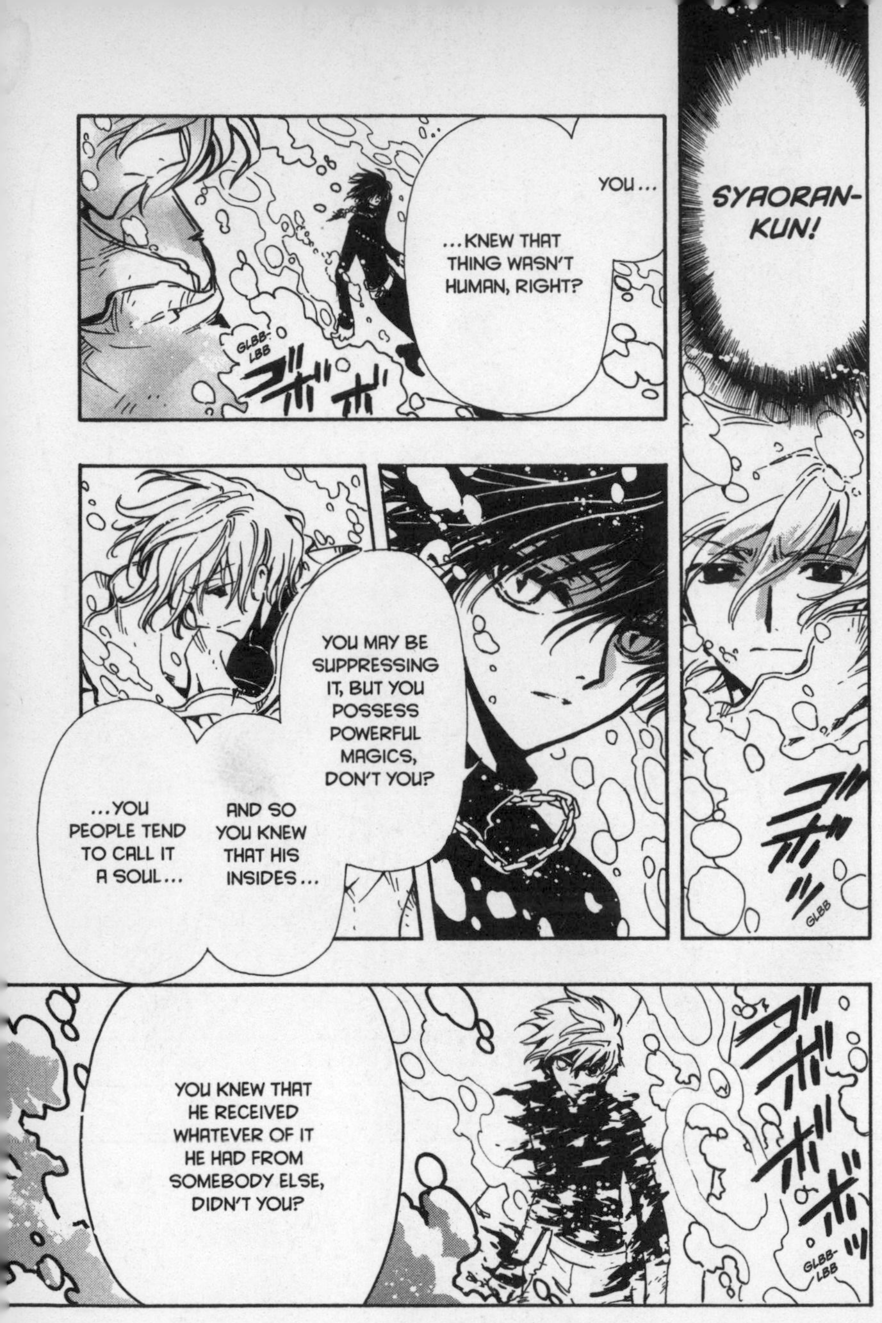
SYAORAN-KUN!
GLBB
YOU…
…KNEW THAT THING WASN'T HUMAN, RIGHT?
GLBB-LBB
YOU MAY BE SUPPRESSING IT, BUT YOU POSSESS POWERFUL MAGICS, DON'T YOU?
AND SO YOU KNEW THAT HIS INSIDES…
…YOU PEOPLE TEND TO CALL IT A SOUL…
GLBB-LBB
YOU KNEW THAT HE RECEIVED WHATEVER OF IT HE HAD FROM SOMEBODY ELSE, DIDN'T YOU?

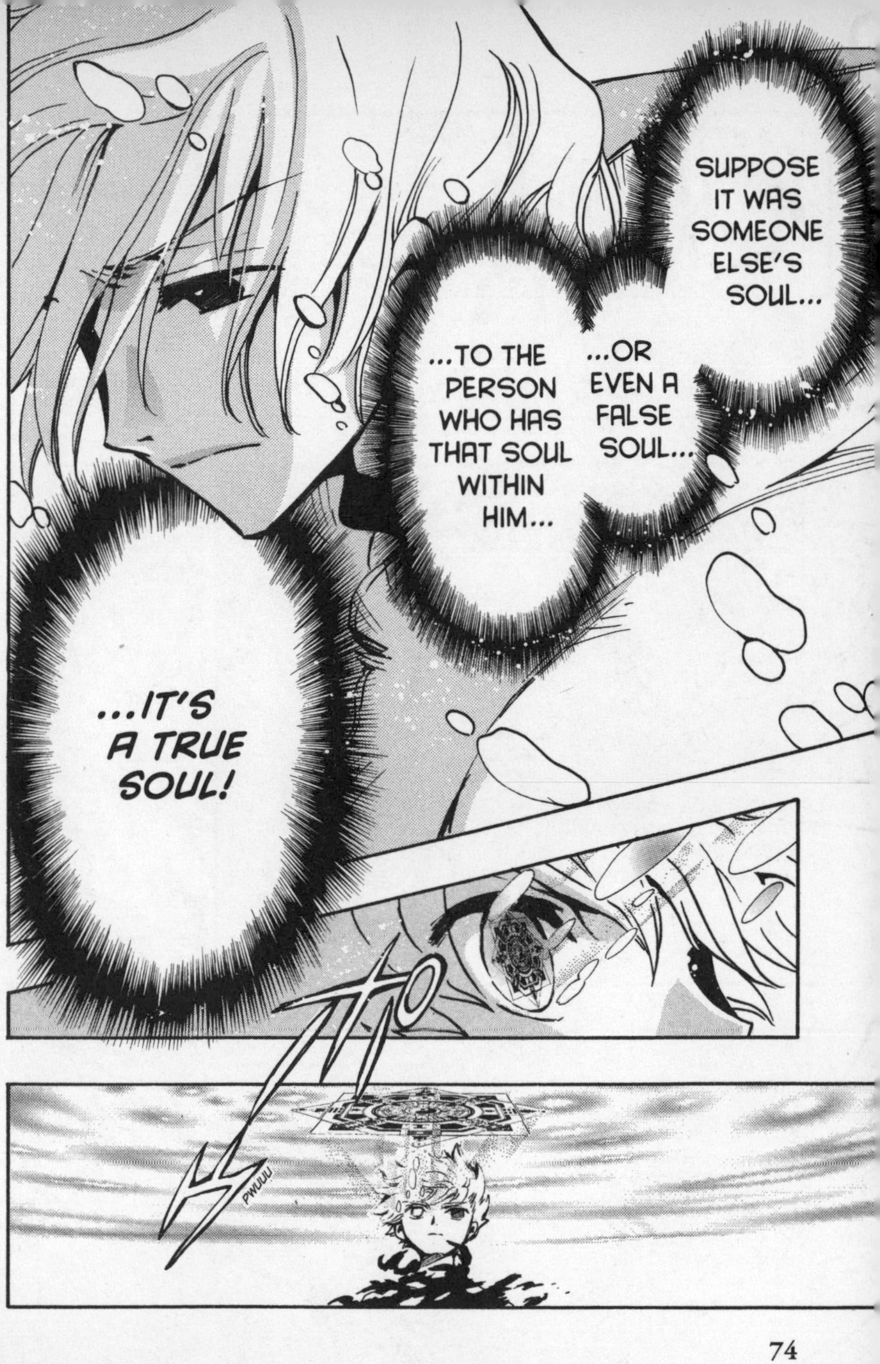
SUPPOSE IT WAS SOMEONE ELSE'S SOUL...
...OR EVEN A FALSE SOUL...
...TO THE PERSON WHO HAS THAT SOUL WITHIN HIM...
...IT'S A TRUE SOUL!
PWUUU

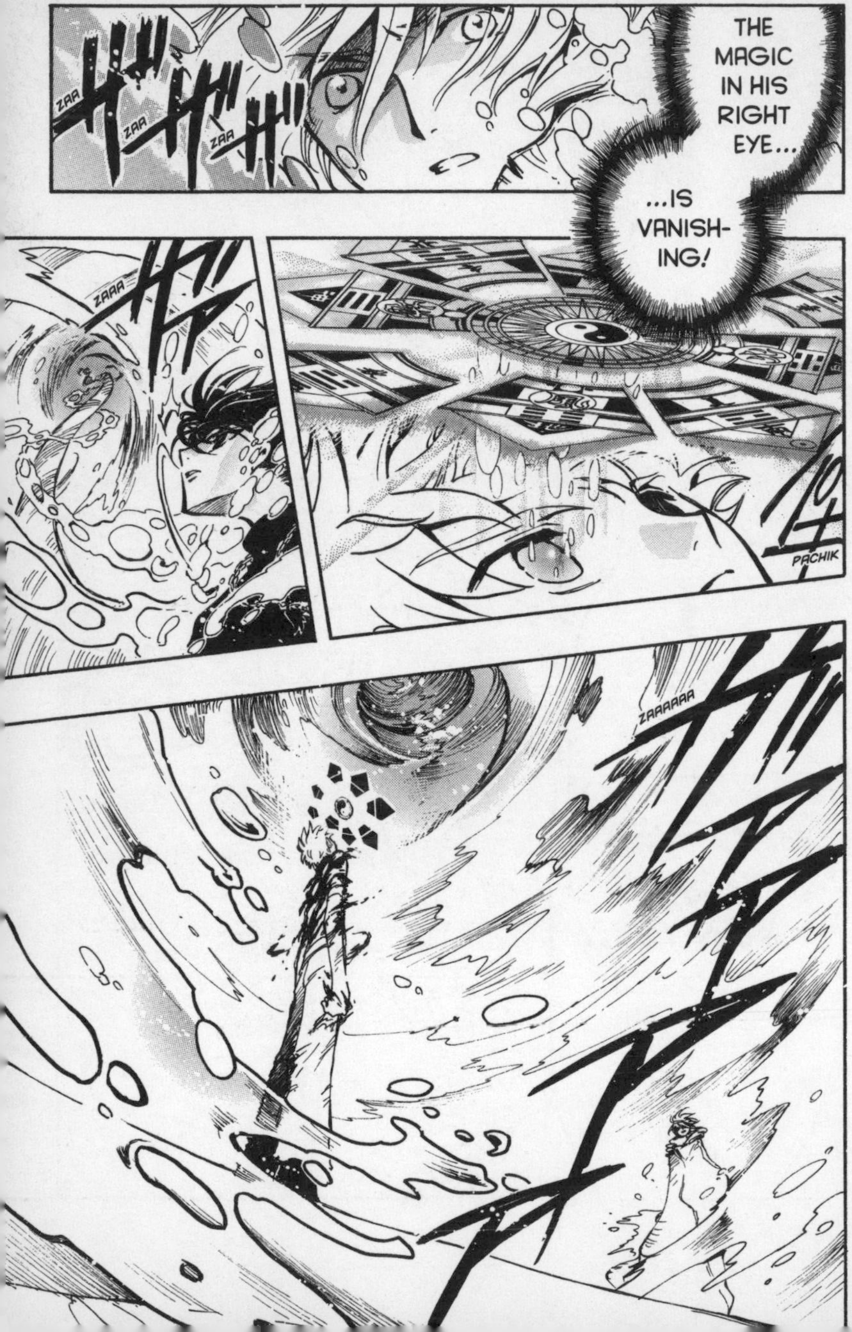
ZAA
ZAA
ZAA
THE MAGIC IN HIS RIGHT EYE...
...IS VANISHING!
PACHIK
ZAAA
ZAAAAAA

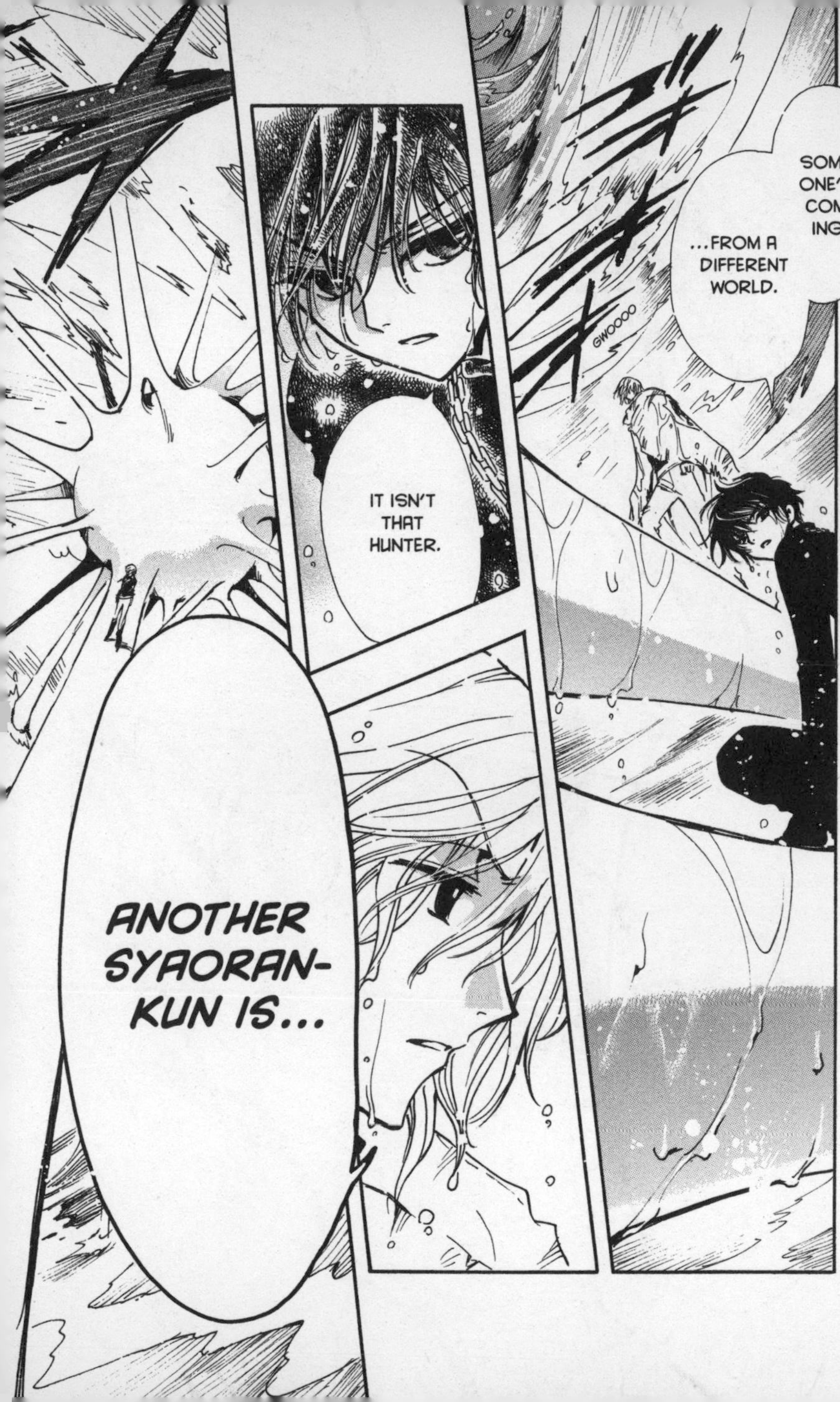
SOME-ONE'S COMING...
...FROM A DIFFERENT WORLD.
GWOOOO
IT ISN'T THAT HUNTER.
ANOTHER SYAORAN-KUN IS...

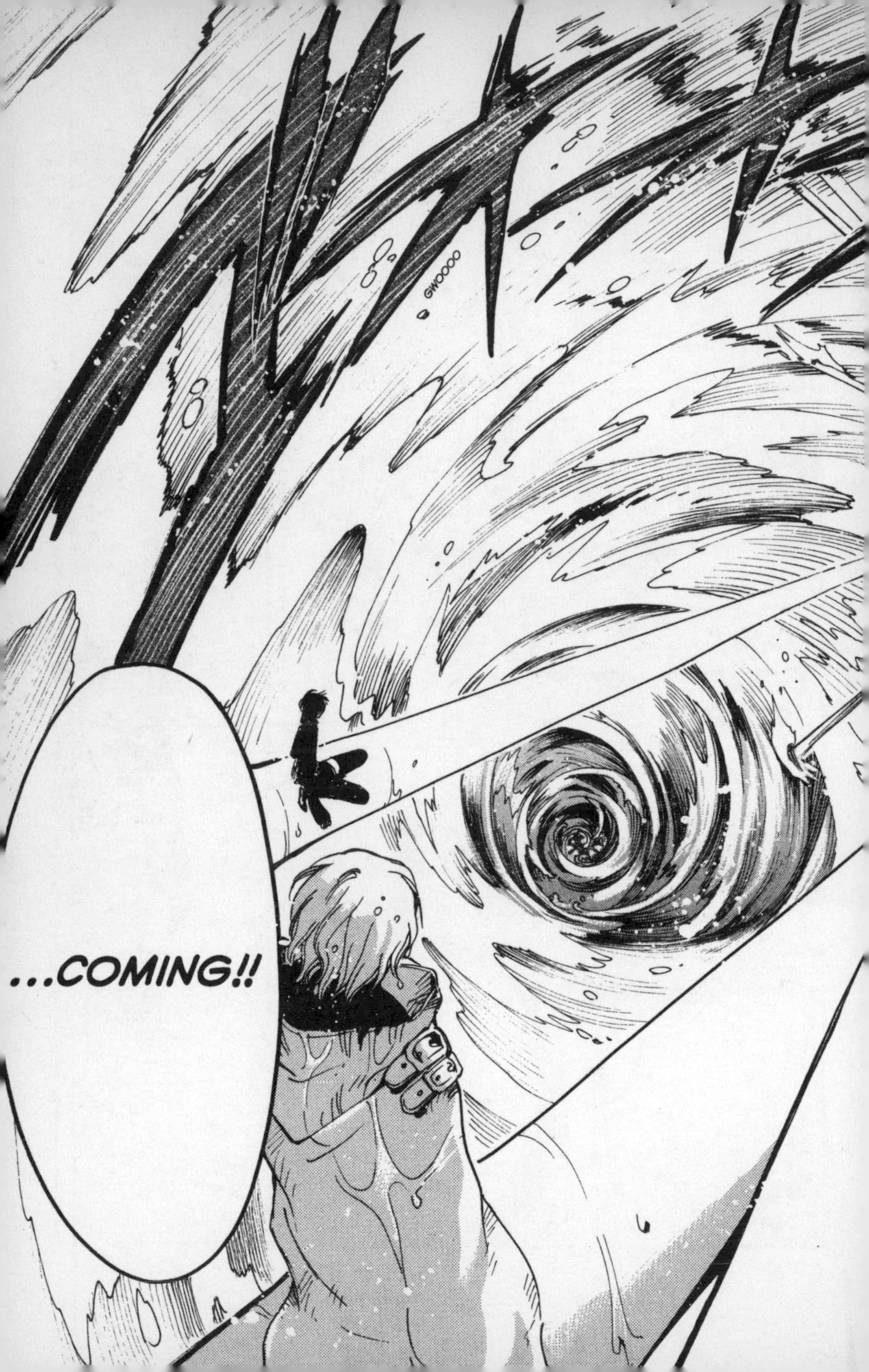
GWOOOO
...COMING!!

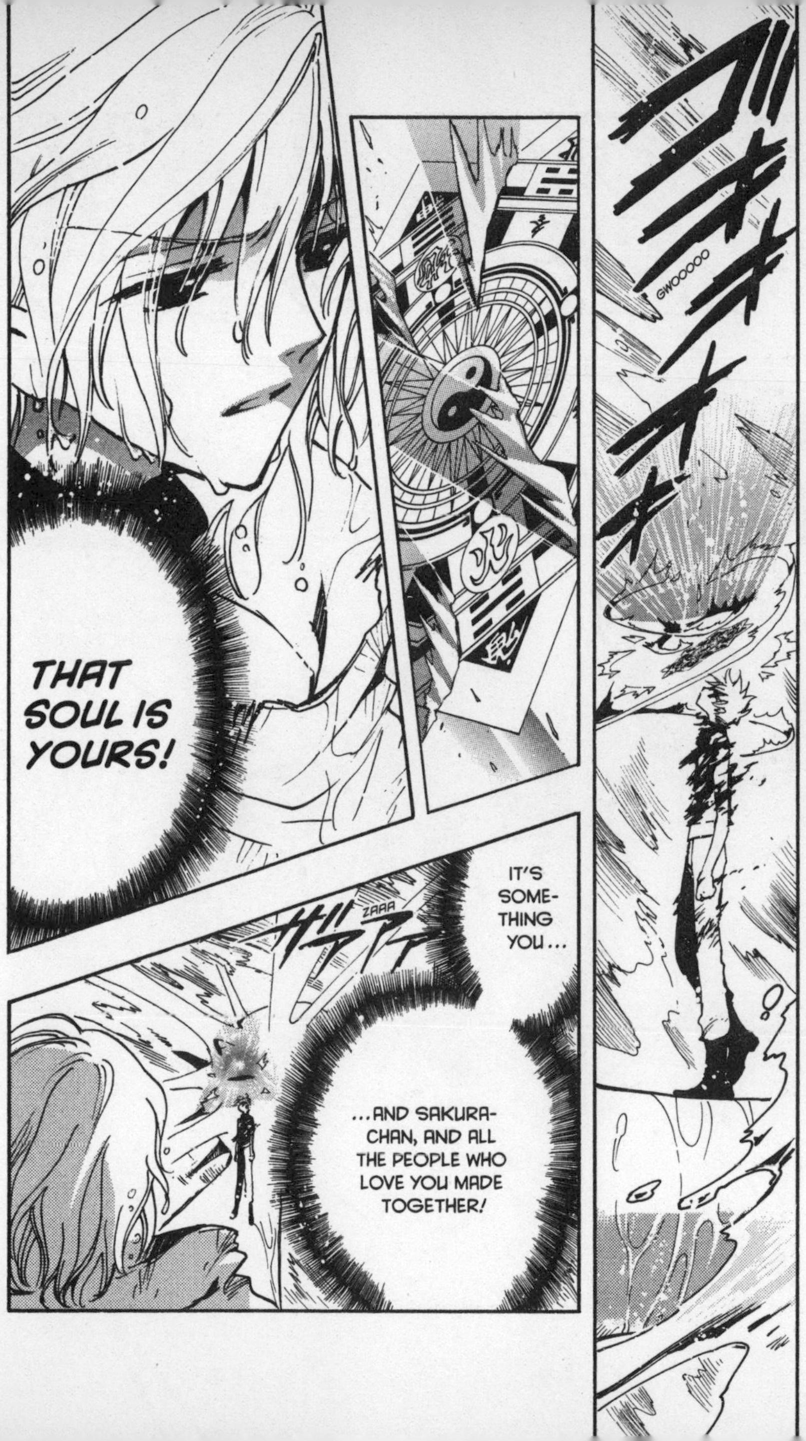
GWOOOOO
THAT SOUL IS YOURS!
IT'S SOME-THING YOU...
ZAAA
...AND SAKURA-CHAN, AND ALL THE PEOPLE WHO LOVE YOU MADE TOGETHER!

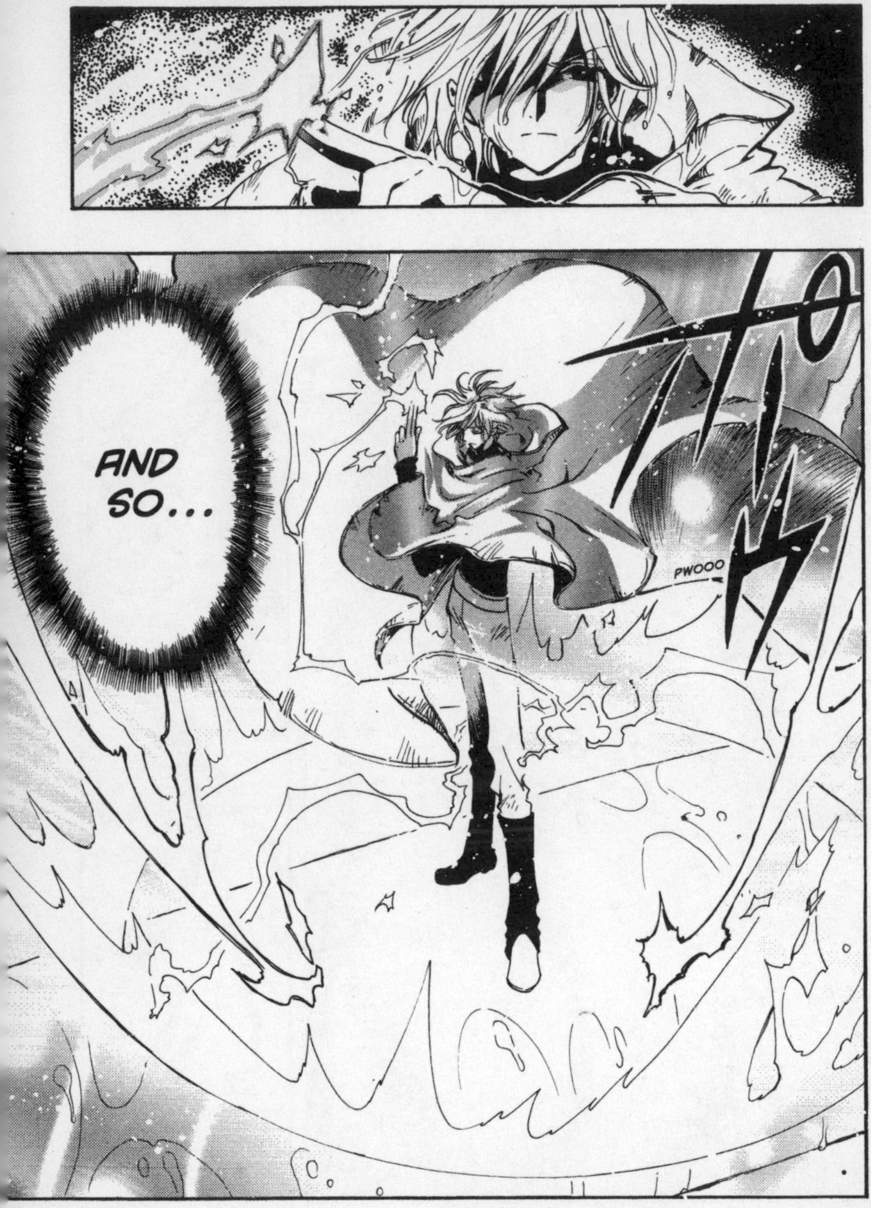
AND SO...
PWOOO

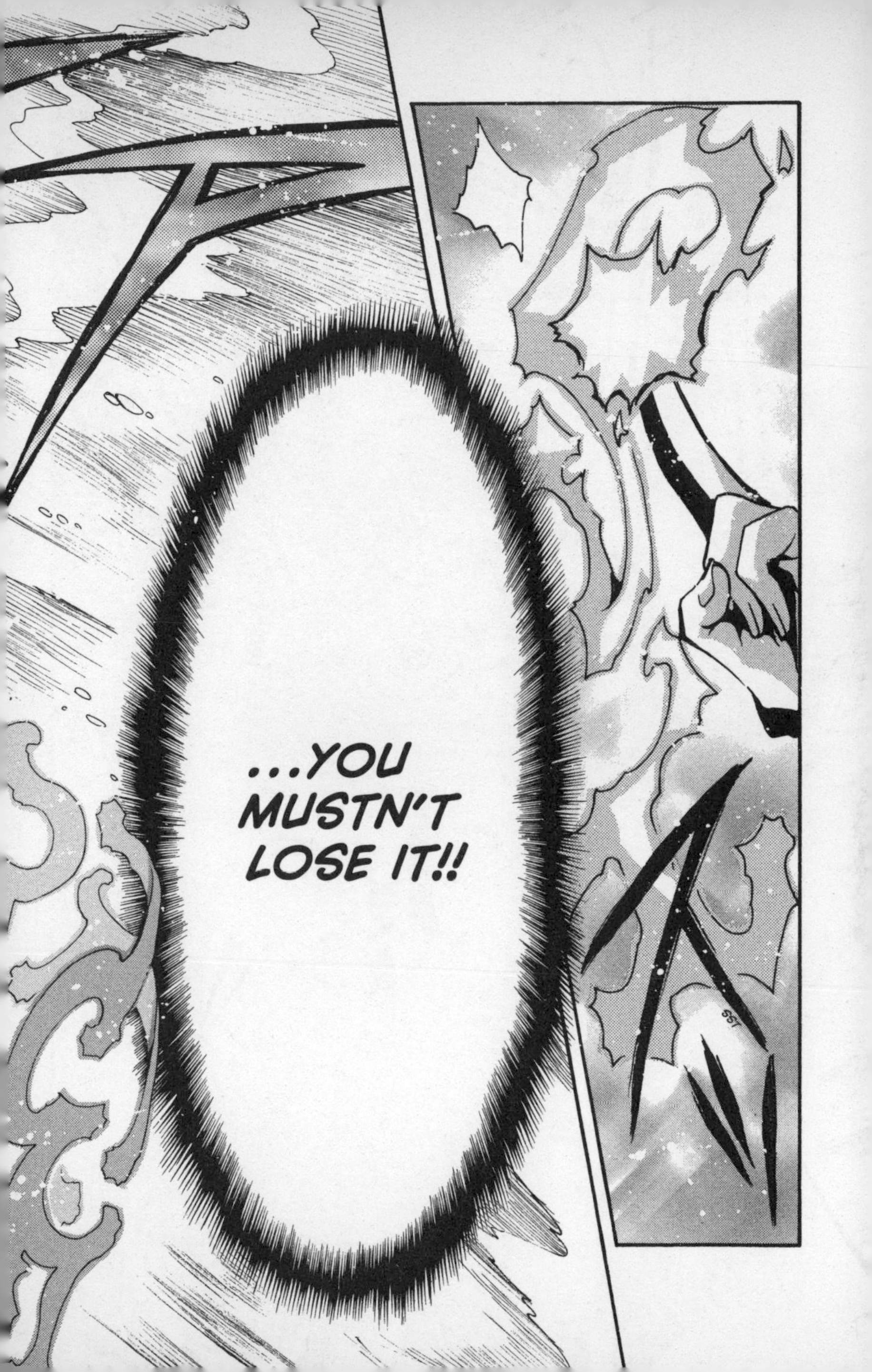
...YOU MUSTN'T LOSE IT!!

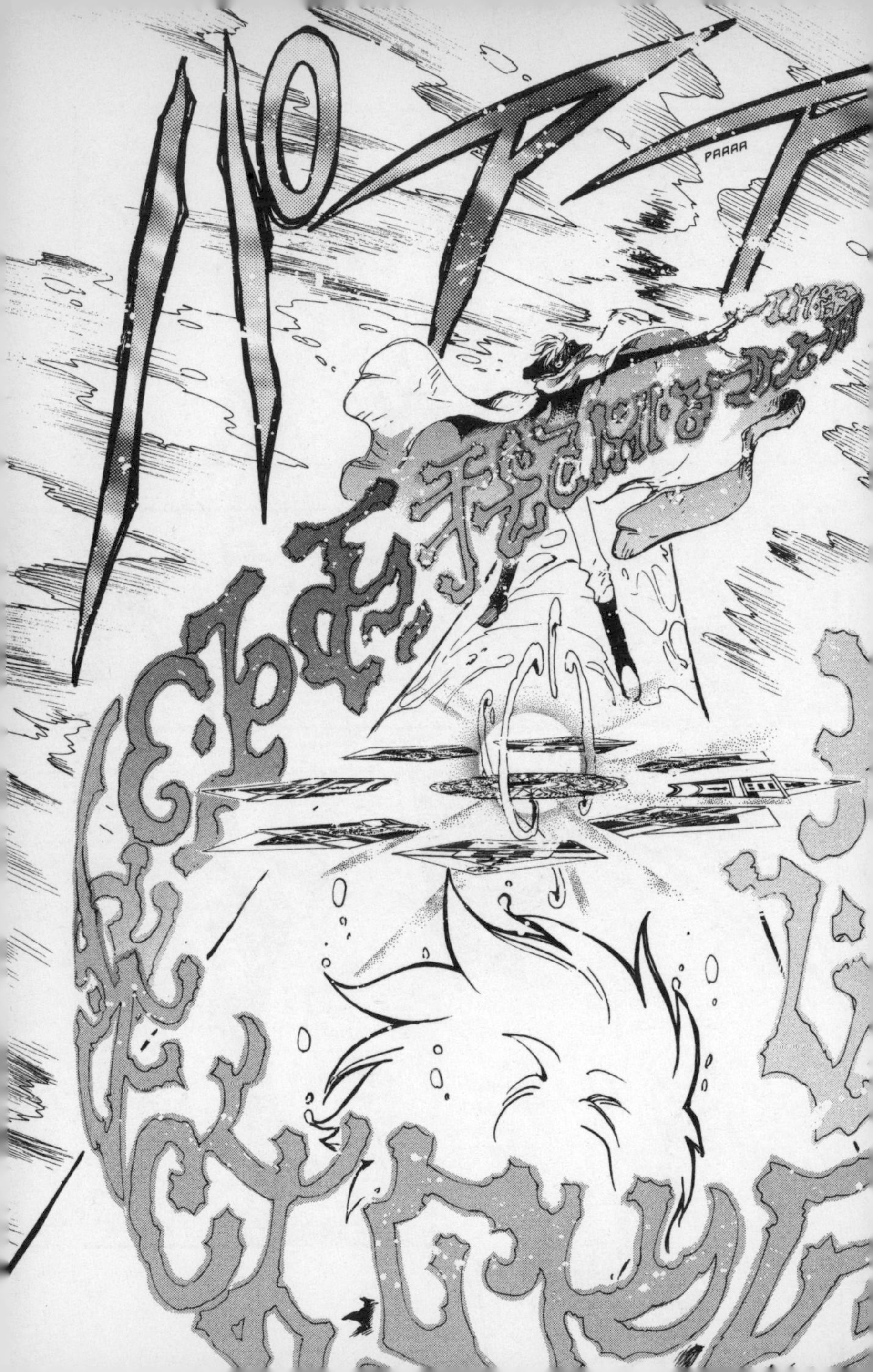
PAAAA

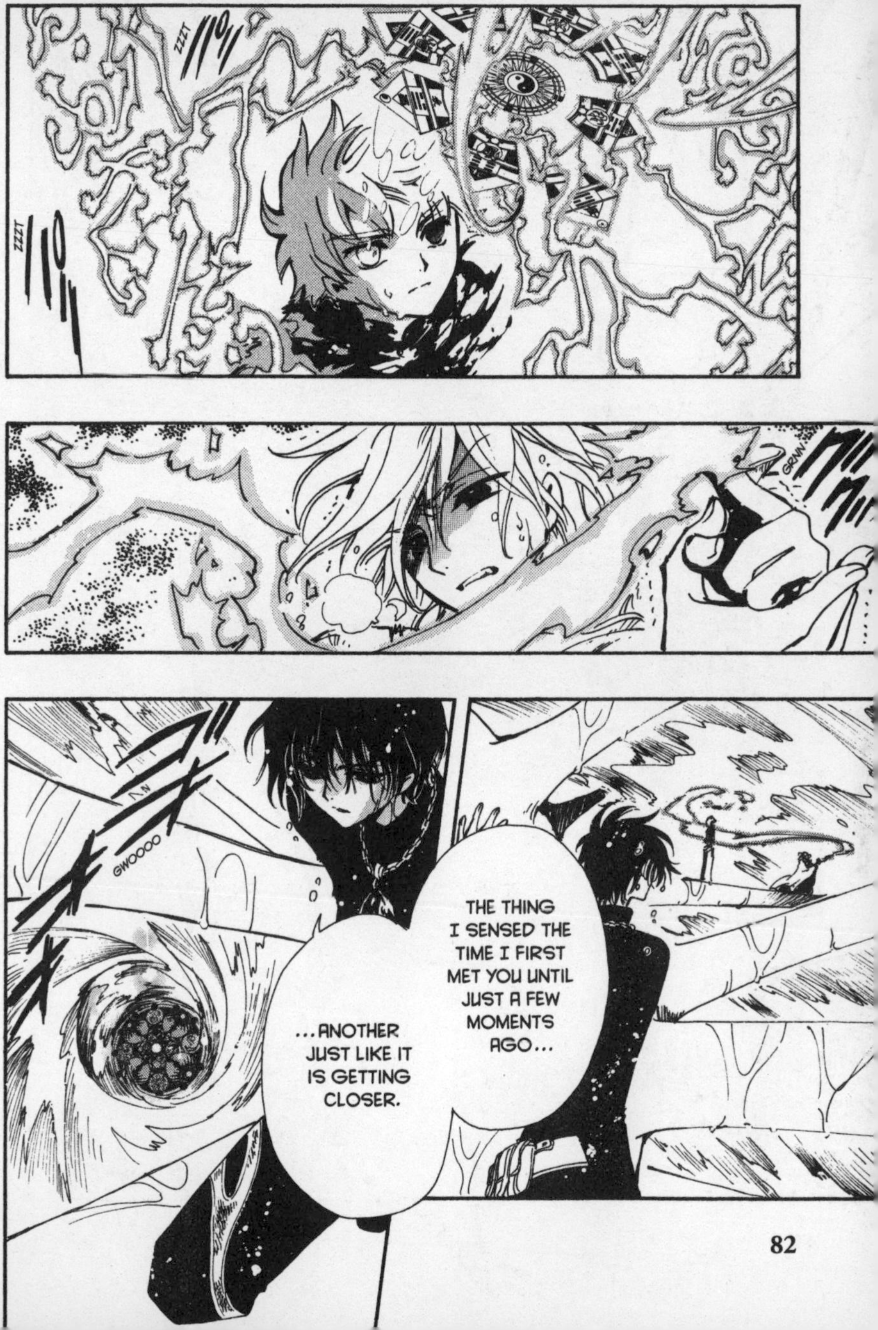
ZZZT
ZZZT
GRNN
THE THING I SENSED THE TIME I FIRST MET YOU UNTIL JUST A FEW MOMENTS AGO...
...ANOTHER JUST LIKE IT IS GETTING CLOSER.
GWOOOO

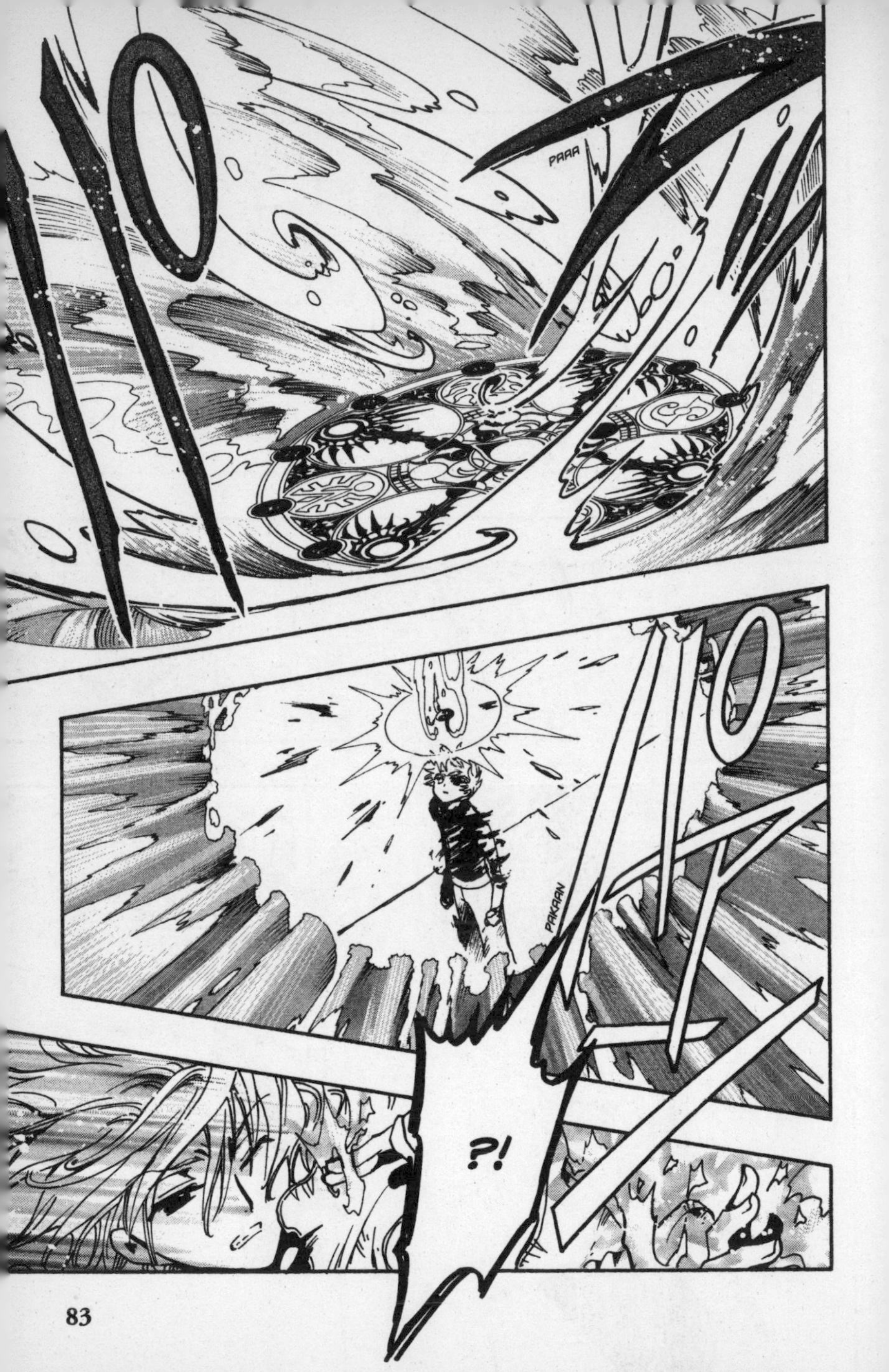
PAAA
PAKAAN
?!

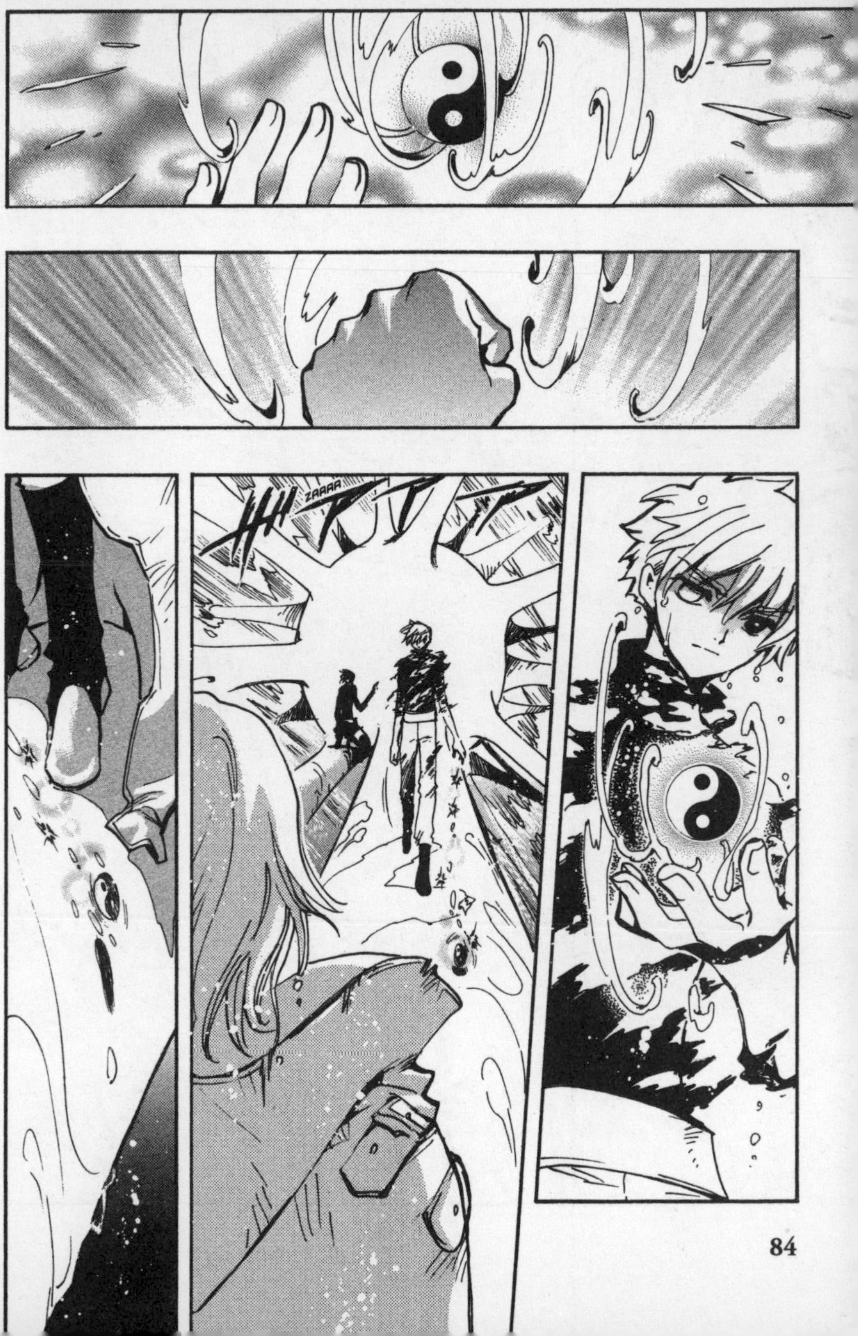
ZAAAA

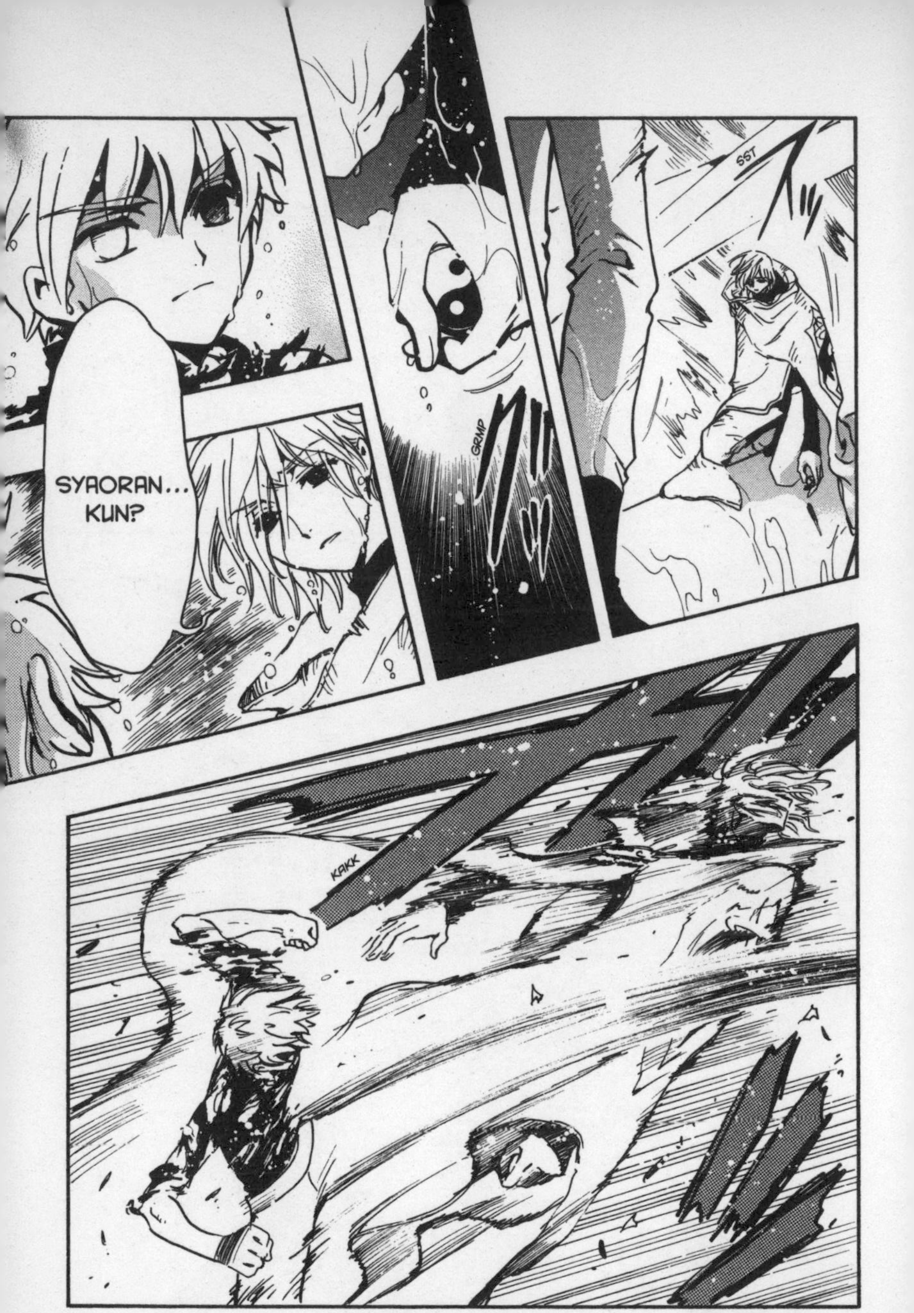
SST
GRMP
SYAORAN... KUN?
KAKK

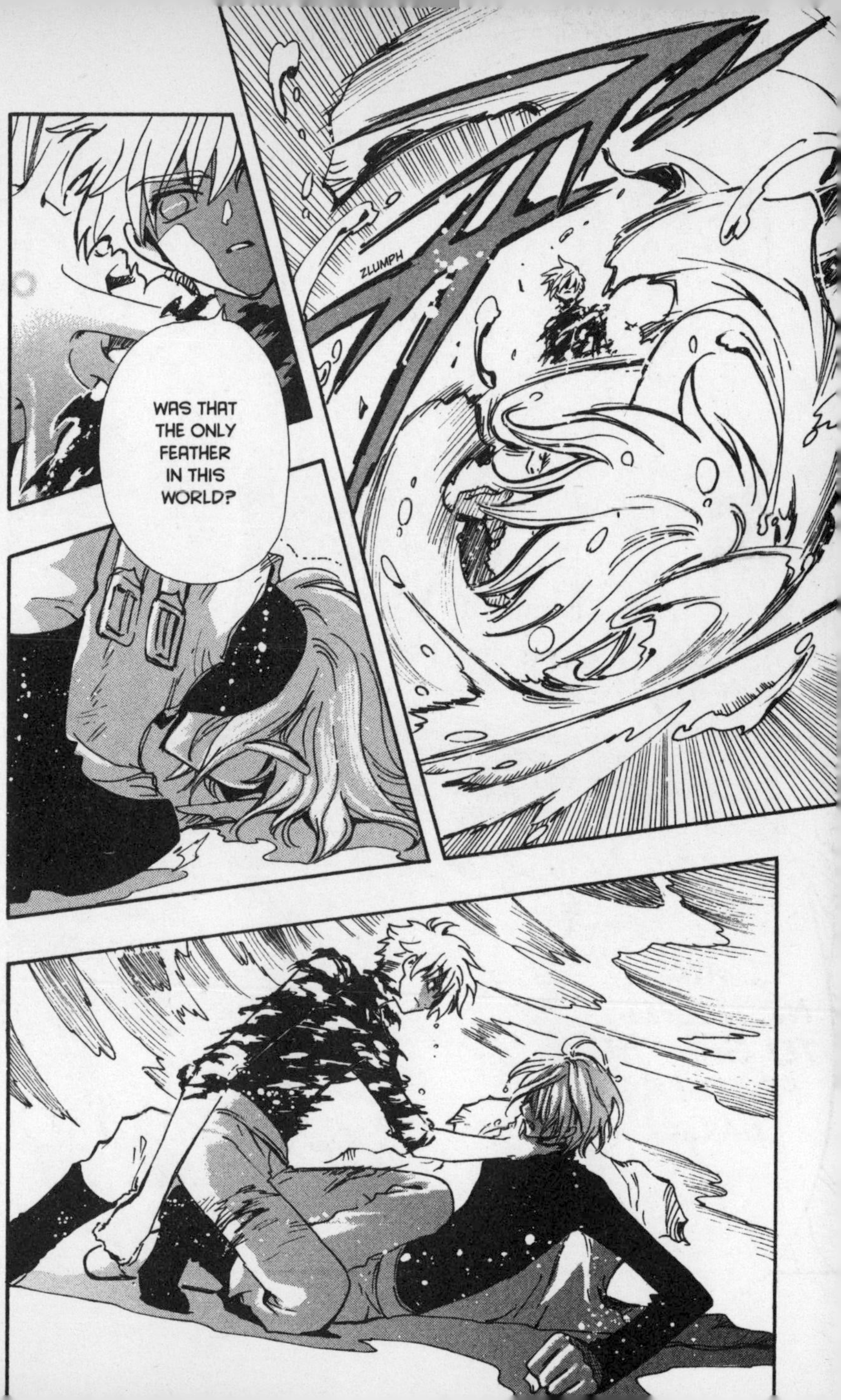
ZLUMPH
WAS THAT THE ONLY FEATHER IN THIS WORLD?

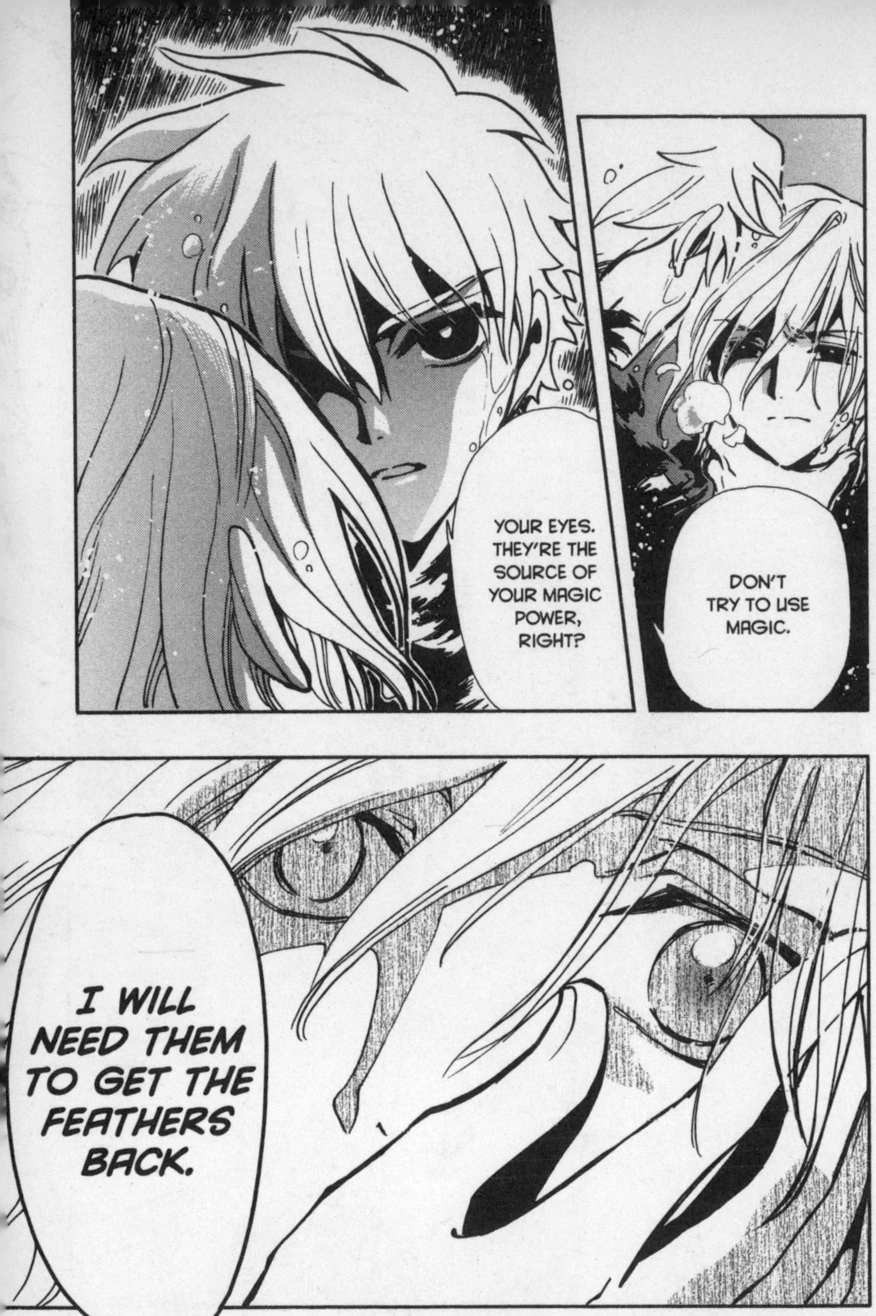
DON'T TRY TO USE MAGIC.
YOUR EYES. THEY'RE THE SOURCE OF YOUR MAGIC POWER, RIGHT?
I WILL NEED THEM TO GET THE FEATHERS BACK.

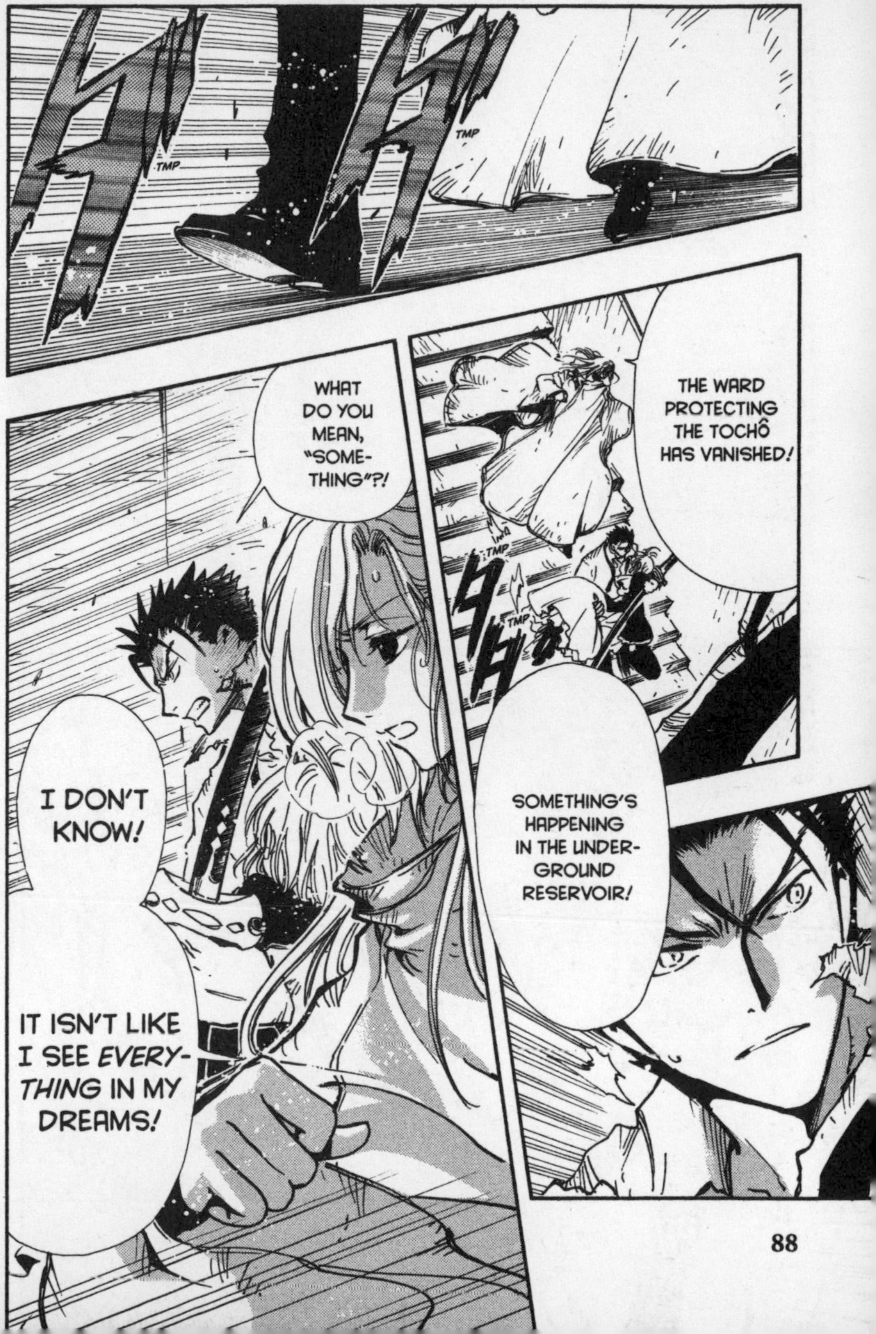
TMP
TMP
THE WARD PROTECTING THE TOCHÔ HAS VANISHED!
TMP
TMP
SOMETHING'S HAPPENING IN THE UNDERGROUND RESERVOIR!
WHAT DO YOU MEAN, "SOMETHING"?!
I DON'T KNOW!
IT ISN'T LIKE I SEE *EVERYTHING* IN MY DREAMS!

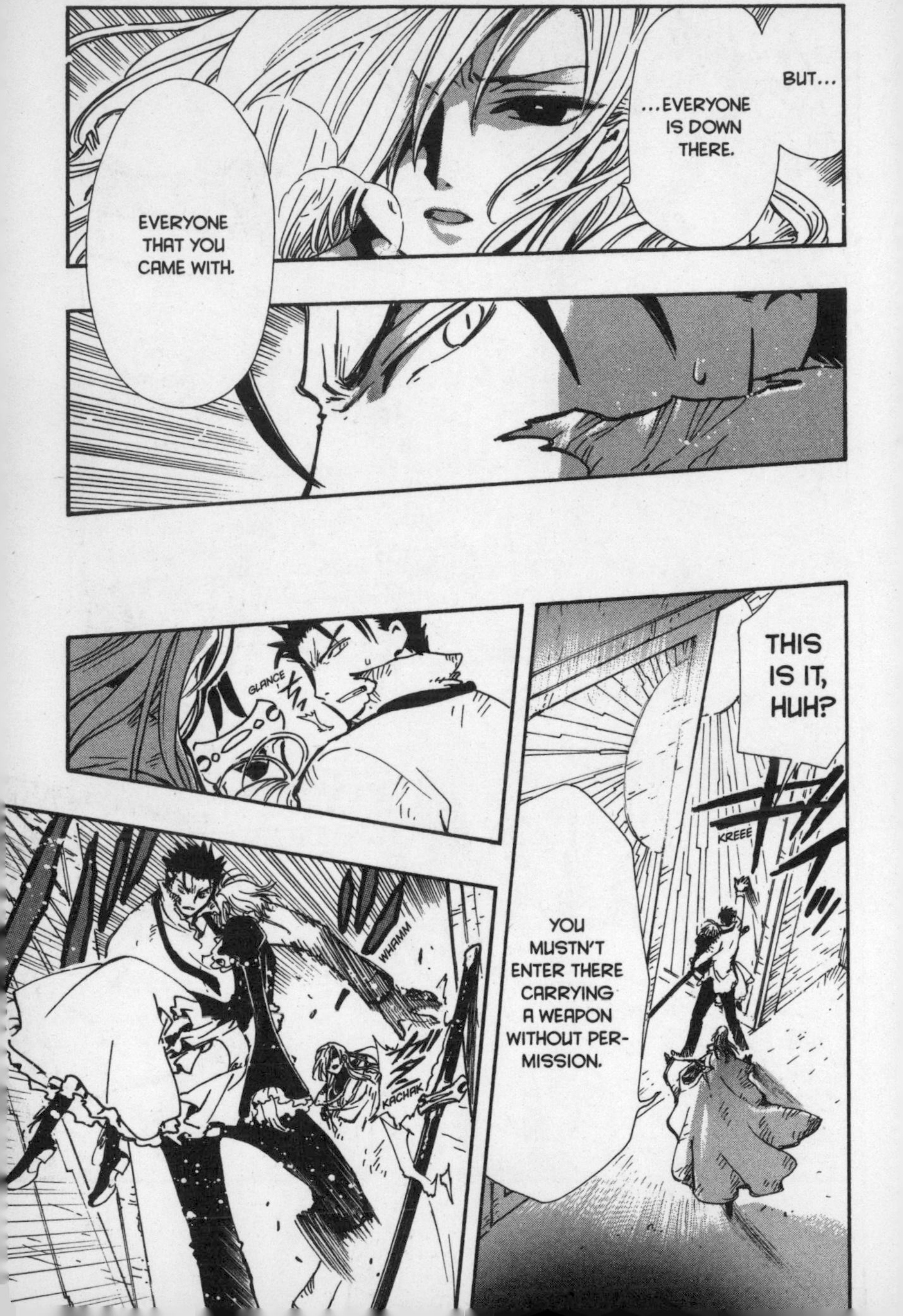
BUT...
...EVERYONE IS DOWN THERE.
EVERYONE THAT YOU CAME WITH.
THIS IS IT, HUH?
KREEE
YOU MUSTN'T ENTER THERE CARRYING A WEAPON WITHOUT PER-MISSION.
GLANCE
WHAMM
KACHAK

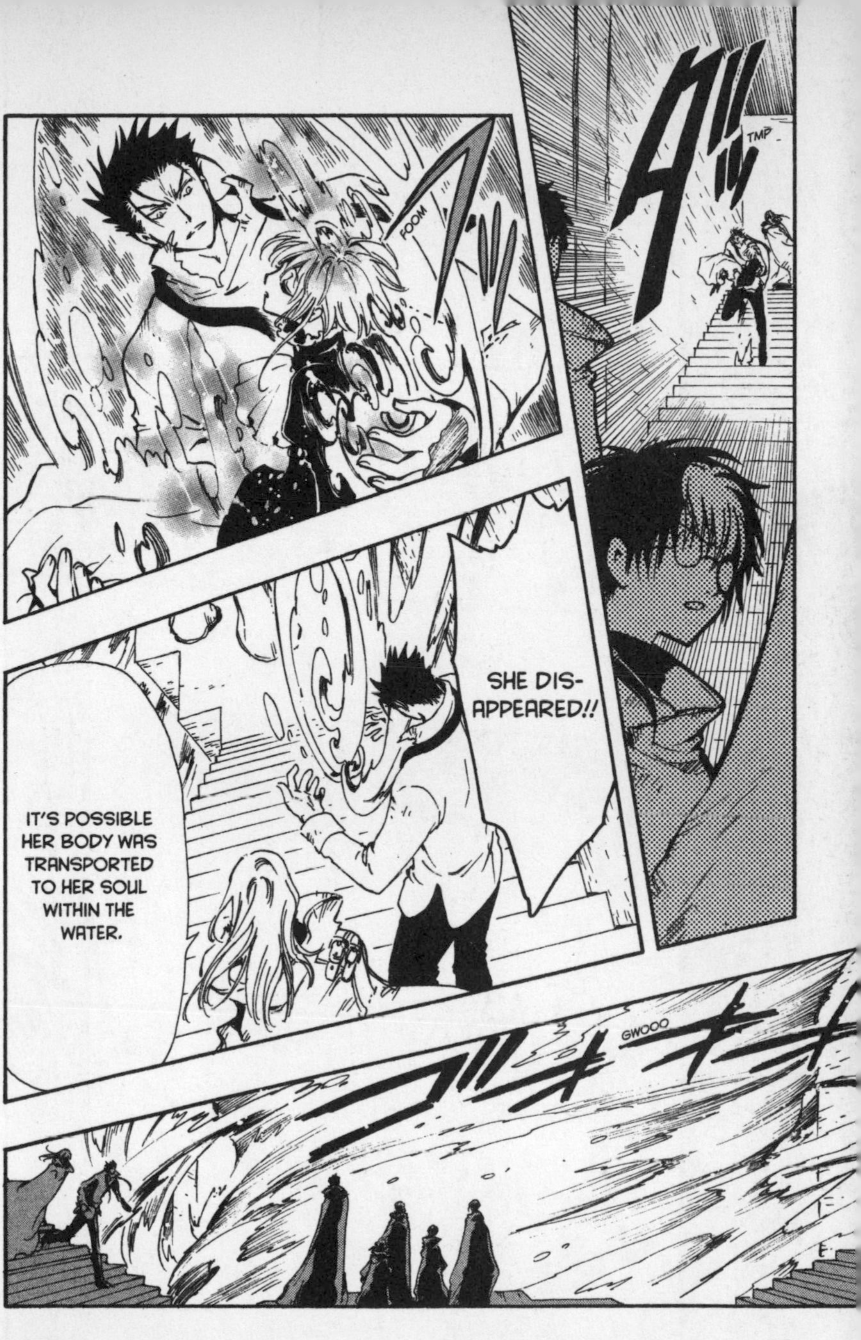
TMP
FOOM
SHE DIS-APPEARED!!
IT'S POSSIBLE HER BODY WAS TRANSPORTED TO HER SOUL WITHIN THE WATER.
GWOOO

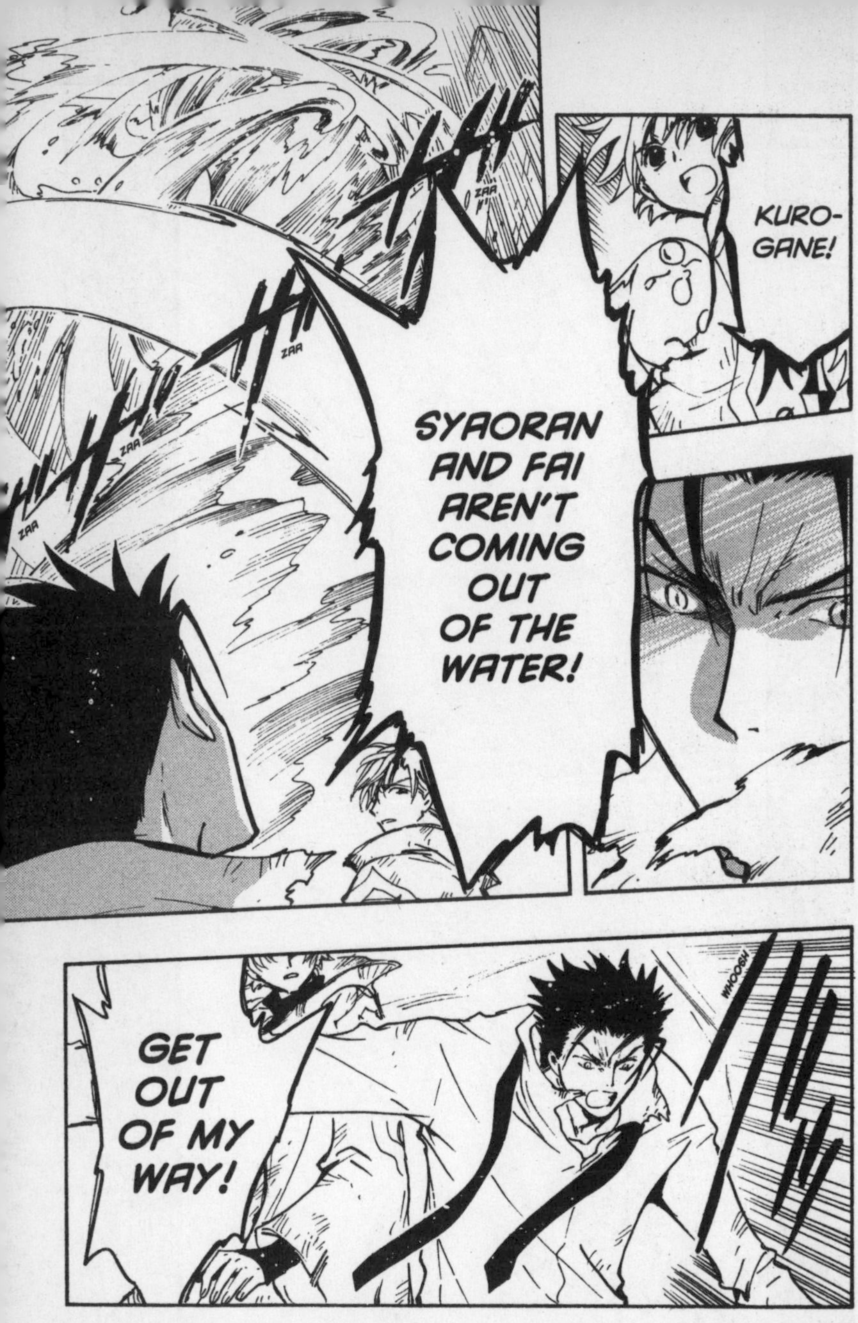
KURO-GANE!
SYAORAN AND FAI AREN'T COMING OUT OF THE WATER!
ZAA
ZAA
ZAA
ZAA
GET OUT OF MY WAY!
WHOOSH

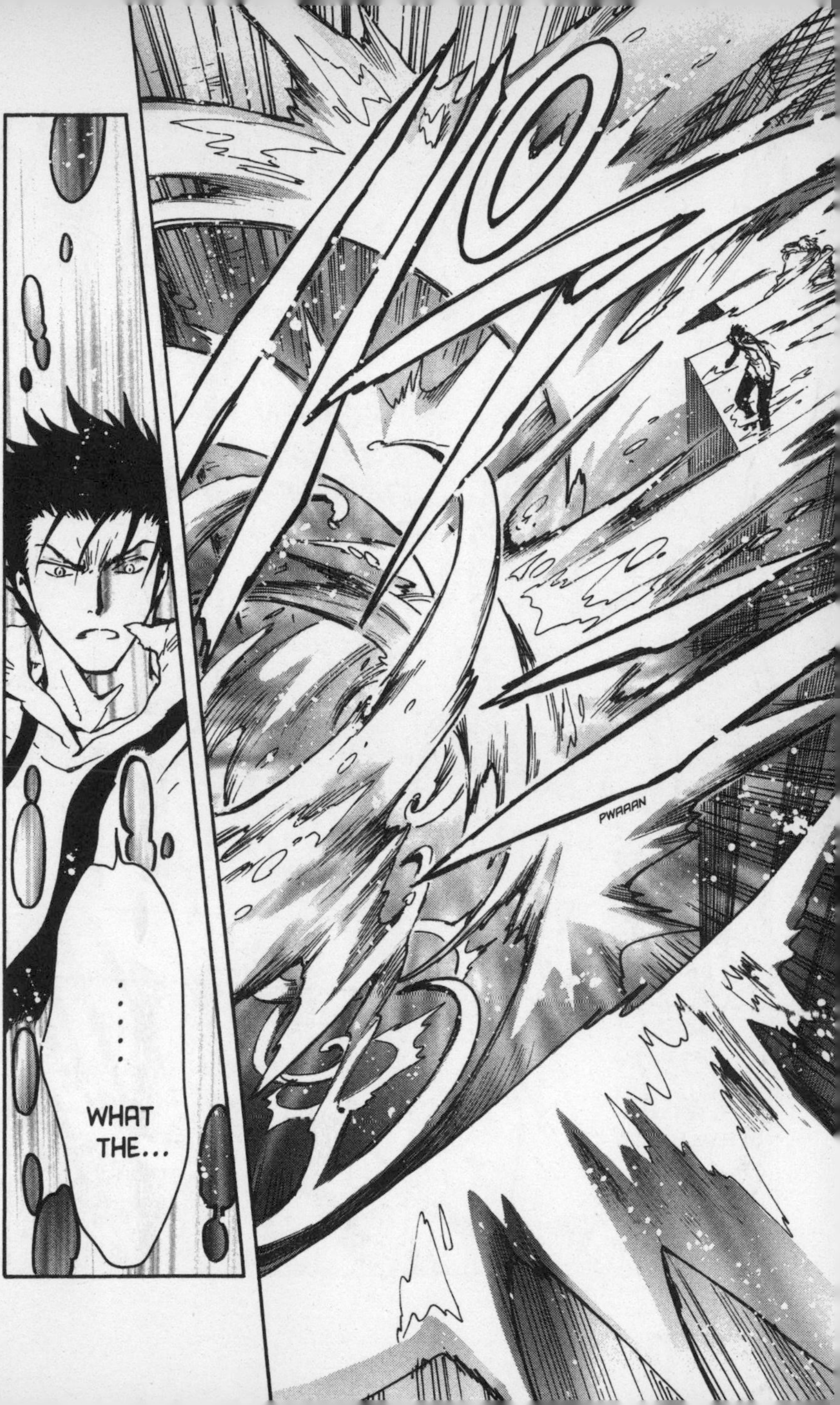
PWAAAN
......
WHAT THE...

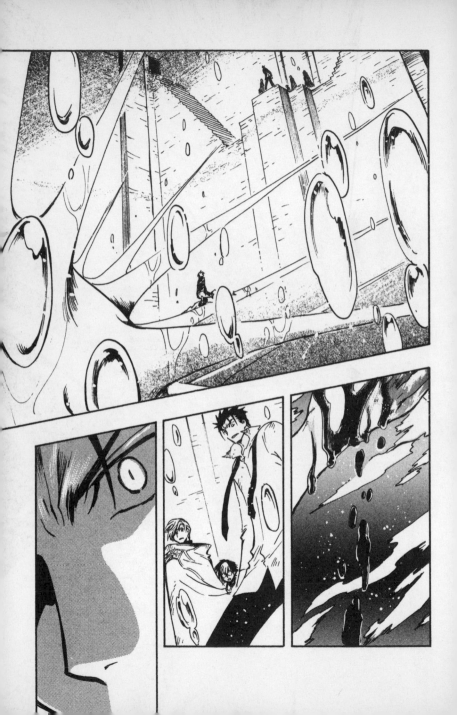

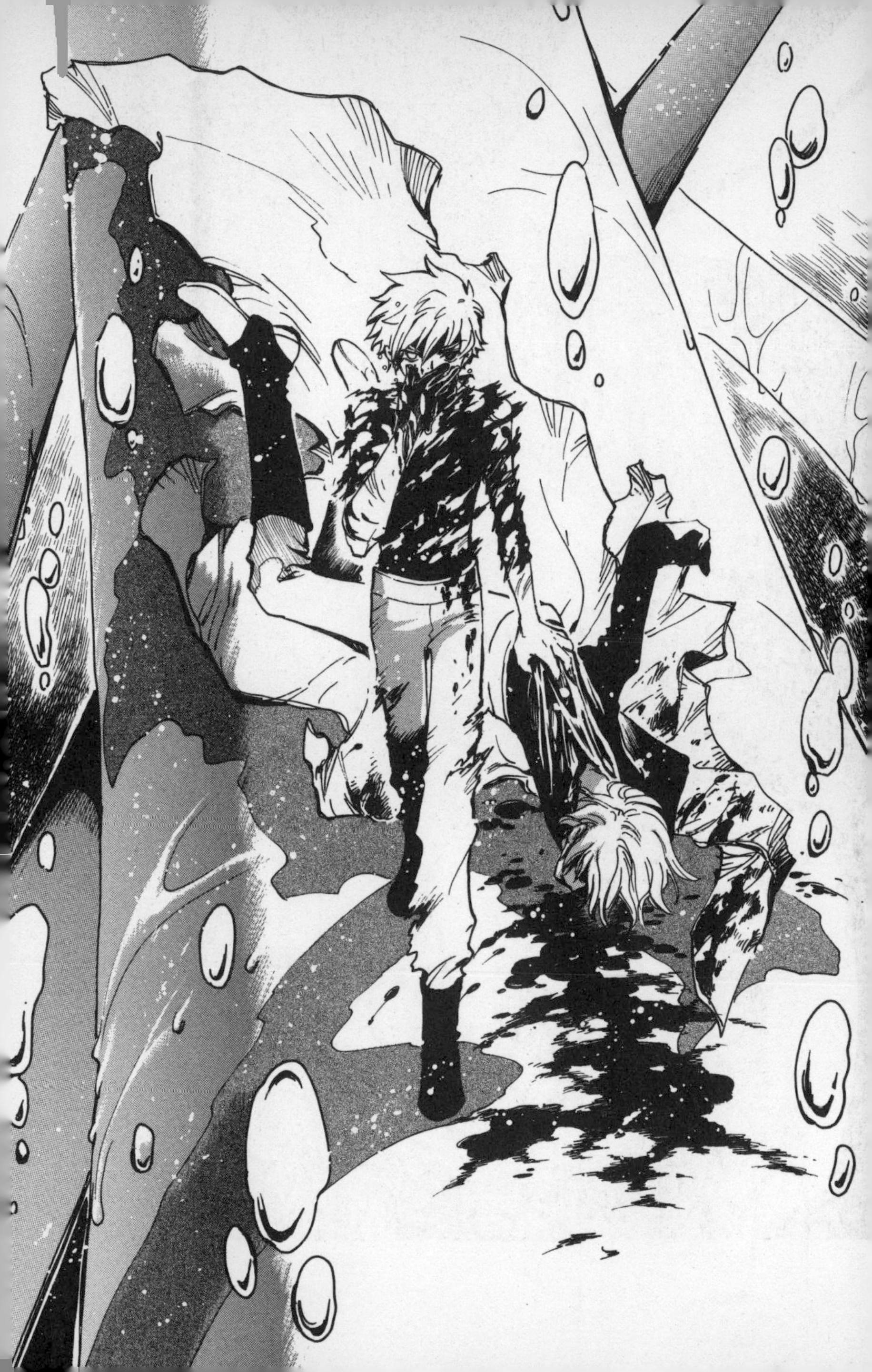

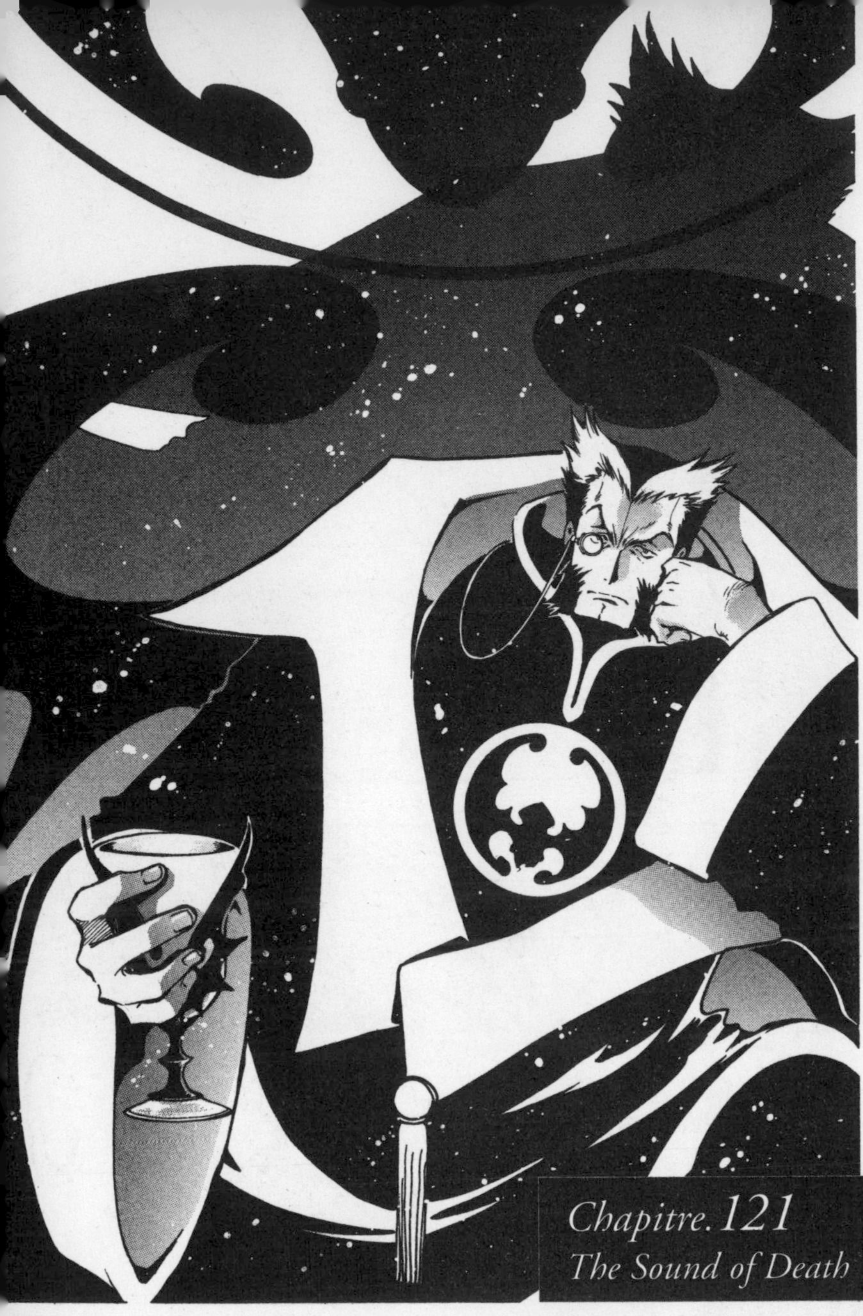
Chapitre. 121
The Sound of Death

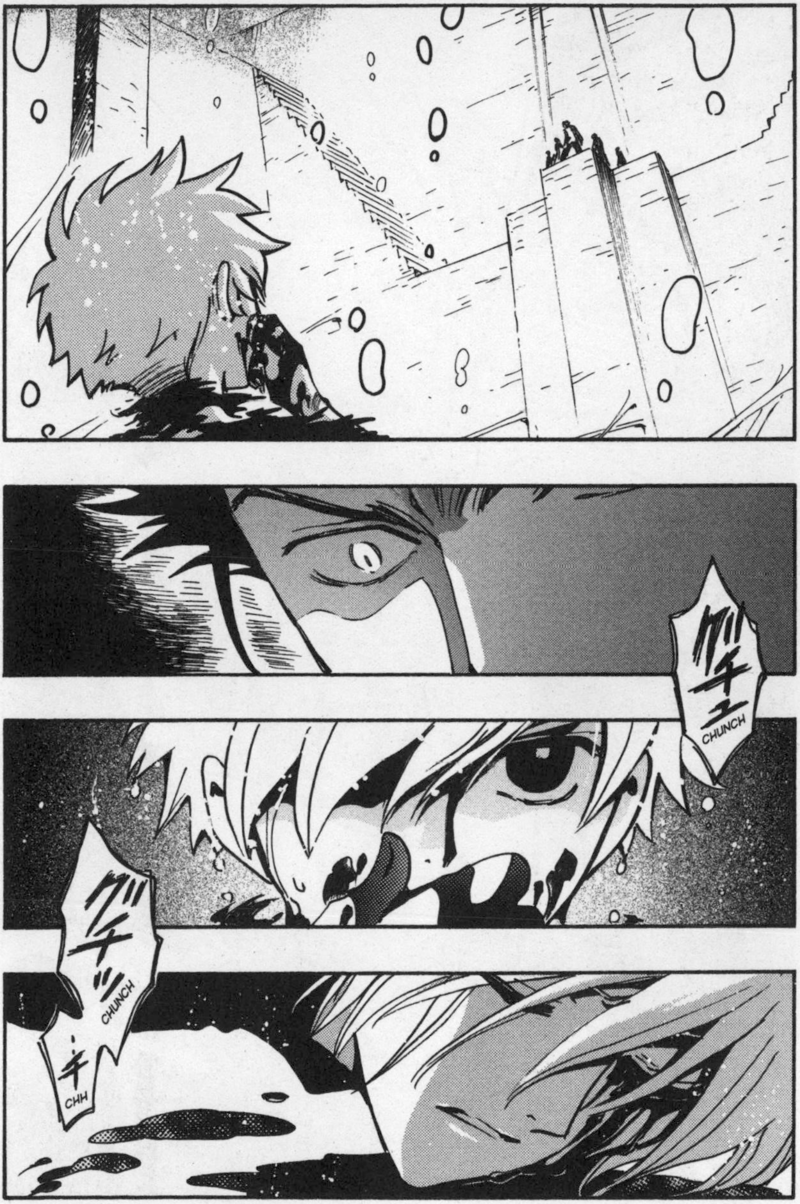
グチュ
CHUNCH
グチッ
CHUNCH
チ
CHH

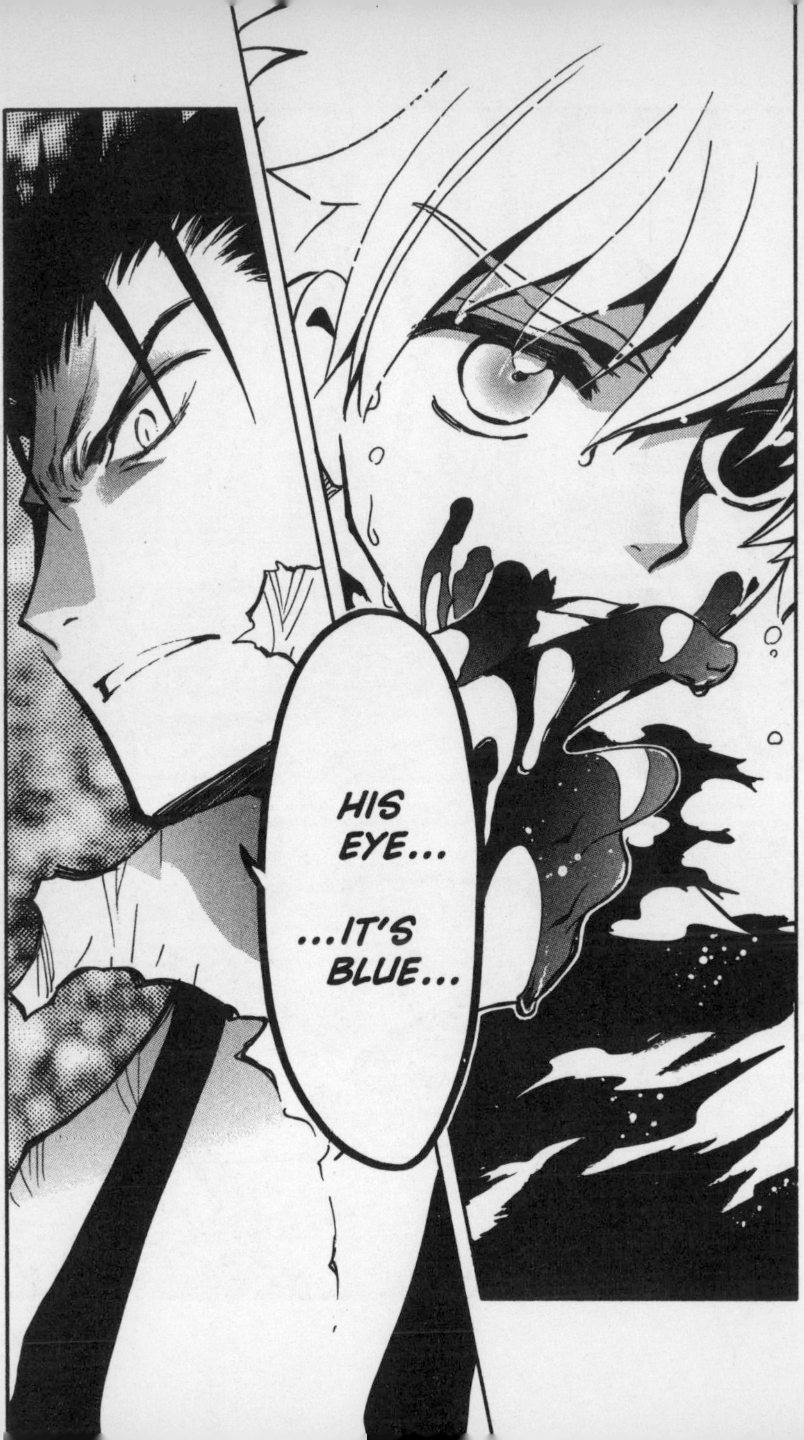
HIS EYE...
...IT'S BLUE...

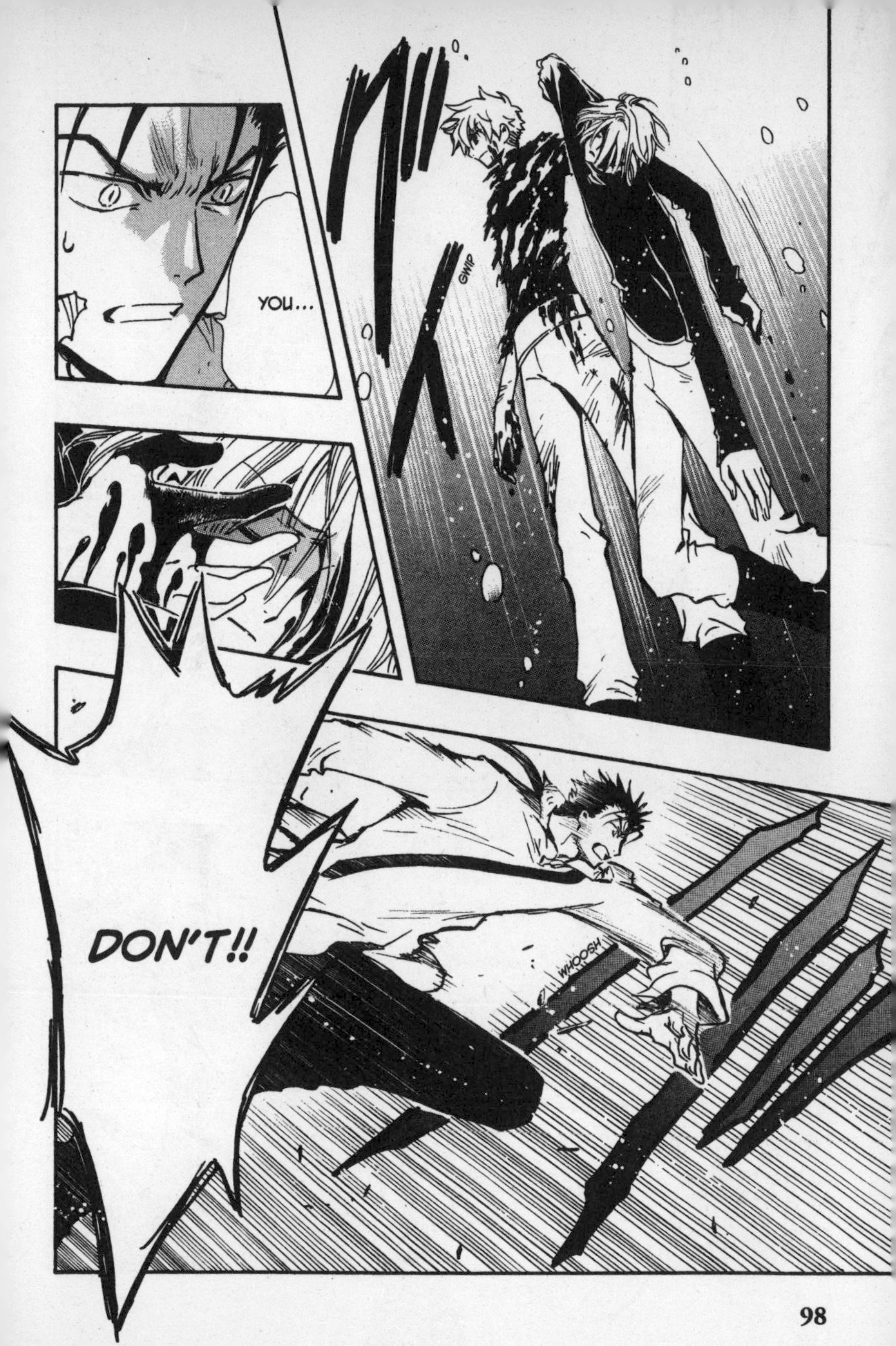
GWIP
YOU...
WHOOSH
DON'T!!

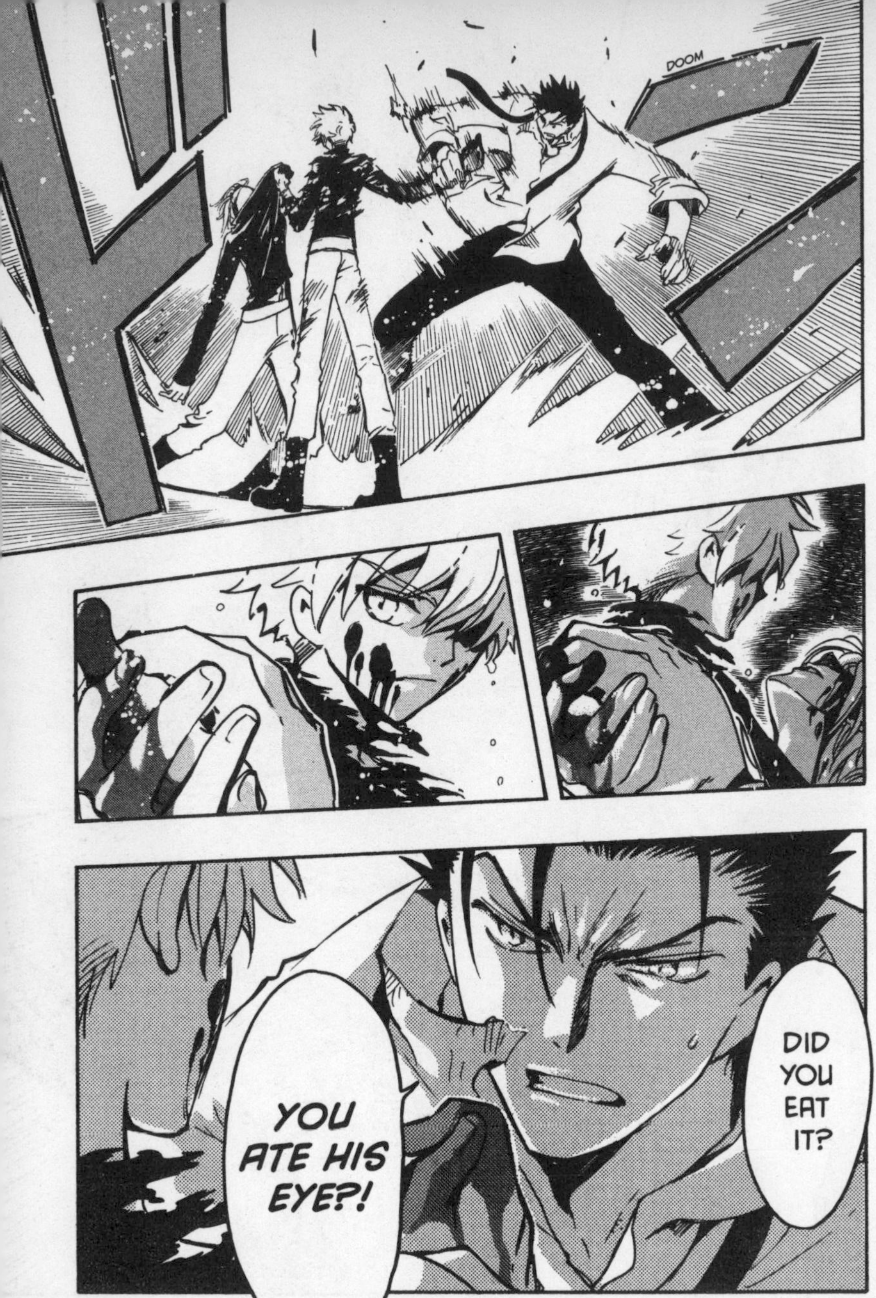
DOOM
DID YOU EAT IT?
YOU ATE HIS EYE?!

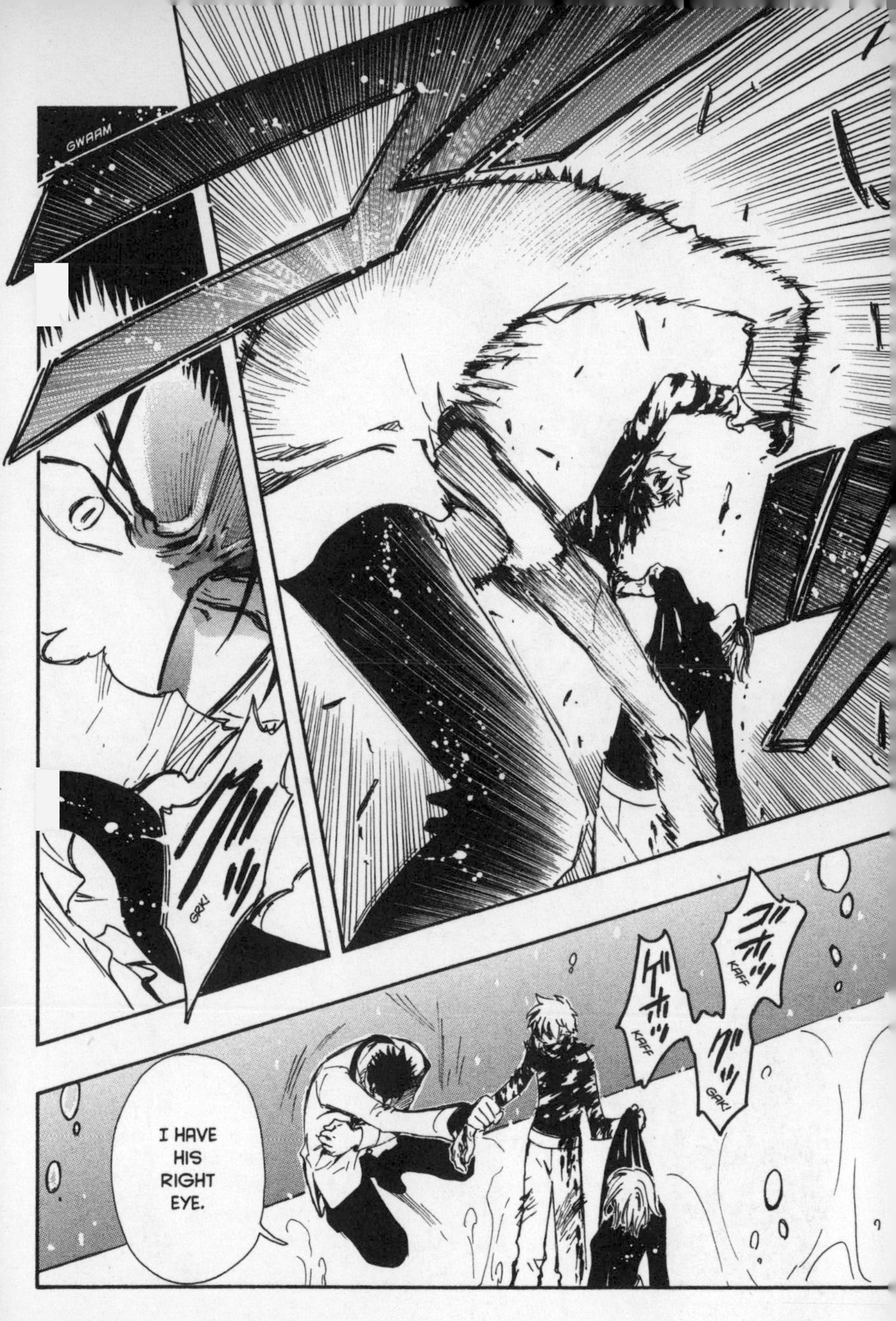
GWAAM
GRK!
KAFF
KAFF
GAK!
I HAVE HIS RIGHT EYE.

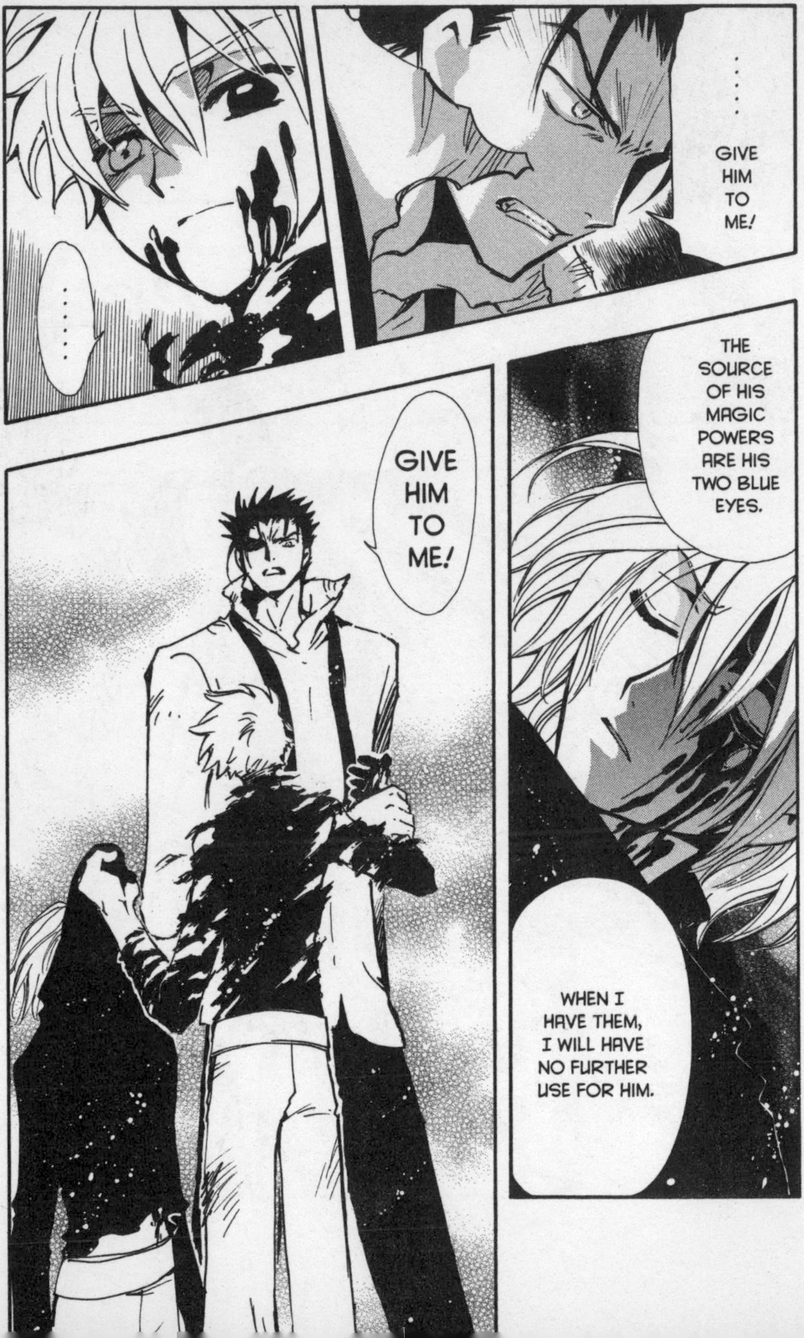
.....
GIVE HIM TO ME!
......
THE SOURCE OF HIS MAGIC POWERS ARE HIS TWO BLUE EYES.
WHEN I HAVE THEM, I WILL HAVE NO FURTHER USE FOR HIM.
GIVE HIM TO ME!

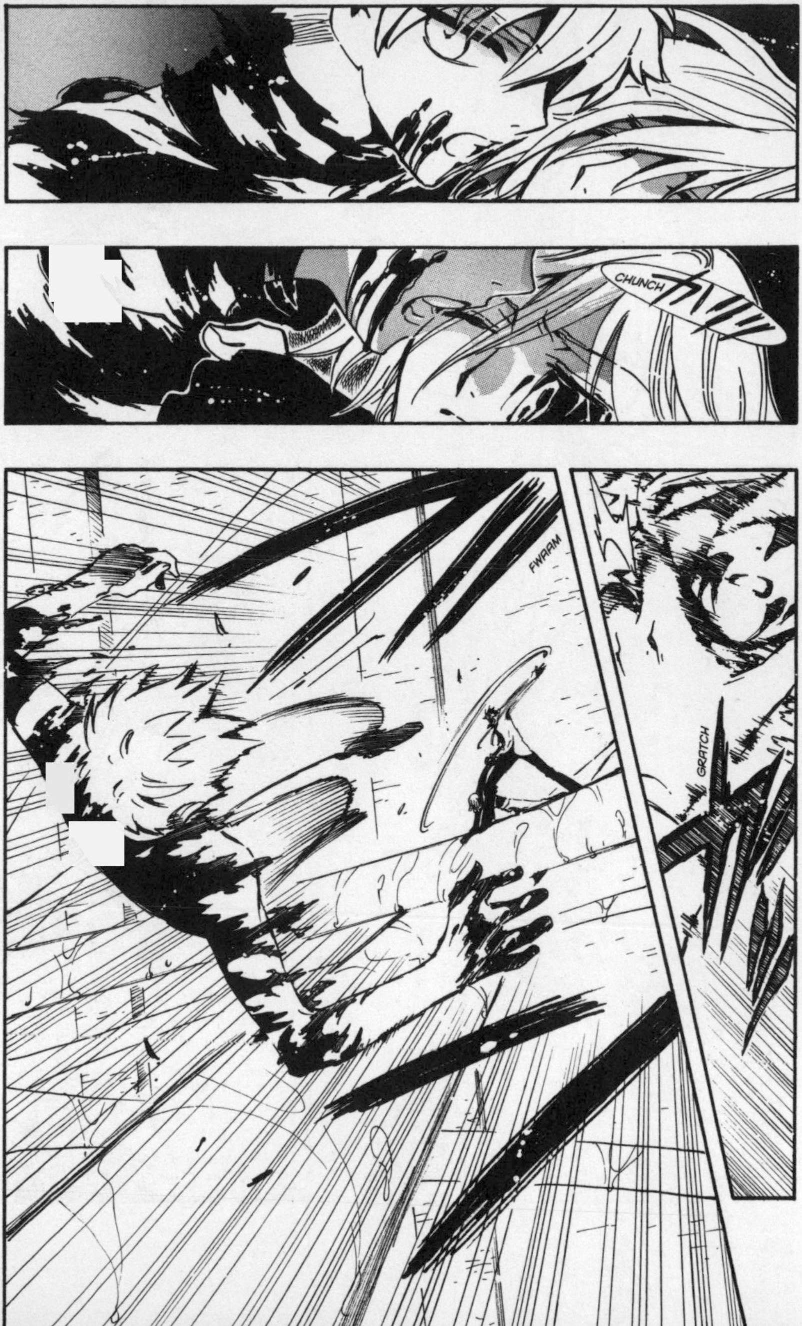
CHUNCH
GRATCH
FWAAM

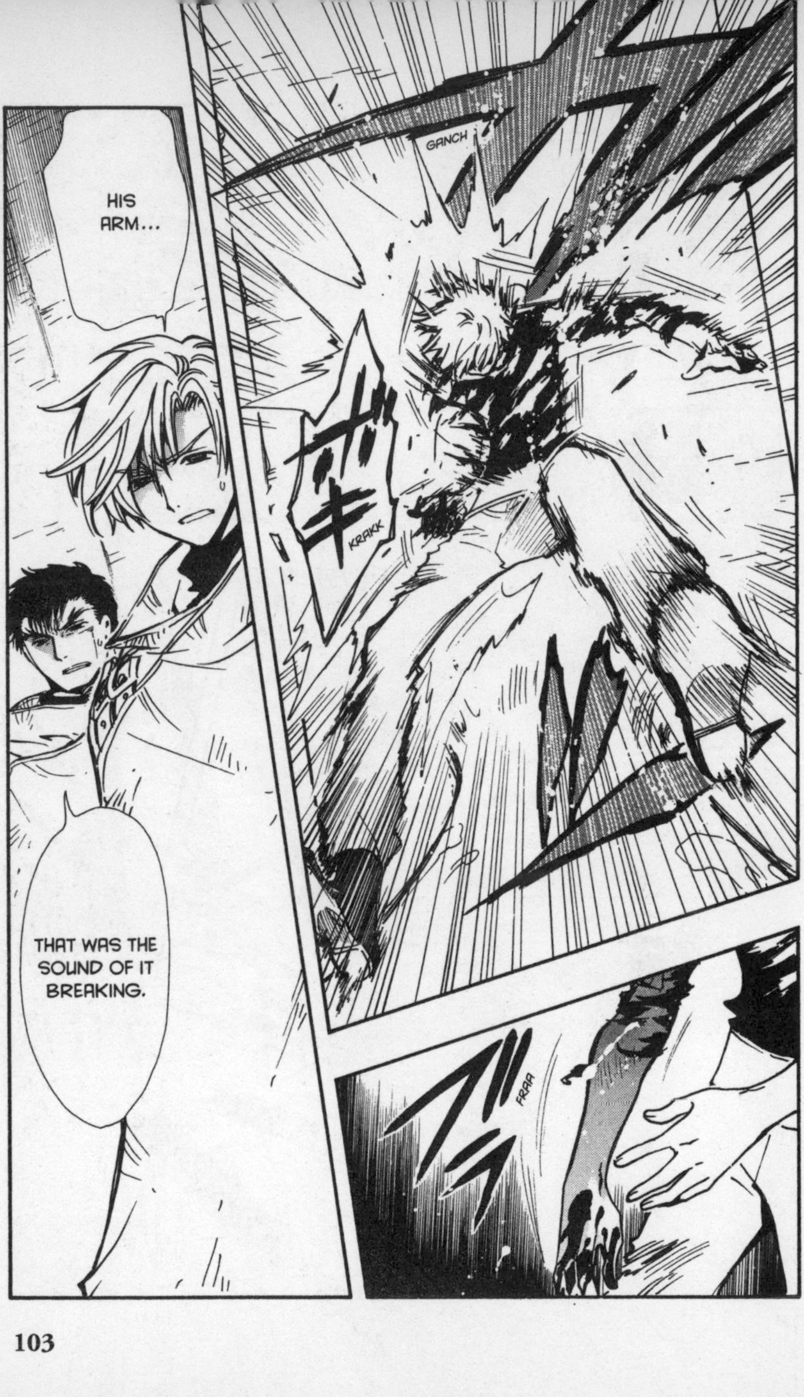
GANCH
KRAKK
FRAA
HIS ARM...
THAT WAS THE SOUND OF IT BREAKING.

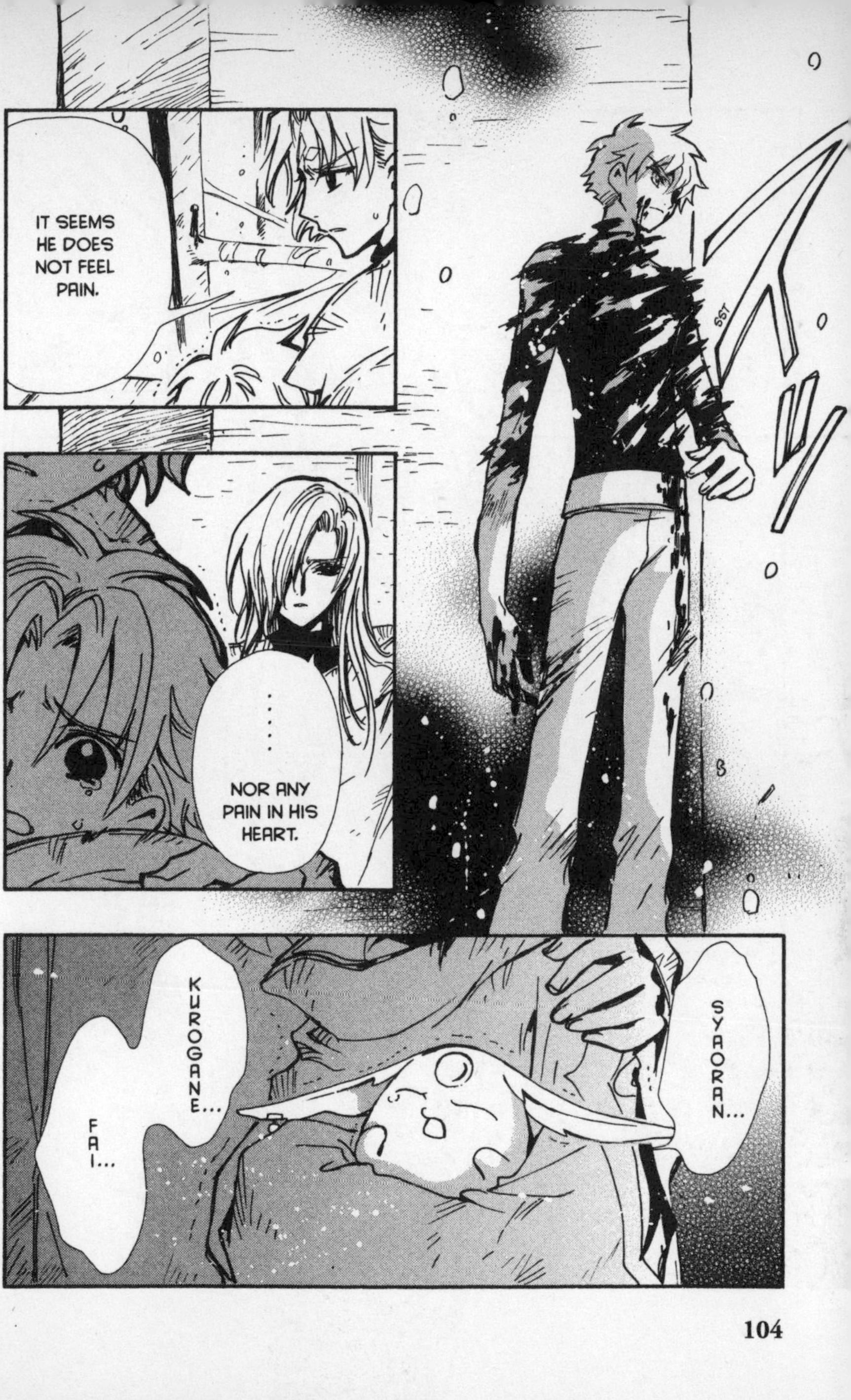

SST
IT SEEMS HE DOES NOT FEEL PAIN.
......
NOR ANY PAIN IN HIS HEART.
SYAORAN...
KUROGANE...
FAI...

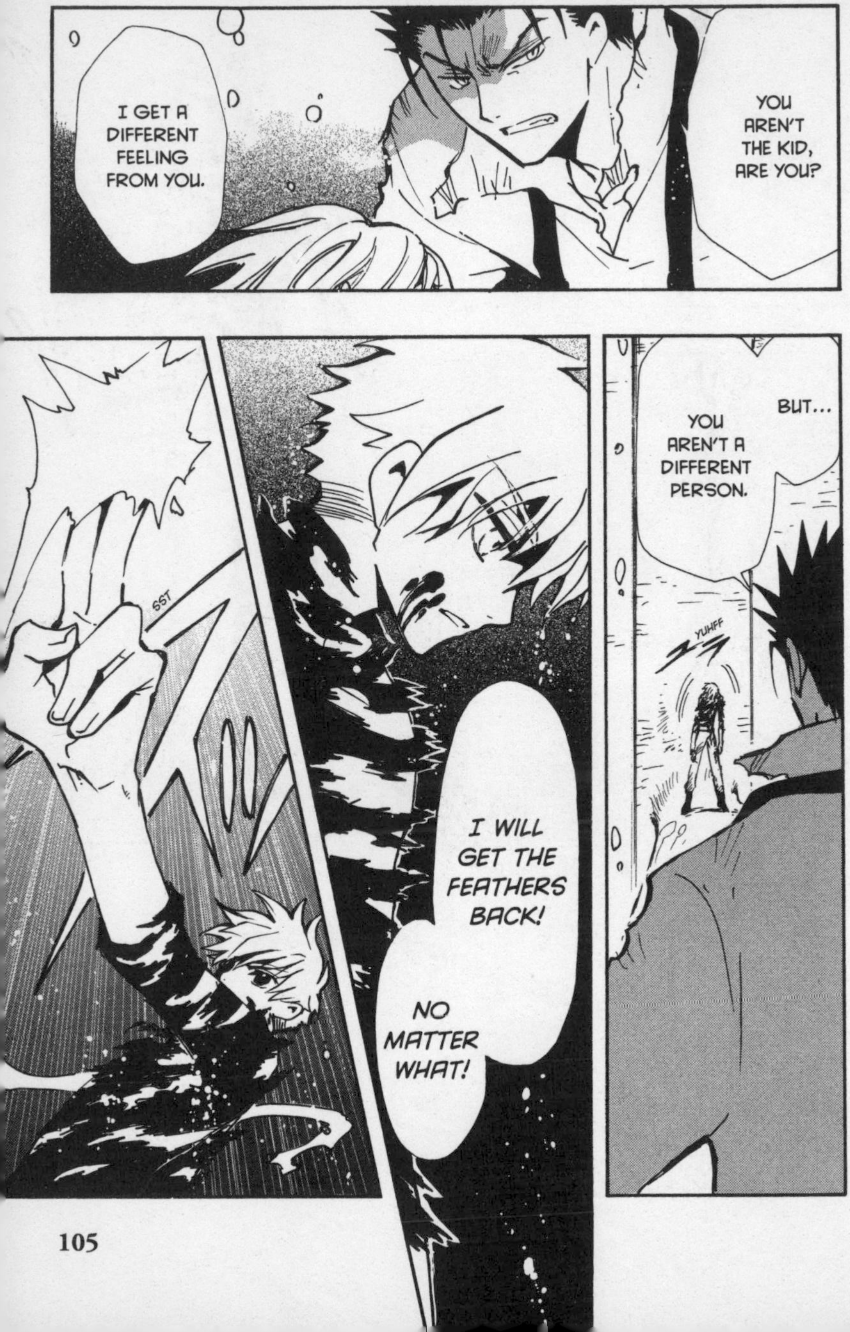
YOU AREN'T THE KID, ARE YOU?
I GET A DIFFERENT FEELING FROM YOU.
BUT...
YOU AREN'T A DIFFERENT PERSON.
YUHFF
I WILL GET THE FEATHERS BACK!
NO MATTER WHAT!
SST

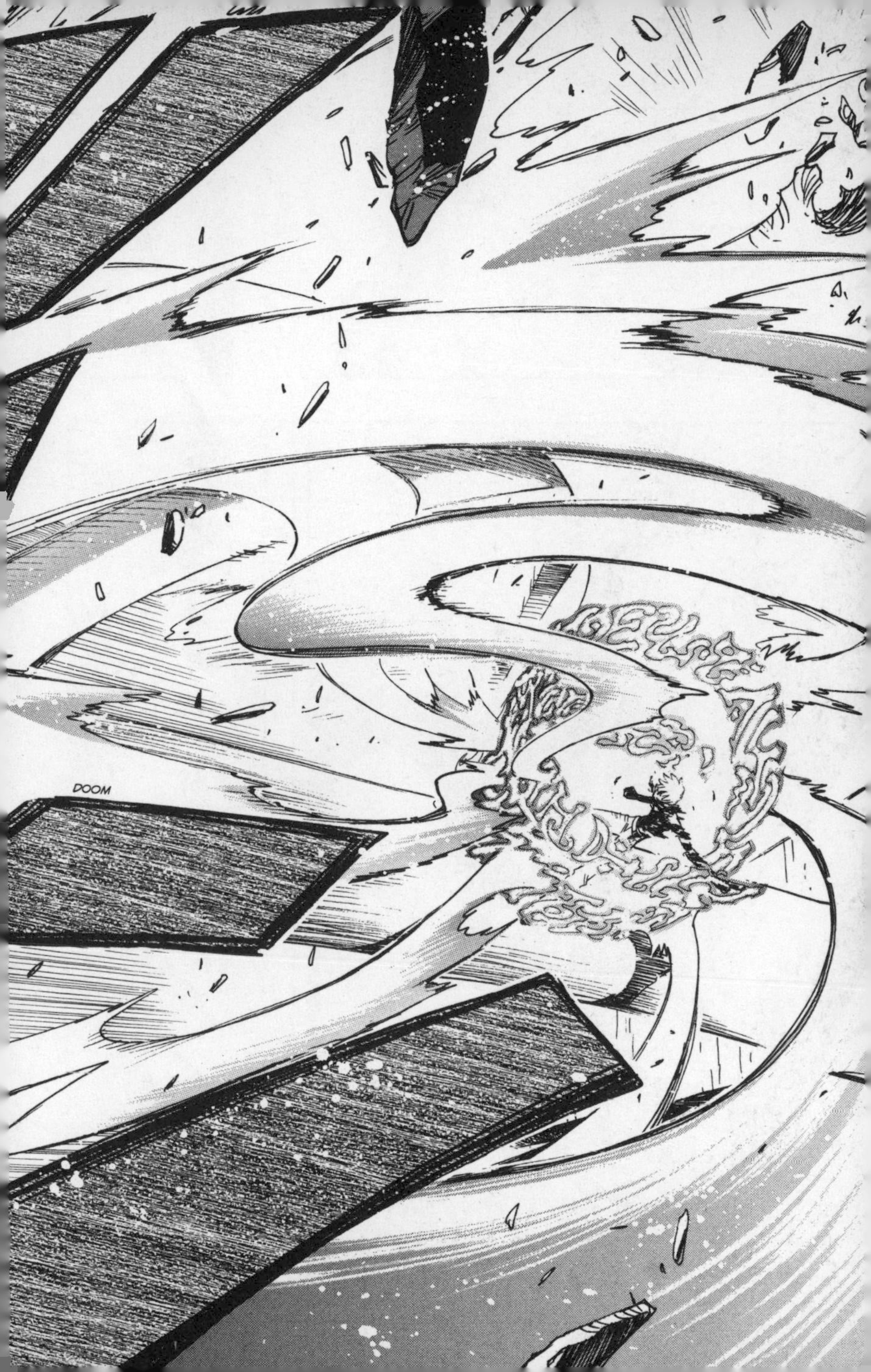
DOOM

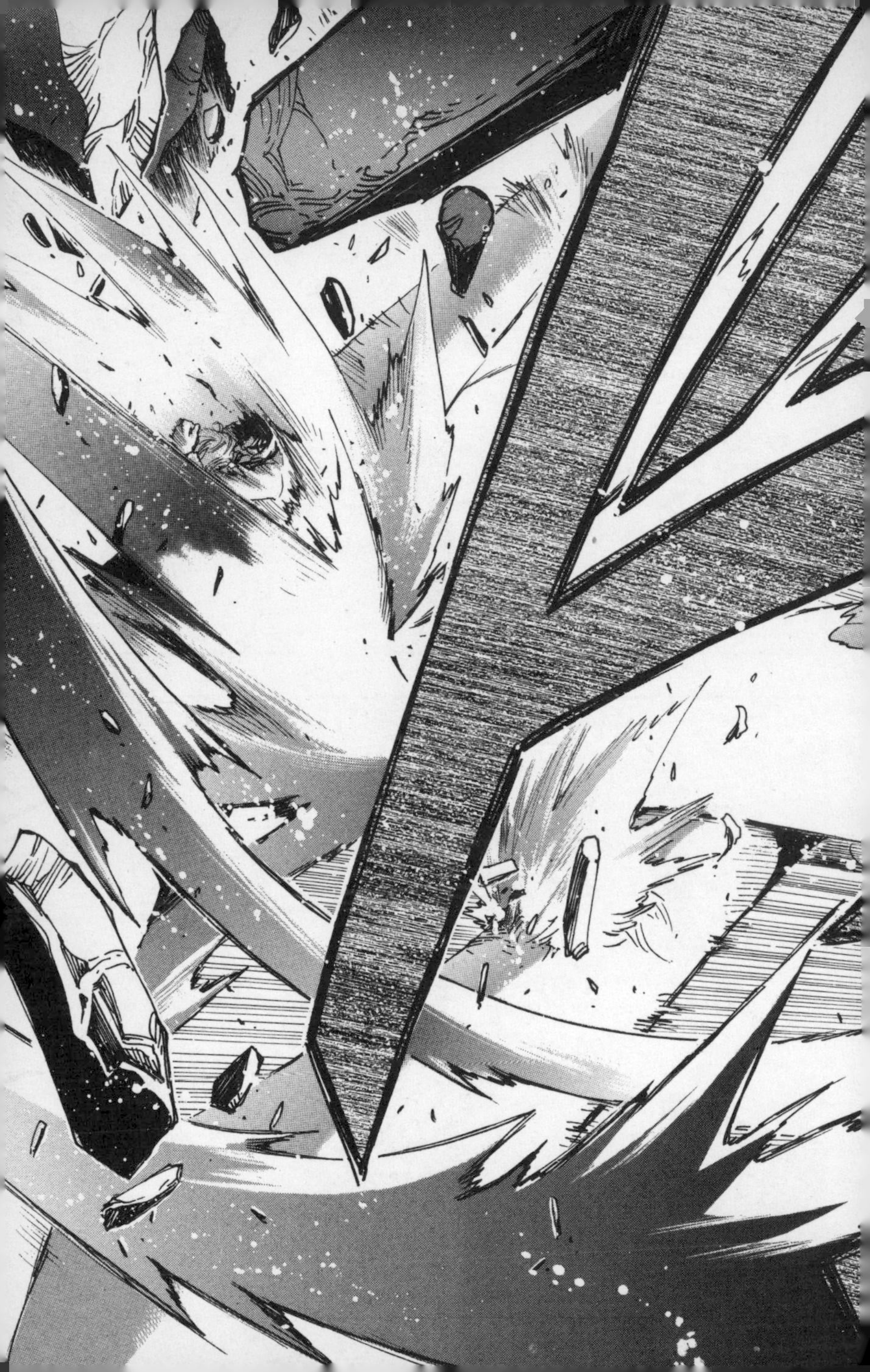

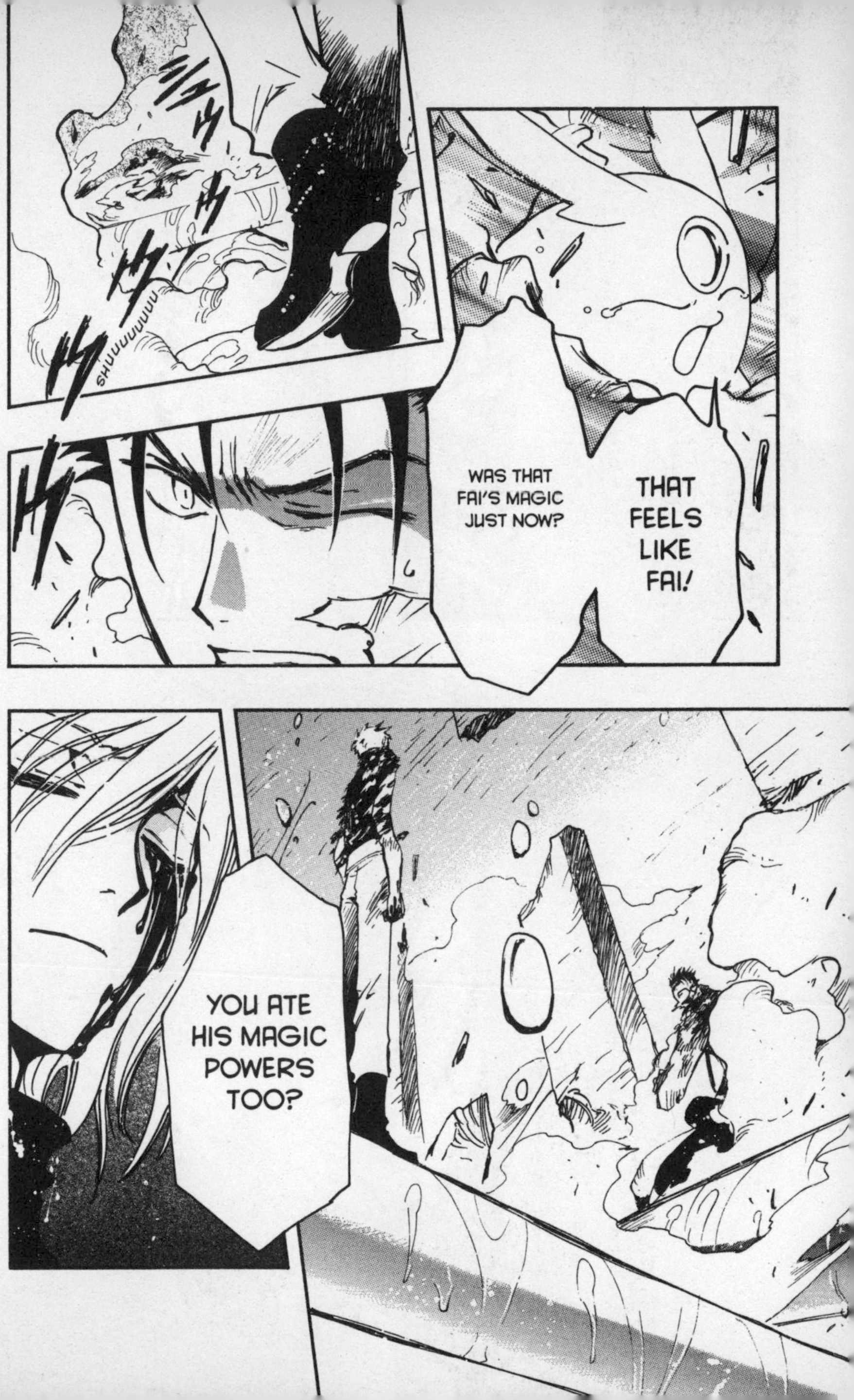
THAT FEELS LIKE FAI!
WAS THAT FAI'S MAGIC JUST NOW?
SHUUUUUUUU
YOU ATE HIS MAGIC POWERS TOO?

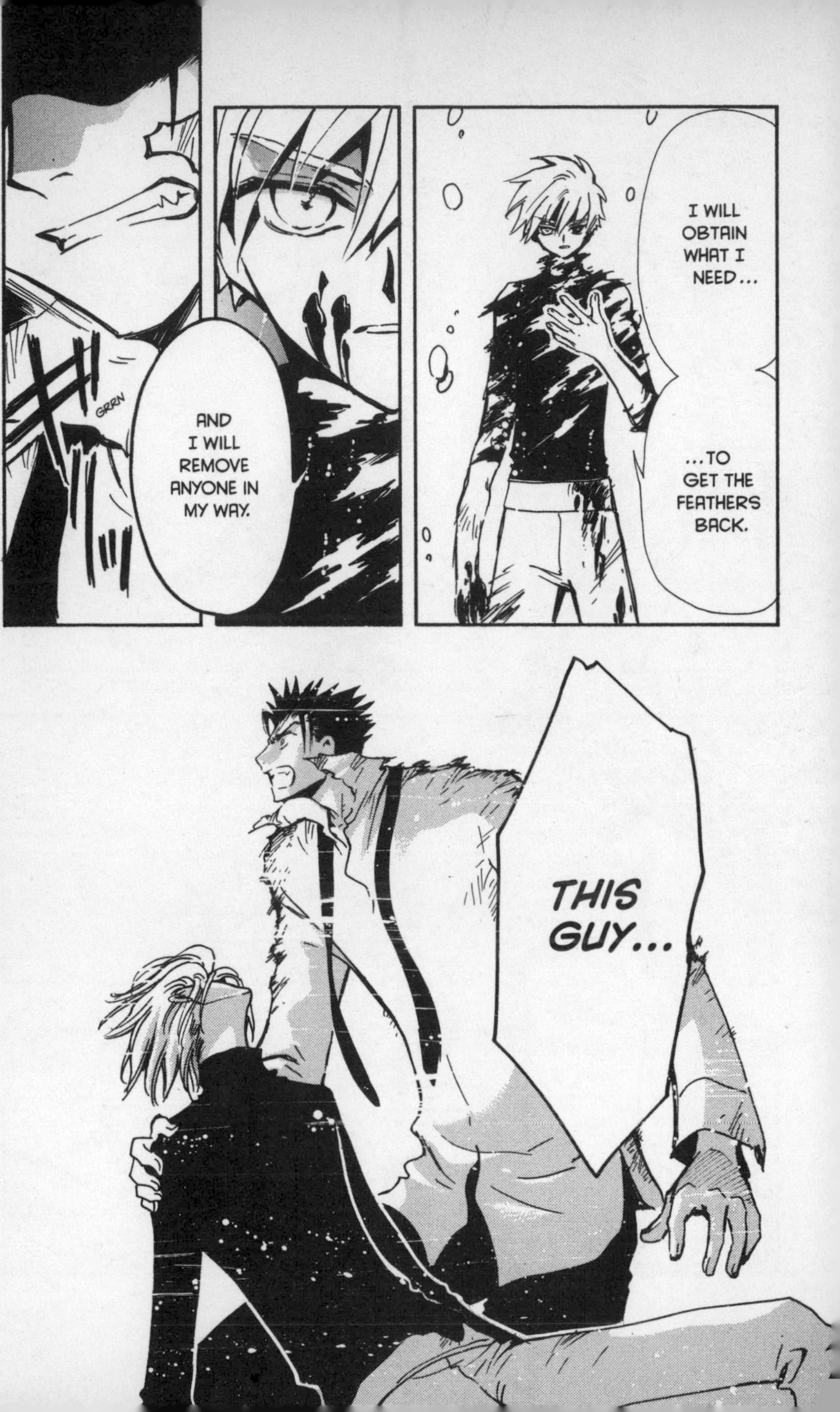
I WILL OBTAIN WHAT I NEED...
...TO GET THE FEATHERS BACK.
AND I WILL REMOVE ANYONE IN MY WAY.
GRRN
THIS GUY...

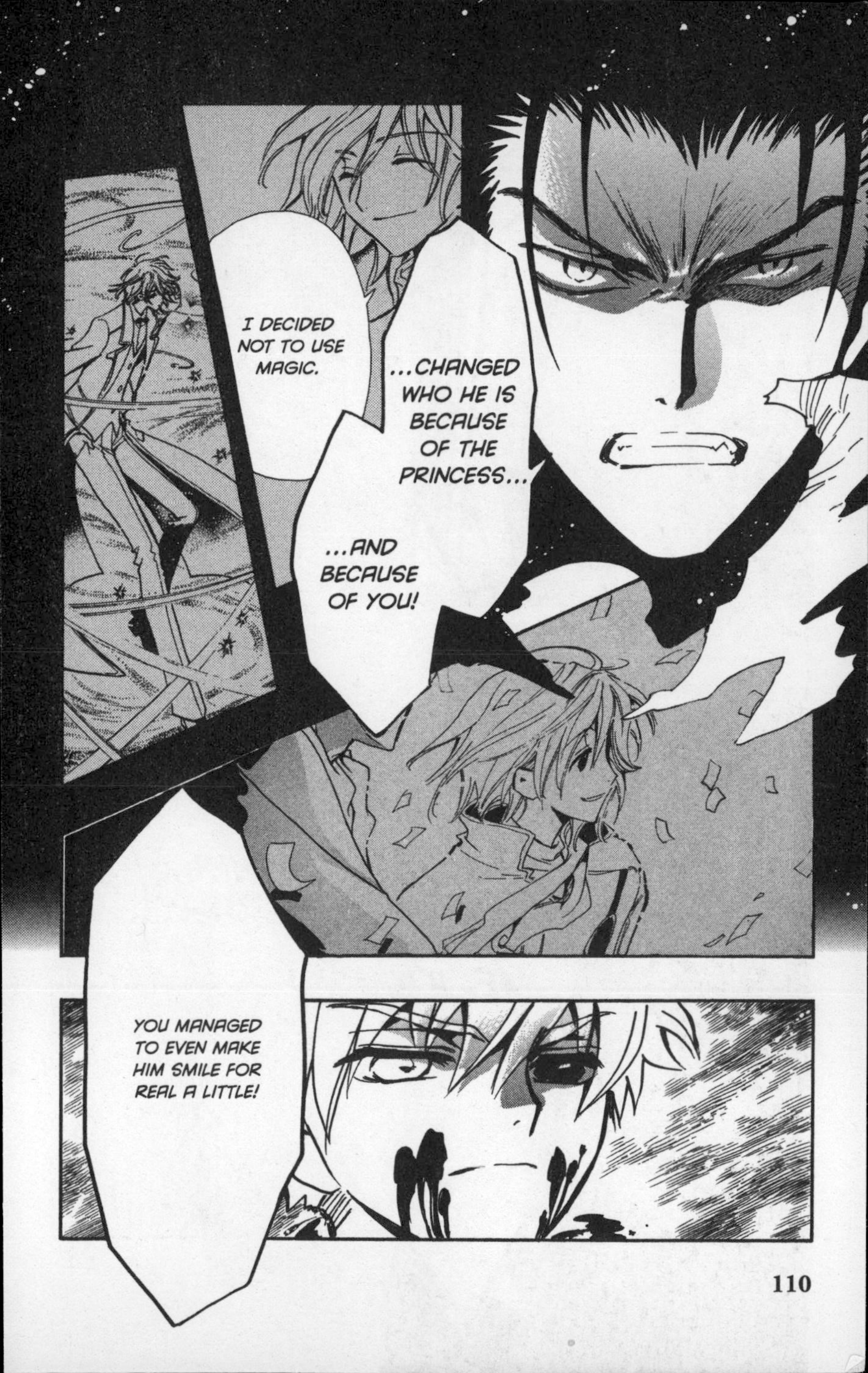
...CHANGED WHO HE IS BECAUSE OF THE PRINCESS...
...AND BECAUSE OF YOU!
I DECIDED NOT TO USE MAGIC.
YOU MANAGED TO EVEN MAKE HIM SMILE FOR REAL A LITTLE!

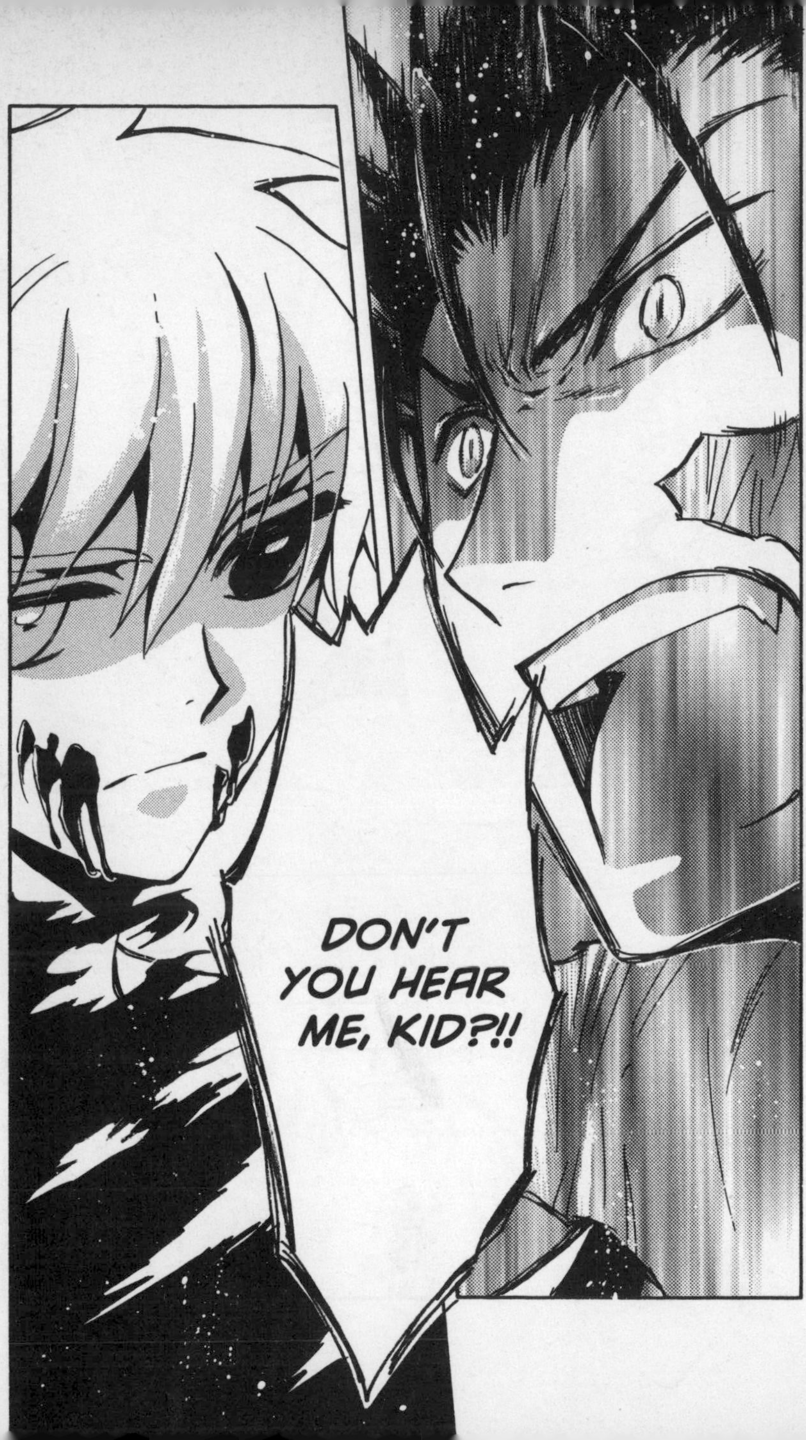
DON'T YOU HEAR ME, KID?!!

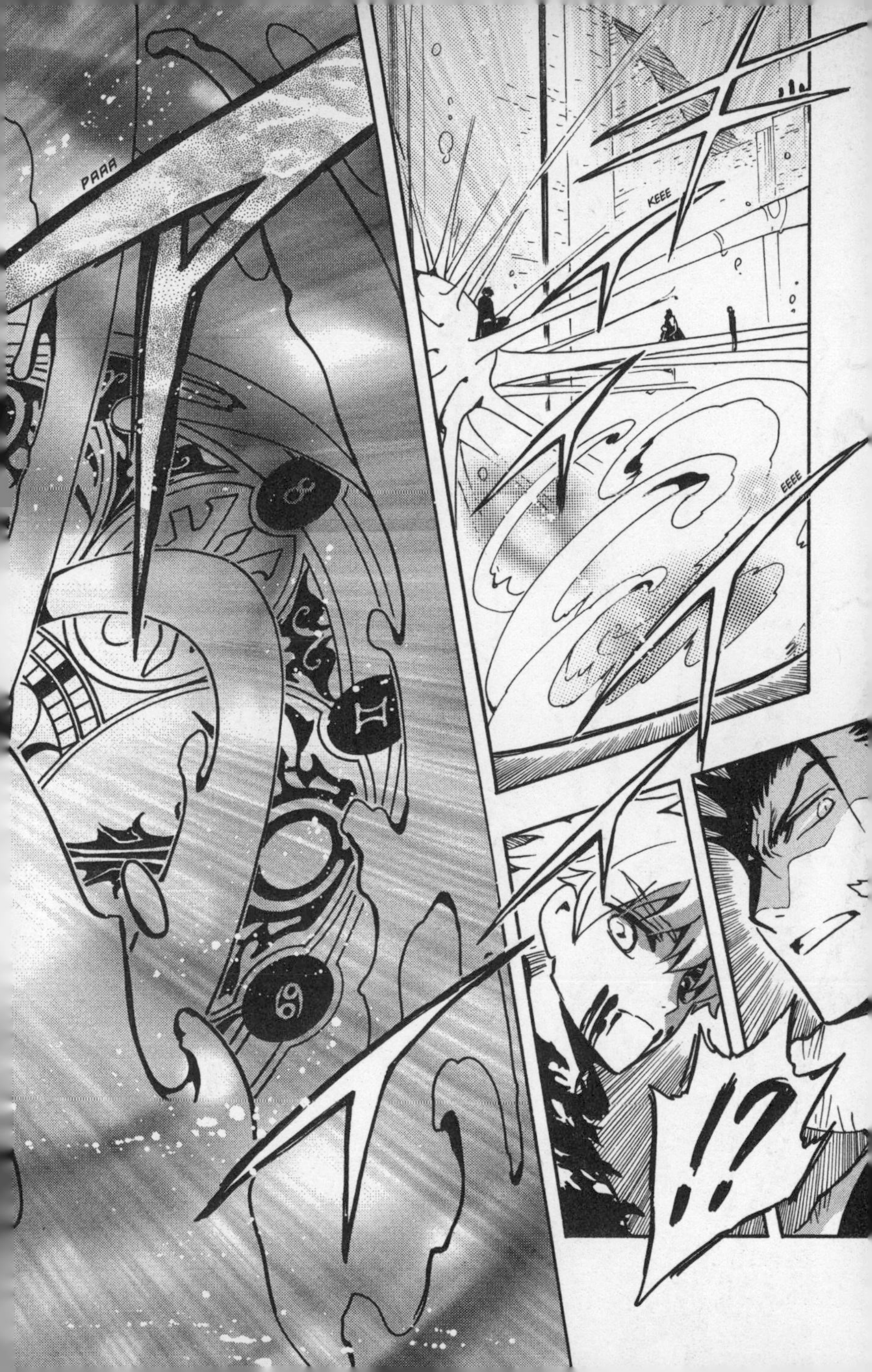
KEEE
EEEE
!?
PAAA

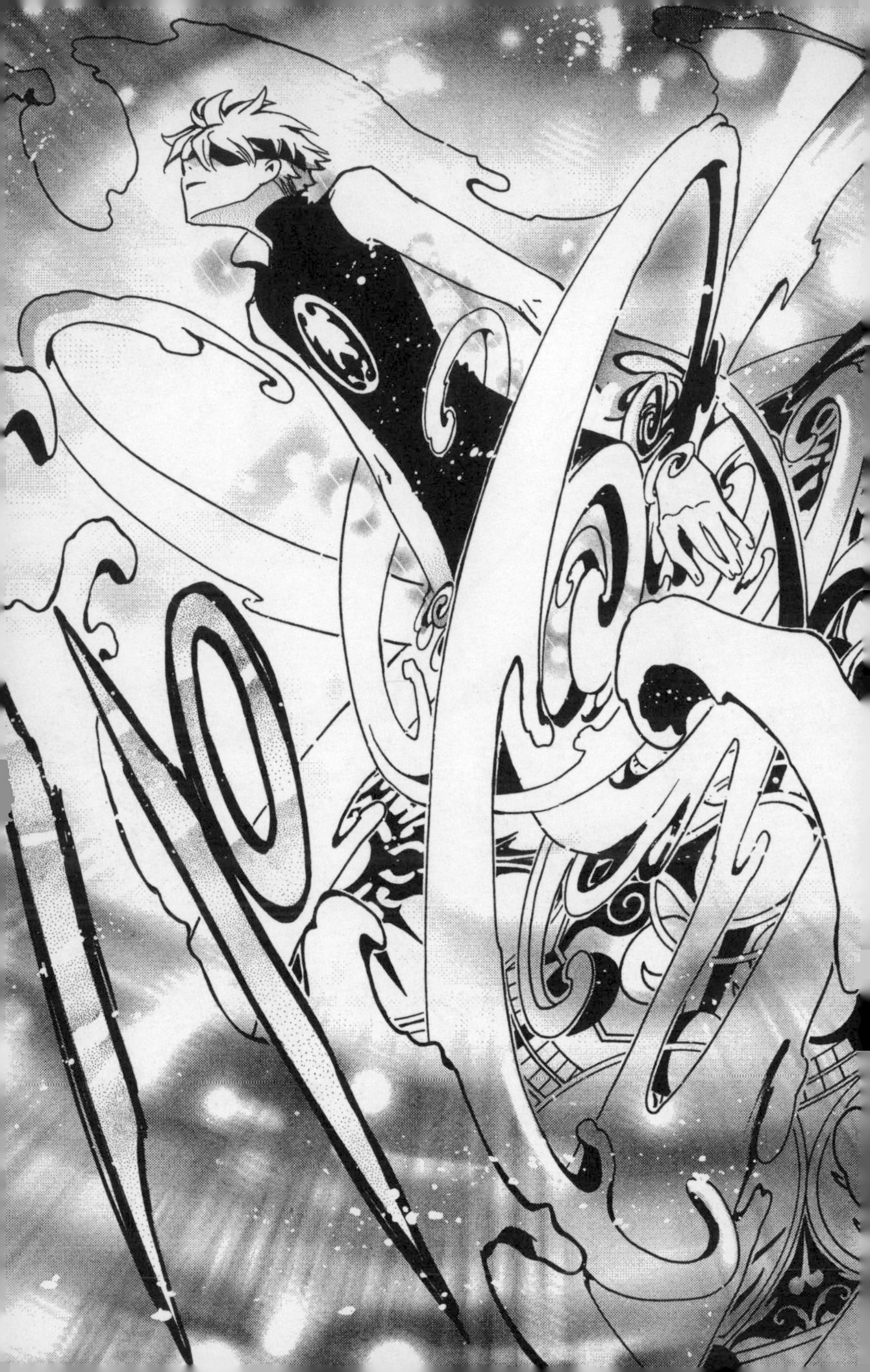

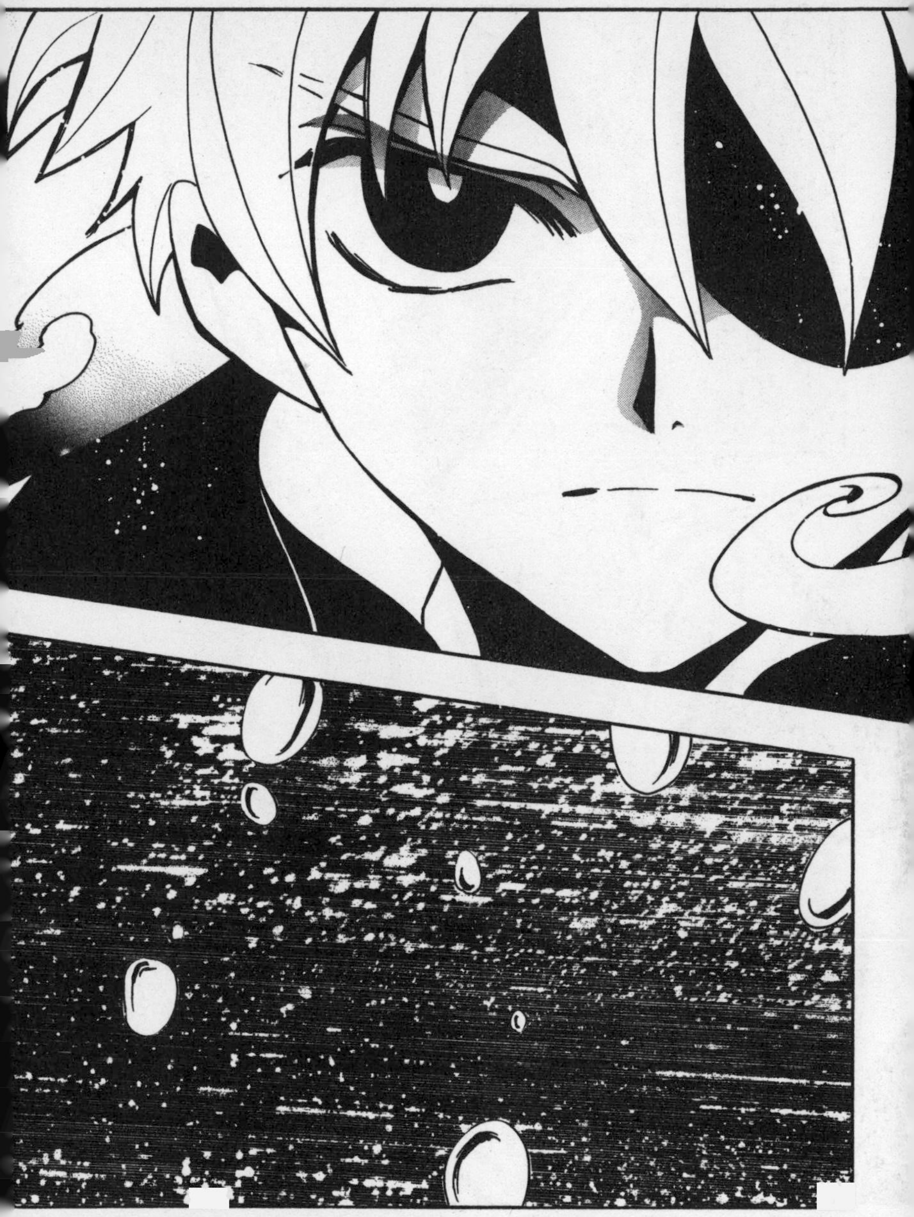

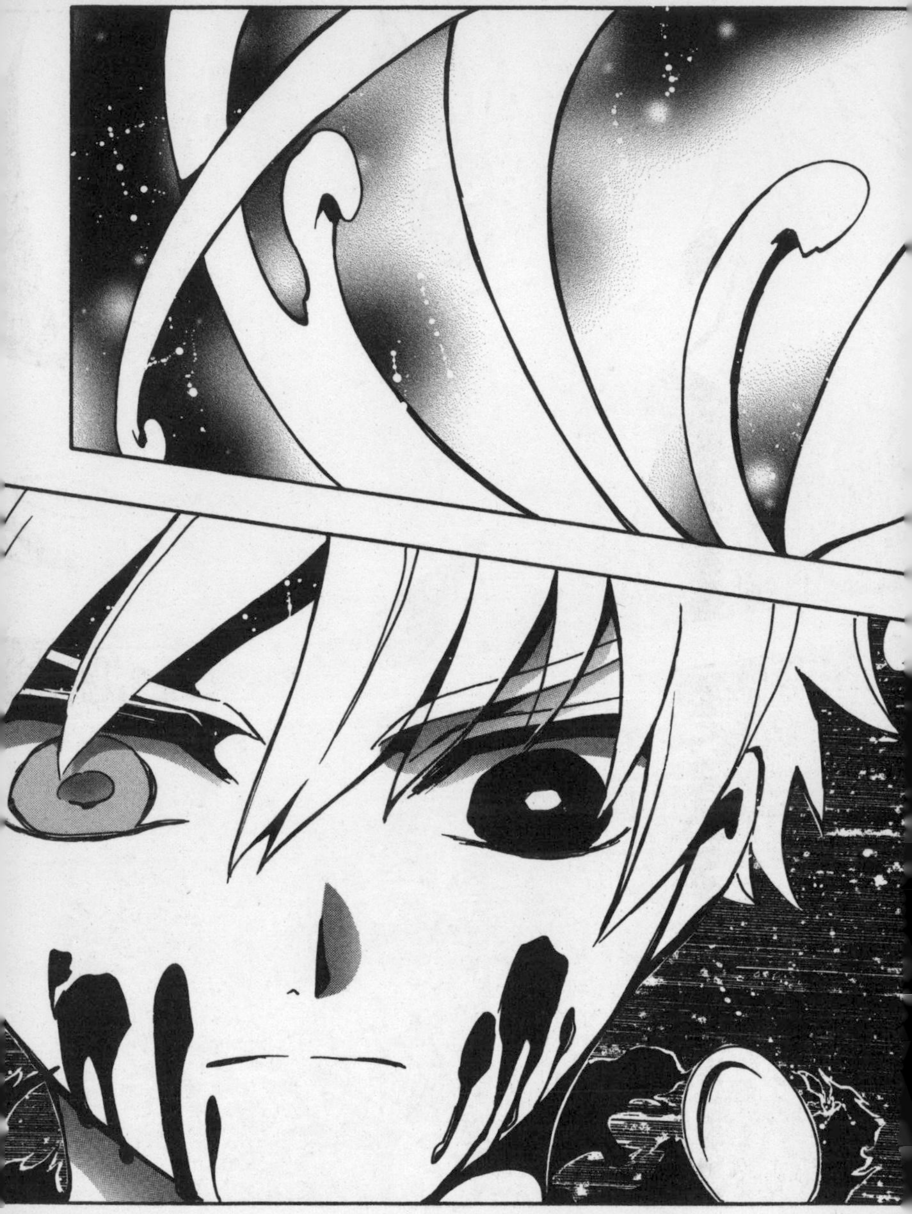

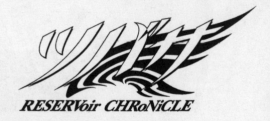
RESERVoir CHRoNiCLE

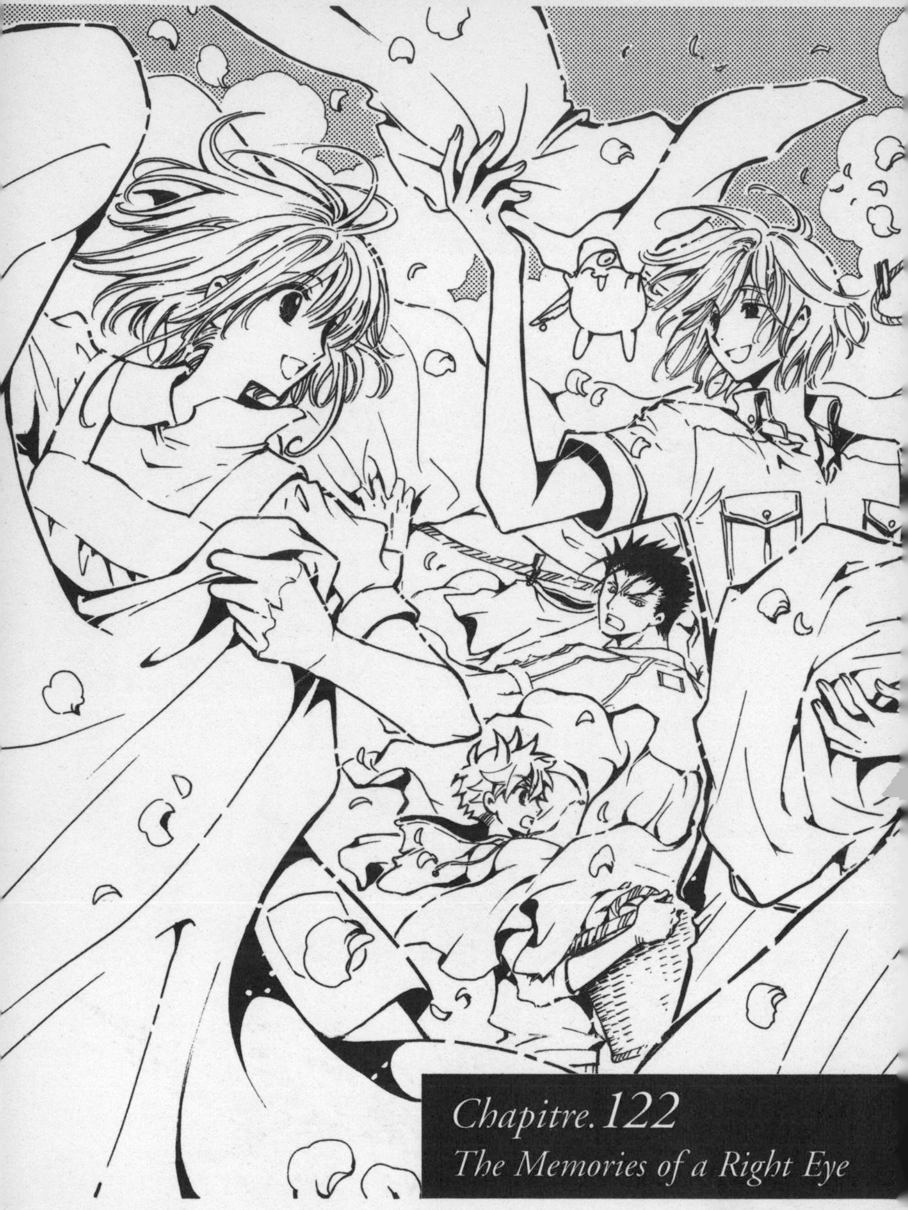
Chapitre. 122
The Memories of a Right Eye

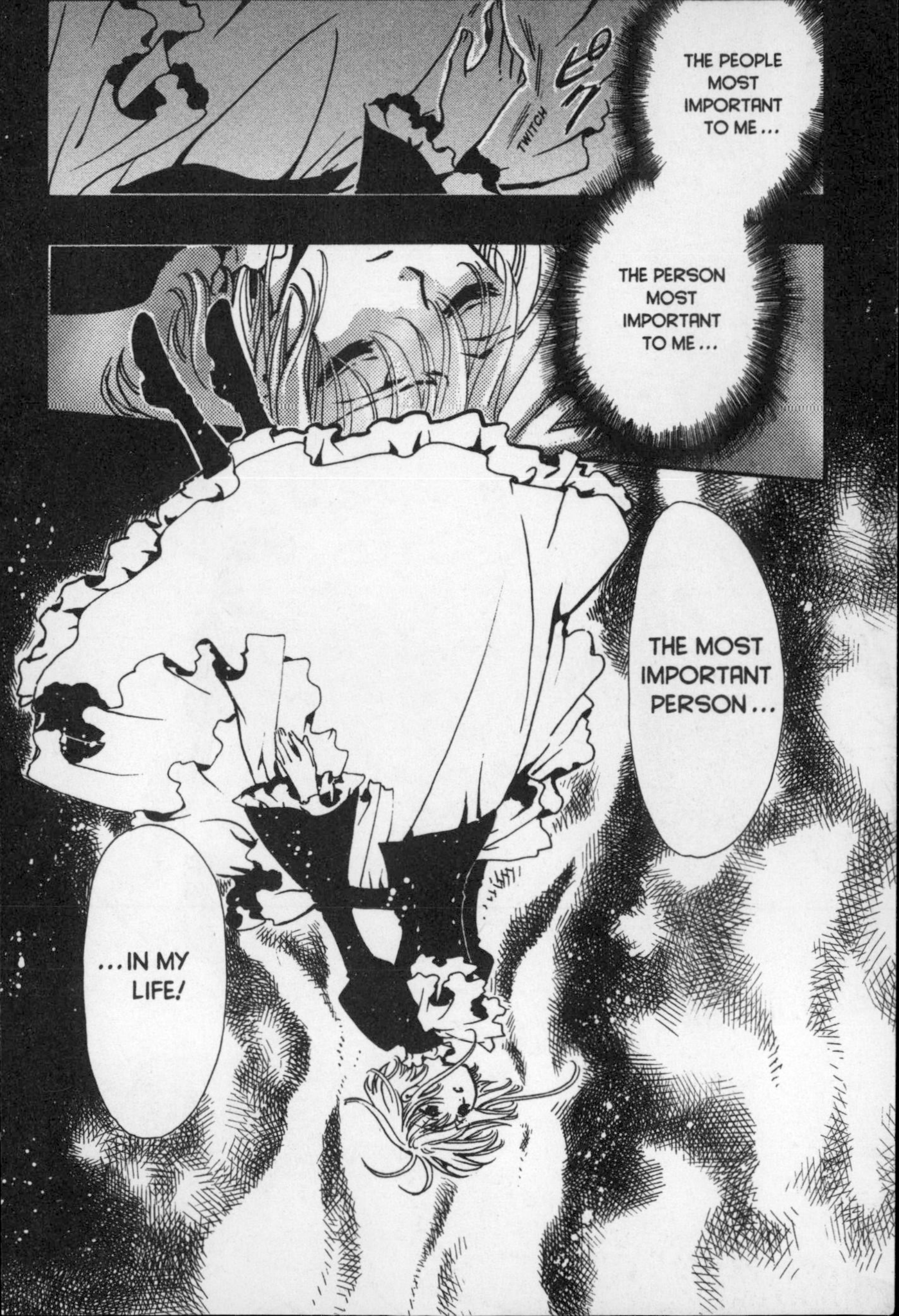
THE PEOPLE MOST IMPORTANT TO ME...
TWITCH
THE PERSON MOST IMPORTANT TO ME...
THE MOST IMPORTANT PERSON...
...IN MY LIFE!

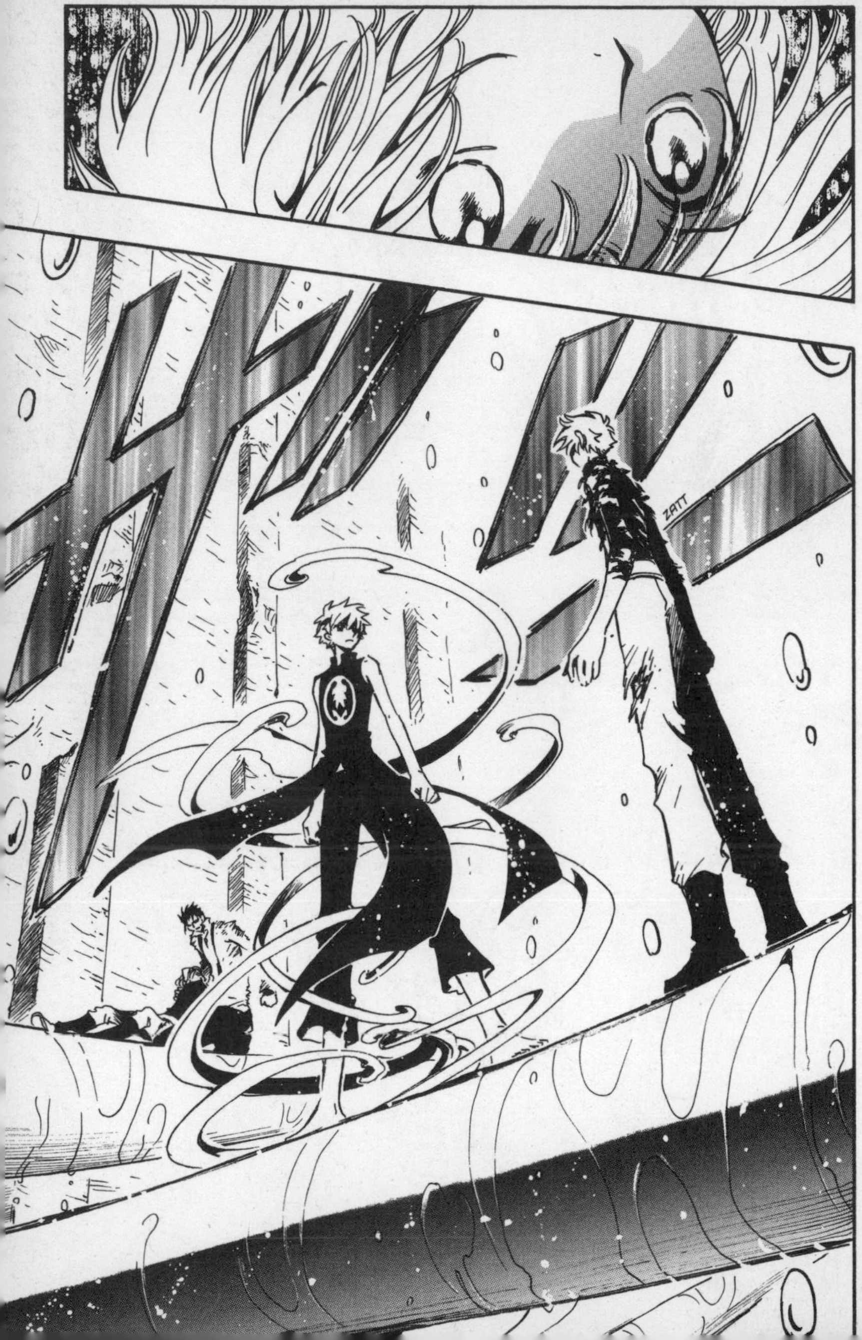
ZATT

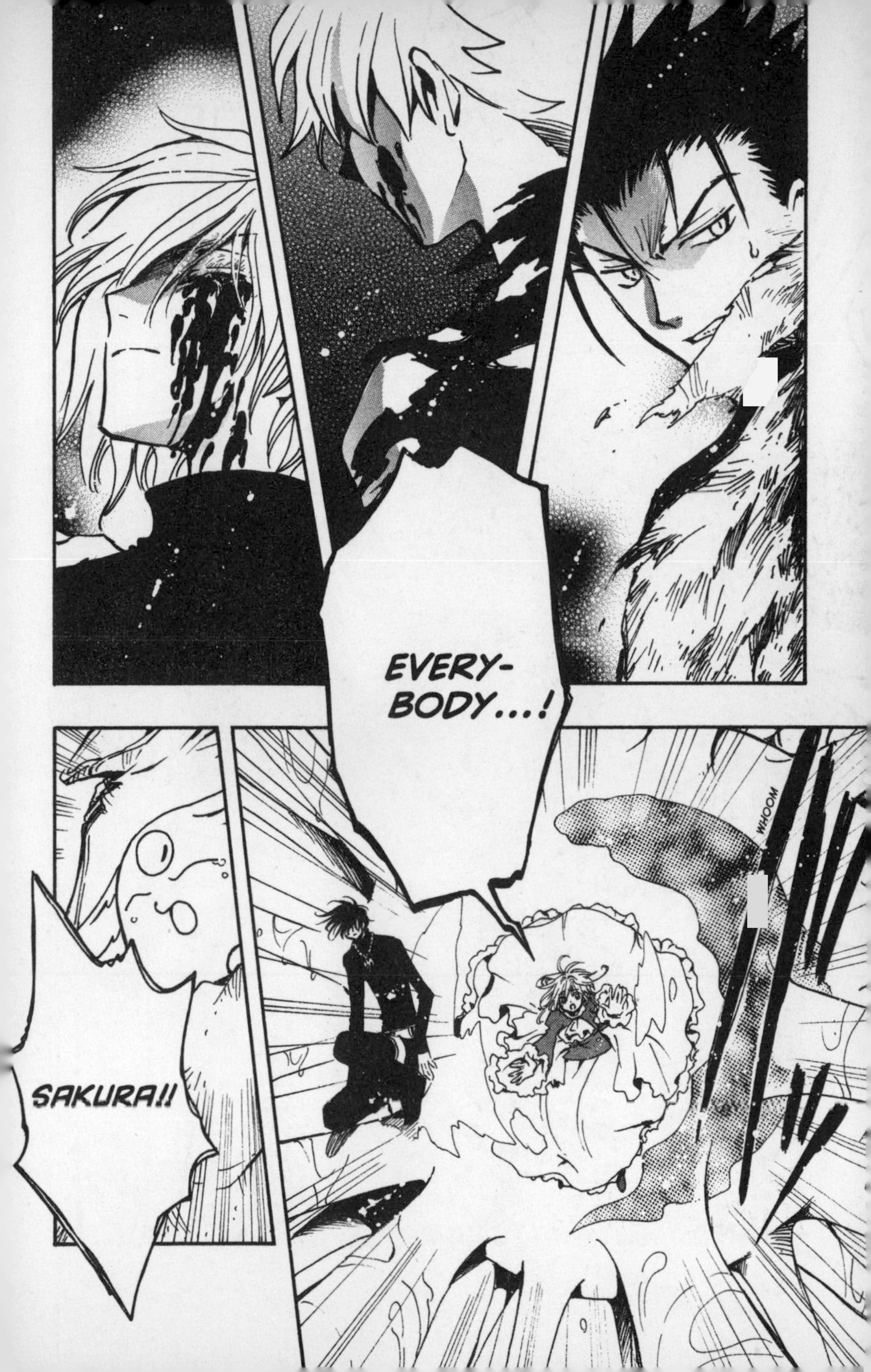
EVERY-
BODY...!
WHOOM
SAKURA!!

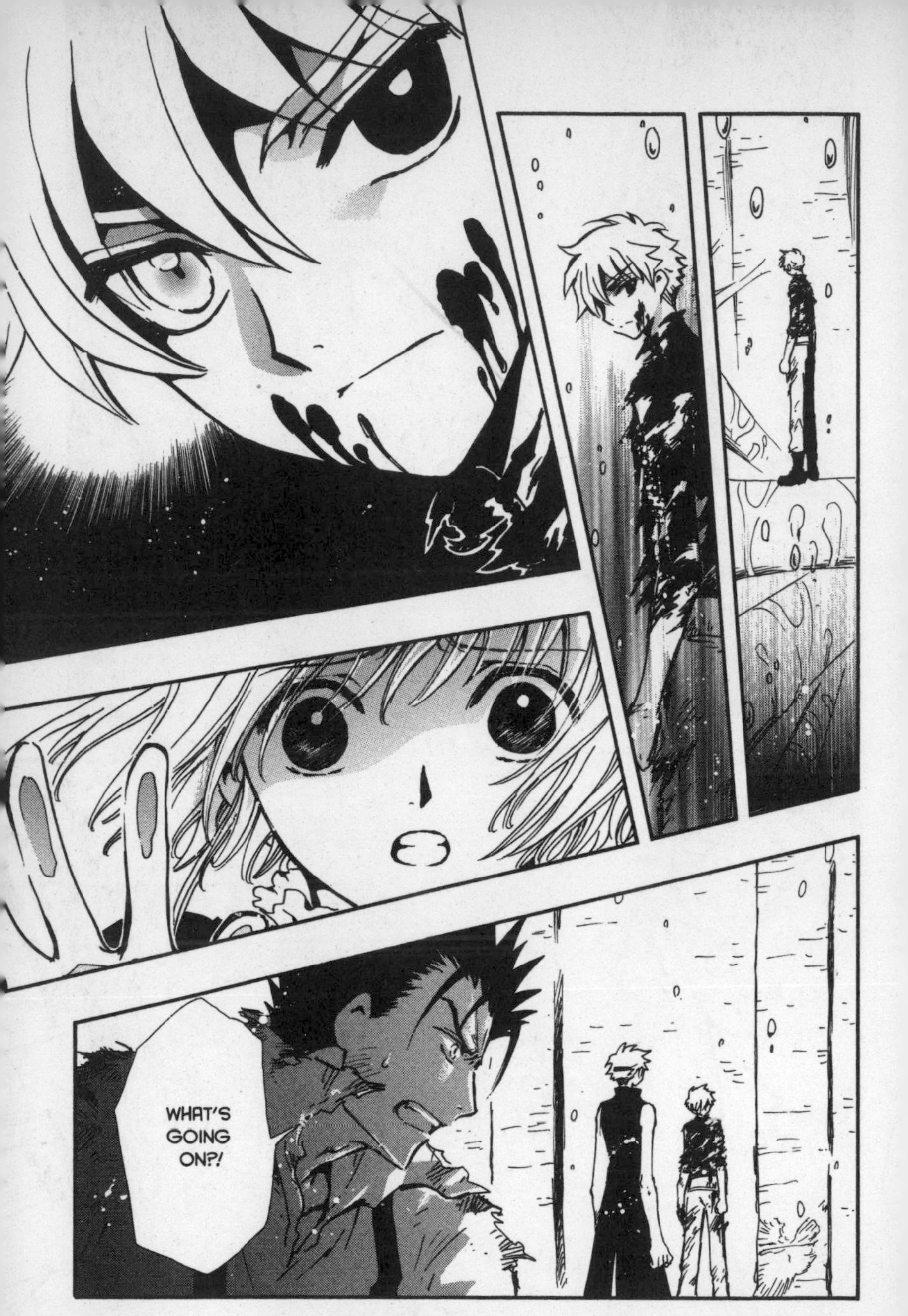
WHAT'S GOING ON?!

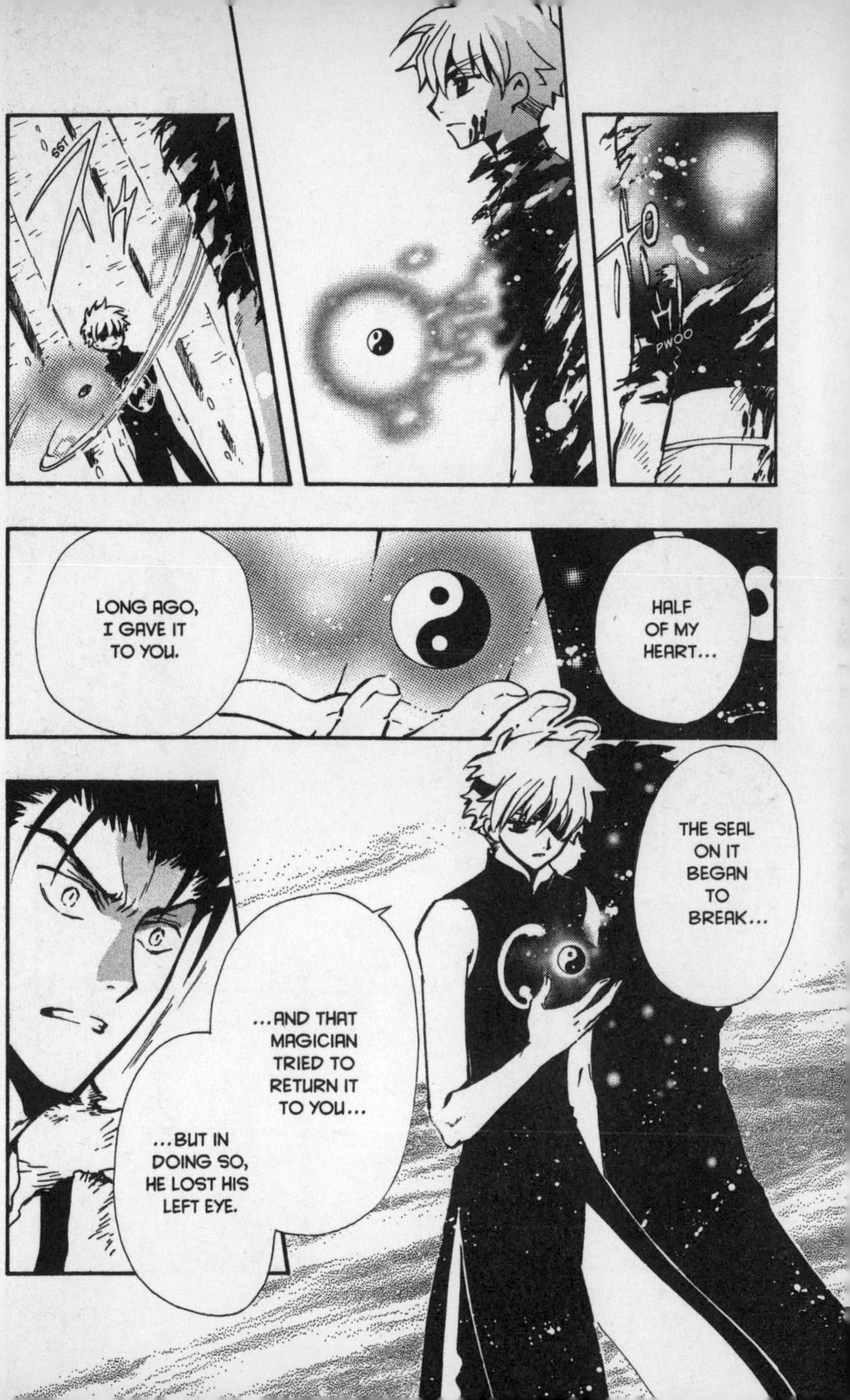
PWOO
SST
HALF OF MY HEART...
LONG AGO, I GAVE IT TO YOU.
THE SEAL ON IT BEGAN TO BREAK...
...AND THAT MAGICIAN TRIED TO RETURN IT TO YOU...
...BUT IN DOING SO, HE LOST HIS LEFT EYE.

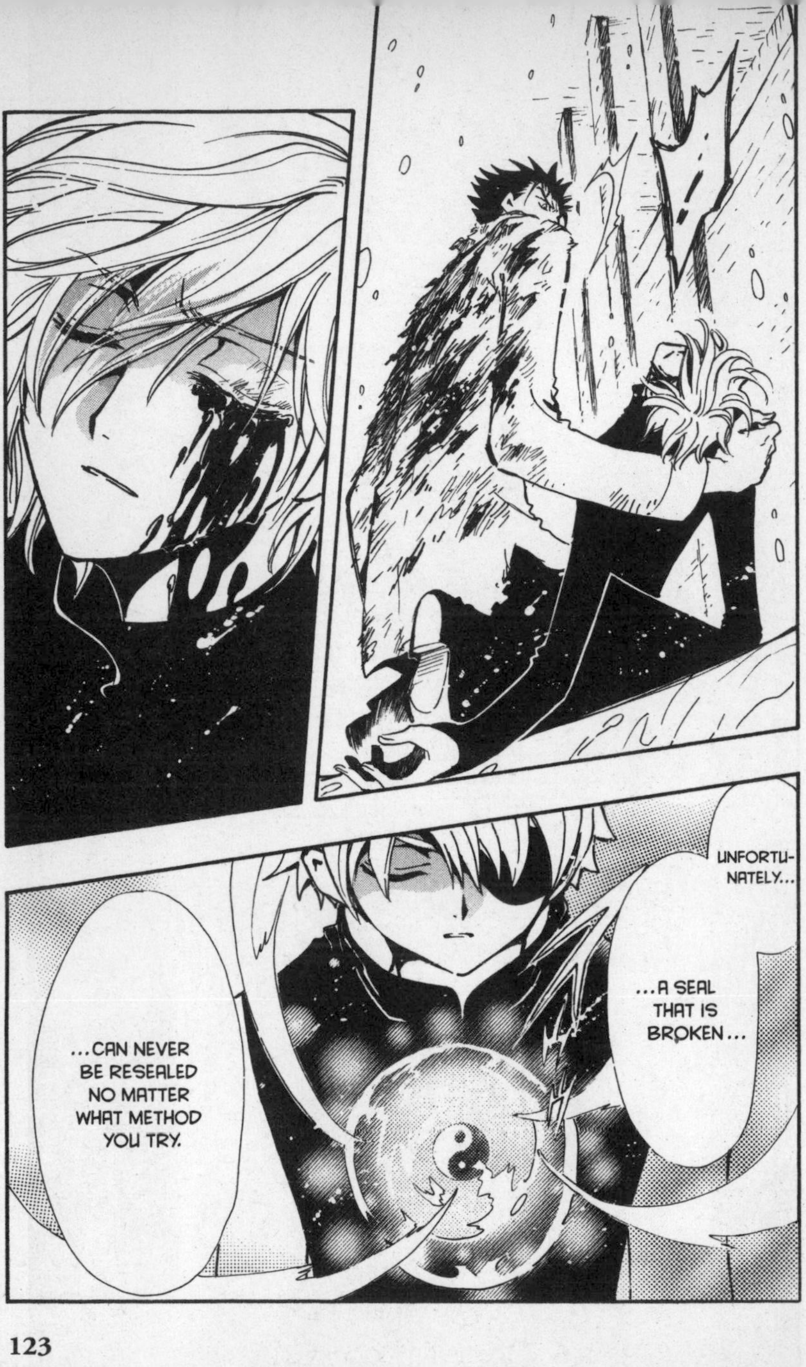
UNFORTU-NATELY...
...A SEAL THAT IS BROKEN...
...CAN NEVER BE RESEALED NO MATTER WHAT METHOD YOU TRY.

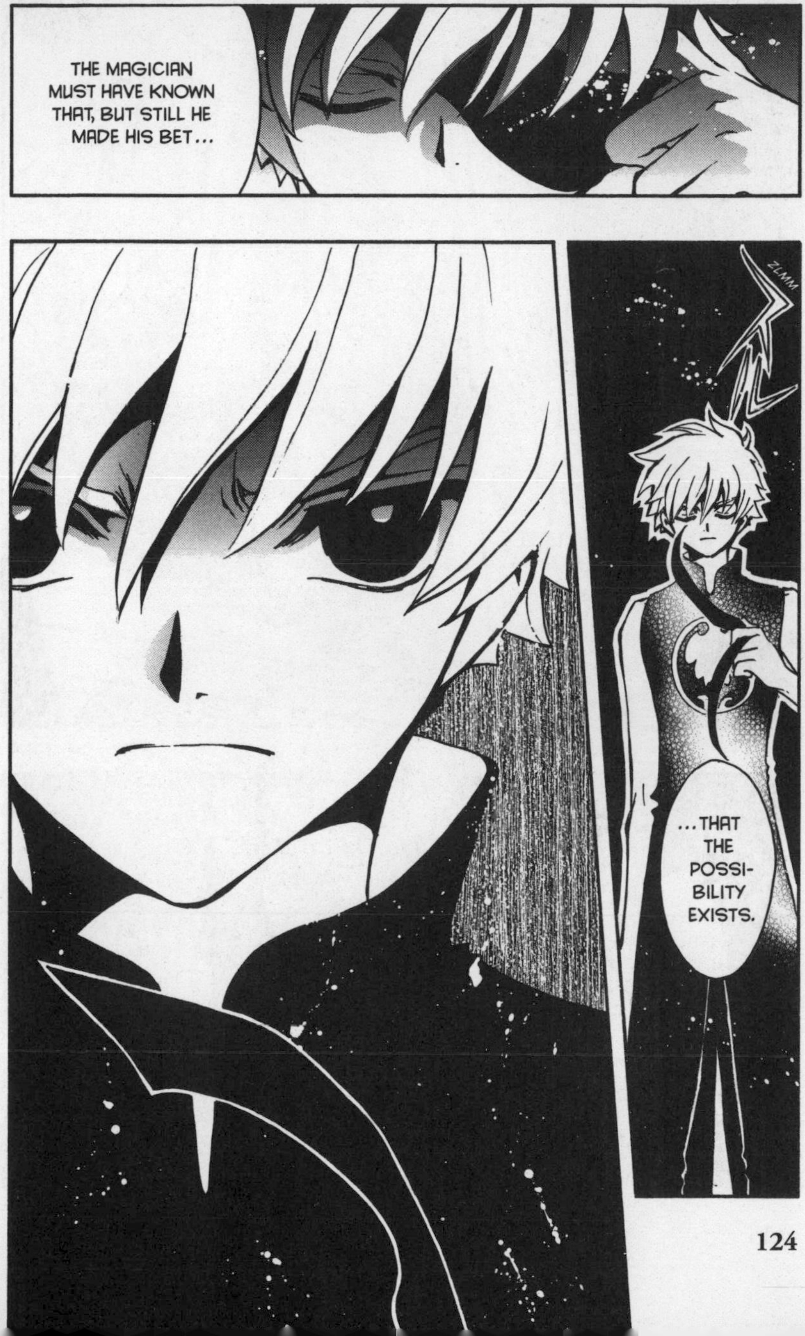
THE MAGICIAN MUST HAVE KNOWN THAT, BUT STILL HE MADE HIS BET…
ZLMM
…THAT THE POSSI-BILITY EXISTS.

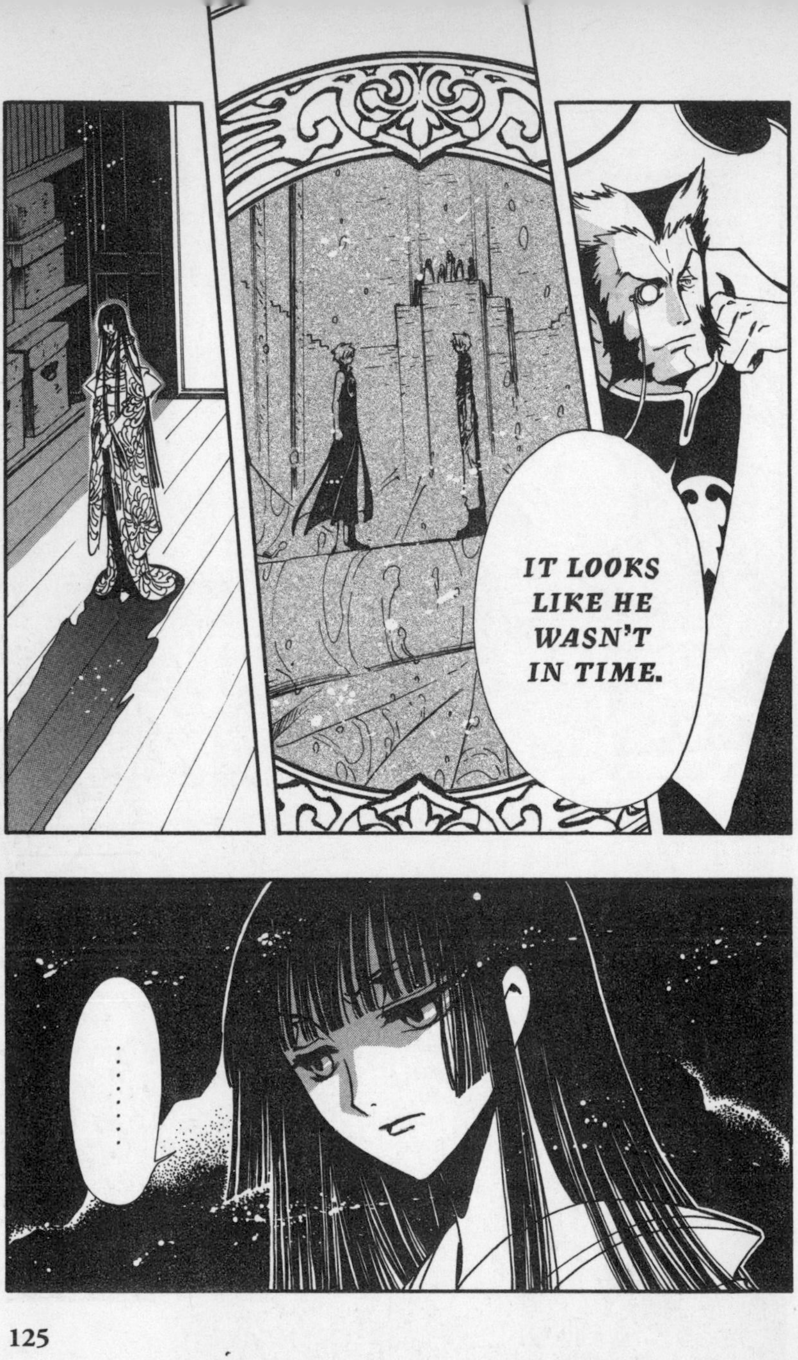
IT LOOKS LIKE HE WASN'T IN TIME.
......

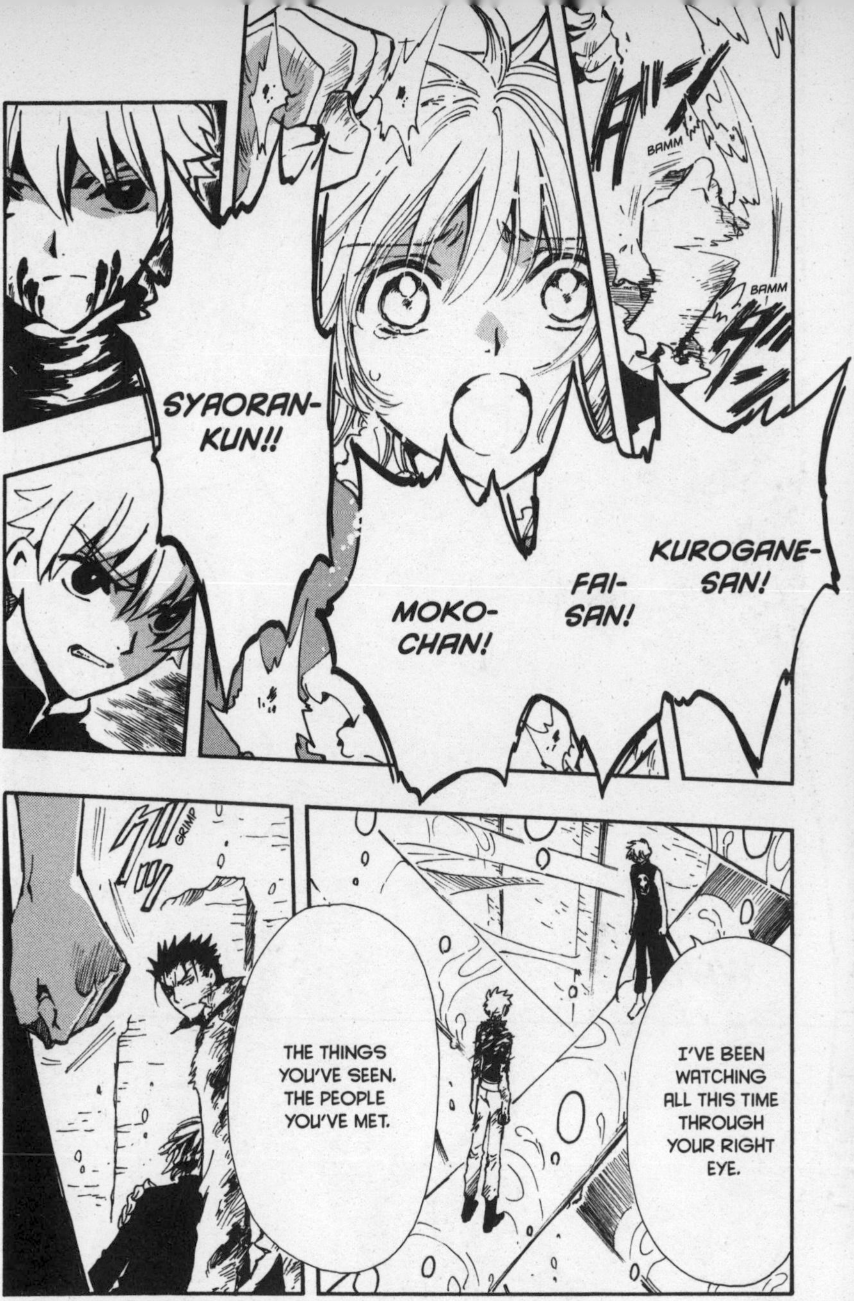
BAMM
BAMM
KUROGANE-SAN!
FAI-SAN!
MOKO-CHAN!
SYAORAN-KUN!!
I'VE BEEN WATCHING ALL THIS TIME THROUGH YOUR RIGHT EYE.
THE THINGS YOU'VE SEEN. THE PEOPLE YOU'VE MET.
GRIMP

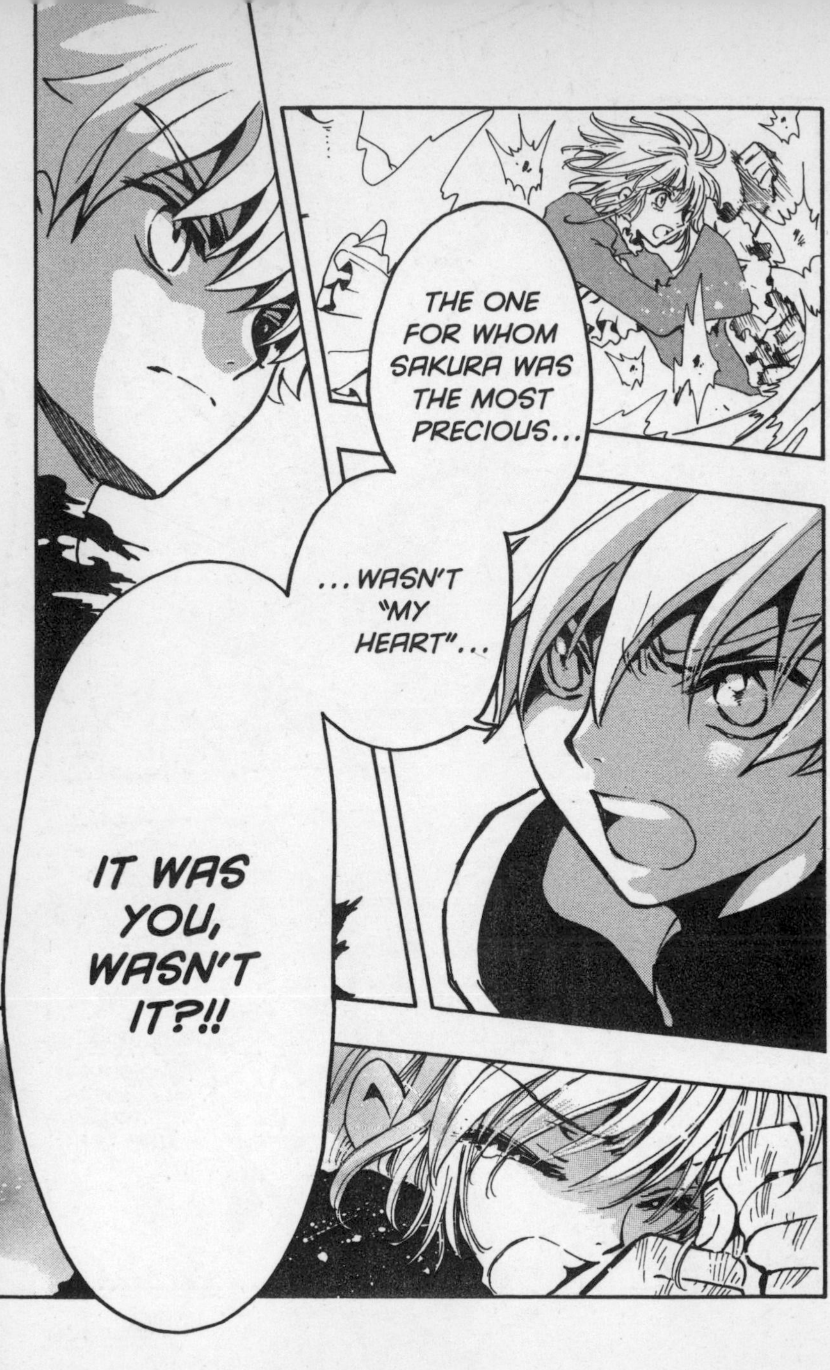
THE ONE FOR WHOM SAKURA WAS THE MOST PRECIOUS...
...WASN'T "MY HEART"...
IT WAS YOU, WASN'T IT?!!

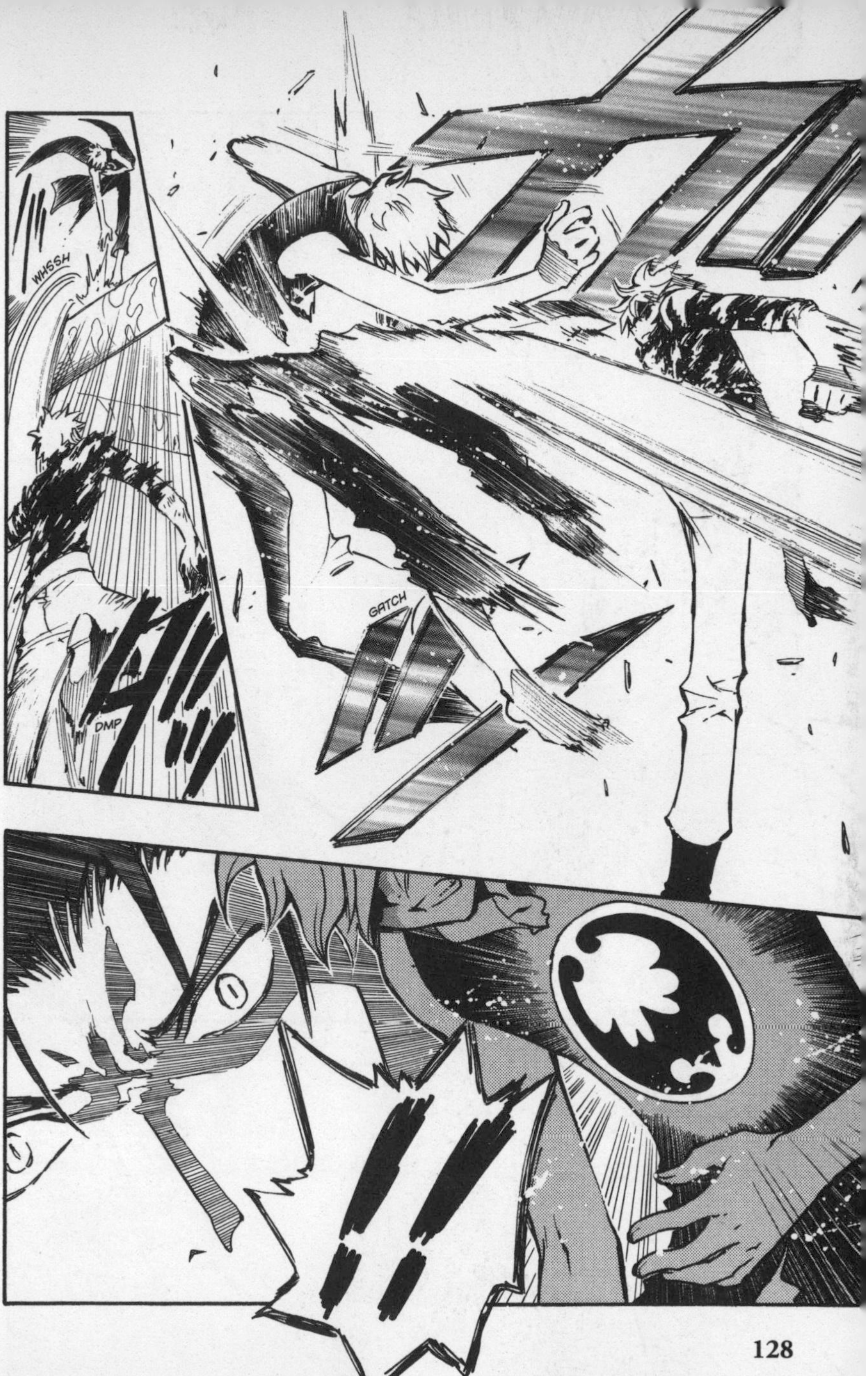
GATCH
WHSSH
DMP

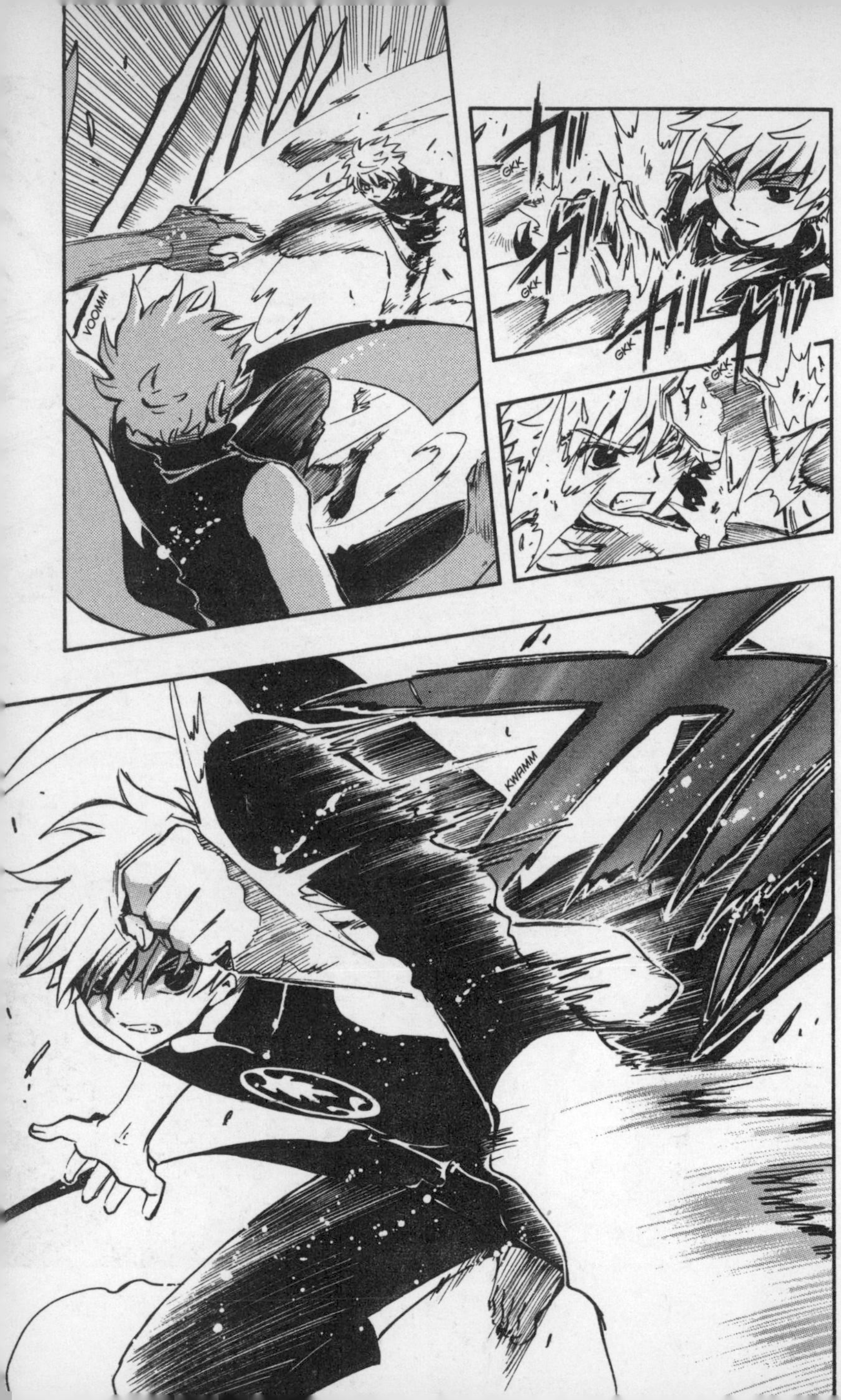
GKK
GKK
GKK
GKK
VOOMM
KWAMM

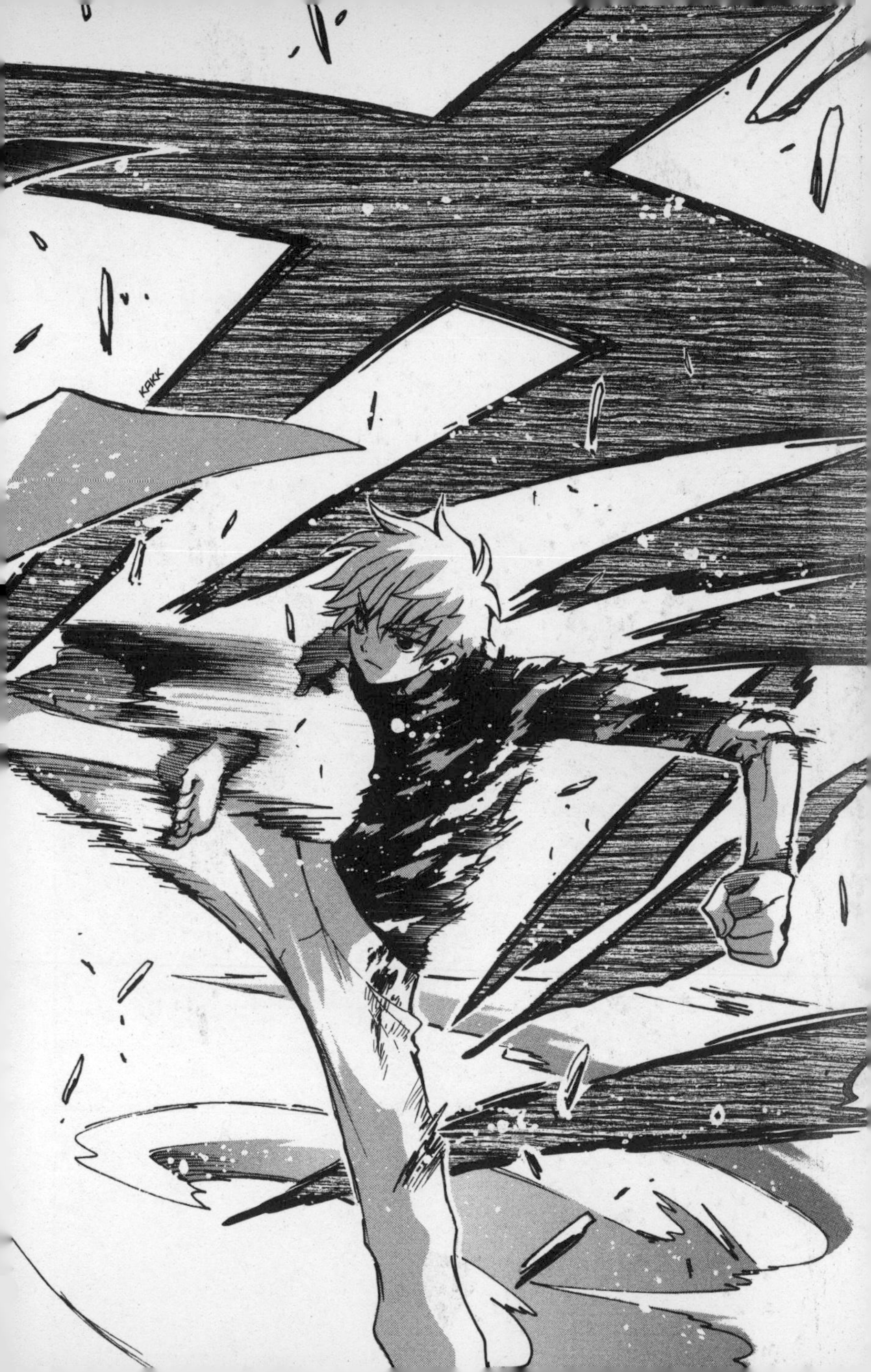
KAKK

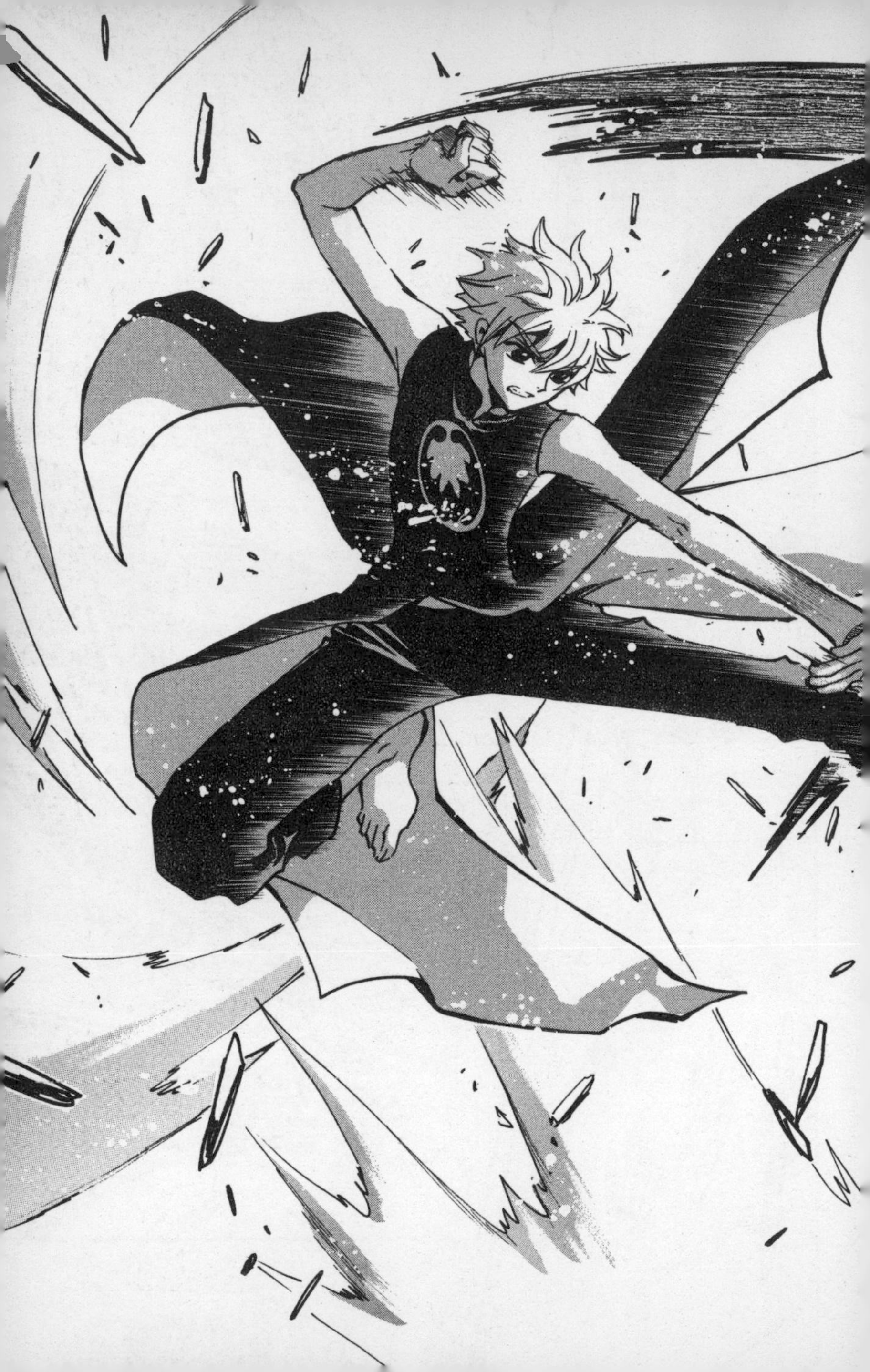

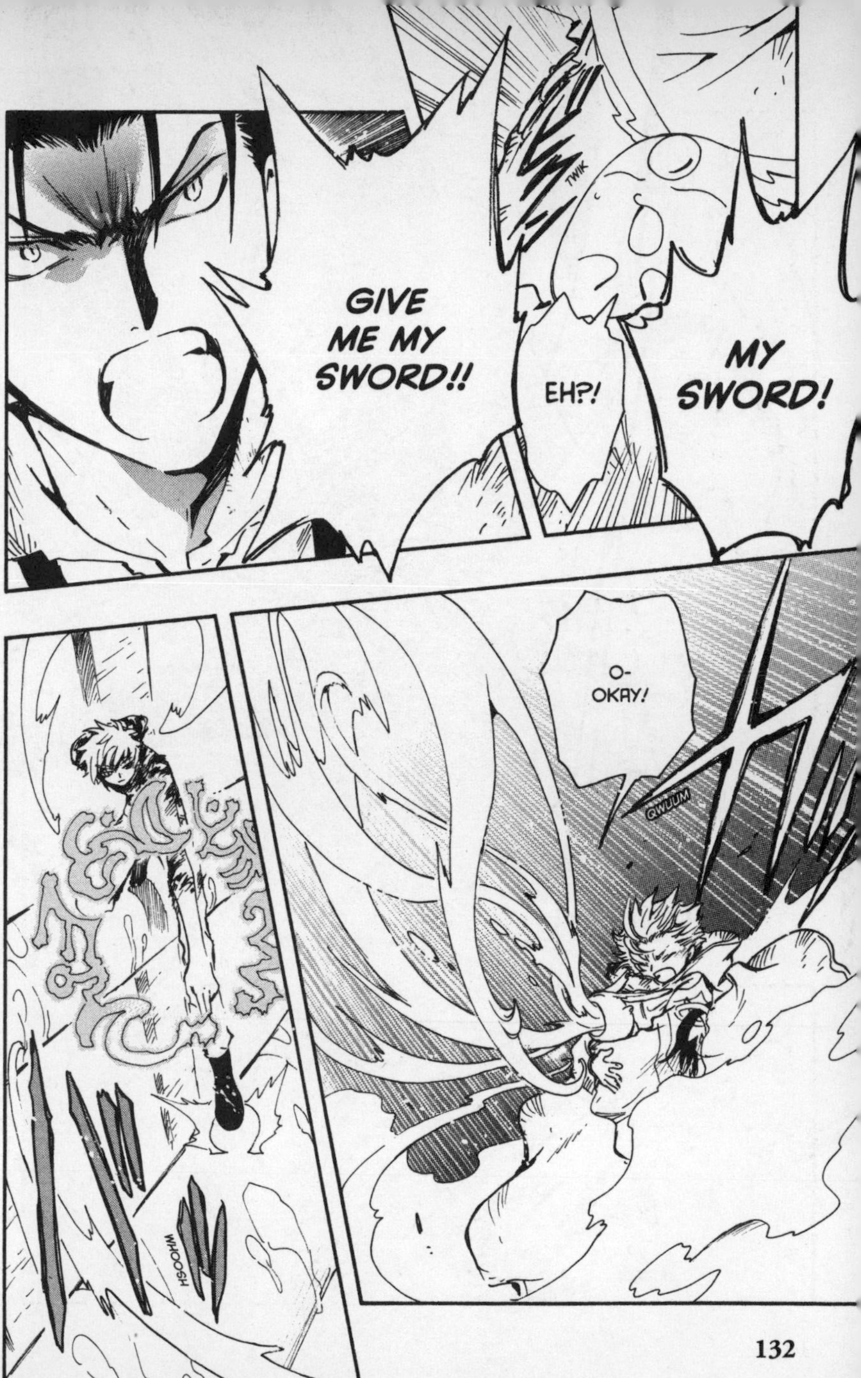
TWIK
MY SWORD!
EH?!
GIVE ME MY SWORD!!
O-OKAY!
QWUUM
WHOOSH

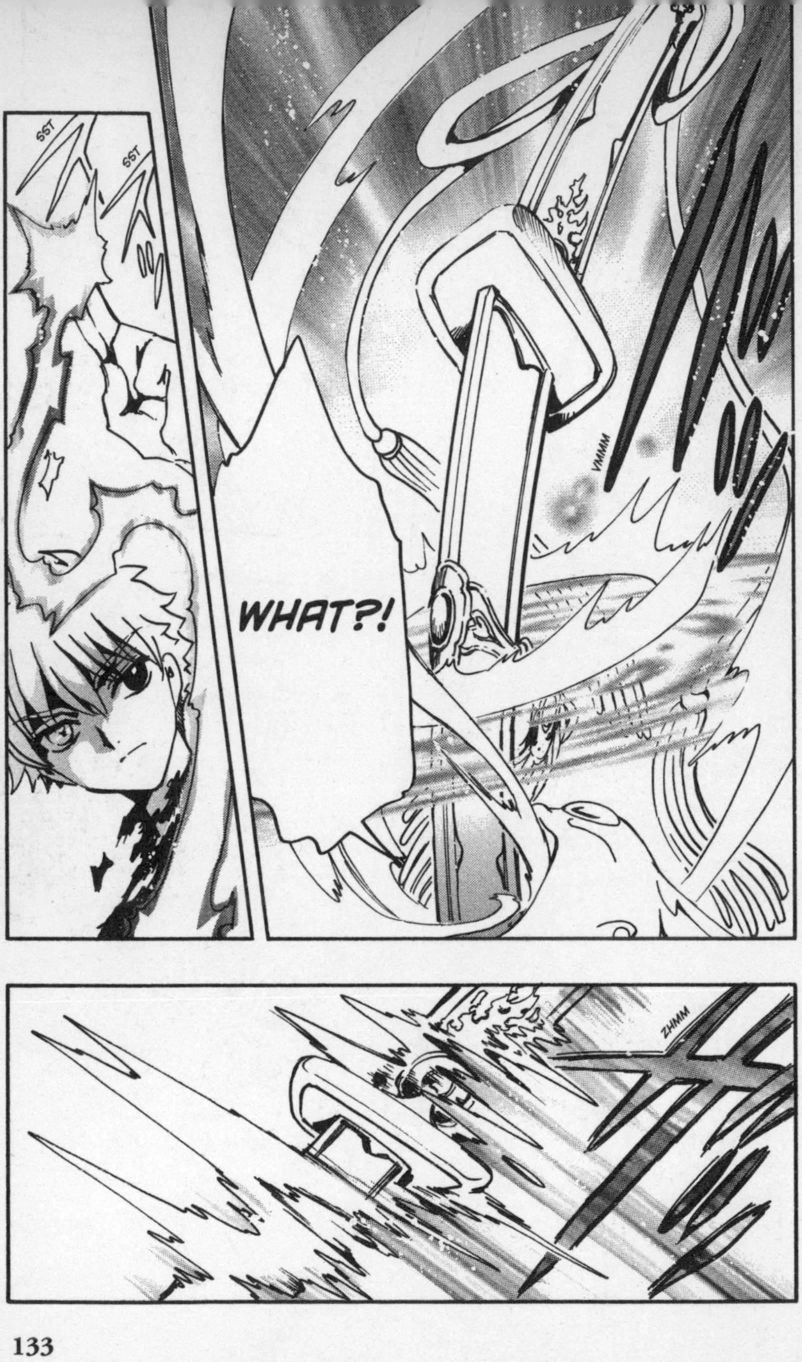
VMMM
WHAT?!
SST
SST
ZHMM

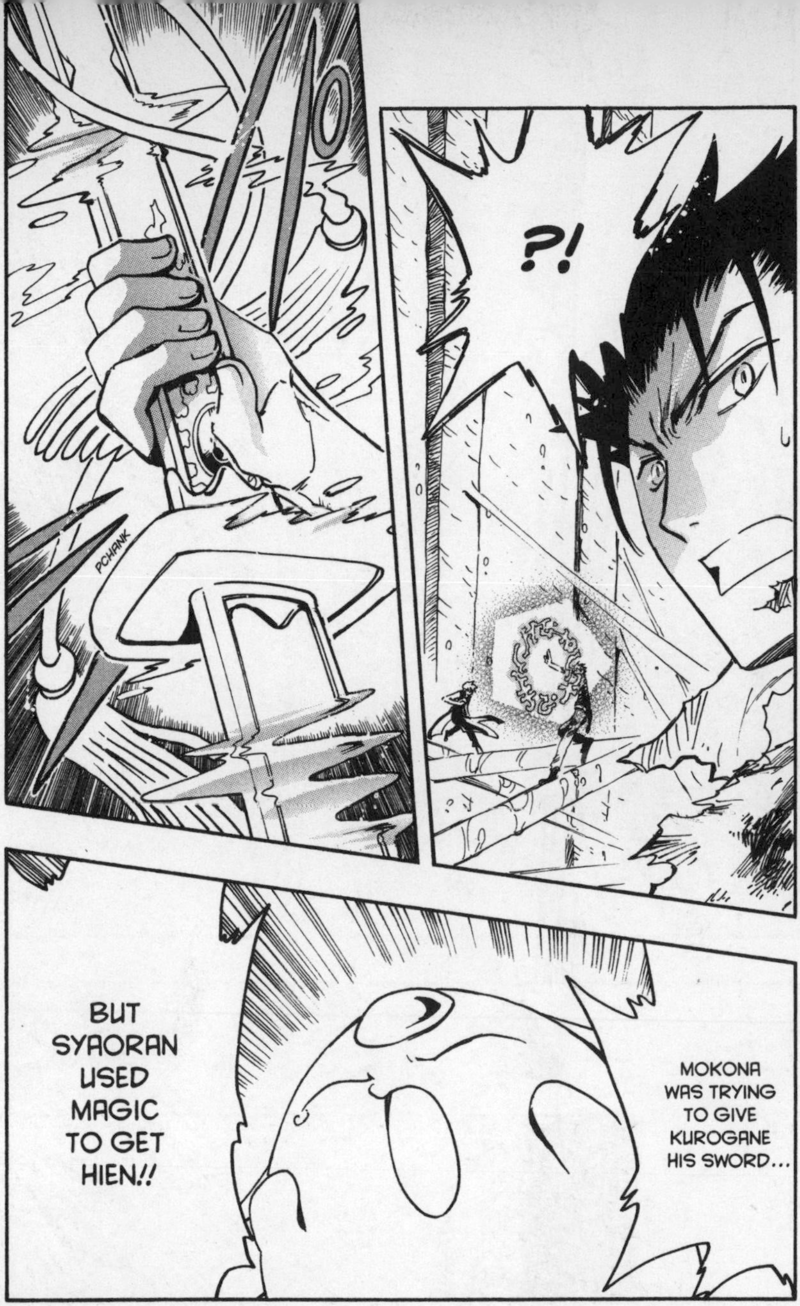
?!
PCHANK
MOKONA WAS TRYING TO GIVE KUROGANE HIS SWORD...
BUT SYAORAN USED MAGIC TO GET HIEN!!

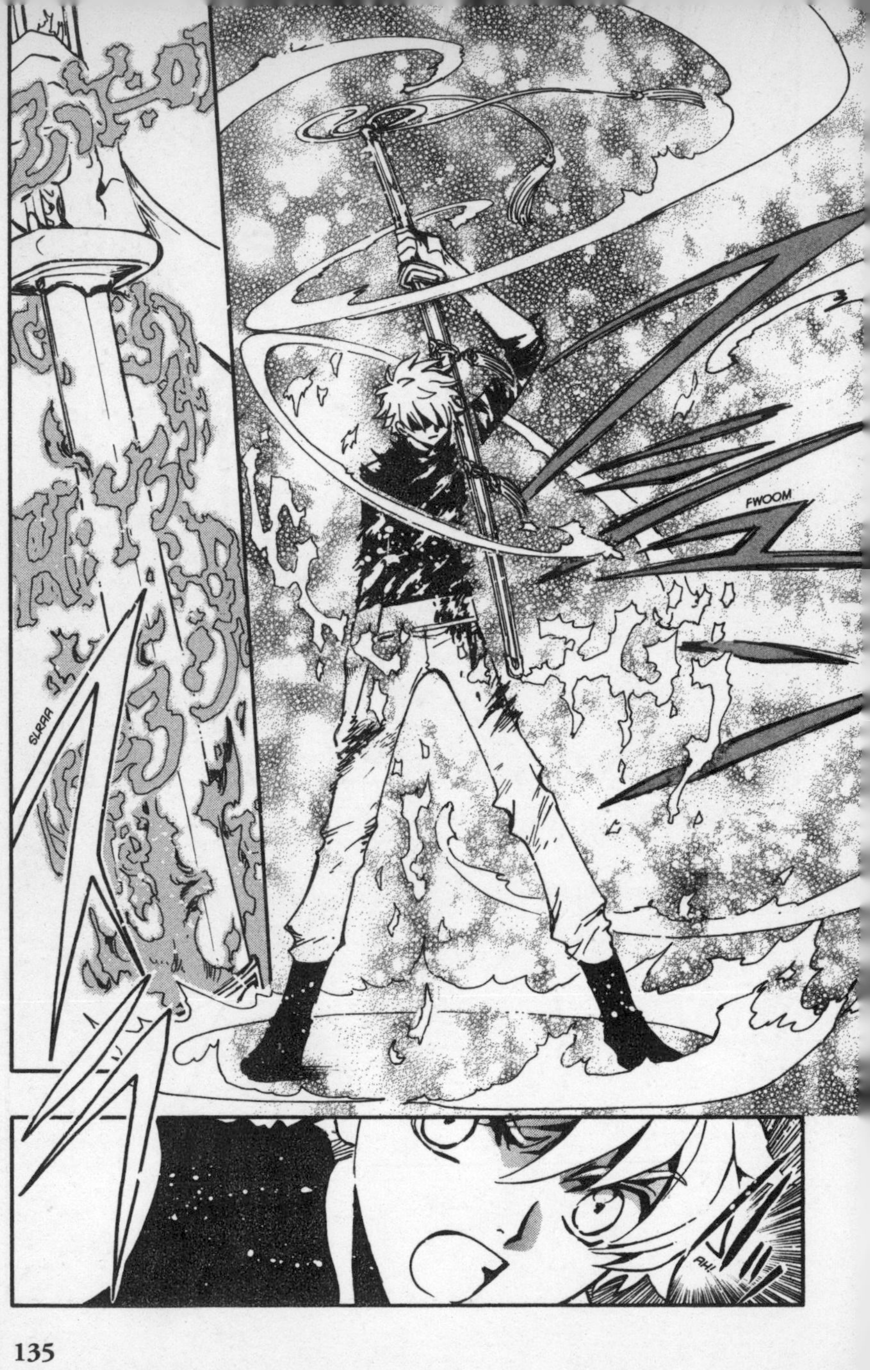
FWOOM
SLRAA
AH!

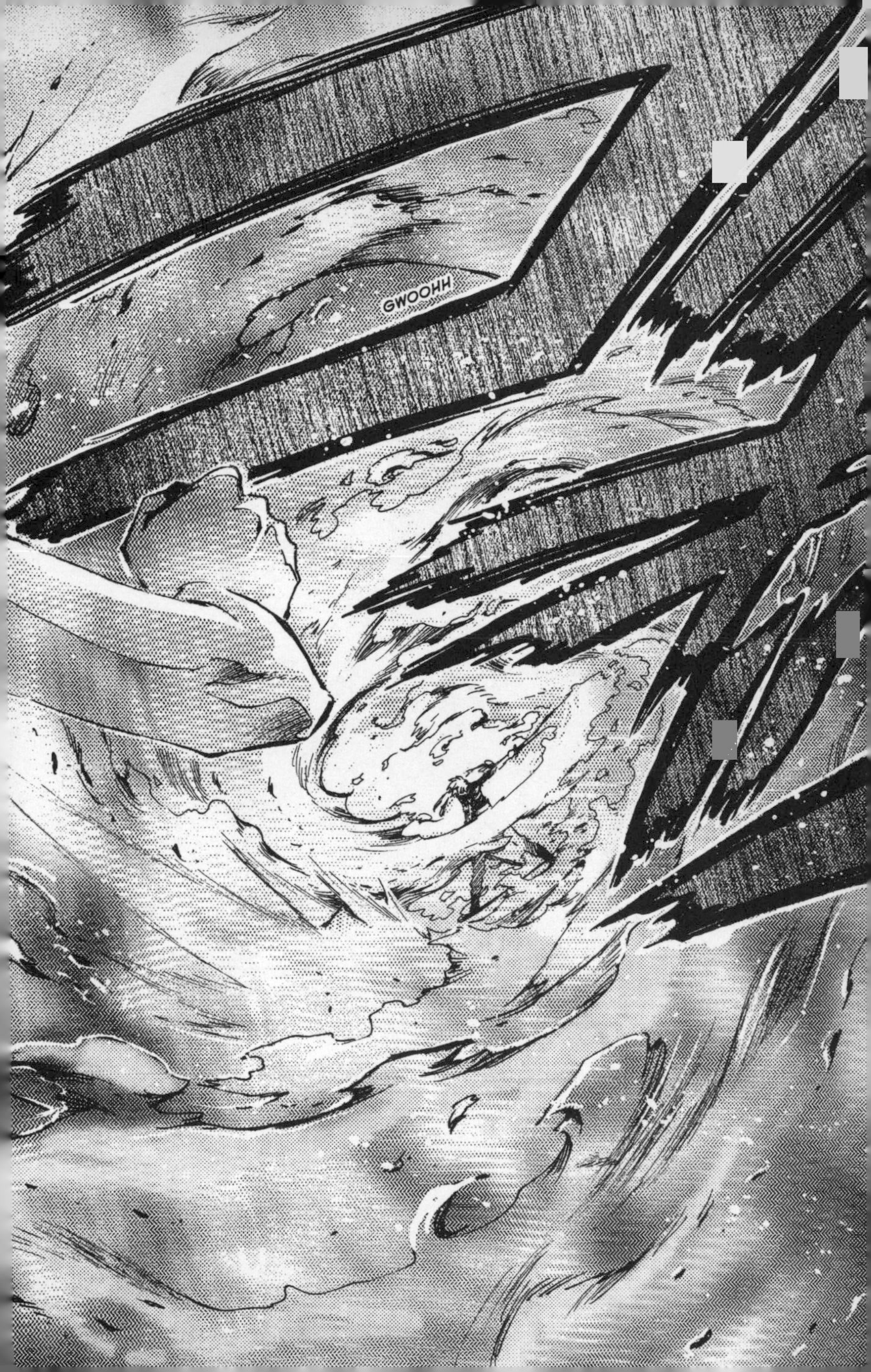
GWOOHH

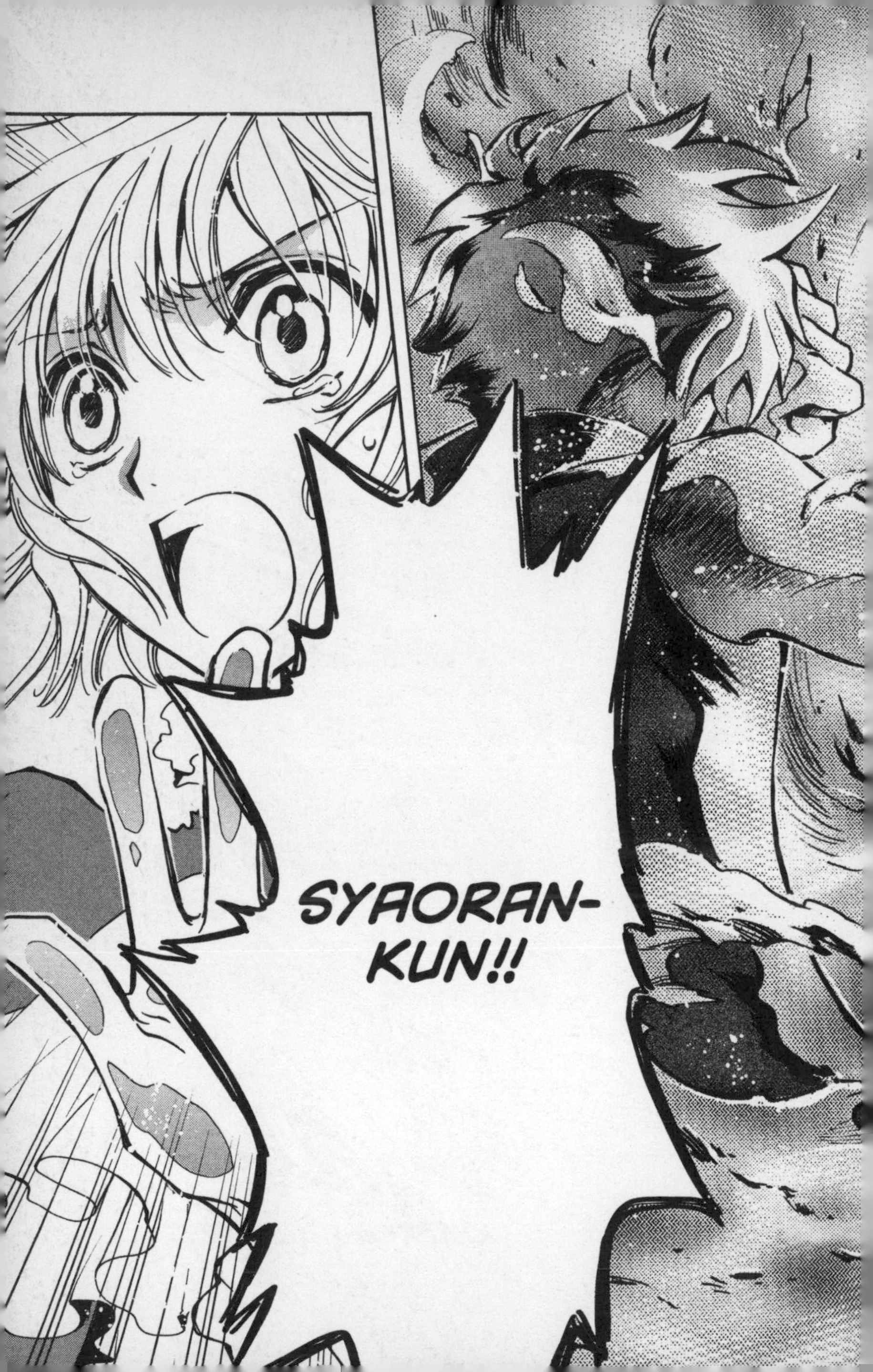
SYAORAN-KUN!!

ツバサ

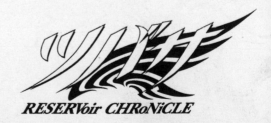

RESERVoir CHRoNiCLE

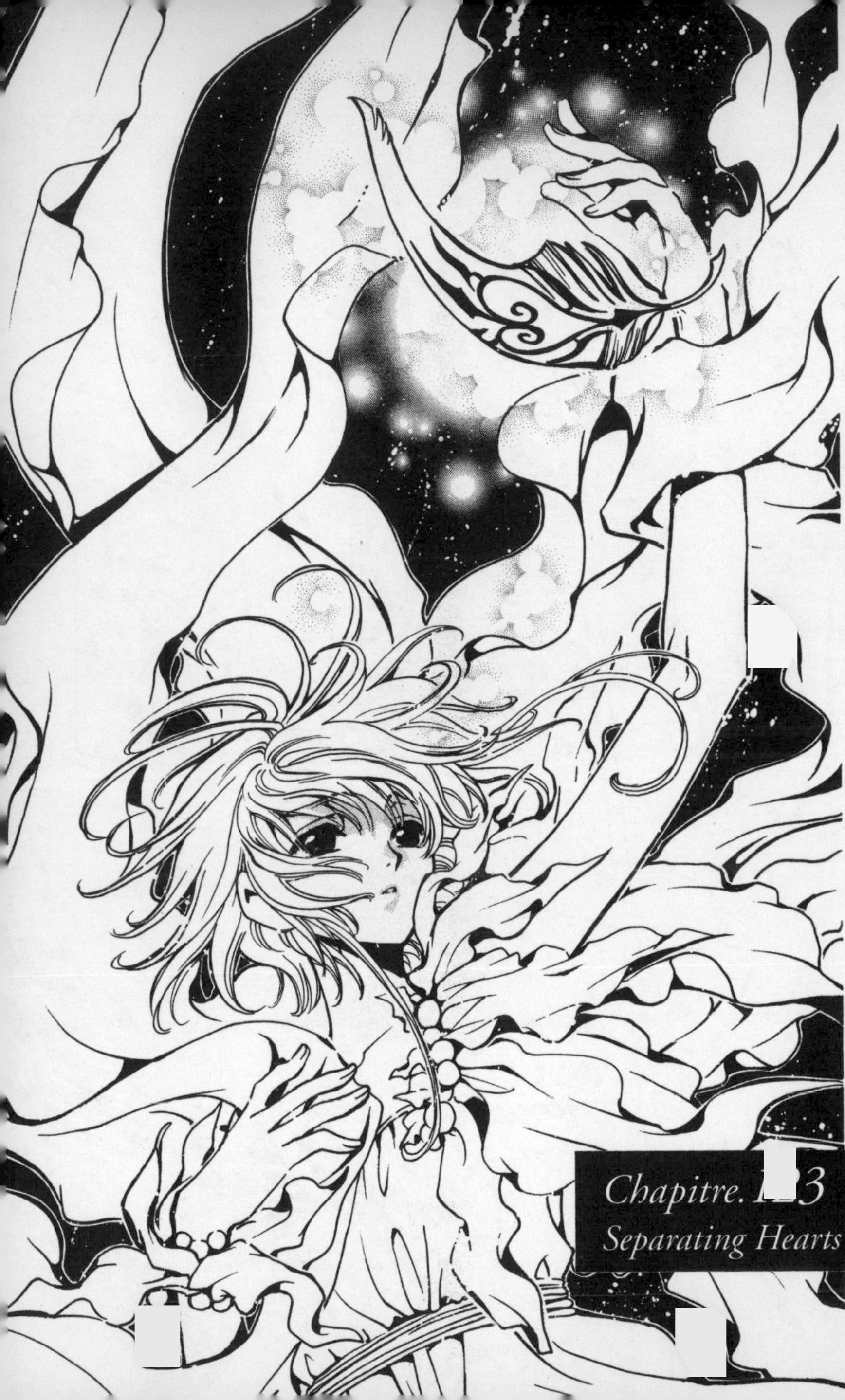

Chapitre. 1[illegible]3
Separating Hearts

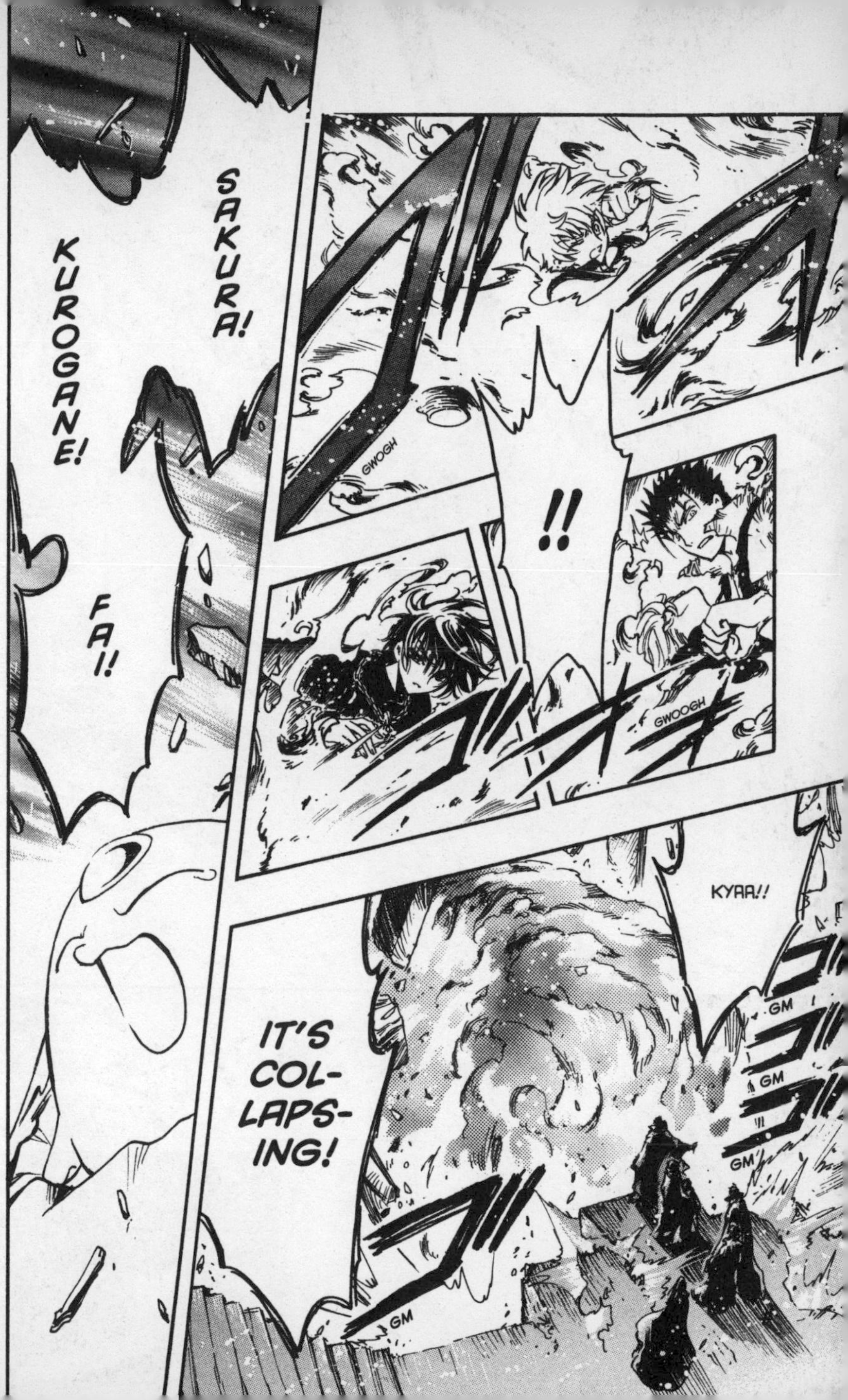
GWOGH
GWOOGH
!!
KYAA!!
GM
GM
GM'
IT'S COL-LAPS-ING!
GM
SAKURA!
KUROGANE!
FAI!

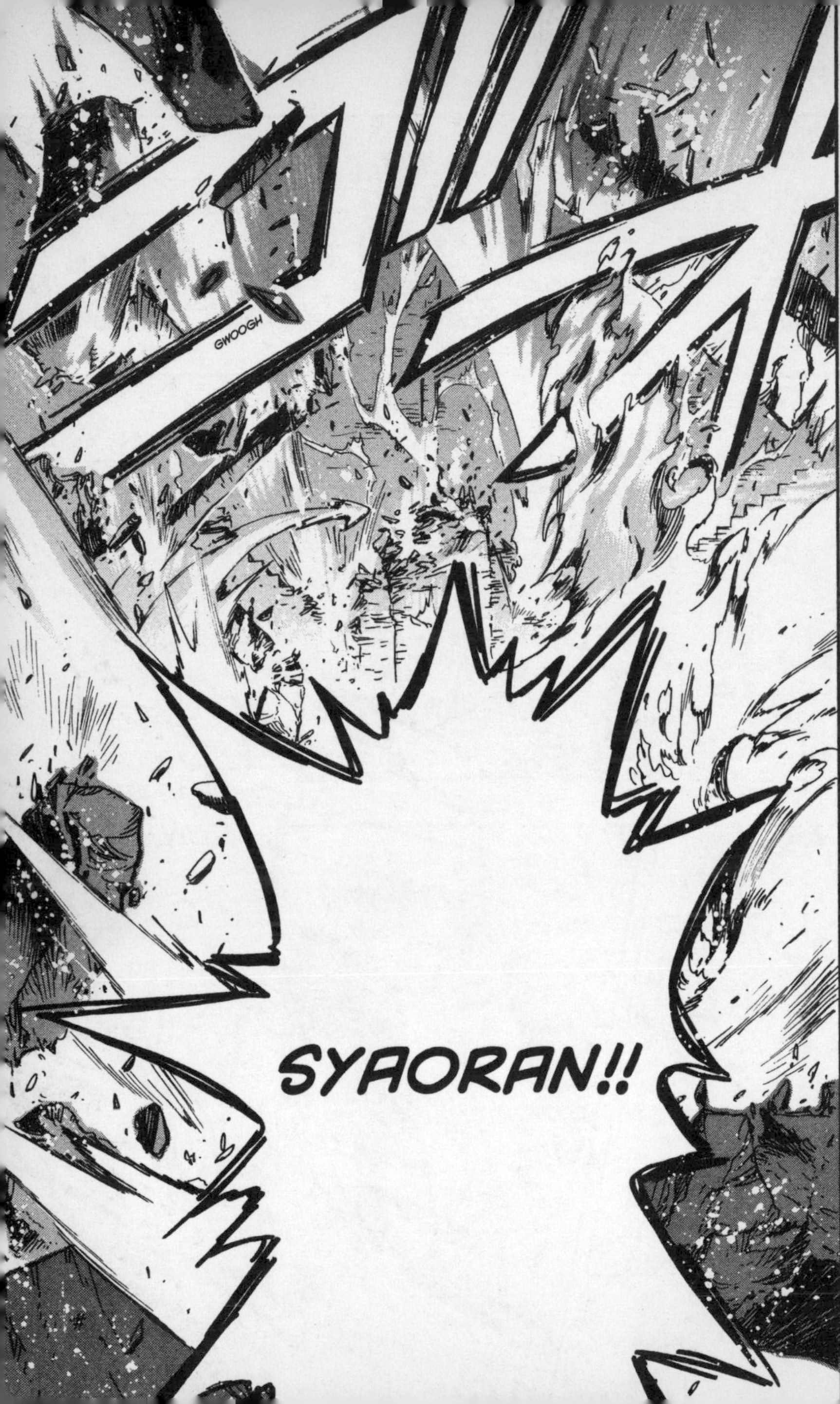
GWOOGH
SYAORAN!!

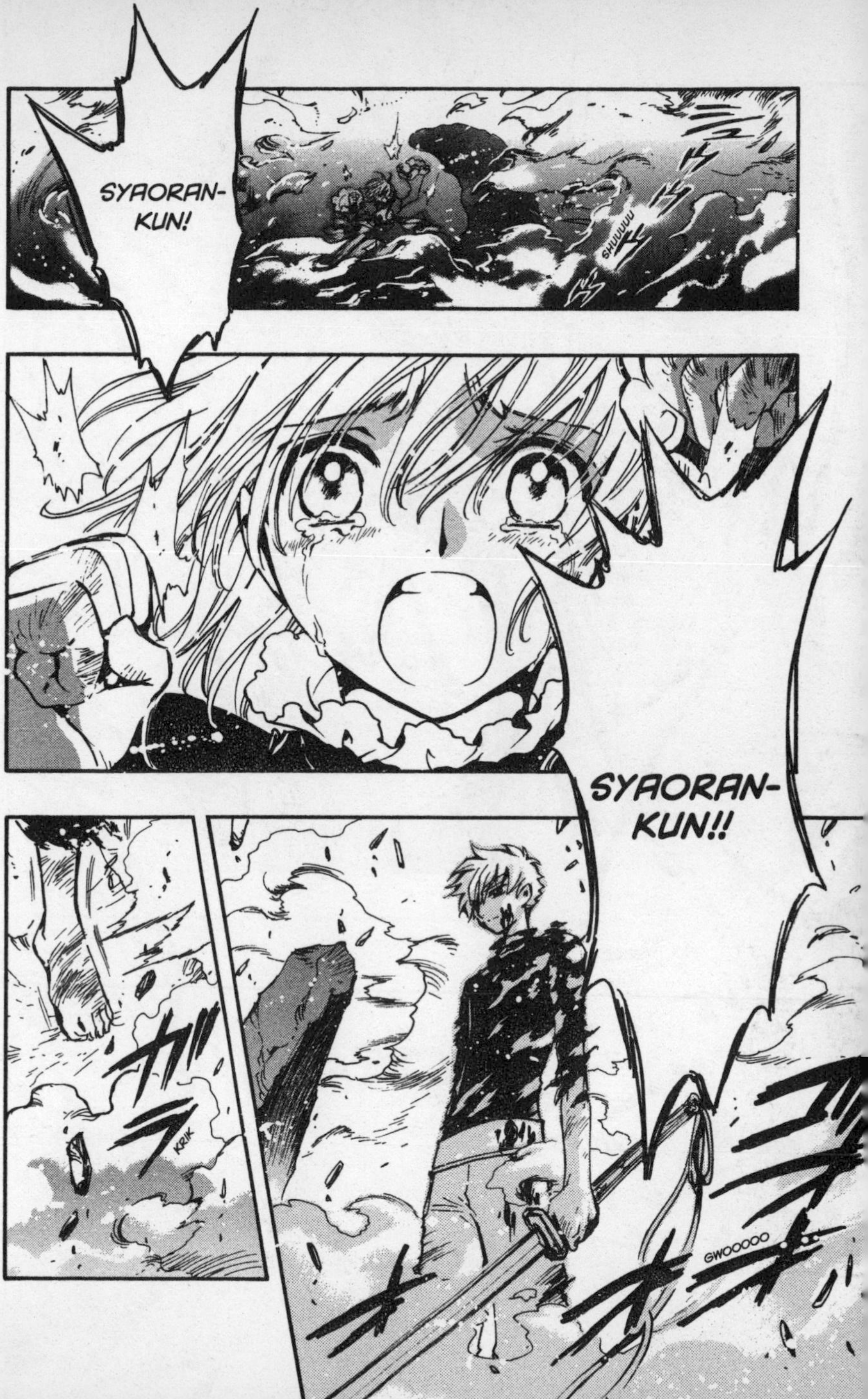
SYAORAN-KUN!
SHUUUUU
SYAORAN-KUN!!
GWOOOOO
KRIK

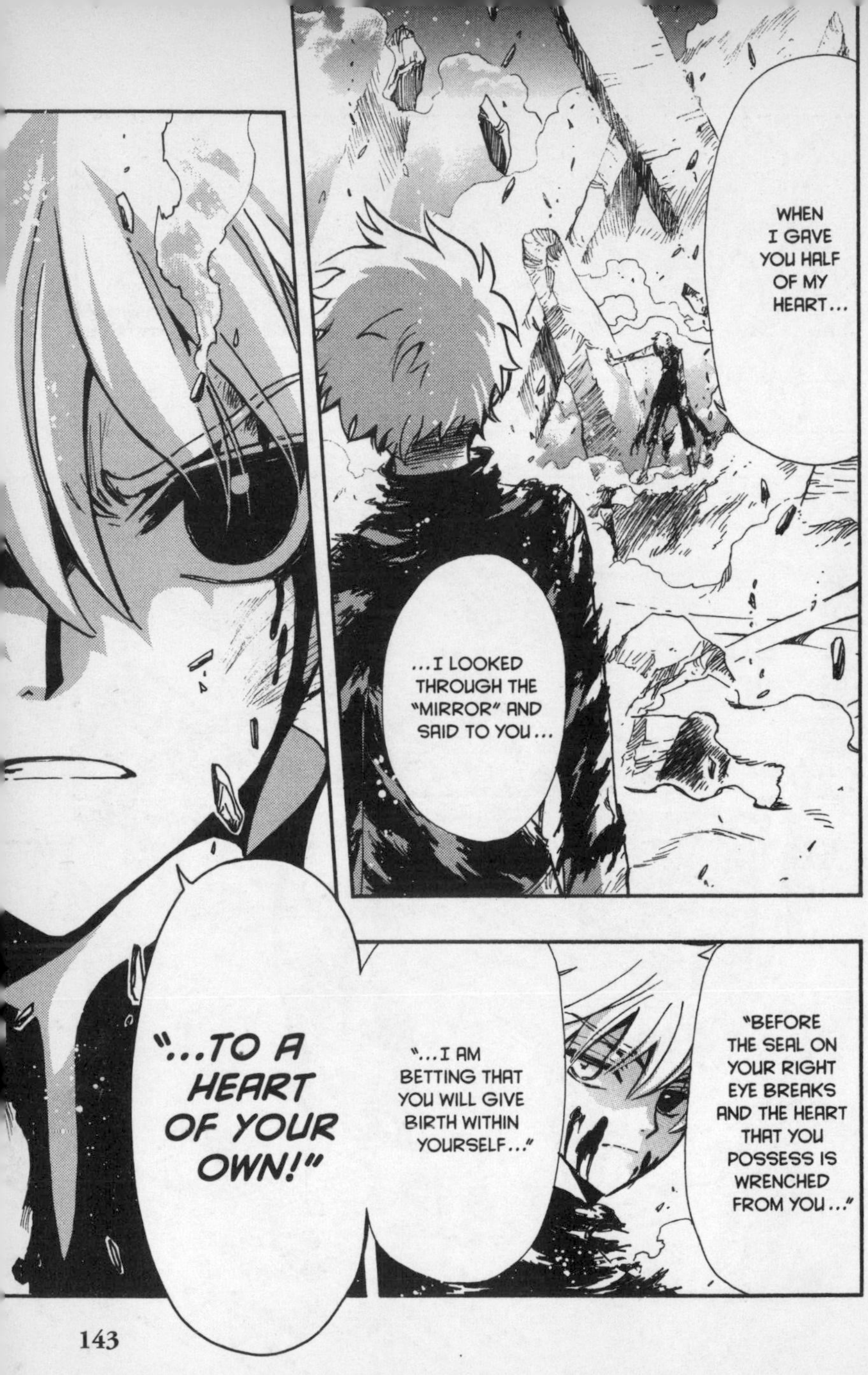
WHEN I GAVE YOU HALF OF MY HEART...
...I LOOKED THROUGH THE "MIRROR" AND SAID TO YOU...
"BEFORE THE SEAL ON YOUR RIGHT EYE BREAKS AND THE HEART THAT YOU POSSESS IS WRENCHED FROM YOU..."
"...I AM BETTING THAT YOU WILL GIVE BIRTH WITHIN YOURSELF..."
"...TO A HEART OF YOUR OWN!"

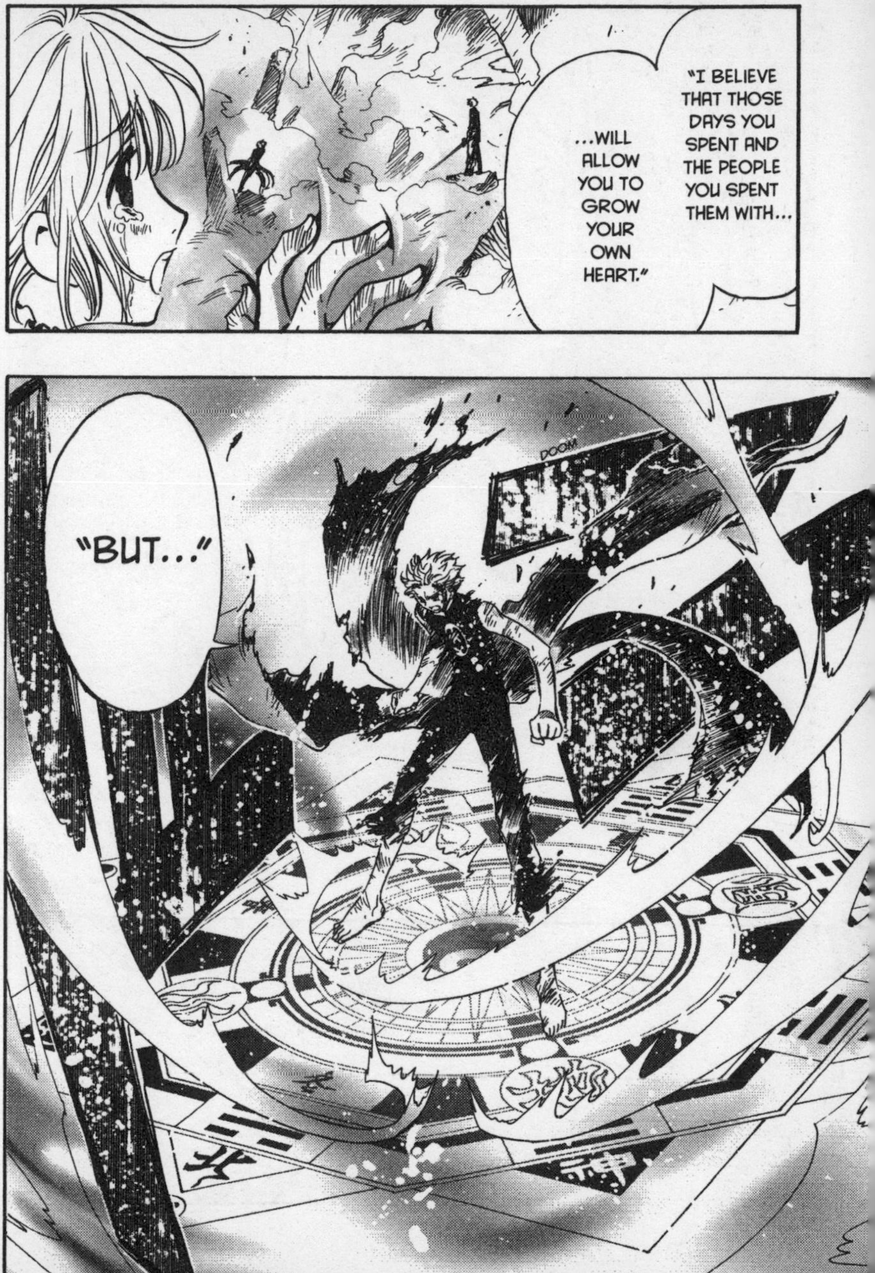
"I BELIEVE THAT THOSE DAYS YOU SPENT AND THE PEOPLE YOU SPENT THEM WITH...
...WILL ALLOW YOU TO GROW YOUR OWN HEART."
DOOM
"BUT..."

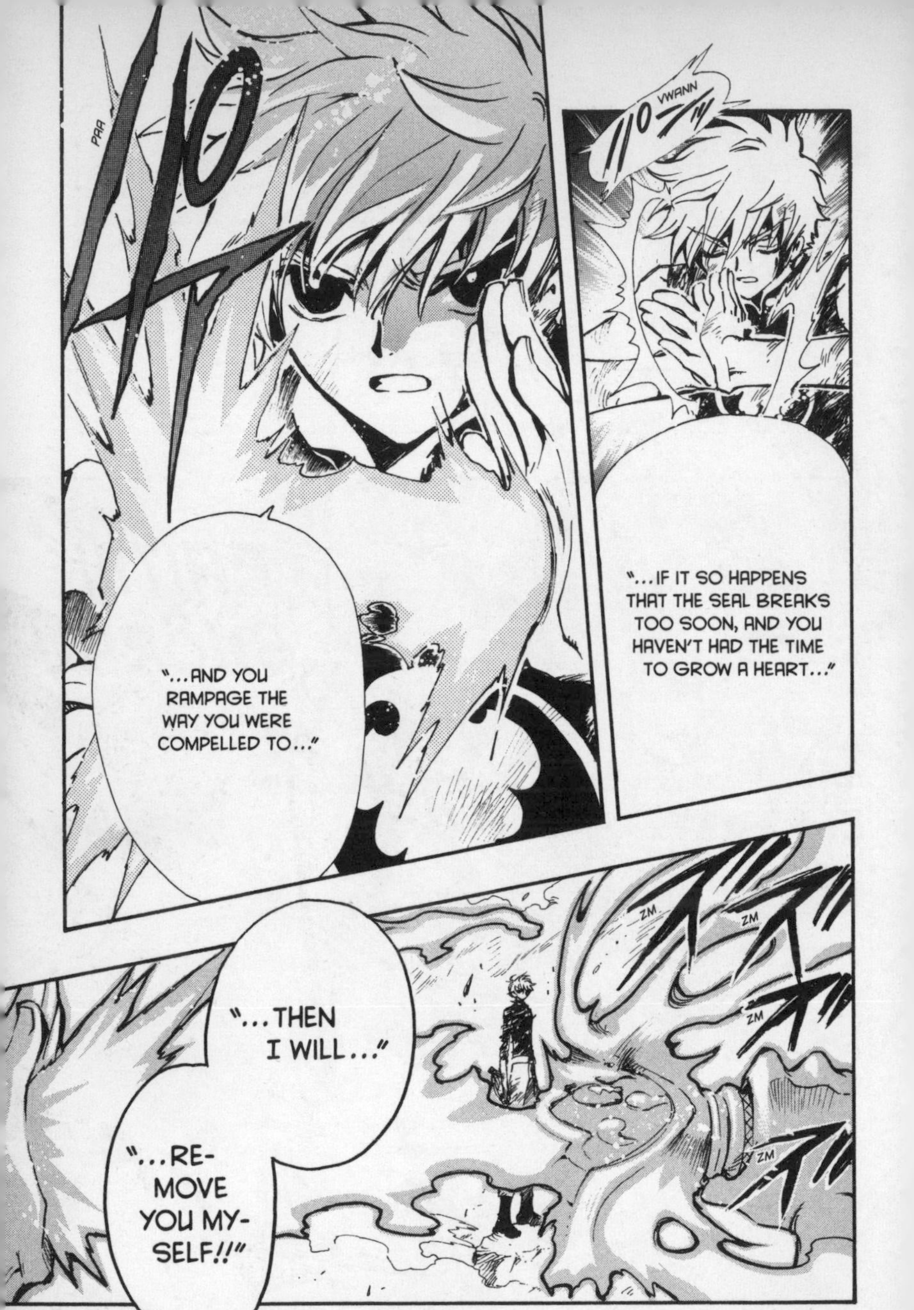
VWANN
"...IF IT SO HAPPENS THAT THE SEAL BREAKS TOO SOON, AND YOU HAVEN'T HAD THE TIME TO GROW A HEART..."
PAA
"...AND YOU RAMPAGE THE WAY YOU WERE COMPELLED TO..."
ZM
ZM
ZM
ZM
"...THEN I WILL..."
"...RE-MOVE YOU MY-SELF!!"

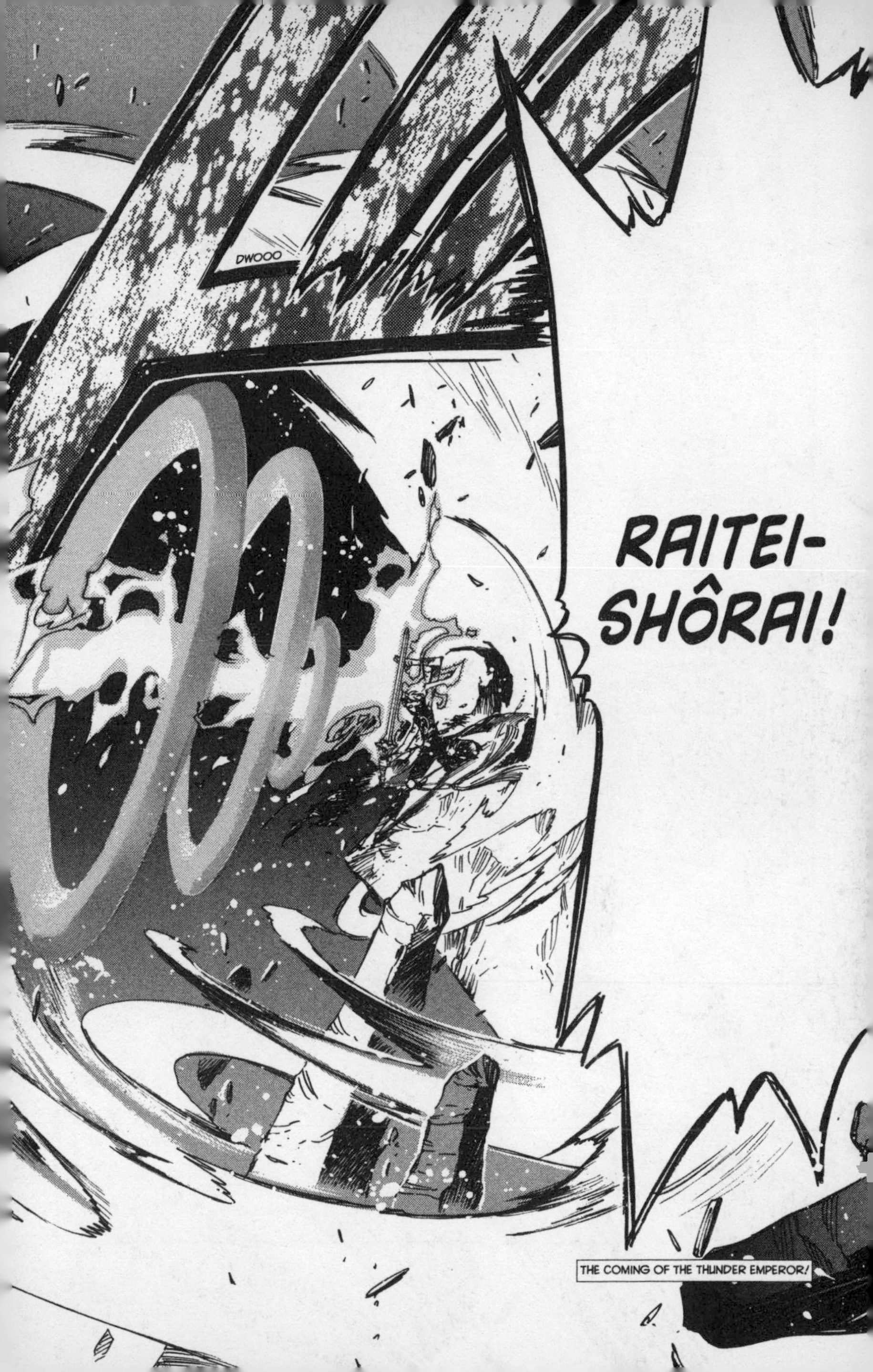
DWOOO
RAITEI-SHÔRAI!
THE COMING OF THE THUNDER EMPEROR!

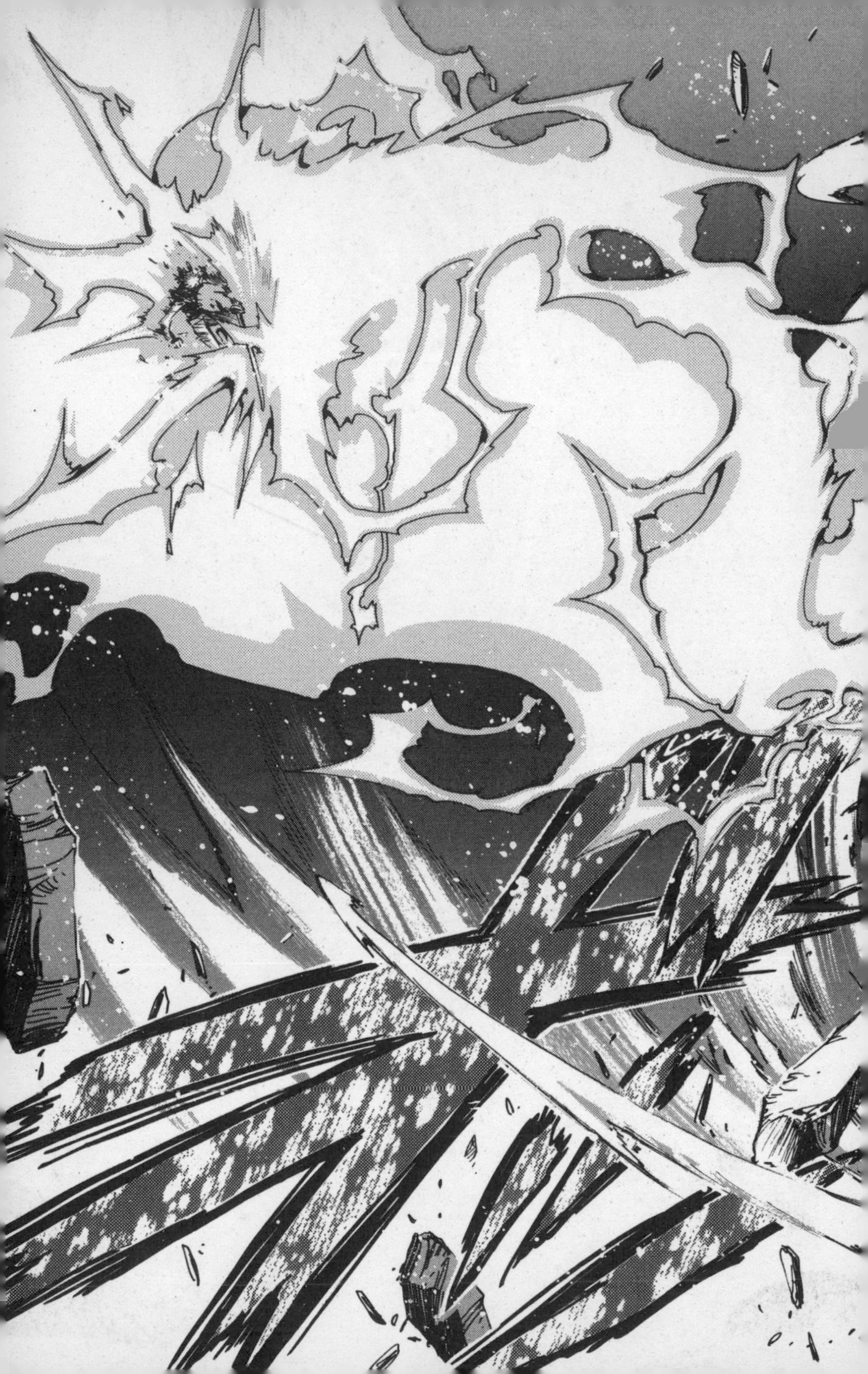

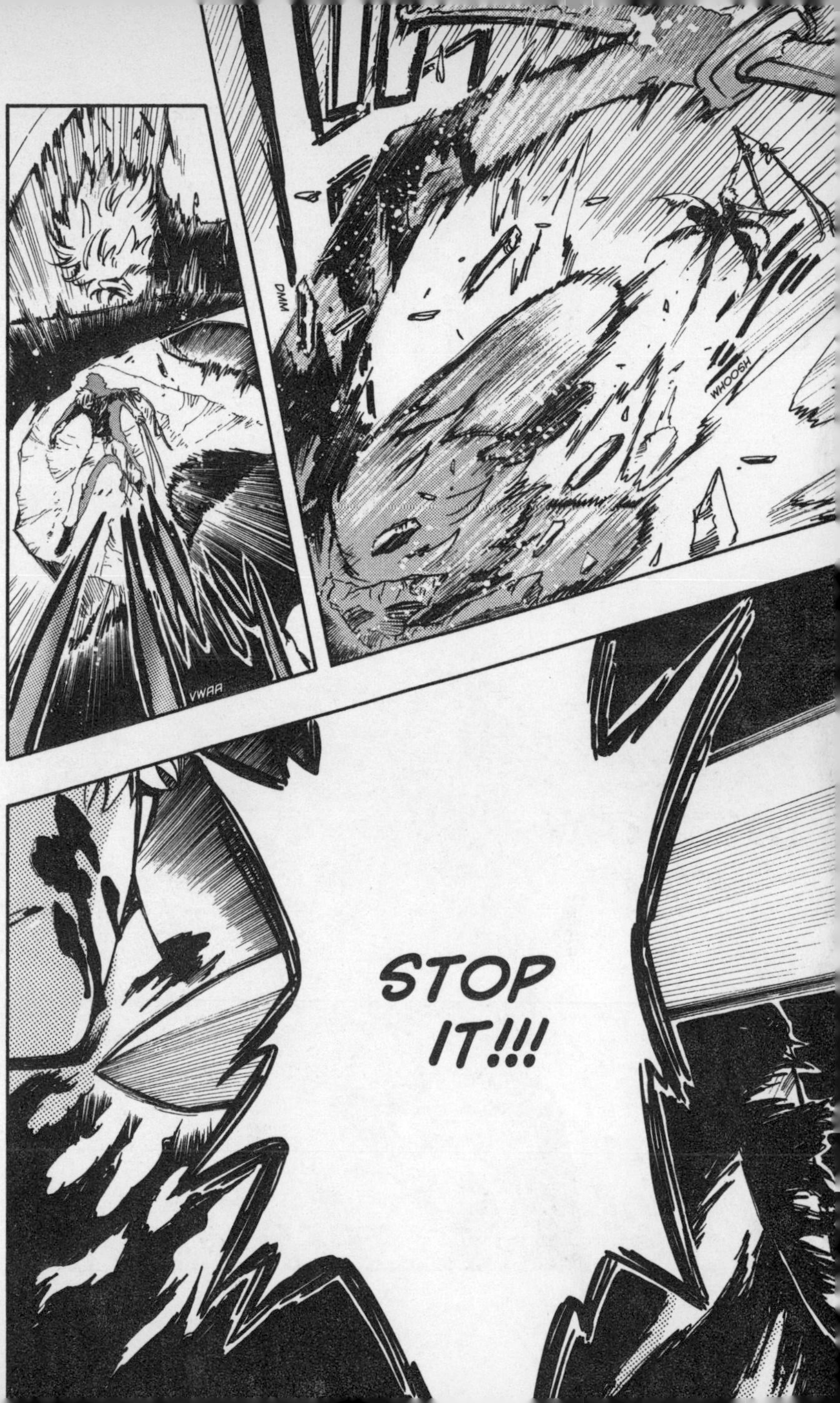
WHOOSH
DMM
VWAA
STOP IT!!!

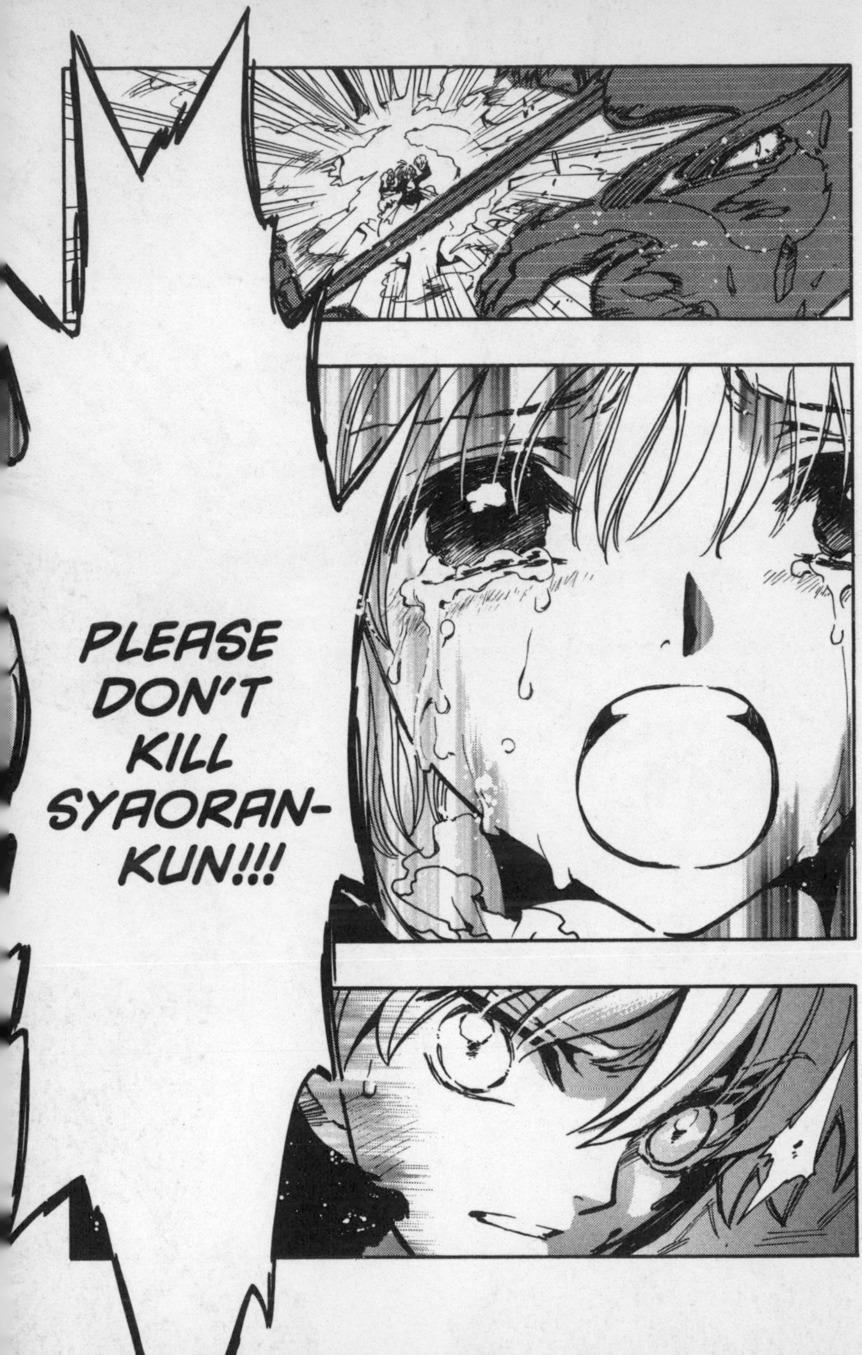
PLEASE DON'T KILL SYAORAN-KUN!!!

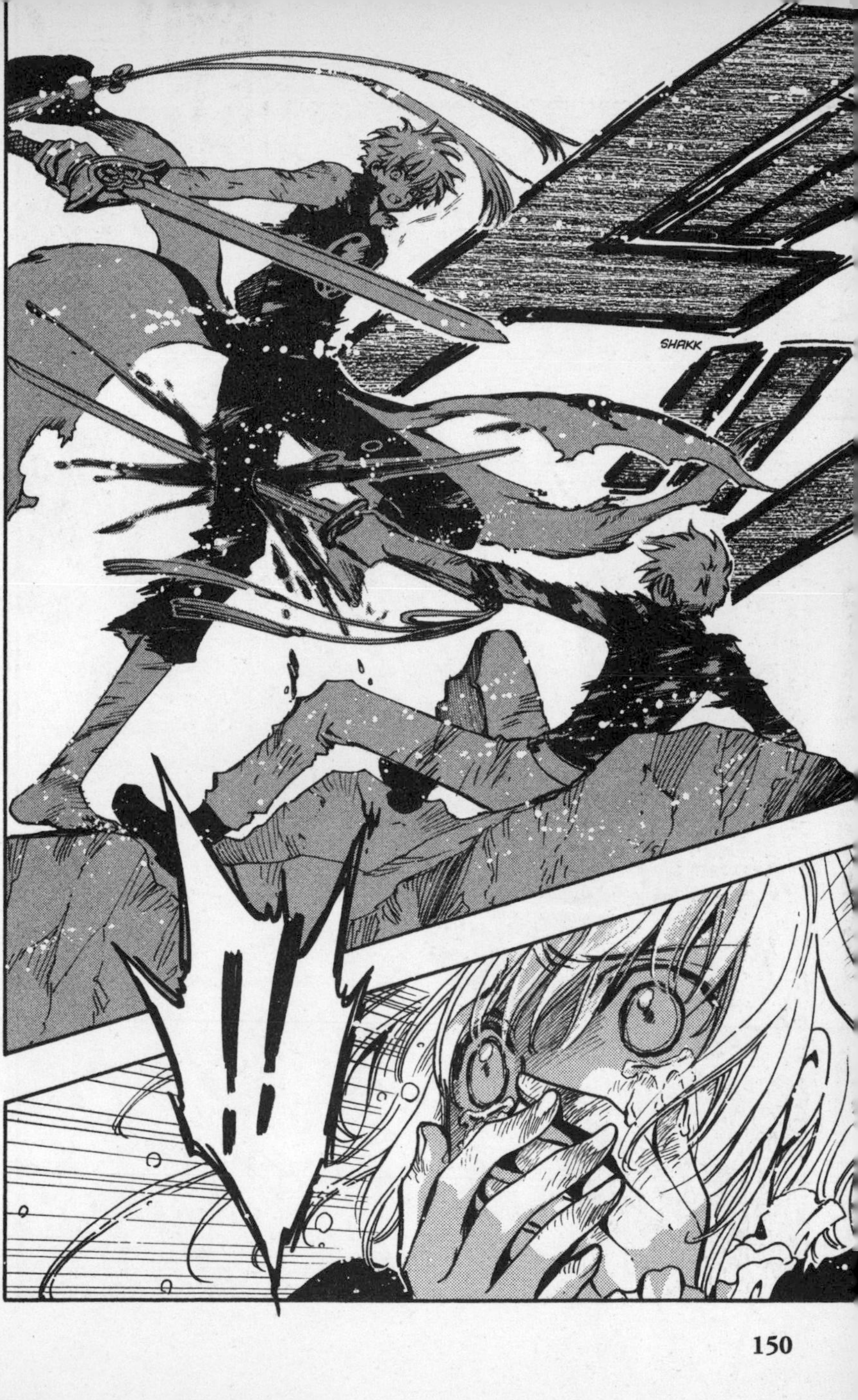
SHAKK
!!

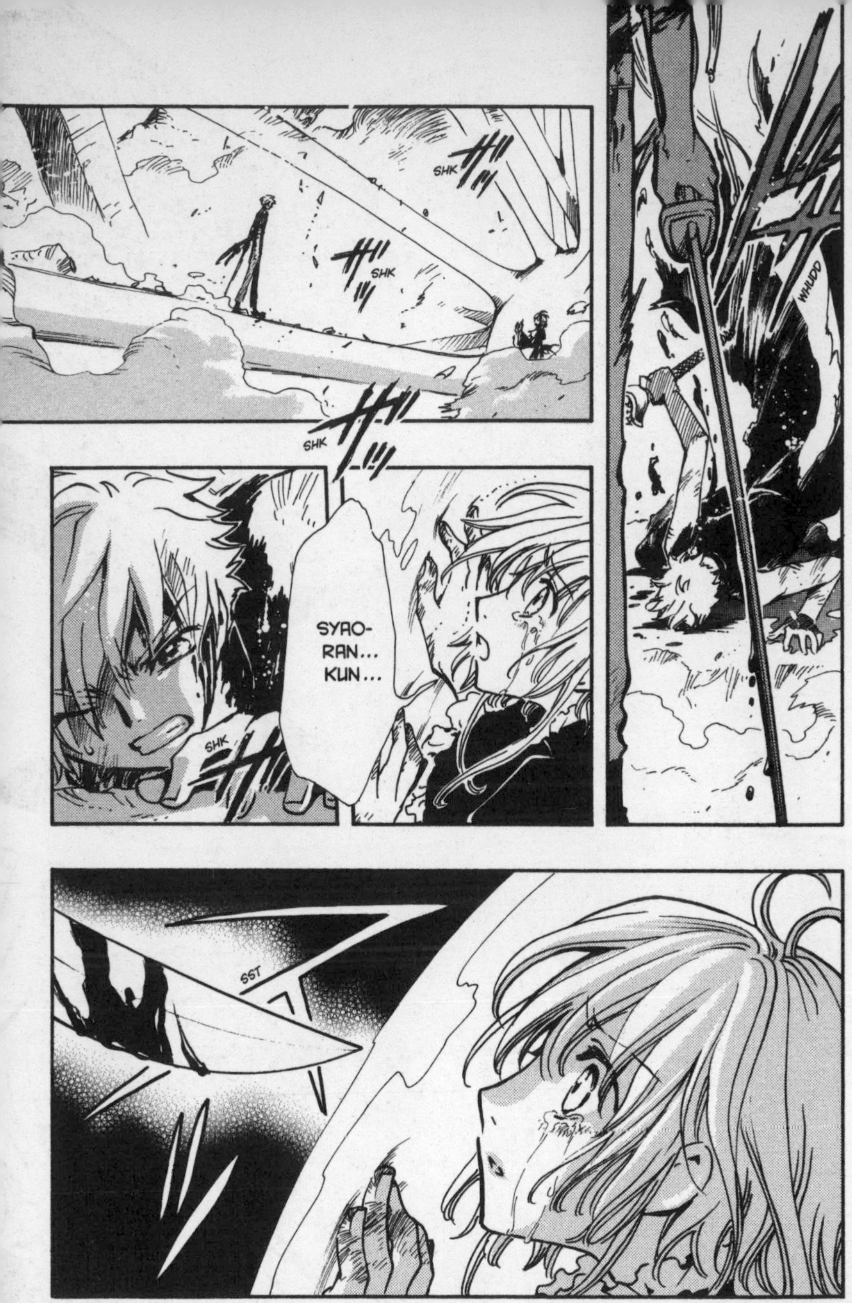
WHUDD
SHK
SHK
SHK
SYAO-
RAN...
KUN...
SHK
SST

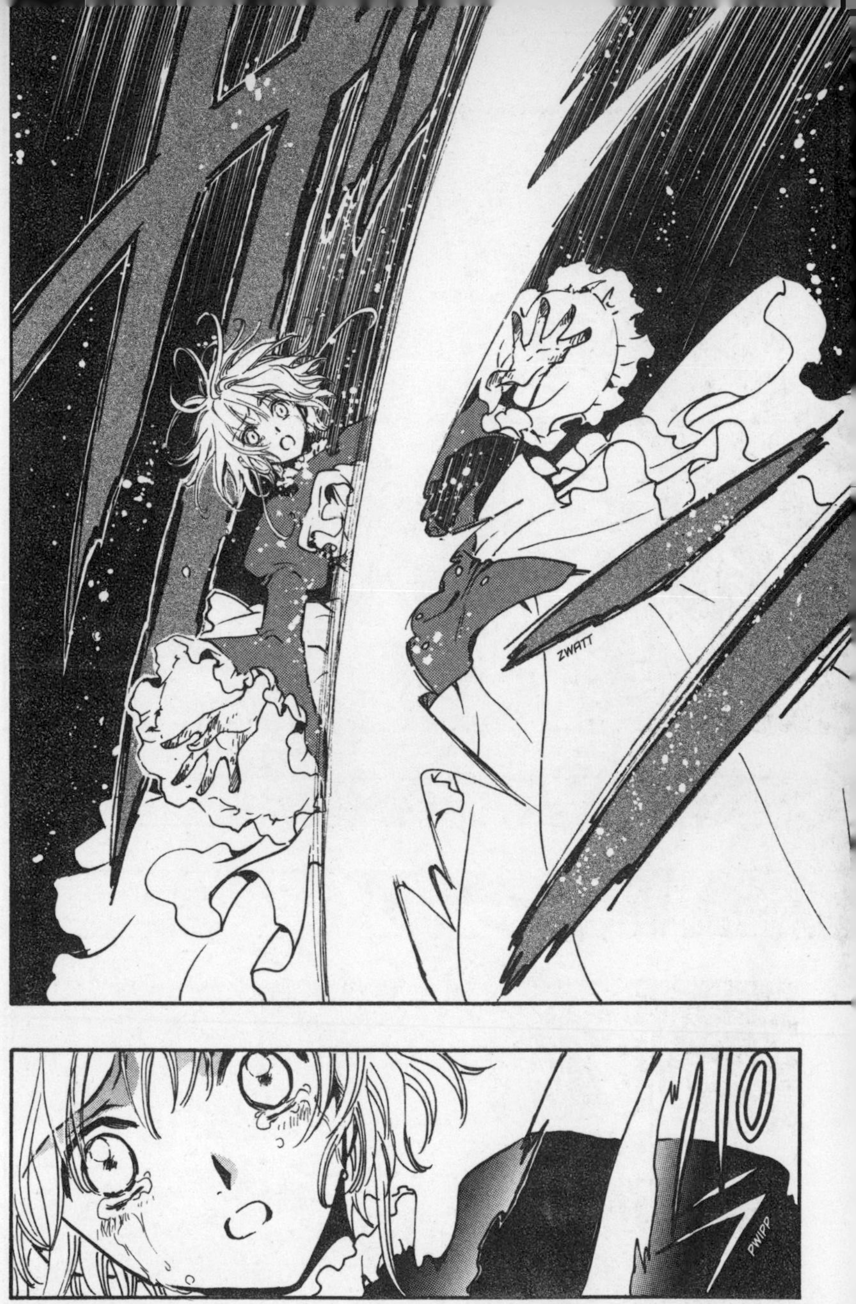
ZWATT
PWIPP

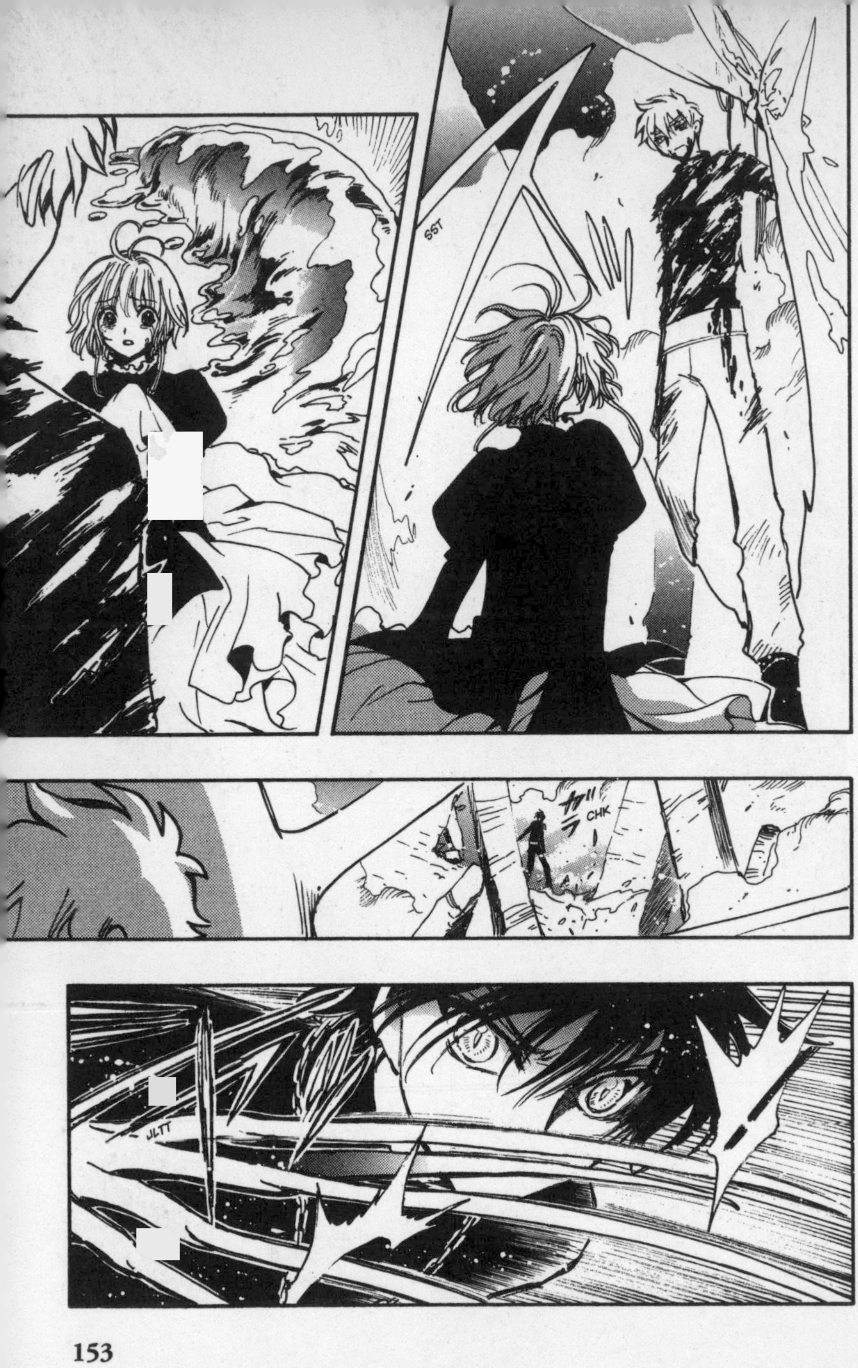
SST
CHK
JLTT

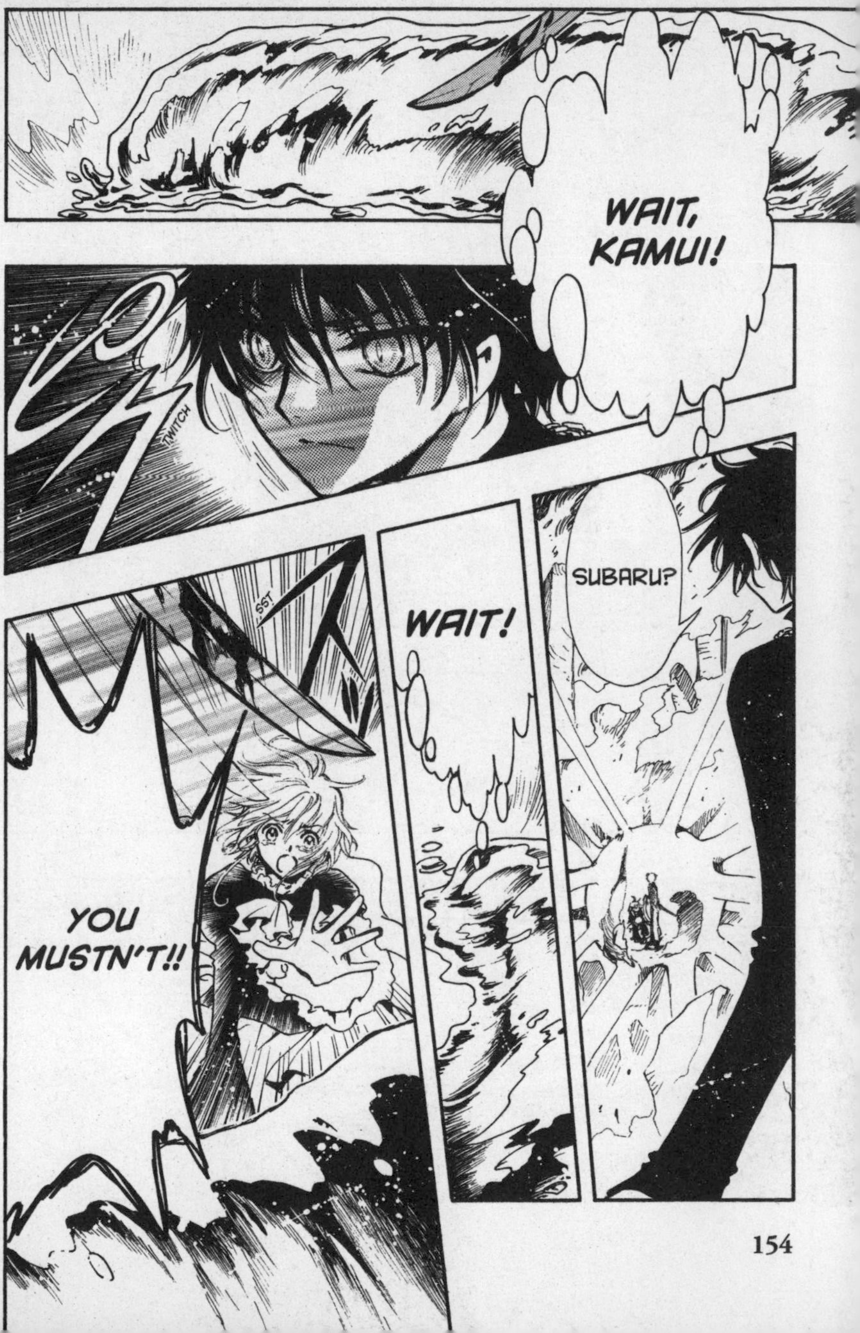
WAIT, KAMUI!
TWITCH
SUBARU?
WAIT!
SST
YOU MUSTN'T!!

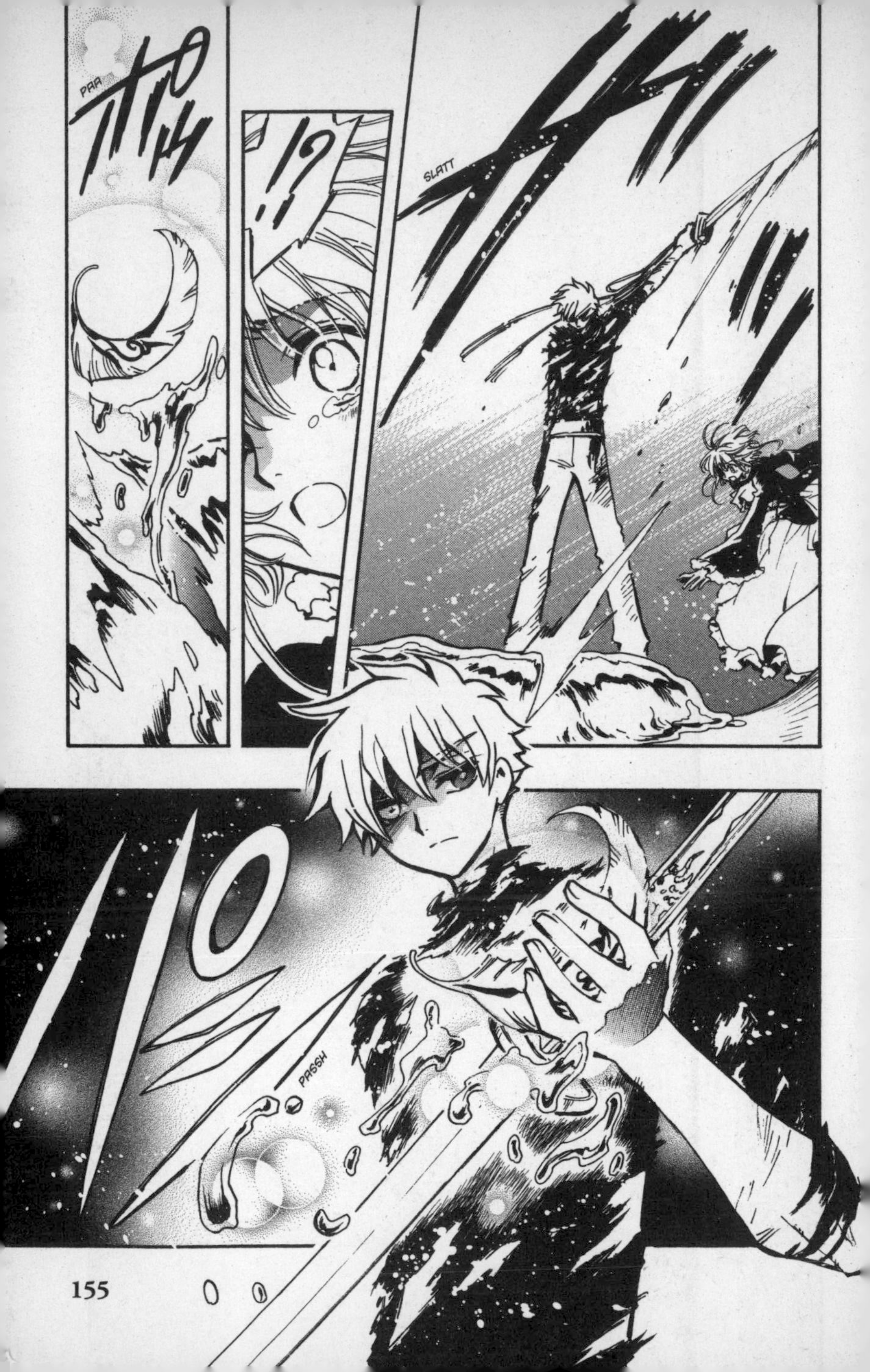
SLATT
!?
PAA
PASSH

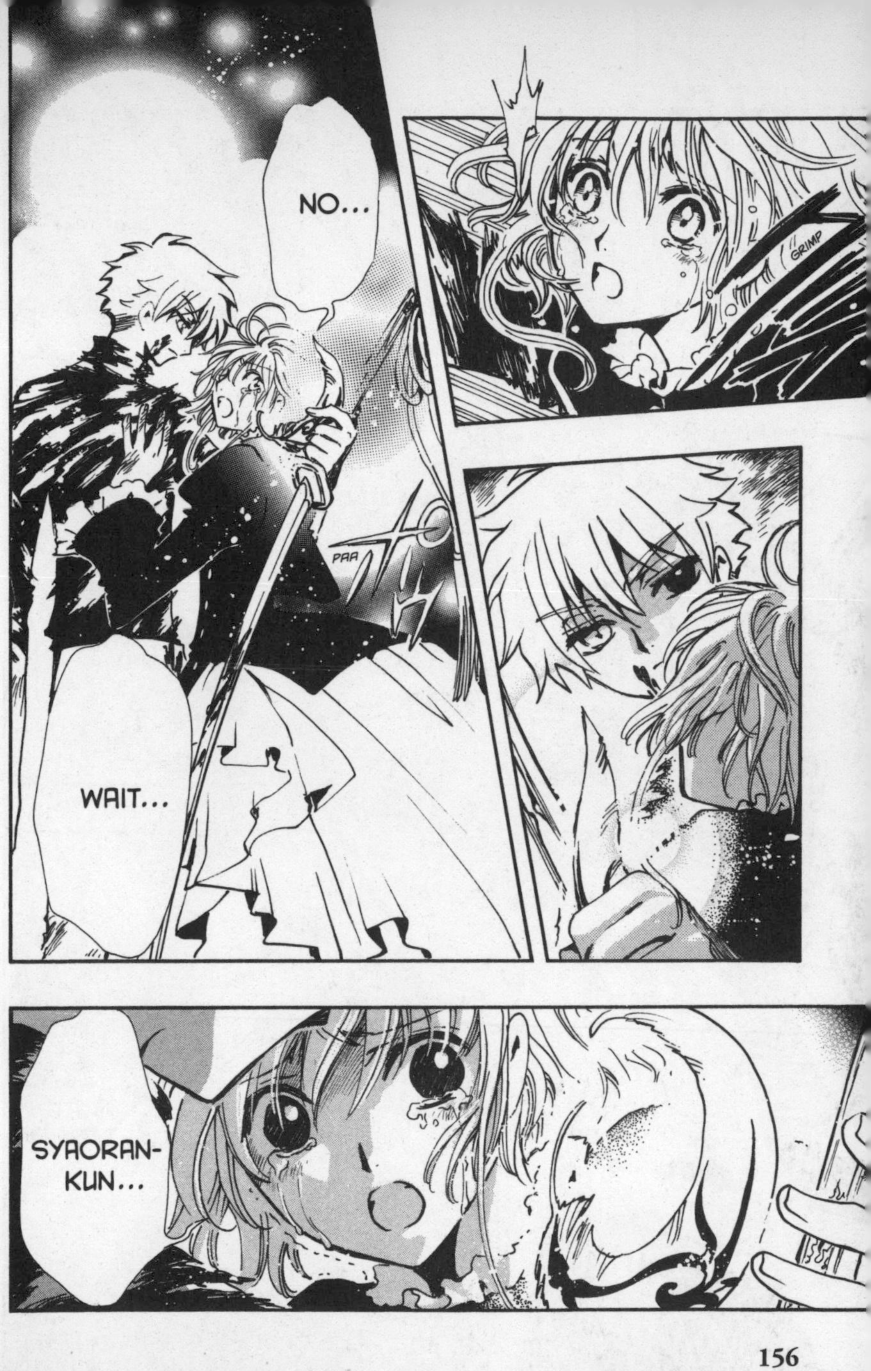
GRIMP
NO...
PAA
WAIT...
SYAORAN-KUN...

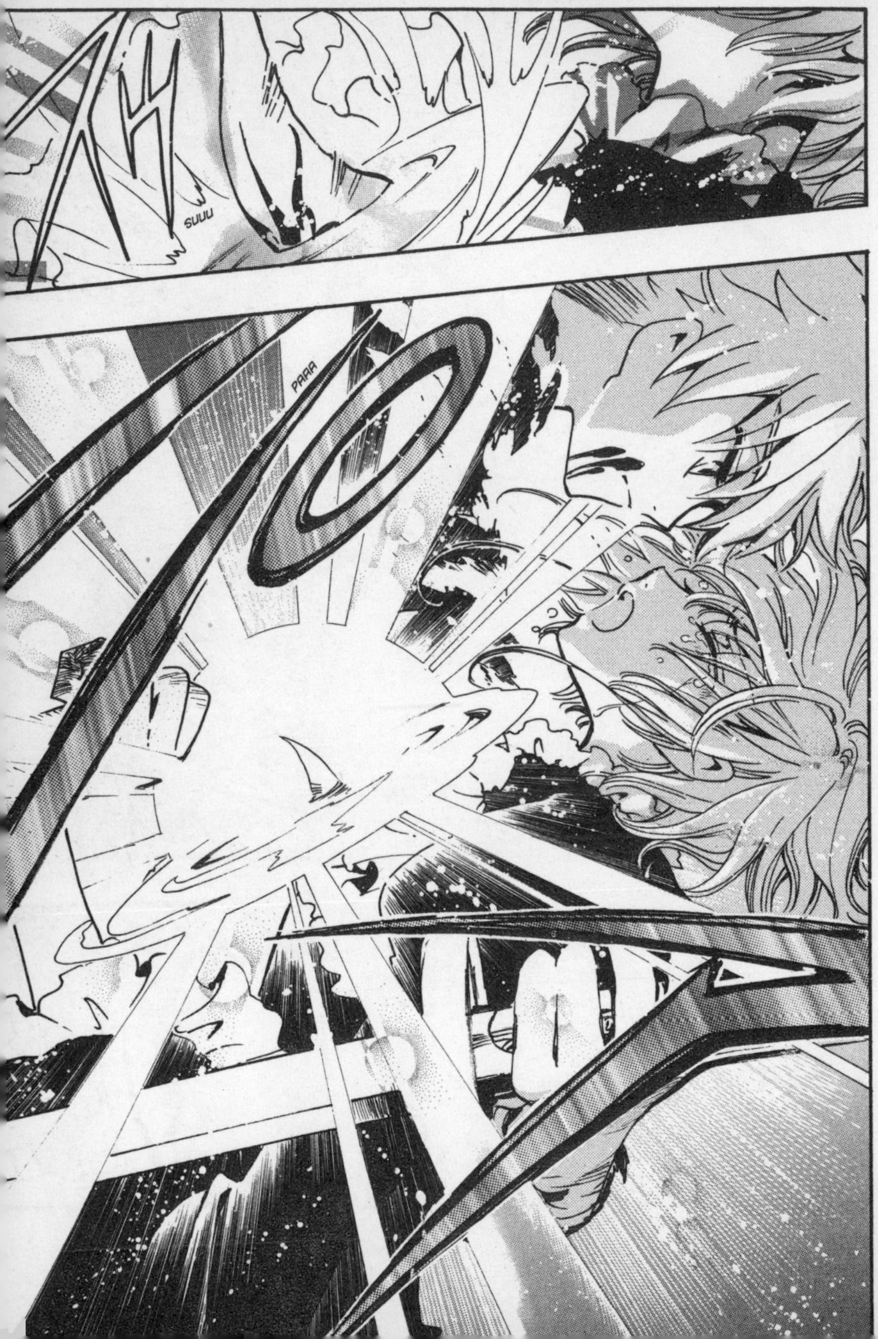
SUUU
PAAA

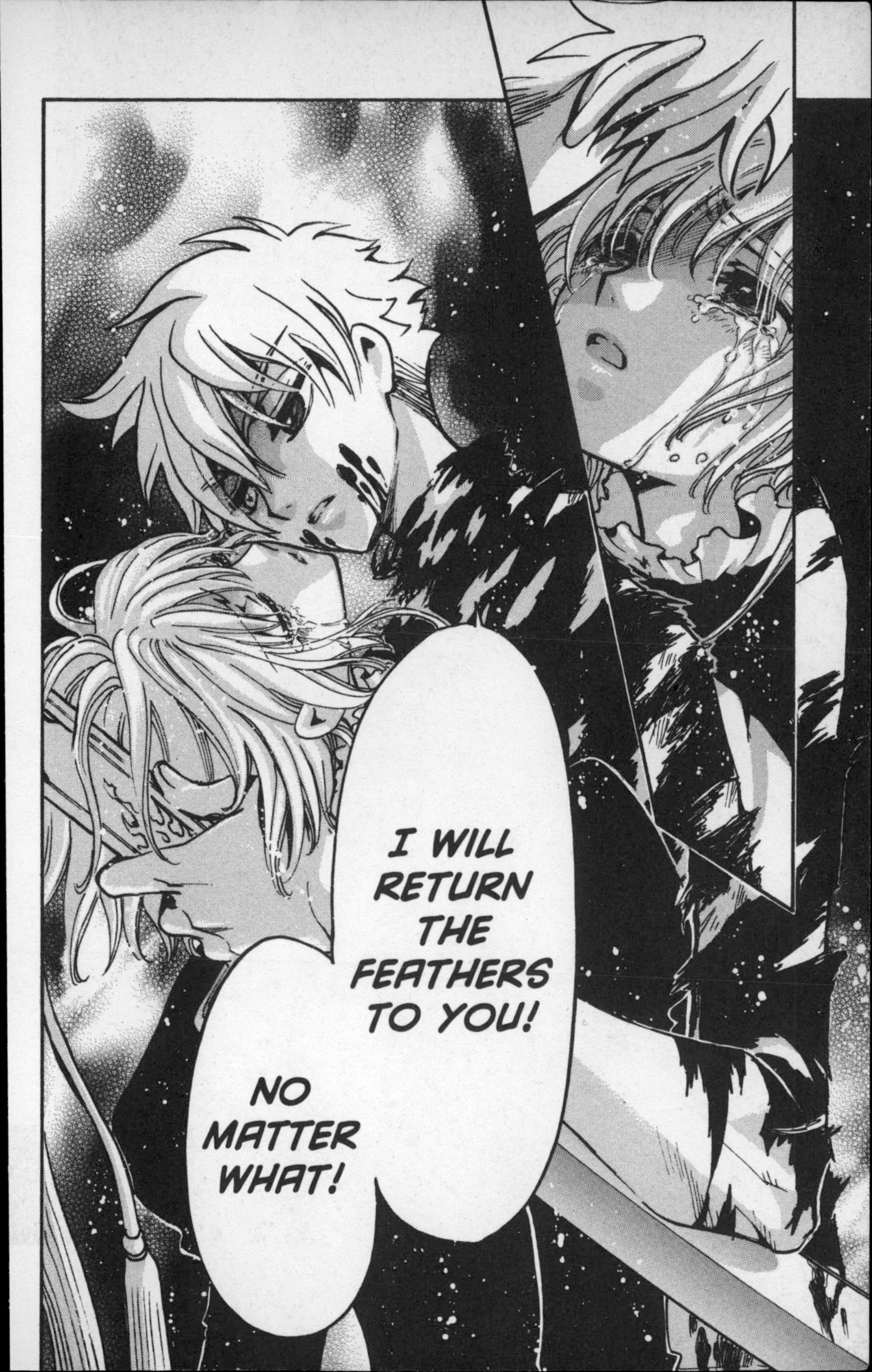
I WILL RETURN THE FEATHERS TO YOU!
NO MATTER WHAT!

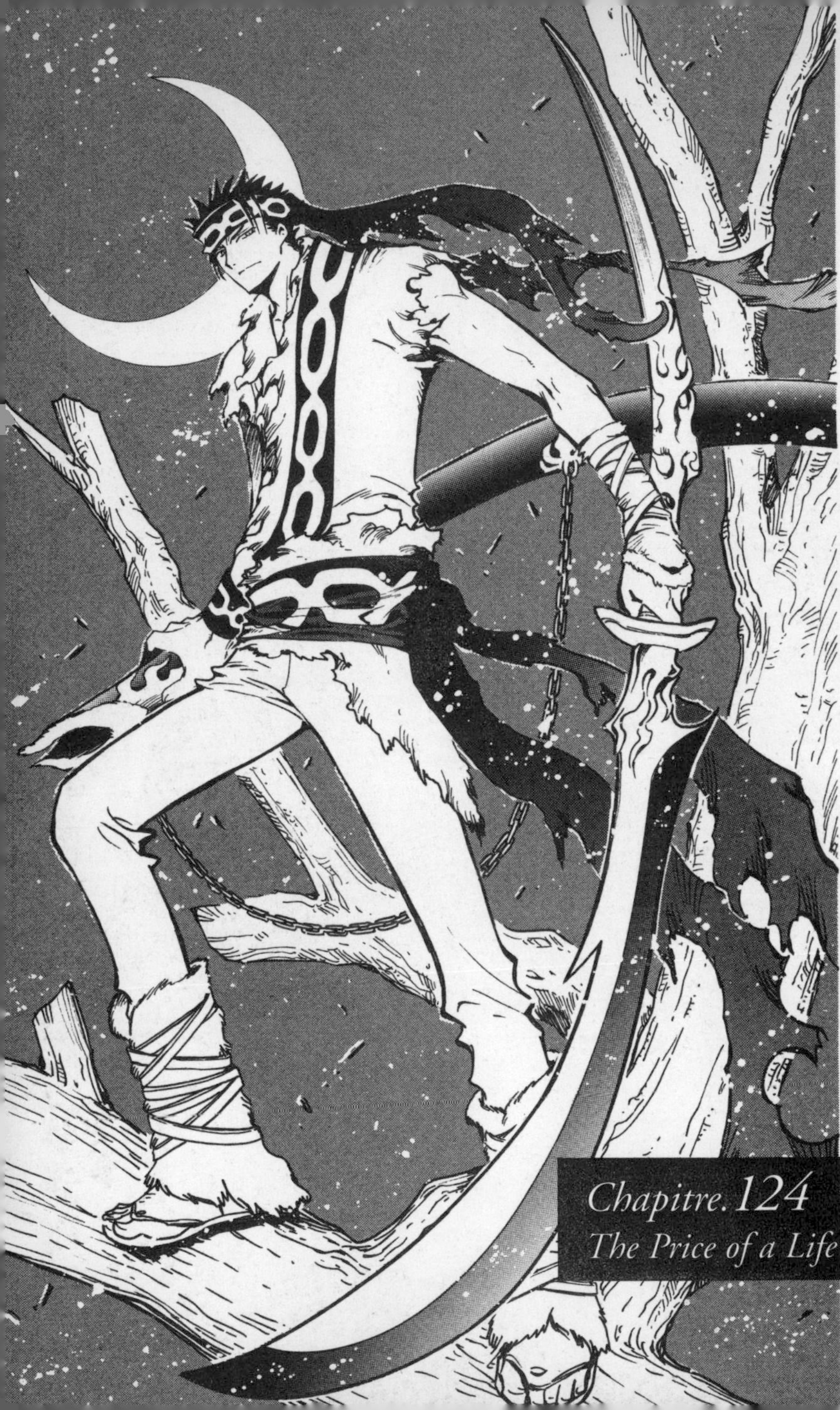
Chapitre. 124
The Price of a Life

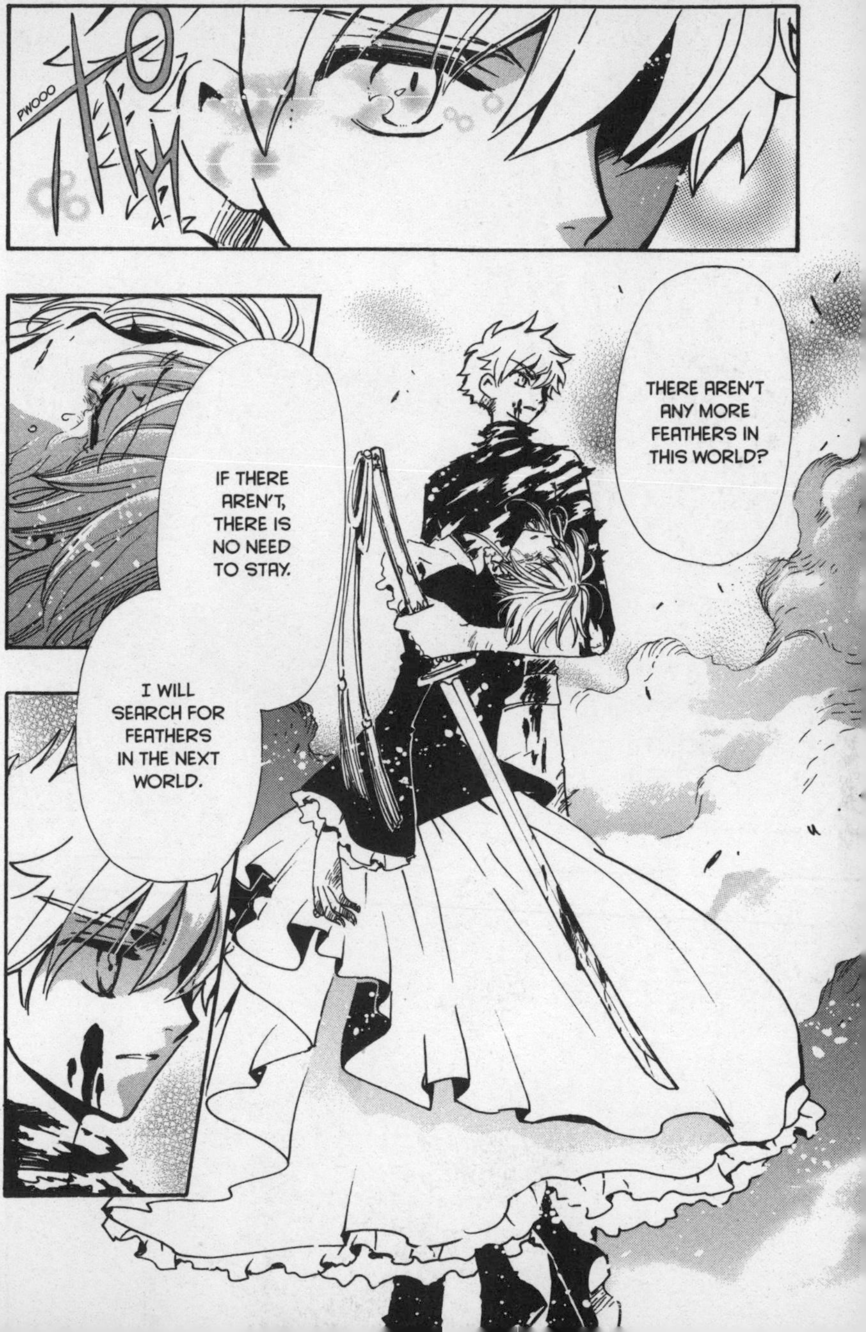
PWOOO
THERE AREN'T ANY MORE FEATHERS IN THIS WORLD?
IF THERE AREN'T, THERE IS NO NEED TO STAY.
I WILL SEARCH FOR FEATHERS IN THE NEXT WORLD.

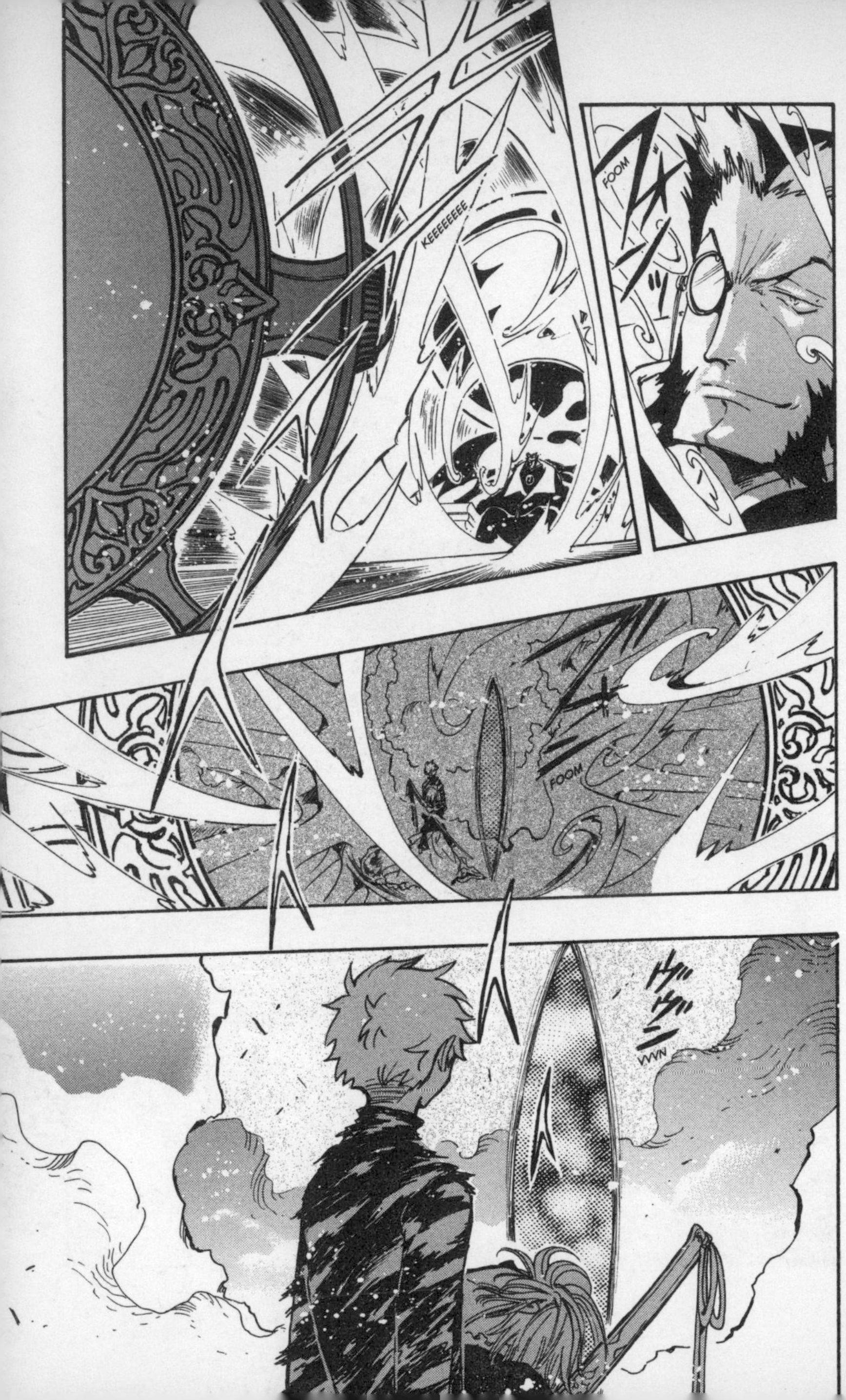
FOOM
KEEEEEEEE
FOOM
VVVN

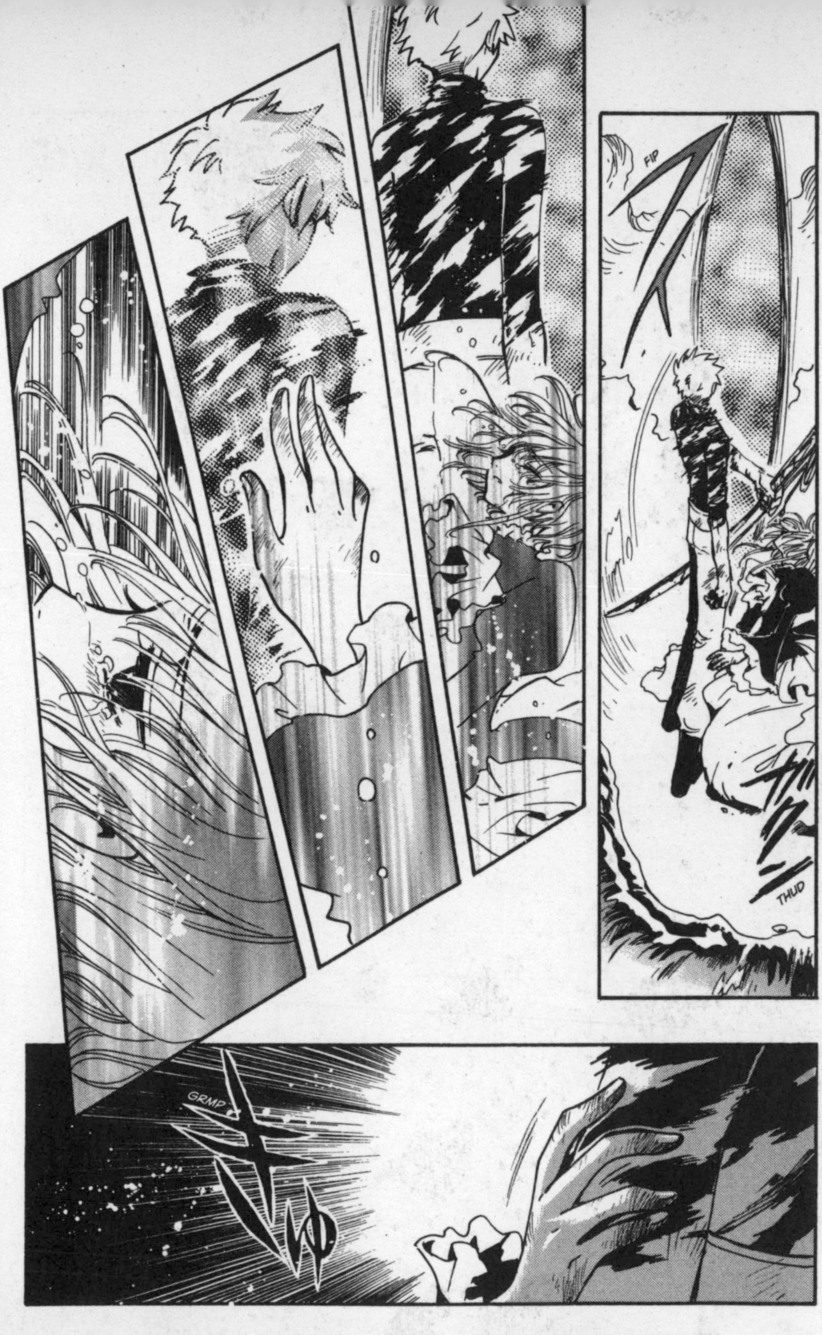
FIP
THUD
GRMP

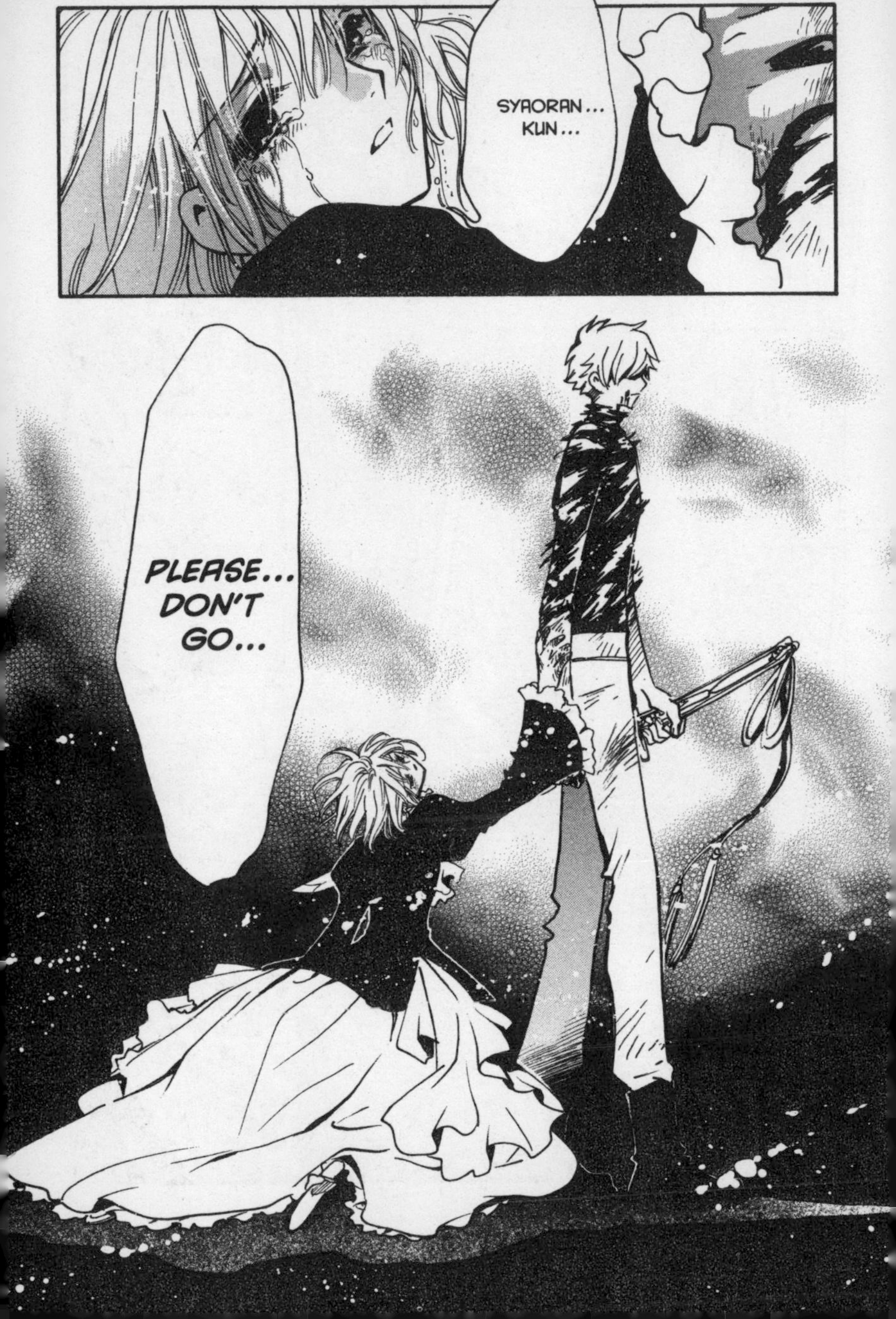
SYAORAN... KUN...
PLEASE... DON'T GO...

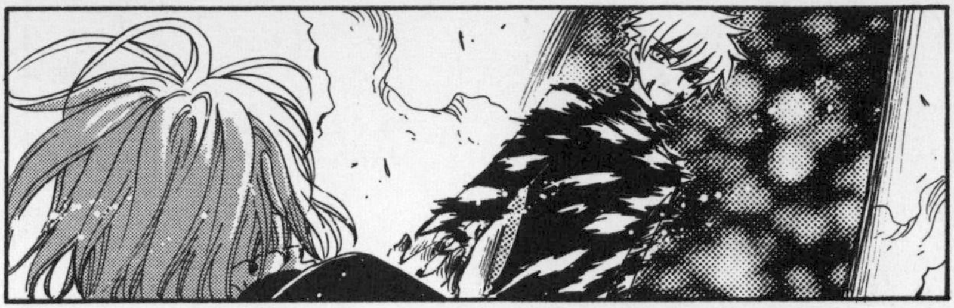
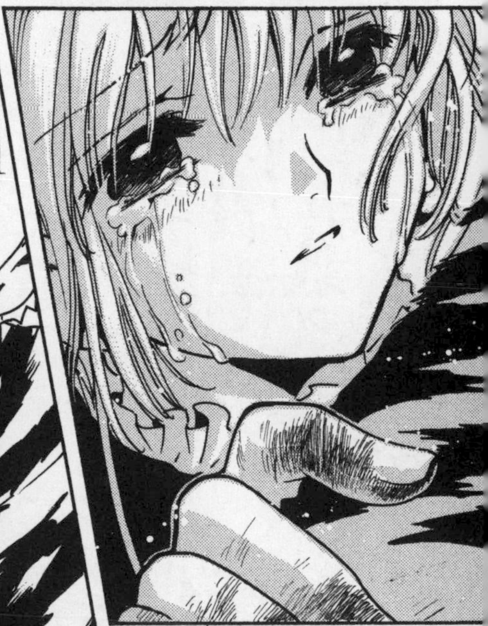
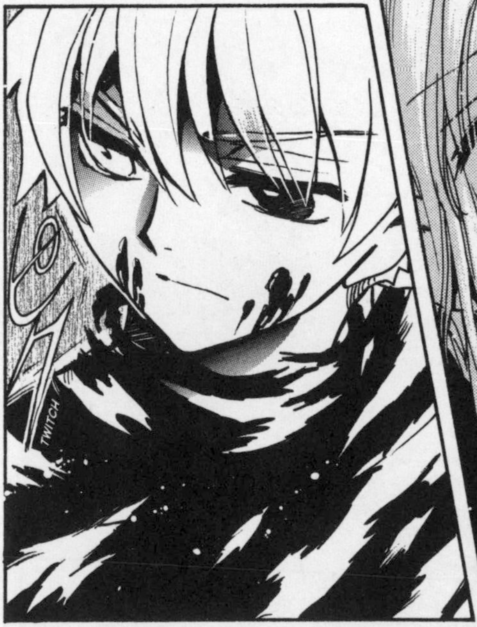
TWITCH
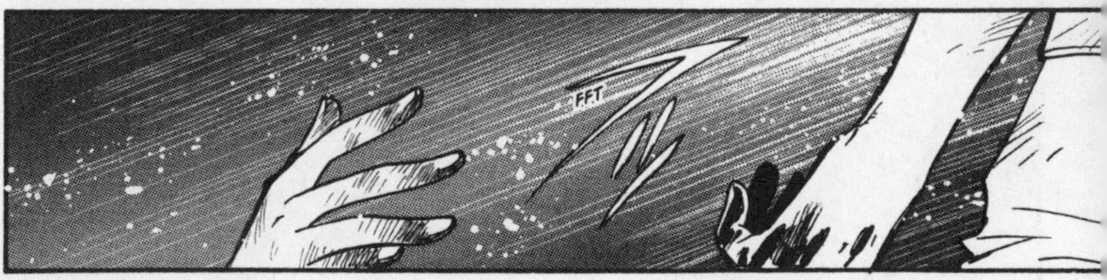
FFT

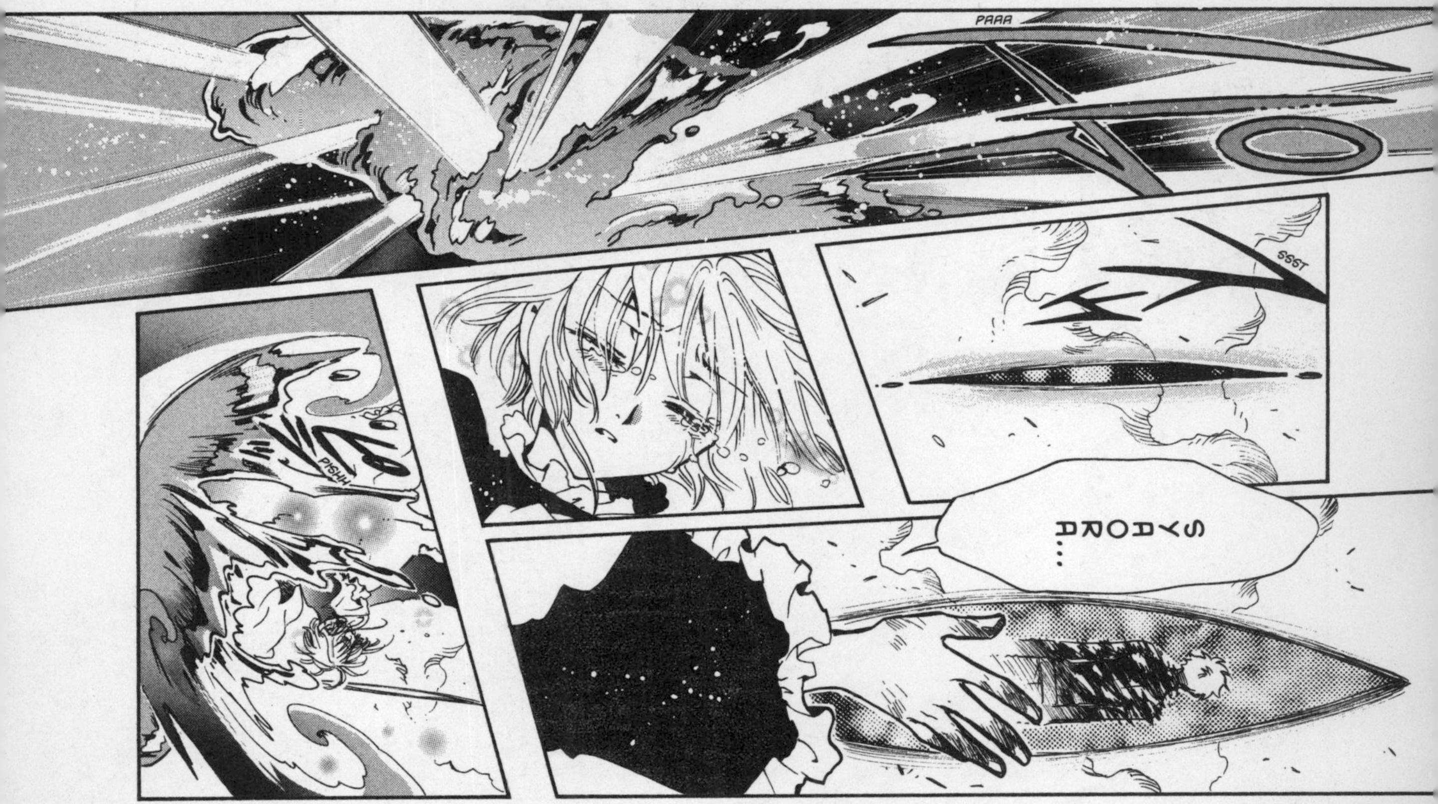
PARR
SSST
SYAORA...
PISHH

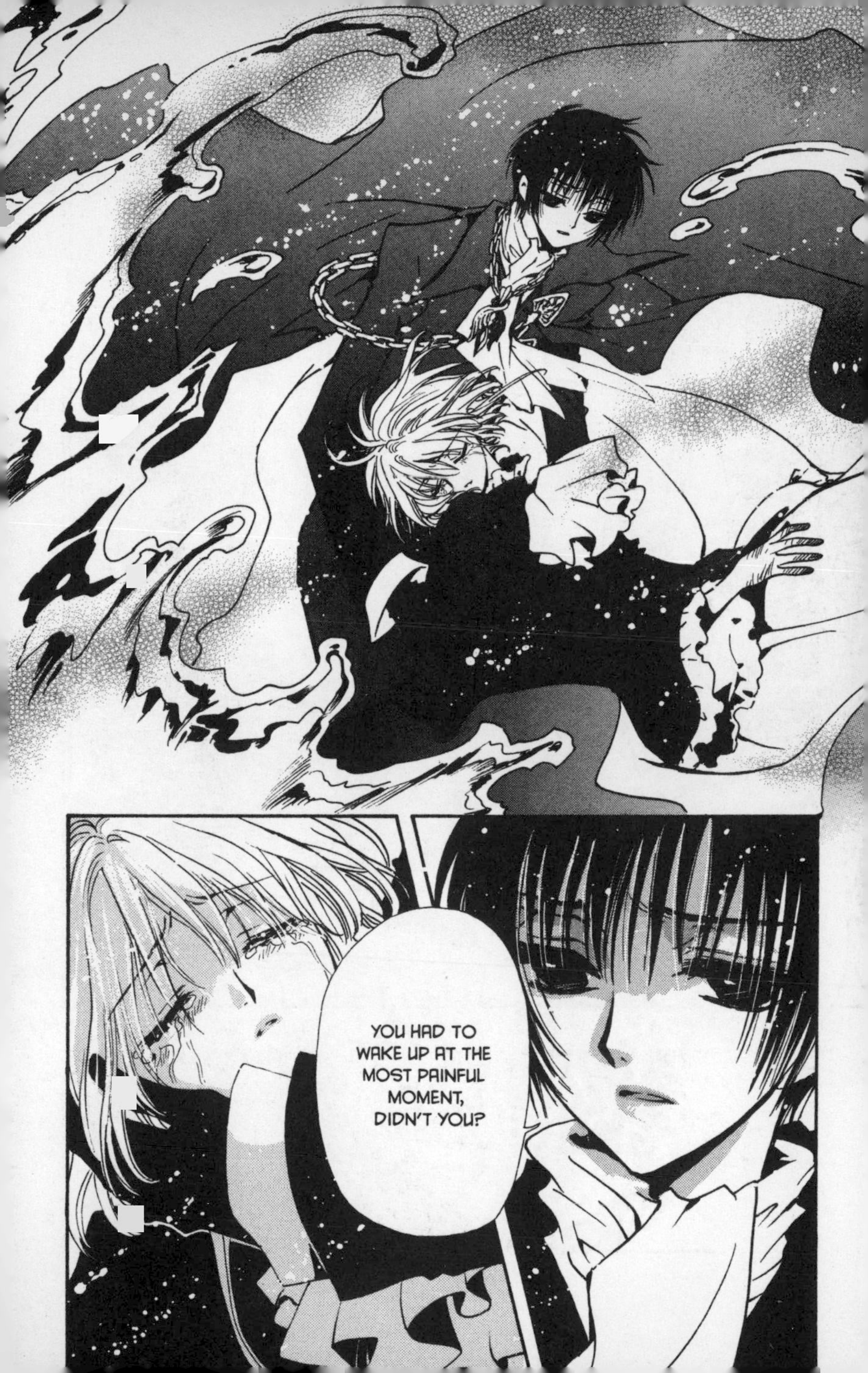
YOU HAD TO WAKE UP AT THE MOST PAINFUL MOMENT, DIDN'T YOU?

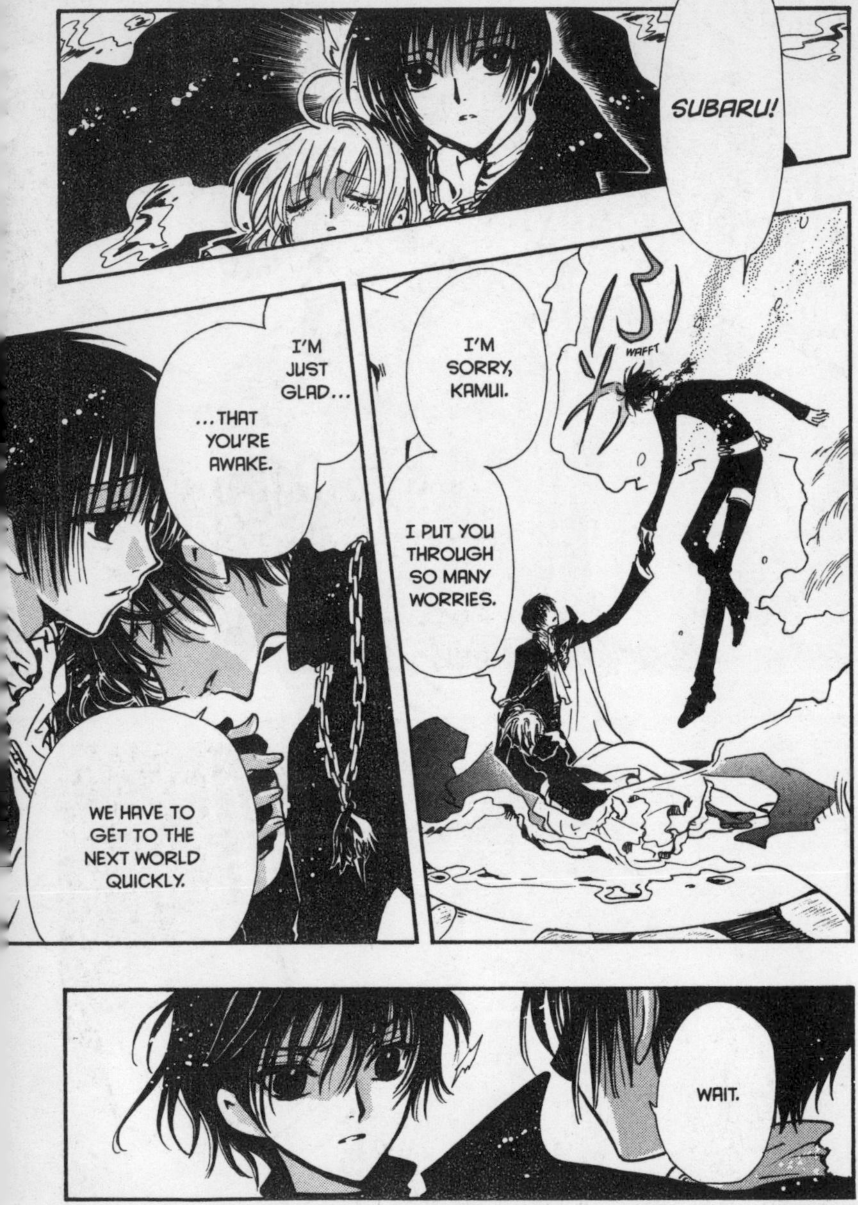
SUBARU!
WAFFT
I'M SORRY, KAMUI.
I PUT YOU THROUGH SO MANY WORRIES.
I'M JUST GLAD...
...THAT YOU'RE AWAKE.
WE HAVE TO GET TO THE NEXT WORLD QUICKLY.
WAIT.

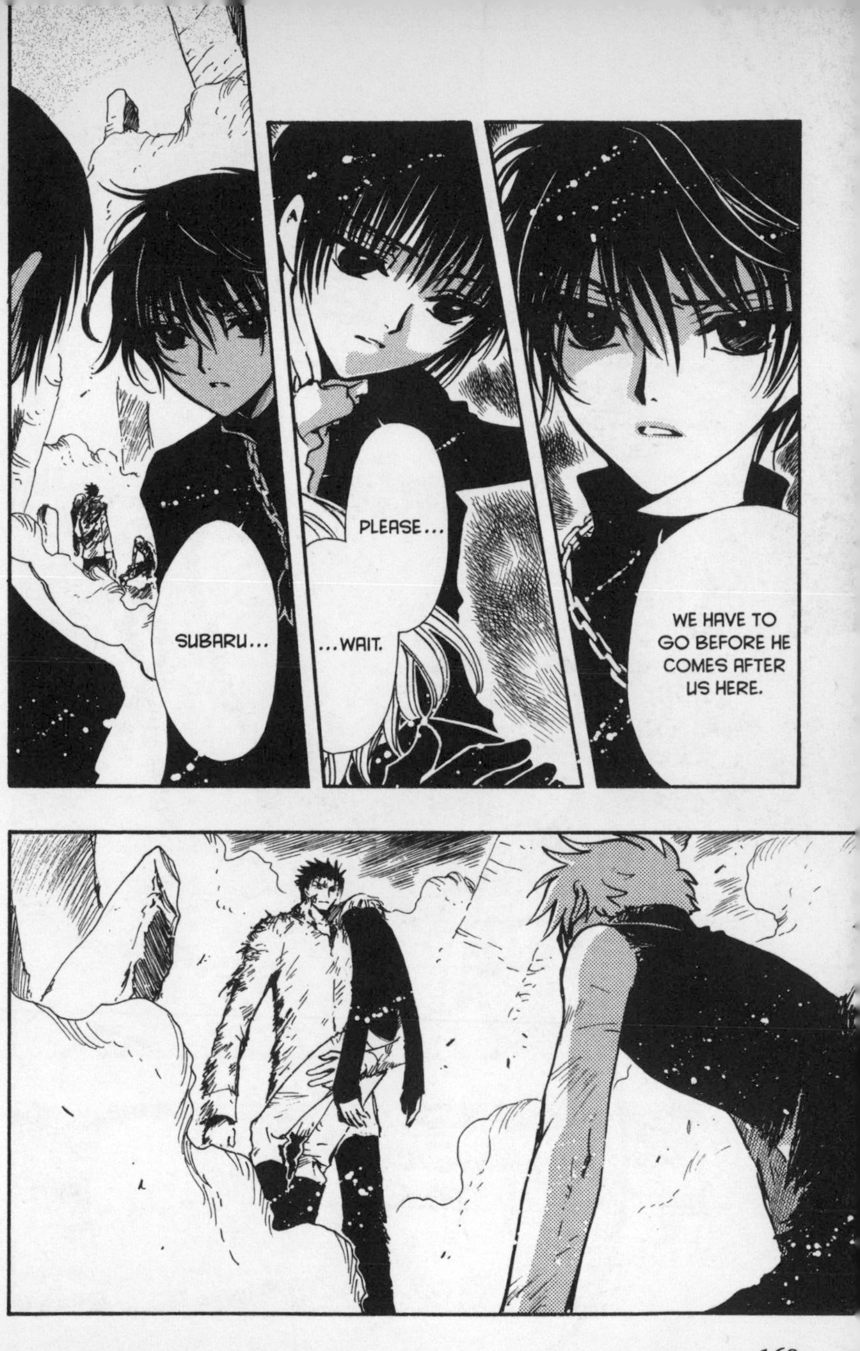
WE HAVE TO GO BEFORE HE COMES AFTER US HERE.
PLEASE...
...WAIT.
SUBARU...

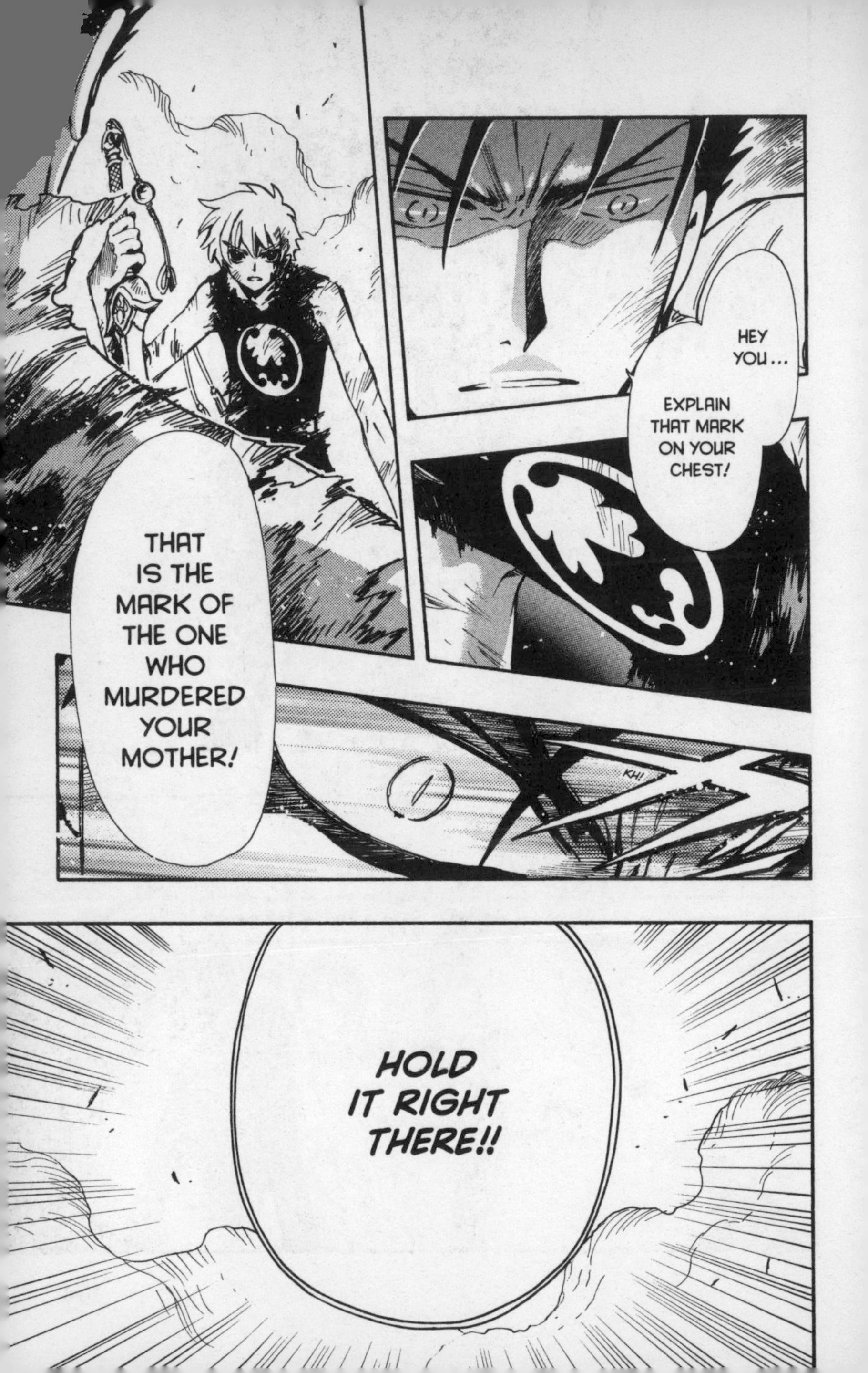
HEY YOU...
EXPLAIN THAT MARK ON YOUR CHEST!
THAT IS THE MARK OF THE ONE WHO MURDERED YOUR MOTHER!
KH!
HOLD IT RIGHT THERE!!

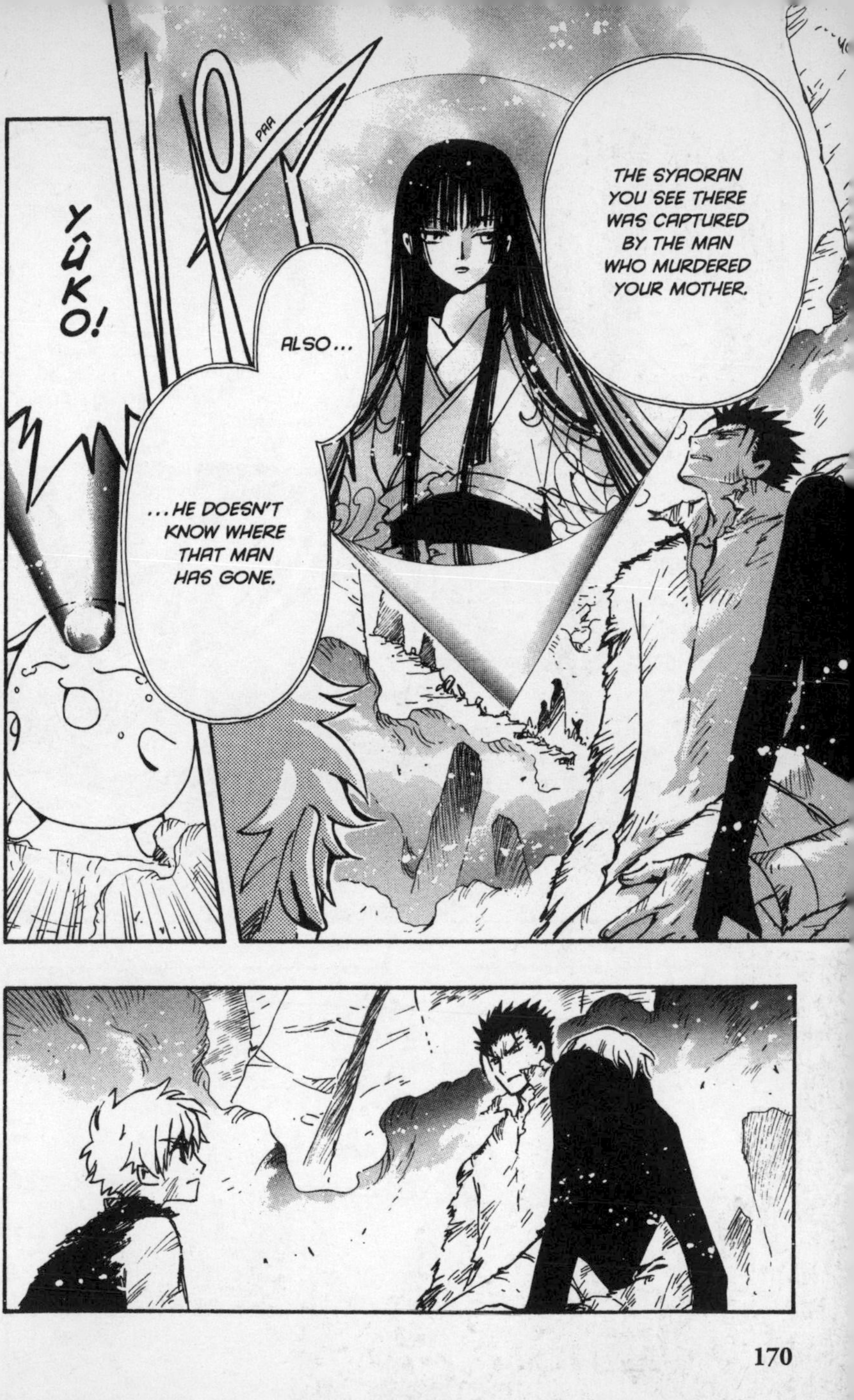
THE SYAORAN YOU SEE THERE WAS CAPTURED BY THE MAN WHO MURDERED YOUR MOTHER.
ALSO...
...HE DOESN'T KNOW WHERE THAT MAN HAS GONE.
PAA
YÛKO!

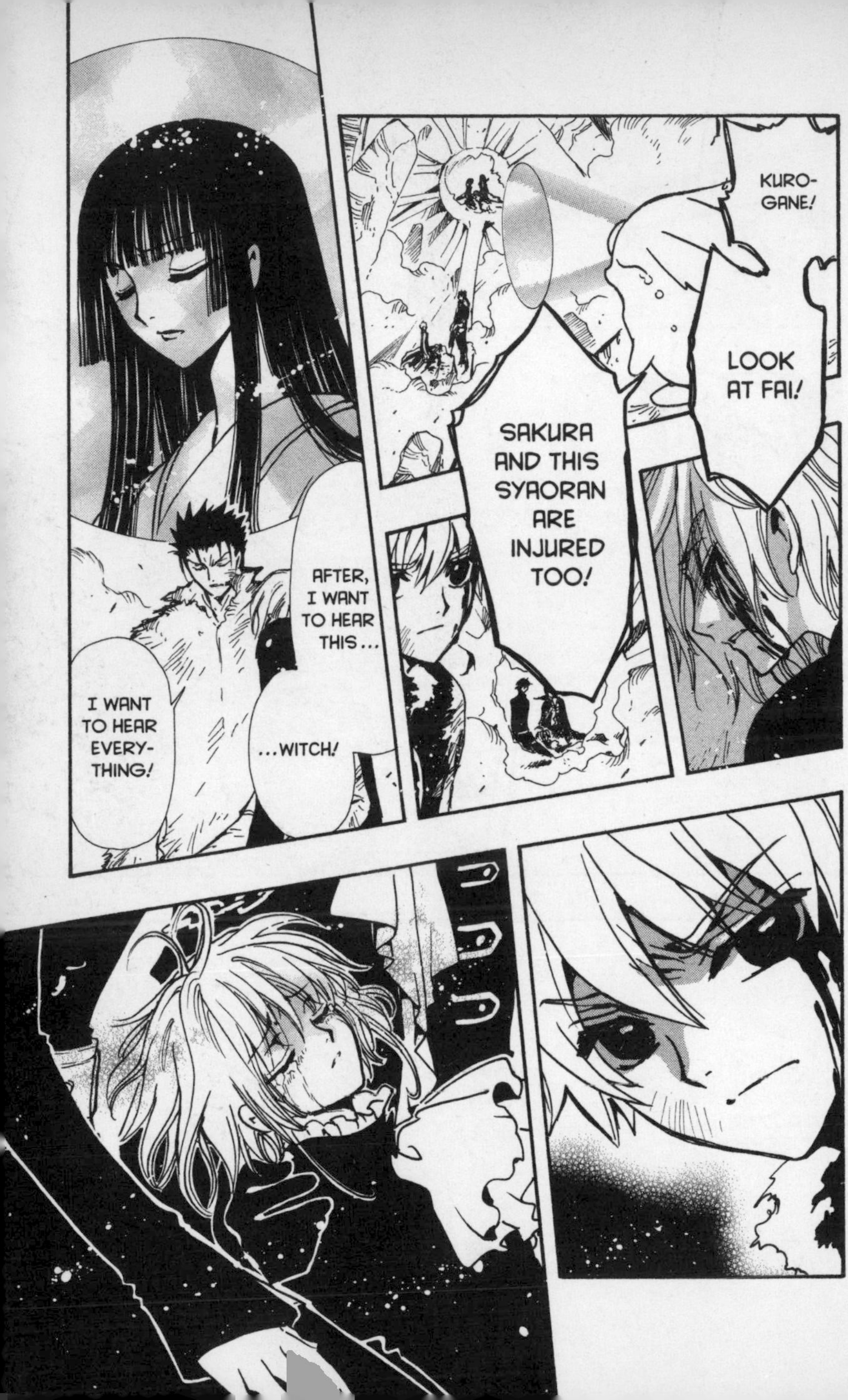
KURO-GANE!
LOOK AT FAI!
SAKURA AND THIS SYAORAN ARE INJURED TOO!
AFTER, I WANT TO HEAR THIS...
...WITCH!
I WANT TO HEAR EVERYTHING!

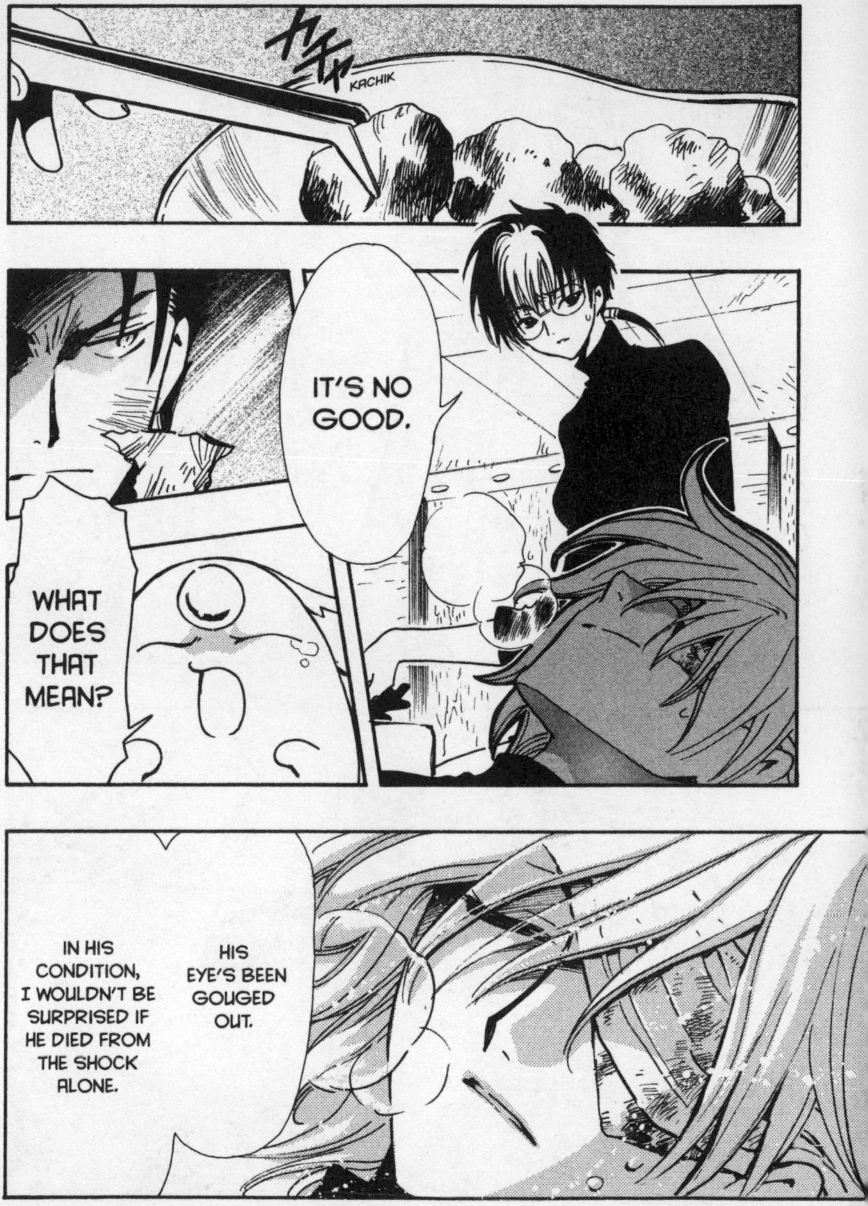
カチャ
KACHIK
IT'S NO GOOD.
WHAT DOES THAT MEAN?
HIS EYE'S BEEN GOUGED OUT.
IN HIS CONDITION, I WOULDN'T BE SURPRISED IF HE DIED FROM THE SHOCK ALONE.

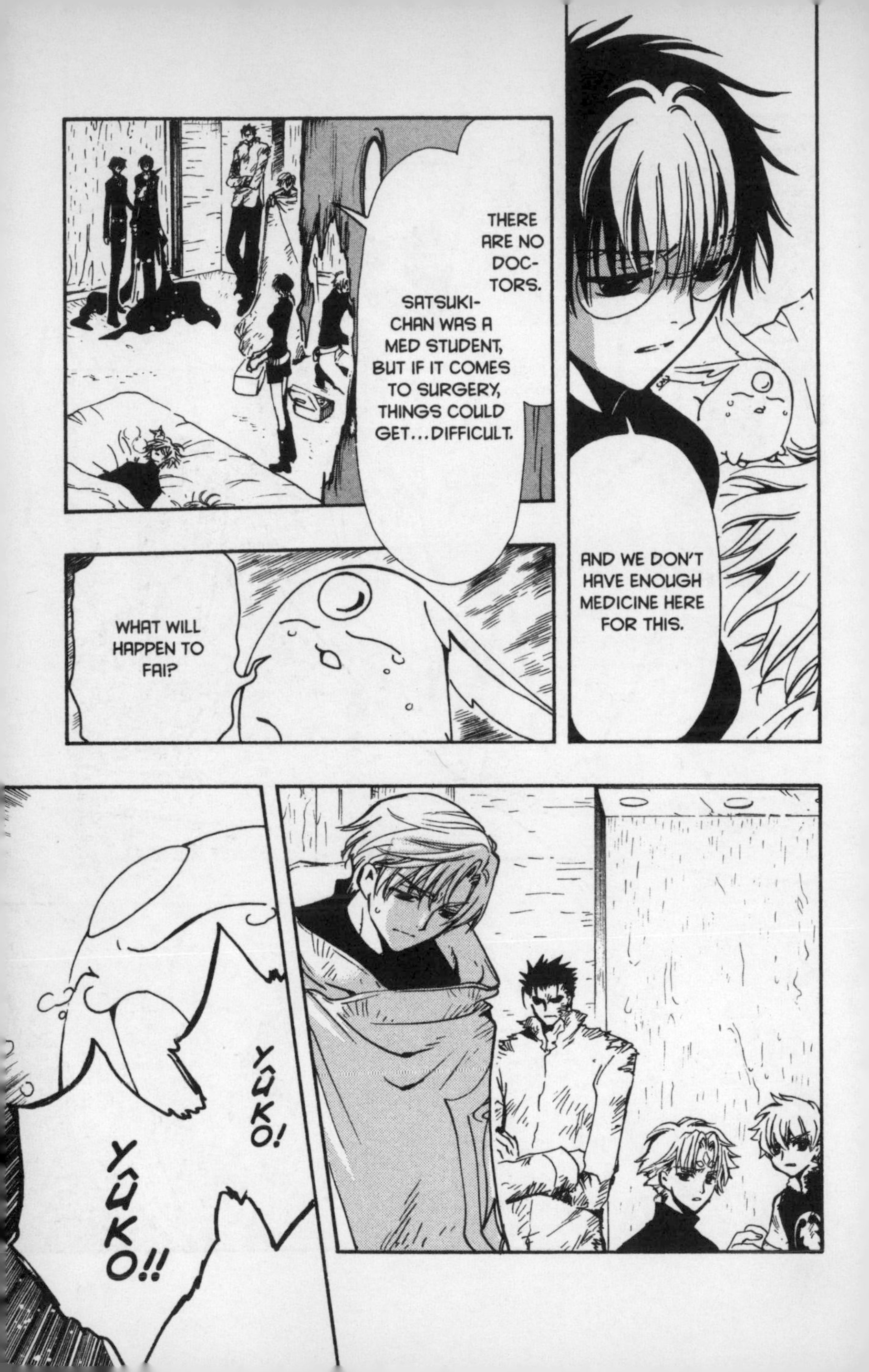
THERE ARE NO DOCTORS. SATSUKI-CHAN WAS A MED STUDENT, BUT IF IT COMES TO SURGERY, THINGS COULD GET...DIFFICULT.
AND WE DON'T HAVE ENOUGH MEDICINE HERE FOR THIS.
WHAT WILL HAPPEN TO FAI?
YÛKO!
YÛKO!!

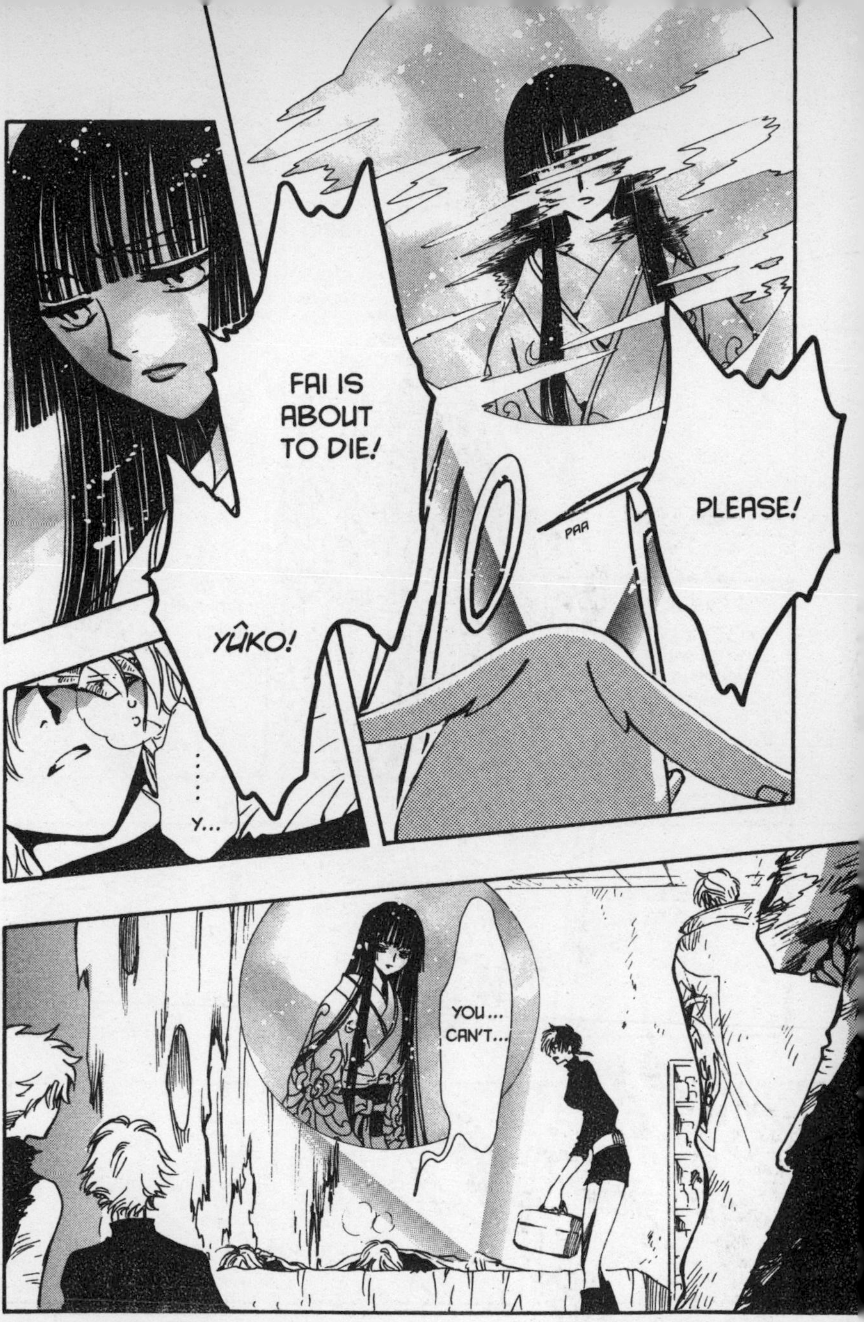
......Y...
YÛKO!
FAI IS ABOUT TO DIE!
PAA
PLEASE!
YOU... CAN'T...

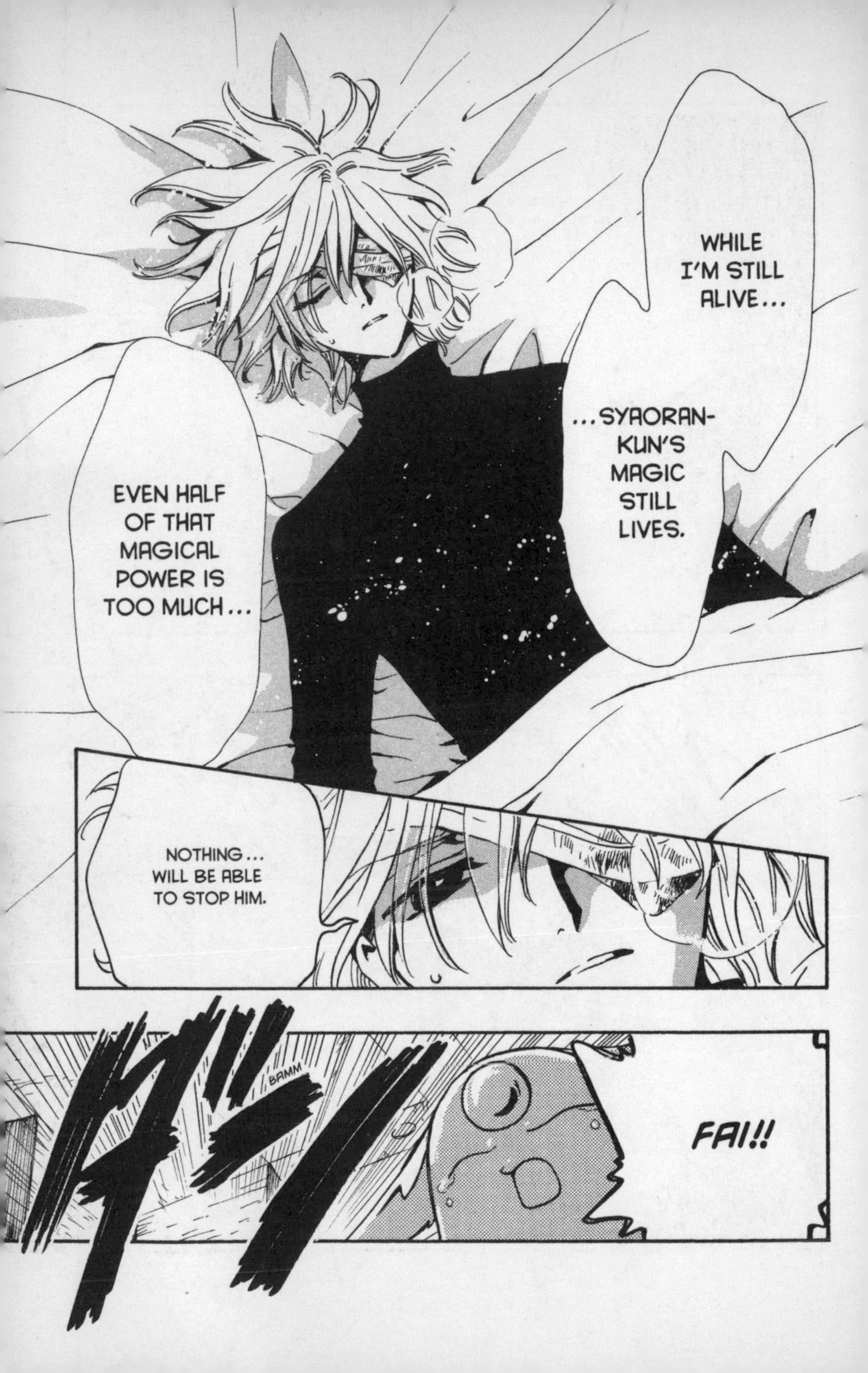
WHILE I'M STILL ALIVE...
...SYAORAN-KUN'S MAGIC STILL LIVES.
EVEN HALF OF THAT MAGICAL POWER IS TOO MUCH...
NOTHING... WILL BE ABLE TO STOP HIM.
FAI!!
BAMM

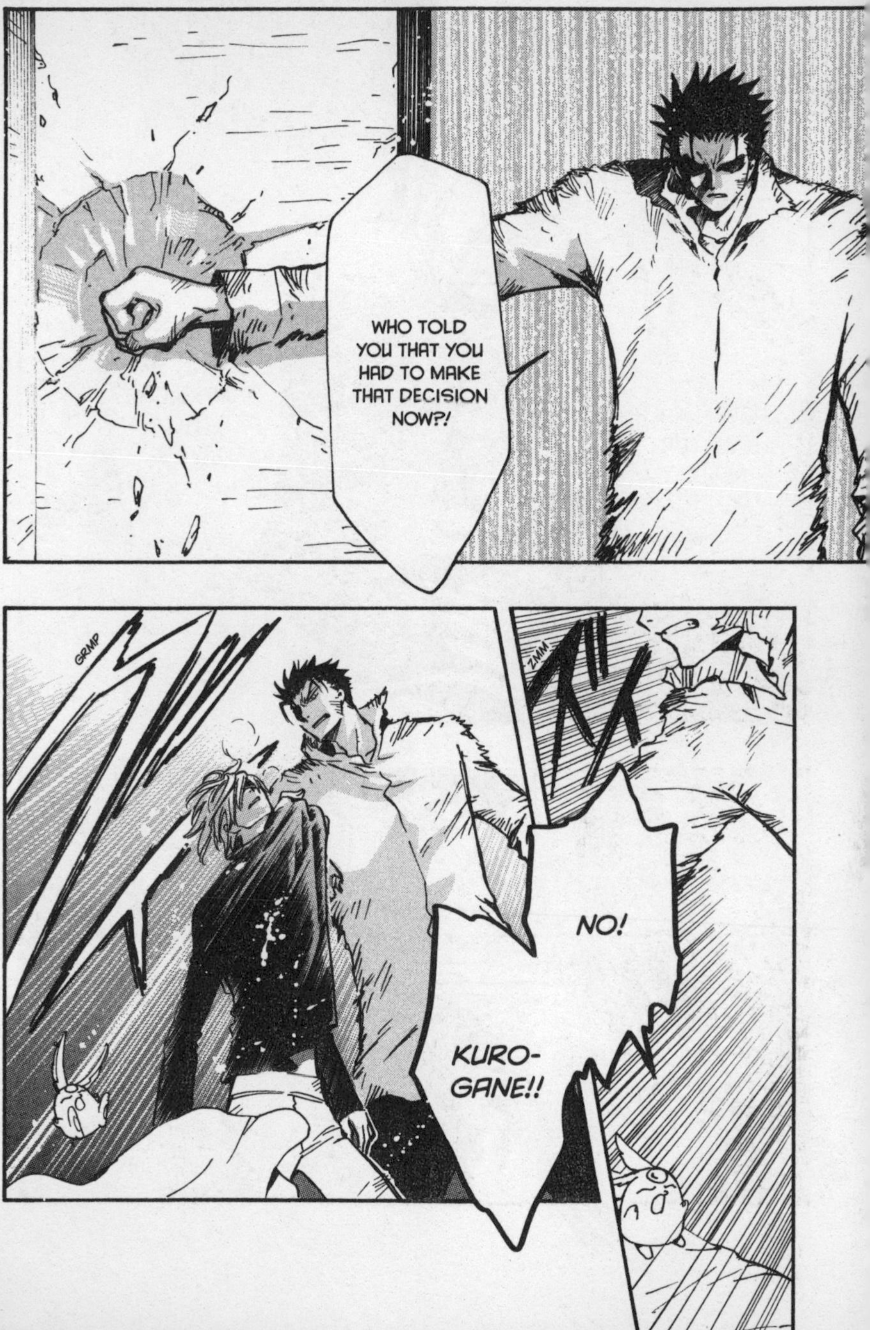
WHO TOLD YOU THAT YOU HAD TO MAKE THAT DECISION NOW?!
ZMM
NO! KURO-GANE!!
GRMP

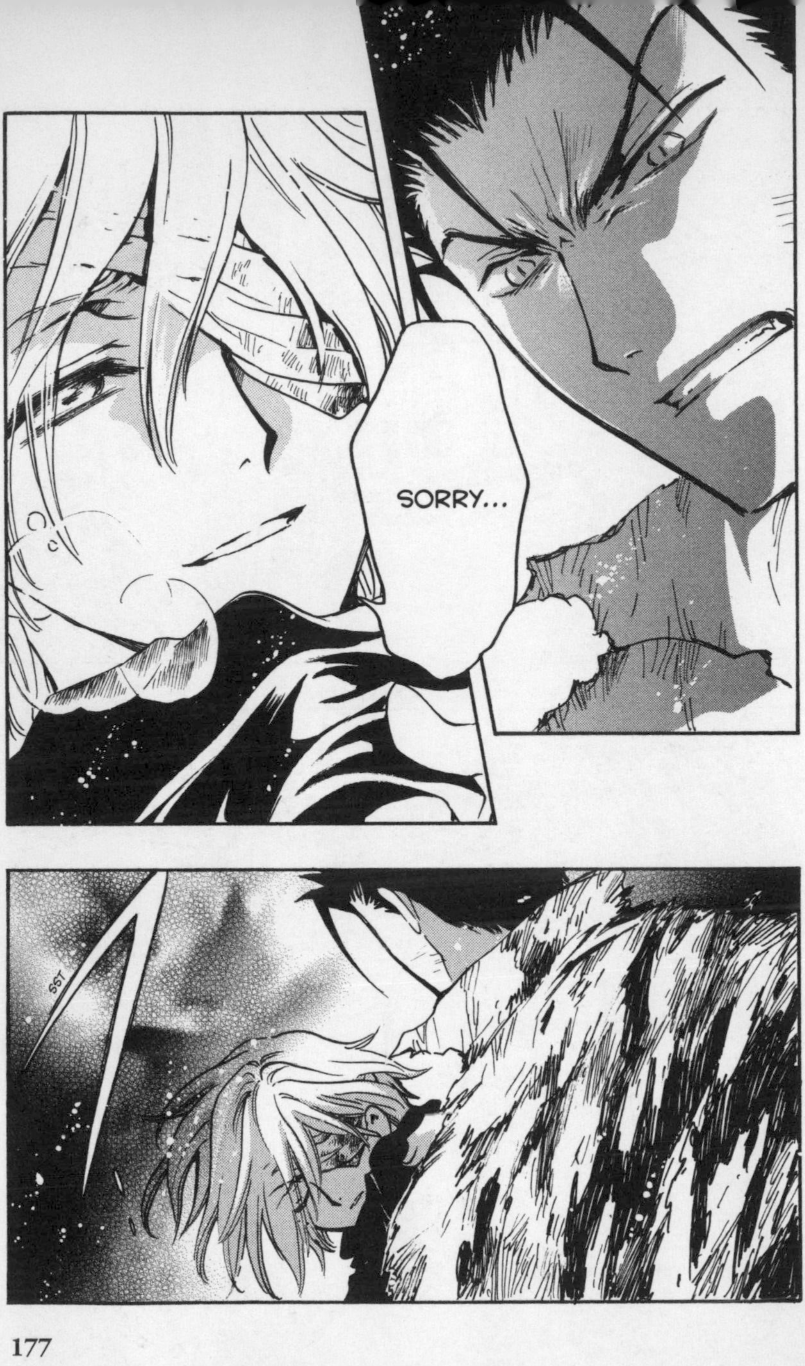
SORRY...
SST

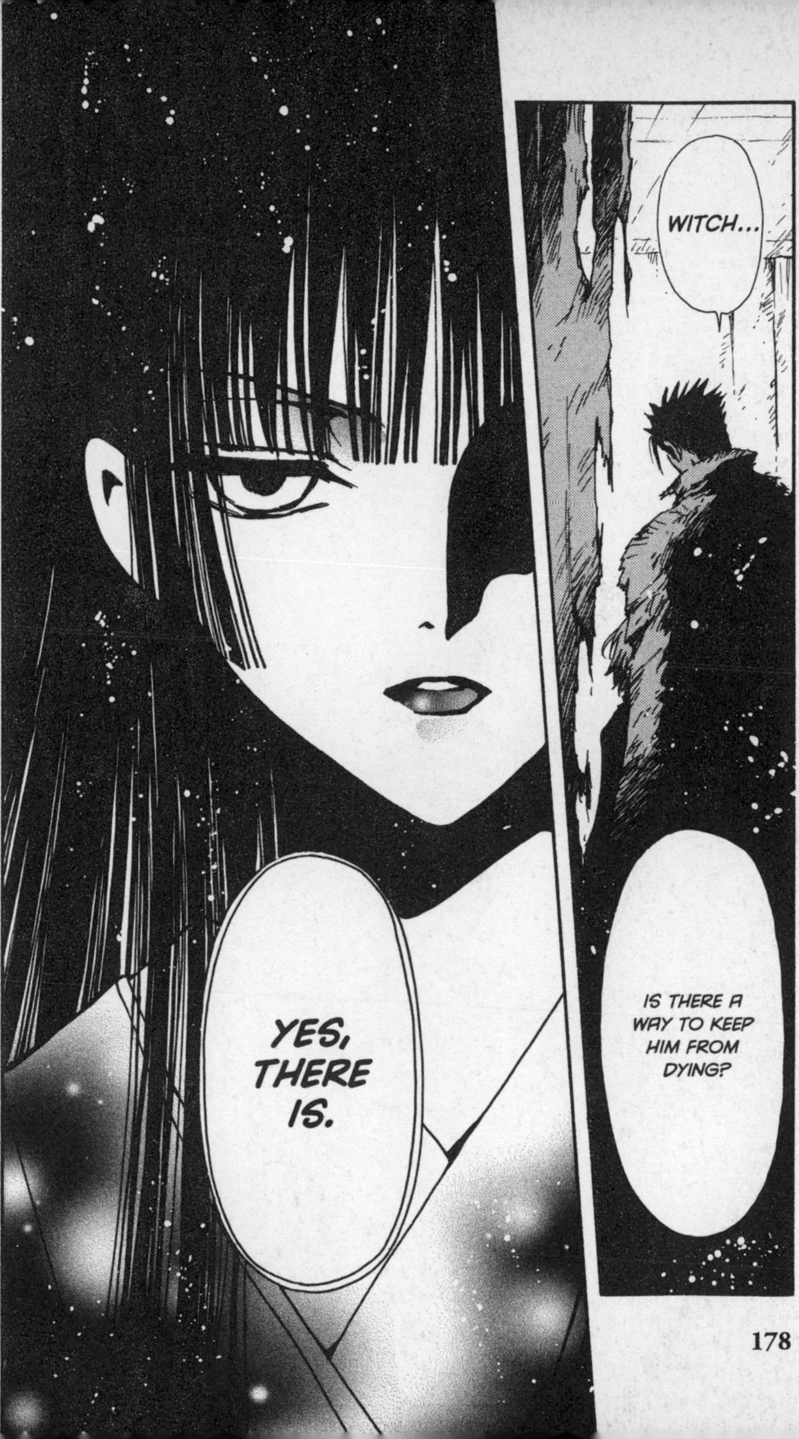
WITCH...
IS THERE A WAY TO KEEP HIM FROM DYING?
YES, THERE IS.

To Be Continued

About the Creators

CLAMP is a group of four women who have become the most popular manga artists in America—Ageha Ohkawa, Mokona, Satsuki Igarashi, and Tsubaki Nekoi. They started out as *doujinshi* (fan comics) creators, but their skill and craft brought them to the attention of publishers very quickly. Their first work from a major publisher was *RG Veda*, but their first mass success was with *Magic Knight Rayearth*. From there, they went on to write many series, including Cardcaptor Sakura and Chobits, two of the most popular manga in the United States. Like many Japanese manga artists, they prefer to avoid the spotlight, and little is known about them personally.

CLAMP is currently publishing three series in Japan: Tsubasa and xxxHOLiC with Kodansha and Gohou Drug with Kadokawa.

Translation Notes

Japanese is a tricky language for most Westerners, and translation is often more art than science. For your edification and reading pleasure, here are notes on some of the places where we could have gone in a different direction in our translation of the work, or where a Japanese cultural reference is used.

Tochô, page 14

As mentioned in the last volume, Tochô is the Japanese name for the double-towered Tokyo Metropolitan Government Building. The word is made up of the kanji *to* which means "city," and *chô* which means "government." This is where the nickname for the building, "City Hall," comes from.

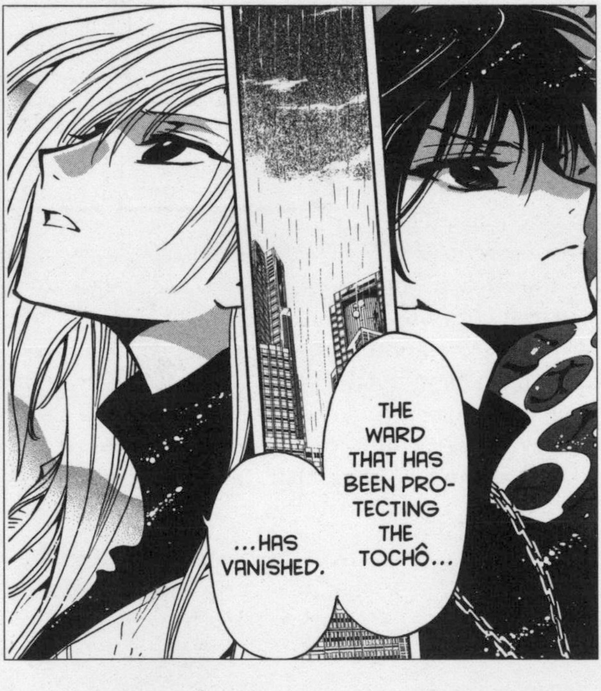
THE WARD THAT HAS BEEN PRO-TECTING THE TOCHÔ...
...HAS VANISHED.

Game, page 22

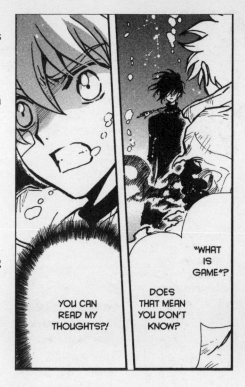

"WHAT IS GAME"?
DOES THAT MEAN YOU DON'T KNOW?
YOU CAN READ MY THOUGHTS?!

As promised in last volume's translation notes, here is the meaning of "game." In Japanese Kamui used the Japanese word "e" spelled in katakana. Out of context, "e" with no kanji could have many meanings including "a picture," "a handle," "an inlet or bay," or "perilla," among other inferred meanings. When Kamui explained its meaning, he finally attached a *kanji* for "e," which fixed the meaning to the word "prey" (as in what a predator eats). Unfortunately, if I had written the word "prey" in the last volume, there would be no reason for Syaoran to be confused at what the word meant. The meaning of the English word "prey" is obvious. Why would Syaoran be confused as he obviously is in the Japanese version? However, "game" (as in big-game hunter) has a very similar meaning to prey while also having a large number of other meanings such that Syaoran (and the reader) would naturally be confused. So while "game" wasn't perfect as far as the meaning of the word, it was the best translation for the situation that this translator could think up.

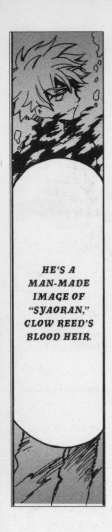

HE'S A
MAN-MADE
IMAGE OF
"SYAORAN,"
CLOW REED'S
BLOOD HEIR.

"Syaoran," page 59

This explanation of who and what the Syaoran we know is was something of a challenge to translate. The only way the Japanese version differentiated between the original Syaoran, who was Clow Reed's successor, and the copy of him was the use of Japanese quotation marks which surrounded Syaoran's name every time it was mentioned. I maintained that convention in the translation. I hope no readers take the quotation marks as the character speaking sarcastically . . .

Image, page 59

In the Japanese version, when referring to the man-made Syaoran, they used the kanji for "photograph," while the pronunciation guide next to the kanji indicated that "photograph" was pronounced as a word meaning something very much like "copy." Since the English word "image" encompasses the meanings for both photograph and copy, it seemed like the best translation to use in this passage.

Fei-Wang gathering souls, page 69

Even as official translator for Tsubasa and xxxHOLiC, I don't have any more inside knowledge of the series than the readers in Japan do. However, for those who don't read xxxHOLiC, in the second story arc of the fifth volume of xxxHOLiC, there was a story of a female high-school student who had her soul stolen from her by a sinister pair of magical wings. An unnamed sorcerer was using the wings to steal souls from humans and gather them for his own purposes. This may be a reference to the events in that story. (But they also may not be . . . CLAMP can be a little difficult to figure out at times.)

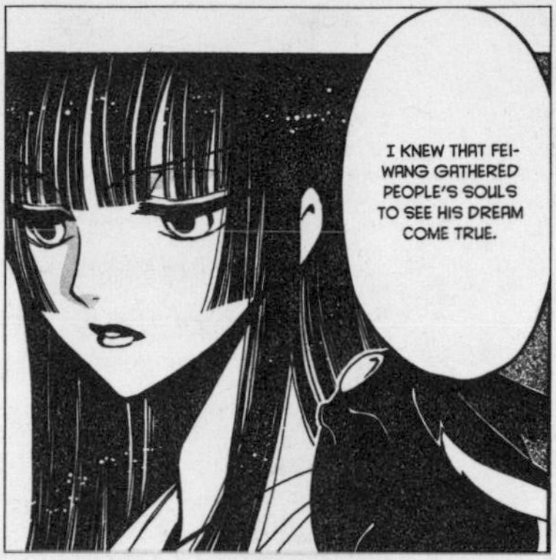
I KNEW THAT FEI-WANG GATHERED PEOPLE'S SOULS TO SEE HIS DREAM COME TRUE.

Syaoran and "Heart," page 122

Although the Japanese words for "soul" and "heart" are used almost interchangeably during Fei-Wang Reed's and Yûko's explanation of the events leading to the creation of the Syaoran "image," Syaoran uses the word "heart" (*kokoro*) exclusively. So to avoid adding confusion to an already confusing explanation, I used the word "soul" in Fei-Wang Reed's and Yûko's explanations, and I reserved the use of the word "heart" for Syaoran alone.

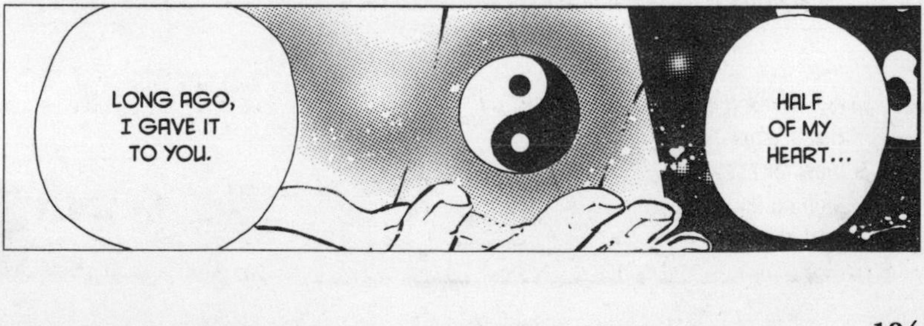
HALF OF MY HEART...
LONG AGO, I GAVE IT TO YOU.

Psycho Busters

MANGA BY AKINARI NAO
STORY BY YUYA AOKI

PSYCHIC TEENS ON THE RUN!

Out of the blue, a beautiful girl asks Kakeru to run away with her. This could be any boy's dream come true, but there's something strange afoot.

It turns out that this girl is on the run from a shadowy government organization intent on using her psychic abilities for its own nefarious ends. But why does she need Kakeru's help? Could it be that he has secret powers, too?

• Story by Yuya Aoki, creator of *Get Backers*

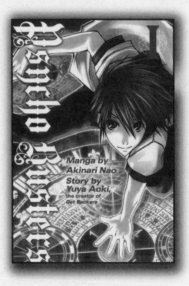

Special extras in each volume! Read them all!

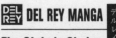

TOMARE!

[STOP!]

You're going the wrong way!

Manga is a completely different type of reading experience.

To start at the *beginning*, go to the *end*!

That's right! Authentic manga is read the traditional Japanese way—from right to left. Exactly the *opposite* of how American books are read. It's easy to follow: Just go to the other end of the book, and read each page—and each panel—from right side to left side, starting at the top right. Now you're experiencing manga as it was meant to be.